T0321217

Critical Issues Impacting Science, Technology, Society (STS), and Our Future

Heather Christina Lum
Pennsylvania State University, USA

A volume in the Advances in Human
and Social Aspects of Technology
(AHSAT) Book Series

Published in the United States of America by
    IGI Global
    Information Science Reference (an imprint of IGI Global)
    701 E. Chocolate Avenue
    Hershey PA, USA 17033
    Tel: 717-533-8845
    Fax: 717-533-8661
    E-mail: cust@igi-global.com
    Web site: http://www.igi-global.com

Library of Congress Cataloging-in-Publication Data

Names: Lum, Heather Christina, 1984- editor.
Title: Critical issues impacting science, technology, society (STS), and our
   future / Heather Christina Lum, editor.
Description: Hershey, PA : Information Science Reference, [2019] | Includes
   bibliographical references.
Identifiers: LCCN 2018041825| ISBN 9781522579496 (hardcover) | ISBN
   9781522579502 (ebook)
Subjects: LCSH: Technology--Social aspects. | Technological
   innovations--Social aspects. | Research--Social aspects.
Classification: LCC T14.5 .C7525 2019 | DDC 303.48/3--dc23 LC record available at https://lccn.
loc.gov/2018041825

This book is published in the IGI Global book series Advances in Human and Social Aspects of Technology (AHSAT) (ISSN: 2328-1316; eISSN: 2328-1324)

British Cataloguing in Publication Data
A Cataloguing in Publication record for this book is available from the British Library.

All work contributed to this book is new, previously-unpublished material.
The views expressed in this book are those of the authors, but not necessarily of the publisher.

For electronic access to this publication, please contact: eresources@igi-global.com.

Advances in Human and Social Aspects of Technology (AHSAT) Book Series

ISSN:2328-1316
EISSN:2328-1324

Editor-in-Chief: Ashish Dwivedi, The University of Hull, UK

MISSION

In recent years, the societal impact of technology has been noted as we become increasingly more connected and are presented with more digital tools and devices. With the popularity of digital devices such as cell phones and tablets, it is crucial to consider the implications of our digital dependence and the presence of technology in our everyday lives.

The **Advances in Human and Social Aspects of Technology (AHSAT) Book Series** seeks to explore the ways in which society and human beings have been affected by technology and how the technological revolution has changed the way we conduct our lives as well as our behavior. The AHSAT book series aims to publish the most cutting-edge research on human behavior and interaction with technology and the ways in which the digital age is changing society.

COVERAGE

- Technoself
- Human Rights and Digitization
- Technology and Freedom of Speech
- ICTs and human empowerment
- Public Access to ICTs
- Computer-Mediated Communication
- Cyber Behavior
- Technology Adoption
- Cultural Influence of ICTs
- Human-Computer Interaction

IGI Global is currently accepting manuscripts for publication within this series. To submit a proposal for a volume in this series, please contact our Acquisition Editors at Acquisitions@igi-global.com or visit: http://www.igi-global.com/publish/.

Titles in this Series

701 East Chocolate Avenue, Hershey, PA 17033, USA
Tel: 717-533-8845 x100 • Fax: 717-533-8661
E-Mail: cust@igi-global.com • www.igi-global.com

Table of Contents

Preface

Science, Technology, and Society (STS) is a topic that has been near and dear to my heart since as long as I can remember. Of course, I did not know what STS was as a discipline when I was a child. What I did know, just as so many other young children who grew up in the '90s knew, is that playing with my Nintendo was a blast. Bouncing up and down on moon shoes with my cousin made us feel like we were astronauts in space. The first time seeing a chemical reaction in class or testing out designs for the best egg protector when falling from a height was the best part of school. For some, this fascination wanes and they turn their attention to other disciplines to study and work in. But for others, science and technology not only remain a passion but ultimately a way of life. They devote your time to building, experimenting, thinking and tweaking to make the world around us faster, better, easier. And these advances in science and technology ultimately affect the world we live in. And the world around us affects the types of technologies we build and the science we pursue. And that is the crux of what STS is.

THE ISSUES

Technology has become ever more present in our society and has enabled such objects as computers and robots to be more relatable to the average person (Osborne, Simon, & Collins, 2003). People born between 1982 and 1998 have been surrounded by and use technology like no other generation in history, with college-aged students now experiencing their academic years more "wired in" than their predecessors (McBride & Nief, 2010). Similarly, technology and robotics companies are now beginning to utilize cutting edge equipment to turn humans into "super humans." For example, the Raytheon Sarcos created an exoskeleton, which allows a human user to increase his or her strength beyond normal human limits with minimal effort (Jacobsen, 2010). Other researchers, like Kevin Warwick from the University of Reading, have gone one step further by implanting a RFI chip into the body. This chip has rewired his brain in a way that allows him to move robots and devices with his mere thoughts (Warwick et al., 2010). Exposure to this constant wave of technological devices may have caused a shift in our thinking from an organic view to a more technological one.

Technology shapes our society in a multitude of ways. It has changed how we communicate with each other, both face to face as well as remotely. Even human-human relationships have been formed through online connections. In 2010, one in six people who got married began his or her relationship online. This is "more than twice the number of people who met at bars, clubs, and other social events combined" (Koford, 2010, p. 1). With regard to television usage, the Nielsen group reports that the average American watches approximately 153 hours of television every month at home and at least 131 million watch on their mobile devices (Nielsen Company, 2017). An even more astounding statistic relates to today's youth and their online usage. According to the New York Times (Lewin, 2010), those between the ages of eight and eighteen years spend more than seven and a half hours a day using a smart phone, computer, television or other electronic devices. According to one 14-year-old, "I feel like my days would be boring without it" (Lewin, 2010, p. 1). Businesses have been impacted equally by technology. Where would we be without the instant access to information via the Internet? The ability to send and receive information via email (over 294 billion sent every day or 2.8 million every second) has forever changed how we work and play (Tschabitscher, 2017).

Given that modern Western society has instant access to nearly anything we can think of, even our perception of time is evolving. As one researcher at UC Berkeley explains, "Because of the ability to instantaneously respond to others, our perception of time has been altered. No longer do we feel like we have enough time in the day. Many find themselves spending their entire work time and even personal time replying to e-mails. Though data proves otherwise, we now feel like there is less than 24 hours in a day. When we are bored, we find ourselves spending our whole time chatting online. By the end of the day, we discover that we have spent hours on the internet" (Meng, 2009, p. 1). We also are facing certain threats that people less than 20 years ago seldom thought about: identity theft and computer viruses. Last year, the FTC estimates that as many as 9 million Americans had their identities stolen, and the primary way of gaining that information was through the internet (Federal Trade Commission, 2017). With this influx of technology in our personal and professional lives, it is clear that we are fundamentally altering what is important to us as well as well as how we interact with each other. For centuries, face to face communication was the only way to interact and learn about each other and the world. But, now we can talk to each other over the phone or online and gain access to any information we want.

This book provides a window into the critical issues impacting and facing us today as well as those that will impact us in the immediate future. Certain chapters dive in to specific technologies such as social media, wearables, and automated vehicles. Others examine the societal impact of such technologies and how they are impacting us. As STS is an interdisciplinary topic, the authors of these chapters come from very different backgrounds with unique takes on what is important and how it will impact us. This book is a small window into the relationship between scientific progress and societal forces and the role of technology and science within people's day-to-day lives.

ORGANIZATION OF THE BOOK

This book is organized into 11 chapters. Below is a brief summary of each chapter:

Chapter 1 starts the book off by discussing the challenges and opportunities that are facing industry. The authors focused on the introduction of the fourth industrial revolution and how it has impacted our society directly and indirectly.

Chapter 2 delves into the concept of blockchain, its purpose and the fundamental concepts surrounding it. Specific types of blockchains from the past, present, and future are then discussed as well as how the adoption of such technology could affect other aspects of our society.

Chapter 3 deals with issues surrounding digital social networking (DSN). The authors discuss the risk-benefit paradox of DSN, the evolution of DSN sites and this chapter intends to serve as a cornerstone towards developing a framework for organizational strategy formulation for DSN.

Chapter 4 examines the future of digital game-based learning (DGBL). This chapter aims at explaining, from theoretical and practical perspectives, the effectiveness of DGBL to enhance intercultural communication skills. The chapter expounds on the effectiveness of utilizing DGBL as a pedagogical tool in education and training.

Chapter 5 identifies the challenges facing international students, specifically as it relates to social media use as an information source. This chapter looks addresses the limited knowledge around the information needs, seeking behavior and use of international students.

Chapter 6 takes a look at "sexting" behaviors of both adolescents and adults. This chapter will examine the prevalence of sexting in the context of existing romantic relationships, and how sexting may relate to features of the relationship.

Chapter 7 specifically focuses on wearable technologies. The authors describe their research surrounding the effects of sensation seeking, intensity, novelty, gender, and prior experience on the workload experienced during one aspect of using wearable fitness trackers, the device installation process.

Chapter 8 examines the impact of automated vehicles and who the likely users are. The authors focus on the trajectory of this technology and the likely outcomes such as the potential for increased energy use, environmental costs, and social inequity.

Chapter 9 brings the book back to an important and wide spread issue surrounding out society which is the digital divide. It dives into the theoretical and practical issues surrounding technology exclusion for certain types of users.

Chapter 10 tackles the issues of designing technology for an aging population. In this chapter, the authors discuss the background research supporting design principles that take into account age-related changes in cognition, movement, and behavior.

Chapter 11 concludes the book by discussing the ergonomic and human factors issues surrounding life and death in terms of 21st century design. In this chapter, the authors describe how current limitations in technologies that are specifically designed to be lethal afford greater pain and suffering than necessary.

Heather C. Lum
Pennsylvania State University, USA

REFERENCES

Federal Trade Commission. (2011). *About identity theft*. Retrieved from http://www. ftc.gov/bcp/edu/microsites/idtheft/consumers/about-identity-theft.html

Jacobsen, S. (2010). *The exoskeleton's super technology*. Retrieved from: http://www.raytheon.com/newsroom/technology/rtn08_exoskeleton/

Koford, B. (2010). *Match.com and Chadwick Martin Bailey 2009 - 2010 studies: recent trends: Online dating*. Retrieved from http://cp.match.com/cppp/media/CMB_Study.pdf

Lewin, T. (2010). *If your kids are awake, they're probably online*. Retrieved from http://www.nytimes.com/2010/01/20/education/20wired.html

McBride, T., & Nief, R. (2010). *Beloit college mindset list, entering class on 2014*. Retrieved from http://www.beloit.edu/mindset/

Meng, J. (2009). *Living in internet time*. Retrieved from http://www.ocf.berkeley.edu/~jaimeng/techtime.html

Nielsen Group. (2009). *Americans watching more tv than ever; web and mobile video up too*. Retrieved from http://blog.nielsen.com/nielsenwire/online_mobile/americans-watching-more-tv-than-ever/

Osborne, J., Simon, S., & Collins, S. (2003). Attitudes towards science: A review of the literature and its implications. *International Journal of Science Education, 25*(9), 1049–1079. doi:10.1080/0950069032000032199

Tschabitscher, H. (2017). *How many emails are sent every day?* Retrieved from http://www.radicati.com/

Warwick, K., Xydas, D., Nasuto, S. J., Becerra, V. M., Hammond, M. W., Downes, J. H., ... Whalley, B. J. (2010). Controlling a Mobile Robot with a Biological Brain. *Defence Science Journal, 1*(60), 5–14. doi:10.14429/dsj.60.11

Chapter 1

Impact of Industry 4.0 Revolution on Science, Technology, and Society (STS):
Challenges and Opportunities in the Industry 4.0 Era

Tuba Ulusoy
Necmettin Erbakan University, Turkey

Esra Yasar
KTO Karatay University, Turkey

Mehmet Aktan
Necmettin Erbakan University, Turkey

ABSTRACT

The Industry 4.0 concept, which leads the Fourth Industrial Revolution, was introduced by Germany in 2011 at the Hannover Messe trade fair and attracted the attention of the world. Since that time, its effects have been seen in different fields, such as science, technology, and society. In this chapter, in order to investigate the effects of Industry 4.0 revolution, answers to the following questions will be presented: Are there any concerns about technological unemployment as a result of Industry 4.0. revolution? Which professions have emerged? How has Industry 4.0 affected society directly or indirectly? What are the technologies of this concept? How do these technologies affect manufacturing and service systems? What are the challenges of implementing the technologies of Industry 4.0? What are the benefits of digitalized manufacturing? Which studies are conducted to accelerate the shift of Industry 4.0 from science to reality? and Which studies have been conducted so far about this concept?

DOI: 10.4018/978-1-5225-7949-6.ch001

BACKGROUND

Numerous studies, which examine Industry 4.0 from various perspectives, can be found in the literature. While some of them focus on the technologies related to Industry 4.0, in some studies, the topic is discussed as based on countries. However, to the best knowledge of the authors of this chapter, there is no study that presents the effects of Industry 4.0 on science, technology, and society together.

This chapter deals with Industry 4.0, which means digital transformation in manufacturing by using high-technology. Since its effects lead to some changes in science, technology, and society, it is important to take attraction to this issue. Many resources indicate that this transformation has both negative and positive impacts. These impacts of Industry 4.0 is presented to shed light on different aspects of the concept of Industry 4.0 in this chapter. In this regard, this chapter can be a guide for the decision makers, who engage with education, industry, and politics.

Introduction

Since Germany, which is one of the European countries, has faced some problems related to product quality and product cost, German government recognized that transformation in the industry is required in order to compete with Eastern countries, like China, which has advantages in terms of low production cost. The concepts of this transformation which lead to the fourth industrial revolution were introduced by Germany in 2011. The transformation is stimulated by the Internet and Cyber-Physical Systems (CPS) which enable digitalized manufacturing and smart factories. The fourth industrial revolution, namely Industry 4.0, has affected not only the manufacturing industry but also the social life. Although it is expected that the technologies related with Industry 4.0 will bring benefits on different aspects, such as economic and social, it brings some concerns related to employment.

The global effects of Industry 4.0 Revolution in science, technology, and society are presented in the remainder of this chapter.

Impact of Industry 4.0 Revolution on Science

In this section, information about scientific studies related to the concept of Industry 4.0 is presented to provide a literature review, which deals with the studies focusing on different aspects of the issue.

German government published an article in November 2011 in which the "Industry 4.0" concept was introduced as a high-tech strategy for 2020 (Zhou, Liu & Zhou, 2015). After this date, papers related to the concept of Industry 4.0 started to be seen in the literature.

When the term "Industry 4.0" is searched in the Web of Science (WoS) database, 1684 papers are found from its core collection. The number of papers for the years from 2012 to 2018 is given in Figure 1.

According to the web of science database, the number of papers has increased year by year. It shows that interest in this issue has continued to be increased since its introduction.

Numbers for types of papers can be seen in Figure 2.

As seen in Figure 2, the largest number of papers are proceedings papers. There is also a significant number of articles in the journals which are indexed by WoS.

As seen in Figure 3, the vast majority of papers are in the categories of Engineering Electrical and Engineering Industrial. While most of the articles published so far are related to the technological aspect of Industry 4.0, the authors of this chapter expect that scientific articles, which investigate the social effects of this concept, will be more common in the near future.

It is recognized that the German term "Industrie 4.0" is used instead of Industry 4.0 in some studies in English. So, it is possible to see "Industrie 4.0" term in this study.

Different definitions of this term can be found in literature. Some of these definitions from various resources are given as follows:

Brettel et al. (2014) emphasized a confusing definition of the term of Industry 4.0 in their study is that "The imminent changes of the industry landscape, particularly in the production and manufacturing industry of the developed world".

Kolberg and Zühlke (2015) describe the terms as that it as a vision of future production.

Figure 1. Number of papers published between 2012 and 2018 (WoS, 2018)

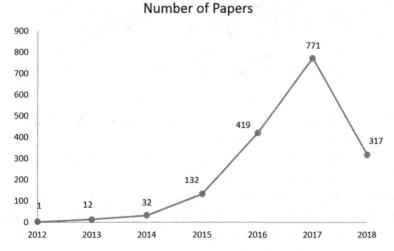

Figure 2. Numbers for types of papers published between 2012 and 2018 (WoS, 2018)

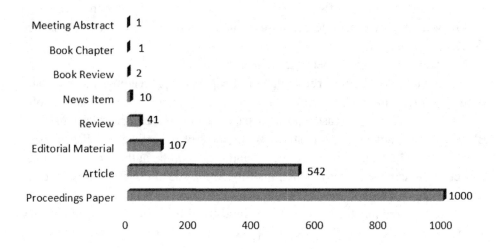

Number of Papers

Figure 3. Number of papers according to web of science categories (WoS, 2018)

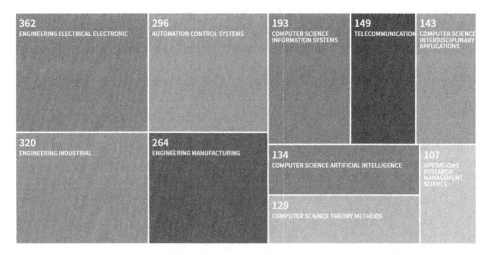

Gilchrist (2016) pointed out that Industry 4.0 refers to the fourth industrial revolution.

Industry 4.0 is described by Lee et al. (2015) as a trend that transforms manufacturing industry to the next generation.

Additionally, the authors of this chapter define the term of "Industry 4.0" as a vision that may lead to a considerably efficient transformation by using high technology, especially in manufacturing.

Selected papers which are about Industry 4.0 are classified in 3 research categories given as follows: Studies on a specific country, applications of Industry 4.0 technologies, and literature reviews.

Some papers focus on the studies related to Industry 4.0 in a country and show observed changes in the 4th industrial revolution so far. Moreover, "Industry 4.0: Building the digital enterprise (Geissbauer, 2015)", and "Time to accelerate in the race toward Industry 4.0 (Lorenz et al., 2016)" reports are presented by Boston Consulting Group (BCG) and PricewaterhouseCoopers (PwC), respectively, which are global consulting management firms. BCG surveyed more than 600 German and American companies, while PwC conducted a survey of more than 2,000 participants from nine major industries in 26 countries, including the United States, Canada, United Kingdom, Germany, France, Brazil, Spain, China, and Japan. The reports, which present the results of these surveys, contain valuable information that enables to see in which stage the countries are in the Industry 4.0 race and the challenges they face when implementing the Industry 4.0.

Some of the studies on a specific country are given as follows:

Sung (2018) advices that companies should consider Industry 4.0 very seriously and suggests policy implications to transition toward Industry 4.0 in Korea.

Li (2018) gives details of "Made-in-China 2025" strategic plan and compares the plan and Germany's "Industry 4.0" vision.

Hereinbefore, Germany is the country that introduced the Industry 4.0 concept to the world. Heng (2014) focuses on Industry 4.0 and Germany and states that Industry 4.0 has potentials that can enhance Germany's industrial capabilities of the firms which already create one-third of the EU's total industrial value added.

The studies that examine Turkey and the concept of Industry 4.0 can be found in the literature. One of them was conducted by Özkan et al. (2018). In the study, effects of the fourth industrial revolution in Turkey are evaluated and the authors state that Turkey is a country, which aims to have one of the ten most powerful economies in the world, so, adoption to the fourth industrial revolution is necessary to realize this aim. Besides, threats and opportunities of Industry 4.0 for Turkey are discussed by Koca (2018).

When technology related studies in the literature are examined, it is thought that these studies can guide the firms on how Industry 4.0 technologies will be implemented. Also, these studies present implementation of these technologies and expected benefits of implementations. The details of some selected studies are given at the remainder of this section.

In the scope of the study of Lee, Kao, & Yang (2014), a systematic prognostics-monitoring system approach is proposed for self-aware and self-maintained machines and implementation of this approach for a heavy-duty equipment vehicle used in mining and construction is presented. It is noted that customers' perception on product innovation, quality, variety, and speed of delivery are affected by information technology and social media networks under Industry 4.0 concept. Self-awareness, self-prediction, self-comparison, self-reconfiguration, and self-maintenance are the capabilities which a factory should have in order to meet the needs of its customers.

Shrouf, Ordieres, & Miragliotta (2014) propose an Internet of Things (IoT) based approach for a smart factory which can help managing energy efficiently. This study is carried out in a manufacturing company in Spain by collecting energy consumption data in real time with several smart meters which are installed at the machine level. It is expected that providing this data for decision makers after analyzing can reduce the wastes.

Schuh, Gartzen, Rodenhauser, & Marks (2015) point out that increasing the integration of working and learning in order to support processes and instruction of new employees are promising approaches. In order to learn the new tasks, Cyber-Physical Systems (CPS) in Industry 4.0 provide work environments with new opportunities. A model including characteristics of Industry 4.0 that support work-based learning is proposed. Application is carried out at the Demonstration Factory of the RWTH Aachen Campus.

Faller & Feldmüller (2015) indicate that Small and Medium-sized Enterprises (SMEs) should be supported to survive in the globalized environment since they face some problems related to Industry 4.0. In order to provide further training in modern technologies enabling Industry 4.0, together with the Schlüsselregion e.V., Bochum University of Applied Sciences established a Campus directly in the Velbert/Heiligenhaus region in which there are SMEs of the lock & key industries. In this campus, mechatronics and information technology are taught, also, students have opportunity work in one of these SMEs.

Literature reviews which examine papers related to the Industry 4.0 according to different aspects can be found in the literature.

One of the literature reviews is conducted by Stock & Seliger (2016). In this study, different opportunities for sustainable manufacturing in Industry 4.0 are covered. Environmental contributions and realizing sustainable industrial value creation on all three sustainability dimensions: economic, social and environmental can be shown as examples of opportunities of this concept.

Hermann, Pentek, & Otto (2016) present a literature review which indicates that Industrie 4.0 does not have a generally accepted definition. A definition of Industry 4.0 is given as "Industrie 4.0 is a collective term for technologies and concepts of value chain organization. Within the modular structured Smart Factories of Industrie 4.0, CPS monitor physical processes, create a virtual copy of the physical world and make decentralized decisions. Over the IoT, CPS communicate and cooperate with each other and humans in real time. Via the IoS, both internal and cross organizational services are offered and utilized by participants of the value chain."

based on the literature review. Interoperability, virtualization, decentralization, real-time capability, service orientation, and modularity are explained as six design principles of Industrie 4.0 in this study.

Rojko(2017), Brettel et al.(2014), Liao et al. (2017), and Lu (2017) mention detailed background and overview of Industry 4.0 from different aspects. Furthermore, research proposals and open research topics can be found in the studies that conducted by Liao et al. (2017) and Lu (2017).

Impact of Industry 4.0 Revolution on Technology

When the historical development of industry is reviewed, it is possible to see that new technologies and methods that come into use in production are the starting points of industrial revolutions.

At the end of the 18th century, the first industrial revolution started with the introduction of mechanical production in which water and steam power were used. Division-based labor mass production with the help of electricity and production lines is assumed as the development which led to the second industrial revolution. The 3rd industrial revolution started with applications of IT and electronics which enabled the automation in production at the 1970s (Lukač, 2015). Presently, the era of the fourth industrial revolution, namely Industry 4.0, is continuing (Lu, 2017). Industry 4.0 which is the subject of this study is associated with the use of Cyber-Physical Systems (CPS) in production systems.

CPS are new generation systems which transform industry. Physical factory floor and the cyber computational space are integrated in these systems that can both monitor and synchronize the information (Lee, Bagheri, & Kao, 2015). With the help of feedback loops, physical processes are affected by computations and physical processes affect computations in CPS (Lee, 2008).

Air- and ground-traffic, discrete and continuous production systems, logistics, medical science, energy production, infrastructure surrounding us, entertainment are application fields of CPS that can affect human life. Also, the fields in which CPS are used may provide better quality of life (Monostori, 2014).

Boston Consulting Group which is a global consulting management firm indicates that there are nine technological advances which transform industrial production in the report titled "Industry 4.0: The Future of Productivity and Growth in Manufacturing Industries" by using case studies from Germany (Rüßmann et al.,2015). These technologies are shown in Figure 4 and the details of them are given as follows:

The Industrial Internet of Things (IIoT): Zhou, Liu & Zhou (2015) described Internet of Things (IoT) as a vision that things "talk" to each other in a network, blending the virtual world with the physical world. Also, it can be described as a

Figure 4. Nine technologies transforming industrial production (Rüßmann et al., 2015)

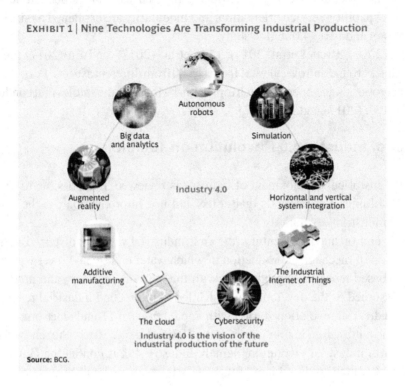

system in which electronics (RFID, tags, sensors, etc.) are embedded in physical items in order to connect Internet (Shrouf, Ordieres, & Miragliotta, 2014).

The Industrial Internet of Things (IIoT) refers to IoT related applications which are used in industry.

Objects with embedded sensors build the information networks which can provide improved business processes that may result in low cost and risks (Chui, Löffler, & Roberts, 2010).

According to Sun (2012), one of the benefits of IoT applications in supply chain management operations is visibility that can improve supply chain transparency. Also, these applications can provide a real-time management, high agility, response to the varied market quickly, and complete integration.

Although IIoT applications offer some advantages to the companies, security and data protection are the concerns associated with both IoT and IIoT.

Cybersecurity: It is expected that as the number of interconnected companies via IoT increases, the number of cyber-attacks will increase as well (Ervural & Ervural, 2018). This situation brings the Cybersecurity on the agenda.

The Cloud: Information technologies, like IoT, required the usage of Cloud computing which enables to provide computing resources, information integration and a data repository for the connected devices (things). Also, Cloud Computing may help to implement new architectures for automation (Givenchi & Jasperneite, 2013).

Additive Manufacturing: This means that a certain material is produced by superimposing. Additive manufacturing (AM) is used in 3D technologies and recently, this issue has attracted much attention because of Industry 4.0. By AM technology disrupting the traditional production, it makes production more specialized and producing small volume and customer specific products efficiently. (Calignano et al., 2017)

Augmented Reality: Augmented reality (AR) is a kind of mixed reality. AR is a technology that enhances the real word environment thanks to computer generated objects. (Krevelen & Poelman, 2010). In the near future, most companies will use AR technology extensively to improve themselves. Especially this technology will be much used in the areas like industrial design and marketing. This technology ensures essentially to produce unlimited new innovative products and ideas.

Big Data and Analytics: Large and complex data is generated by the elements of Industry 4.0, including the equipment, machines, production, applications, products and services. Analytics are necessary in order to extract value from the huge data, namely Big Data. Big Data and analytics can enable to optimize processes, reduce costs, and improve operational efficiencies (Zhou, Liu & Zhou, 2015).

Simulation: Simulation is the process of creating the environment by transferring the actual living data to a computer system. It provides advantages in terms of time, cost and risk management since it can make the development of the processes traceable (Celen, 2017).

Horizontal and Vertical System Integration: While the integration of a resource and an information network within the value chain is called "Horizontal integration", "Vertical integration" refers to networked manufacturing systems within the intelligent factories of the future and personalized custom manufacturing. Man to man, man to machine, machine to machine or service to service are the interconnections within CPS that may help integration in order to maximize customization (Zhou, Liu & Zhou, 2015).

According to Rüßmann et al. (2015), most of today's IT systems are not fully integrated, but Industry 4.0 will make companies, departments, functions, and capabilities integrated.

Autonomous Robots: Robots have been preferred in manufacturing systems for a long time, but, they are not as simple as before. New robots are self-sufficient, autonomous, interactive, flexible, and cooperative (Gilchrist, 2016; Rüßmann et al. 2015).

Artificial Intelligence (AI) also plays important role in today's manufacturing. Robots with donated AI can perform the tasks which can be unsafe and unsuitable for a human. This may help to increase occupational safety.

To ensure safety and security in the transportation of hazardous materials, to increase the quality of packaging used in food transport with smart containers, to prevent damage with sensors on machine in predictive maintenance, to provide easy and affordable repair with remote control in elevator maintenance, to update devices with remote control, to manage traffic flows, water flows, air quality, air security in smart cities can be opportunities provided by Industry 4.0 technologies.

Impact of Industry 4.0 Revolution on Society

One of the biggest impacts of the Industry 4.0 will be on society since with the development of technology, lifestyles of people also change. The change in the way of life is reflected as a radical change in the society. (Ortega,2018) So far, it can be observed that society has been affected by developments of science and technology, since it must integrate its life to these changes which have both positive and negative impacts.

As technology brings speed with it, fast communication and transportation were realized. While this situation has stepped up community communication, it is falsifying and eternal verities are not improving at the same time.

New technology may have problems, such as loss of personality and laziness of people.

These can be considered as negative effects of Industry 4.0 on society. On the other hand, Industry 4.0 also has positive impacts. It has increased cultural development because it provides easier access to areas of interest. Since development of technology helps people to save time, they can spend their time on self-development.

Convenience has increased in many areas of society. For example; social assistance organizations are popularized and the forms of assistance to these organizations have been transformed into a message.

Today, the effect of Industry 4.0 is observed in every country and adaptation processes are studied on the basis of countries. However Japan has not acted radically in this regard. It has been a partner of CeBIT, one of the world's most comprehensive technology fairs in Germany and in this fair Society 5.0 philosophy was introduced by Japan. (Pîrvu & Zamfirescu, 2017) Thus, a report prepared by the Federation of Japanese Economic Organizations Keidanren tried to introduce this concept to the world (Keidanren, 2016). Within the scope of this report; from the moment when the society started to be established up to now, 5 divisions were presented as shown in Figure 5.

Figure 5. The representation of the historical development of society (Keidanren, 2016)

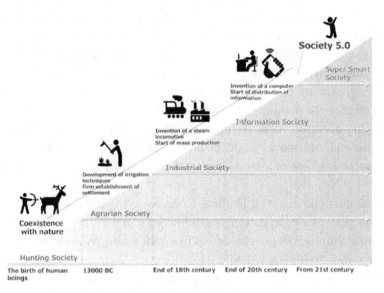

These sections are hunting society, agrarian society, industrial society, information society and super smart society. Society initially originated as a hunter society (Fujii et al,2018). They used only animals as food supplies and had to hunt. After that, the agriculture period started and the agrarian society was formed by passing to resident life. With the invention of steam technology, industrial society transfer was provided. With the development of production and technology, the period of information society has begun. Finally, with the emerge and development of the Industry 4.0, super smart society concept was formed. The reason why Japan introduces this concept is that Industry 4.0 integrates the society and uses the technology that Industry 4.0 has brought. (Shiroishi et al,2018) The aim of this philosophy is to produce solutions against the aging world population, to find solutions for environmental pollution and natural disasters, to use the internet in order to collect the objects effectively and to integrate the virtual world with the real world.

There was often job concern within the society since a new cycle began in every age, especially in terms of production systems. But this has always been the opposite. For example, the introduction of steam power made the people move into new business lines. For the new period, the same concepts of technological unemployment become the main topics of conversation and job concern among the society (Pfeiffer, 2017).

Constitutively; unemployment is a level of employment created by people who want to work and who cannot find a job despite the desire and ability to work. Unemployment is mainly divided into open unemployment and closed unemployment.

Closed unemployment occurs when there is no significant reduction in production in a situation where a part of the workforce is removed from production (İçerli, 2007).

Open unemployment is a condition in which a person cannot find a job despite being willing. Among open unemployment, the most commonly found types of unemployment in the literature are given as follows:

Temporary unemployment: Temporary employment, studies on projects as well as fixed-time and subcontract work, are unrestricted work relationships. Temporary unemployment is a type of unemployment that occurs in this context. (Virtanen et al., 2005)

Seasonal unemployment: It happens to decrease in production due to slowing of economic activity due to natural conditions or social events in the types of jobs where regular shifts do not exist in sectors like agriculture, construction and tourism (Mourdoukoutas, 1988; Unay, 2001)

Structural unemployment: It is the type of unemployment that is caused by the economic structure of a country (Jackman,Roper, 1987) and experienced in such cases some sectors are making progress, while some sectors are declining; therefore, labour demand is experienced in developing sectors while labour loss is observed in declining sectors. (Oktay, 2002)

Cyclical unemployment: The economy does not stay at the same level, there are developments such as recession and stagnation. In these periods there is a surplus of demand and this leads to a decrease in production. Thus, temporary or long term unemployment occurs. This type of unemployment is called cyclical unemployment. (Lilien,1982; Yıldırım, Karaman,2001)

Technological unemployment: As technology developing, labour can be replaced by machines or new technology, this situation may cause the employees to become unemployed or working in new business lines. The type of unemployment in this period is called technological unemployment.

Of the types of unemployment described here; technological unemployment is the type of unemployment that is concerned about living with Industry 4.0 and Society 5.0. In the literature, there are estimating studies about the current and near future on this subject. In some studies, it is predicted that technological unemployment will take place for a temporary period of 3 years; some studies have made estimates over the professions (Feldmann, 2013; Walsh, 2017; Frey & Osborne, 2017).

With the integration of emerging technology into the way of life as Industry 4.0 and Society 5.0 inductivities, everything people use is renewing or changing in general terms. New occupations are also emerging to fully adapt to these innovations or changes. While some occupations lose their significance or disappear, some occupations come into prominence or are born. This transformation of the industrial era is in fact reflected in all areas of society.

For example, in the academic sense, Industry 4.0 courses have been added by some schools at undergraduate level. Some of the pre-licensing periods have been added to the curriculum subject and is foreseen to be necessary in the new age. In the case of the example, even this situation reveals the need for a specialist teacher. Occupations to be newly formed are stated in some sources as follows (Lueth, 2015):

- **Industrial Data Scientist:** This profession is based on Big Data management. This analyses the data and works to make the results of the analysis useful to the companies.
- **Robot Coordinator:** They undertake the task of supervising the production robots and ensuring their regular checks.
- **Cloud Computing Expertise:** It ensures that cloud computing works unproblematic so that all data from any point can be accessed with persistent internet servers.
- **Wearable Technology Design:** They work with the advancement of technology. Wearable products are technologically advanced, and at the same time can be designed by the costumer as desired (Eğer, n.d.)
- **3-D Printer Engineering:** They undertake the task of developing new printers (Eğer, n.d.).

Expectations in future job opportunities are in the direction of the reduction of jobs based on physical strength and the increase in employment of specialist and skilled workers. According to the World Economic Forum, with Industry 4.0, life satisfaction of each employee will increase, people will have more individual time and more hobbies.

As a result of the study conducted by BCG, the potential impact of job growth by occupational and industry groups by 2025 is shown in Figure 6 (Lueth, 2015). According to the results, while the increase in professions related to R&D and IT can be seen, a decline in the manufacturing labor force is expected.

Considering that one of the most important society related issues is education, the impact of Industry 4.0 on education should be mentioned in this section.

Penprase (2018) emphasized that some changes are required in the science and technology curriculum of higher education in order to make the students more skilled in the rapidly emerging areas of genomics, data science, AI, robotics, and nanomaterials. Besides analyzing and breaking a technical or scientific problem into its constituent parts, the interconnections between each scientific problem across global scales and interrelations between physical, chemical, biological and economic dimensions of a problem must be taken into account in the higher education.

Figure 6. The potential impact of job growth by occupational and industry groups by 2025 (Lueth, 2015)

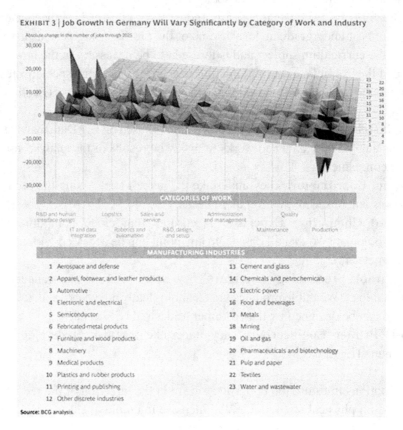

DISCUSSION

The developments in the Industry 4.0 revolution have raised numerous discussions. Some of the major questions are how this technology can be used effectively by society and about technological unemployment.

The first main subject is how technology of Industry 4.0 can be used effectively by society. In fact, the Society 5.0 put forward by Japan has been raised to answer this question. As technology develops; at the same time, society must also adapt to this technology. In the other words, technology producers should turn technology into the condition that can be used by society.

The second main subject is technological unemployment. As mentioned above, there are three different opinions about the technological unemployment. The first is that the technological unemployment will be occur, the second is that it will be occur temporarily, the third is that it will not be occur. But; the general expectation is that it will be occur temporarily. Because in previous industrial revolutions, it was only temporary; after a certain period, people have turned to new professions. Development leads to improvement, and this become a transformation. Adaptation to new professions will not happen suddenly, people will need a certain time to learn about these professions and to get used to it.

In addition to this discussion; Schwab, mentioned that the technological developments in the field of biology are of concern in his book he wrote. (Schwab, 2016) He worries about that we will use this developing technology only to repair our wounds, or we will use it to make ourselves a better person. In second case, personality confusion may occur, parental education can be destroyed. Therefore, technology should be managed in such a way that people do not change their personalities.

We have expressed concerns on the issues of technology. But it should not be forgotten that this development of the technology in this industry revaluation is very faster, wider and deeper than the other industrial ages. It is possible that this development will be more effective than other ages. So, the new technology change will be effective in every aspect of life.

Technology is development that makes the life of people easier if people use it. People can spend more time with them as they adapt to the technology. Thus, the hobbies of people are increasing, and people can specialize in a specific area. This situation makes life easier and happier. However; there are also opinions that suggests otherwise. For example; Professor Stephen Hawking, a scientist, is concerned that artificial intelligence can bring an end to humanity. Because Hawking argued that artificial intelligence could continue to improve itself and even reshape itself. Therefore he thinks that humanity cannot compete this such force. (Cellan,John, 2014). Also, Kolberg and Zühlke (2015) claim that some people are skeptical or even hostile towards the Industry 4.0. There are a lot of people who are afraid that new technology would bring the end of humanity. Abusing of technology is one of the most common and valid reasons that make people think of that way.

CONCLUSION

Companies and countries which cannot adapt to Industry 4.0 revolution concept can be left behind by their rivals in both national and international markets. Failure in the competitiveness may affect adversely not only themselves but also the society they are in. Because the development of societies depends on the strategies of the county; to adapt to the technology, to follow the developments should become government policy. Thereby, governments can develop a roadmap that can help them toward the fourth industrial revolution. At the same time, companies should develop both products and production process. It is clear that using Industry 4.0 technologies bring a range of benefits to companies. However, these technologies require large amounts of investments. So, while making investment decisions, companies should analyze their current status, sector, and expectations carefully.

In the process of development, both countries and companies should be in interaction with each other. In addition, it is important for states to develop their own technologies and not to buy them from another country in terms of maintaining development.

Although Industry 4.0 revaluation is associated with the technological changes in the manufacturing industry, it has crucial effects on society. Although there are worries that the technologies used in production will bring about problems that will negatively affect the society, such as unemployment, it is also important to consider that new business models will emerge, innovations have to be applied in the field of education in order to equip the workforce with the skills required by this concept.

REFERENCES

Brettel, M., Friederichsen, N., Keller, M., & Rosenberg, M. (2014). How virtualization, decentralization and network building change the manufacturing landscape: An Industry 4.0 Perspective. *International Journal of Mechanical. Industrial Science and Engineering*, *8*(1), 37–44.

Calignano, F., Manfredi, D., Ambrosio, E. P., Biamino, S., Lombardi, M., Atzeni, E., ... Fino, P. (2017). Overview on Additive Manufacturing Technologies. *Proceedings of the IEEE*, *105*(4), 593–612. doi:10.1109/JPROC.2016.2625098

Çelen, S., (2017), Sanayi 4.0 ve Simülasyon. *International Journal of 3D Printing Technologies and Digital Industry*, (1), 9-26.

Cellan-Jones. (2014). Retrieved from https://www.bbc.com/news/technology-30290540

Chui, M., Löffler, M., & Roberts, R. (2010), *Internet of Things*, Retrieved from https://www.mckinsey.com/industries/high-tech/our-insights/the-internet-of-things.

EğerE. (n.d.). Retrieved from http://www.endustri40.com/endustri-4-0-ile-birlikte-gelecek-10-yeni-meslek/

Ervural, B. C., & Ervural, B. (2018). Overview of Cyber Security in the Industry 4.0 Era. In Industry 4.0: Managing The Digital Transformation (pp. 267-284). Springer.

Faller, C., & Feldmüller, D. (2015). Industry 4.0 learning factory for regional SMEs. *Procedia CIRP*, *32*, 88–91. doi:10.1016/j.procir.2015.02.117

Feldmann, H. (2013). Technological unemployment in industrial countries. *Journal of Evolutionary Economics*, *23*(5), 1099–1126. doi:10.100700191-013-0308-6

Frey, C. B., & Osborne, M. A. (2017). The future of employment: How susceptible are jobs to computerisation? *Technological Forecasting and Social Change*, *114*, 254–280. doi:10.1016/j.techfore.2016.08.019

Fujii, T., Guo, T., & Kamoshida, A. (2018, August). A Consideration of Service Strategy of Japanese Electric Manufacturers to Realize Super Smart Society (SOCIETY 5.0). In *International Conference on Knowledge Management in Organizations* (pp. 634-645). Springer. 10.1007/978-3-319-95204-8_53

Geissbauer, R., Vedso, J., & Schrauf, S. (2015). *Industry 4.0: Building the digital enterprise*. Retrieved from https://www.pwc.com/gx/en/industries/industry-4.0.html

Gerbert, P., Lorenz, M., Rüßmann, M., Waldner, M., Justus, J., Engel, P., & Harnisch, M. (2015). *Industry 4.0: The future of productivity and growth in manufacturing industries*. Boston Consulting Group. Retrieved from https://www.bcg.com/publications/2015/engineered_products_project_business_industry_4_future_productivity_growth_manufacturing_industries.aspx

Gilchrist, A. (2016). Introducing Industry 4.0. In: Industry 4.0. Apress.

Givehchi, O., & Jasperneite, J. (2013). Industrial automation services as part of the Cloud: First experiences. *Proceedings of the Jahreskolloquium Kommunikation in der Automation–KommA*.

Heng, S. (2014). *Industry 4.0: Upgrading of Germany's Industrial Capabilities on the Horizon*. Academic Press.

Hermann, M., Pentek, T., & Otto, B. (2016, January). Design principles for industrie 4.0 scenarios. In *System Sciences (HICSS), 2016 49th Hawaii International Conference on* (pp. 3928-3937). IEEE.

İçerli, M. K. (2007). *Çalışma Ekonomisi*. İstanbul: BETA Yayınevi.

Jackman, R., & Roper, S. (1987). Structural unemployment. *Oxford Bulletin of Economics and Statistics*, *49*(1), 9–36. doi:10.1111/j.1468-0084.1987.mp49001002.x

Keidanren. (2016, April). *Toward realization of the new economy and society*. Japan Business Federation.

Koca, K. C. (2018). Sanayi 4.0: Türkiye Açısından Fırsatlar ve Tehditler. *Sosyoekonomi*, *26*(36), 245–252. doi:10.17233osyoekonomi.2018.02.15

Kolberg, D., & Zühlke, D. (2015). Lean automation enabled by industry 4.0 technologies. *IFAC-PapersOnLine*, *48*(3), 1870–1875. doi:10.1016/j.ifacol.2015.06.359

Lee, E. (2008). *Cyber Physical Systems: Design Challenges*. University of California, Berkeley Technical Report No. UCB/EECS-2008-8. Retrieved from http://www.eecs.berkeley.edu/Pubs/TechRpts/2008/EECS-2008-8.html, 2008.

Lee, J., Bagheri, B., & Kao, H. A. (2015). A cyber-physical systems architecture for industry 4.0-based manufacturing systems. *Manufacturing Letters*, *3*, 18–23. doi:10.1016/j.mfglet.2014.12.001

Lee, J., Kao, H. A., & Yang, S. (2014). Service innovation and smart analytics for industry 4.0 and big data environment. *Procedia Cirp*, *16*, 3–8. doi:10.1016/j.procir.2014.02.001

Li, L. (2018). China's manufacturing locus in 2025: With a comparison of "Made-in-China 2025" and "Industry 4.0". *Technological Forecasting and Social Change*, *135*, 66–74. doi:10.1016/j.techfore.2017.05.028

Liao, Y., Deschamps, F., Loures, E. D. F. R., & Ramos, L. F. P. (2017). Past, present and future of Industry 4.0-a systematic literature review and research agenda proposal. *International Journal of Production Research*, *55*(12), 3609–3629. doi:10.1080/00207543.2017.1308576

Lilien, D. M. (1982). Sectoral shifts and cyclical unemployment. *Journal of Political Economy*, *90*(4), 777–793. doi:10.1086/261088

Lorenz, M., Küpper, D., Rüßmann, M., Heidemann, A., & Bause, A. (2016). *Time to Accelerate in the Race Toward Industry 4.0*. Retrieved from: https://www.bcgperspectives.com/content/articles/lean-manufacturing-operations-time-accelerate-race-toward-industry-4/

Lu, Y. (2017). Industry 4.0: A survey on technologies, applications and open research issues. *Journal of Industrial Information Integration*, *6*, 1–10. doi:10.1016/j.jii.2017.04.005

LuethK. L. (2015). Retrieved from https://iot-analytics.com/top-5-new-industrial-iot-jobs/

Lukač, D. (2015, November). The fourth ICT-based industrial revolution" Industry 4.0"—HMI and the case of CAE/CAD innovation with EPLAN P8. In *Telecommunications Forum Telfor (TELFOR), 2015 23rd* (pp. 835-838). IEEE.

Monostori, L. (2014). Cyber-physical production systems: Roots, expectations and R&D challenges. *Procedia Cirp, 17*, 9–13. doi:10.1016/j.procir.2014.03.115

Mourdoukoutas, P. (1988). Seasonal employment, seasonal unemployment and unemployment compensation: The case of the tourist industry of the Greek islands. *American Journal of Economics and Sociology, 47*(3), 315–329. doi:10.1111/j.1536-7150.1988.tb02044.x

Oktay, E., (2002). *Makro İktisat Teorisi ve Politikası.* Maltepe Üniversitesi İ.İ.B.F. Yayınları No: 2, 3. Baskı, Ege Reklam Basım Sanatları Ltd. Şti., Eylül, İstanbul.

Ortega, A., Pérez, F. A., & Turianskyi, Y. (2018). *Technological justice: A G20 agenda (No. 2018-58).* Economics Discussion Papers.

Özkan, M., Al, A., & Yavuz, S. (2018). Uluslararası Politik Ekonomi Açısından Dördüncü Sanayi-Endüstri Devrimi'nin Etkileri ve Türkiye. *Siyasal Bilimler Dergisi, 1*(1), 1–30. doi:10.14782/marusbd.418669

Penprase, B. E. (2018). *Higher Education in the Era of the Fourth Industrial Revolution.* Singapore: Springer.

Pfeiffer, S. (2017). The vision of "Industrie 4.0" in the making—A case of future told, tamed, and traded. *NanoEthics, 11*(1), 107–121. doi:10.100711569-016-0280-3 PMID:28435474

Pîrvu, B. C., & Zamfirescu, C. B. (2017, August). Smart factory in the context of 4th industrial revolution: Challenges and opportunities for Romania. *IOP Conference Series. Materials Science and Engineering, 227*(1), 012094. doi:10.1088/1757-899X/227/1/012094

Rojko, A. (2017). Industry 4.0 concept: Background and overview. *International Journal of Interactive Mobile Technologies, 11*(5), 77–90. doi:10.3991/ijim.v11i5.7072

Rüßmann, M., Lorenz, M., Gerbert, P., Waldner, M., Justus, J., Engel, P., & Harnisch, M. (2015). Industry 4.0: The future of productivity and growth in manufacturing industries. Boston Consulting Group.

Schuh, G., Gartzen, T., Rodenhauser, T., & Marks, A. (2015). Promoting work-based learning through industry 4.0. *Procedia CIRP*, *32*, 82–87. doi:10.1016/j.procir.2015.02.213

Schwab, K. (2016). The 4th industrial revolution. In *World Economic Forum*. New York: Crown Business.

Shiroishi, Y., Uchiyama, K., & Suzuki, N. (2018). Society 5.0: For Human Security and Well-Being. *Computer*, *51*(7), 91–95. doi:10.1109/MC.2018.3011041

Shrouf, F., Ordieres, J., & Miragliotta, G. (2014, December). Smart factories in Industry 4.0: A review of the concept and of energy management approached in production based on the Internet of Things paradigm. In *Industrial Engineering and Engineering Management (IEEM), 2014 IEEE International Conference on* (pp. 697-701). IEEE.

Stock, T., & Seliger, G. (2016). Opportunities of sustainable manufacturing in industry 4.0. *Procedia Cirp*, *40*, 536–541. doi:10.1016/j.procir.2016.01.129

Sun, C. (2012). Application of RFID technology for logistics on internet of things. *AASRI Procedia*, *1*, 106–111. doi:10.1016/j.aasri.2012.06.019

Sung, T. K. (2018). Industry 4.0: A Korea perspective. *Technological Forecasting and Social Change*, *132*, 40–45. doi:10.1016/j.techfore.2017.11.005

Unay, C. (2001). *Makro Ekonomi*. Bursa: Vipaş.

Van Krevelen, D. W. F., & Poelman, R. (2010). A survey of augmented reality technologies, applications and limitations. *International Journal of Virtual Reality*, *9*(2), 1.

Virtanen, M., Kivimäki, M., Joensuu, M., Virtanen, P., Elovainio, M., & Vahtera, J. (2005). Temporary employment and health: A review. *International Journal of Epidemiology*, *34*(3), 610–622. doi:10.1093/ije/dyi024 PMID:15737968

Walsh, T. (2017). Expert and Non-Expert Opinion about Technological Unemployment. *International Journal of Automation and Computing*, 1-6.

Web of Science. (n.d.). Retrieved from www.webofknowledge.com

Zhou, K., Liu, T., & Zhou, L. (2015, August). Industry 4.0: Towards future industrial opportunities and challenges. In *Fuzzy Systems and Knowledge Discovery (FSKD), 2015 12th International Conference on* (pp. 2147-2152). IEEE.

Chapter 2
Blockchain:
Past, Present, and Future

Duarte Teles
🆔 https://orcid.org/0000-0002-9171-7343
The Instituto Politécnico do Porto, Portugal

Isabel Azevedo
The Instituto Politécnico do Porto, Portugal

ABSTRACT

This chapter provides a conceptual understanding of blockchain, its purpose, and fundamental concepts before discussing two prominent blockchains, Bitcoin and Ethereum, which are, respectively, representative of the first and second generations of this technology. Some applications that are characteristic of the third generation are presented along with their potential and limitations. They also serve to substantiate some of the problems that are discussed later. Thus, the current developments that are addressing the most pressing current issues and the approaches to overcome them are discussed in the vision of the future of blockchain. What will be the fourth generation, with obligatory resolution or mitigation of many of these problems, which could lead to a widespread adoption of the technology in several other sectors, is described.

INTRODUCTION

A significant amount of public attention has been devoted to blockchain, a technology that has been impacting many sectors of activity; with the promise of revolutionizing even more in the near to distant future. Finance, education, health (Cisneros,

DOI: 10.4018/978-1-5225-7949-6.ch002

Aarestrup, & Lund, 2018), (Suberg, 2015), the government sector (Walport, 2016), and communications (Yrjölä, 2017) are a few of the sectors of activity greatly impacted by blockchain technology. For instance, in finance, it offers several key advantages including speeding up and simplifying cross-border payments (Eysden & Boersma, 2016) and to improve online identity management (Boersma, 2016). In Education, MIT has recently started issuing diplomas using this technology (Durant & Trachy, 2017).

As a public, distributed ledger, blockchain essentially stores transactions between two or more unknown parties. Common knowledge is that this technology is often associated with illegal and criminal undergrounds, more specifically drug and weapons trafficking such as the infamous Silk Road marketplace (Norry, 2017). Moreover, the public also links the term blockchain with a means to send value without knowing the parties involved at the speed one can send data over the Internet. Some even try to make a quick profit akin to investing in the stock market, with the idea of getting rich in a quick, easy manner. Moreover, blockchain allows developers to create trust-less, corruption-free, and transparent decentralized software applications (DApps).

As with any modern technology, blockchain faces some significant problems that must be tackled which can slow its massive adoption in the near future. These include scalability, electricity, security and the importance of data protection and its subset data privacy.

The remaining of this chapter is divided into three main parts. The section" Overview of Blockchain Technology" introduces the core concepts of a blockchain, the section "The Past and the Present", contains two subsections: "Blockchain and its Problems", where some of the blockchain's problems are analyzed and reviewed, and "Successful Examples of Blockchain Technology", where it is presented some of its most notable applications. The last section, "The Future", starts with the current state of the most predominant blockchain problems with the aim to overview what the future holds for the blockchain technology. Finally, the last section summarizes the main points discussed in this chapter with some concluding remarks.

OVERVIEW OF BLOCKCHAIN TECHNOLOGY

A blockchain is essentially a public ledger of every transaction ever taken place or, in other terms, a list of records linked together via cryptography called blocks. Each contains transaction data, a timestamp and a cryptographic hash to the previous block (a link), as displayed in Figure 1. Every previous block cannot be altered, changed or edited; cryptography ensures that any change to the contents of a previous block in the chain would invalidate the data in every block after it. This way, a blockchain is by design resistant to modification of its data; it is also immutable and distributed.

Figure 1. The blockchain: several valid blocks linked together

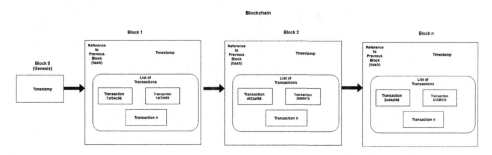

A blockchain uses peer-to-peer technology for multiple computers to be connected between them. It can be therefore described as a peer-to-peer network composed of computers (or more commonly known as nodes) where anyone can join, freely and anonymously. This way, it embraces the distributed nature of a computer network, where there is no central authority controlling it and is therefore highly resistant to censorship. For this reason, a blockchain is often characterized as a decentralized network.

A blockchain is maintained by other special computers in the network called "miners", or network "nodes", which are competing between each other to solve complex mathematical problems --- that are highly difficult to solve but easily verifiable and therefore are energy-intensive --- to ensure a transaction is valid and can, therefore, be added to a new block. These results are shared across all other computers on the network, where they must agree on the solution, hence the term "consensus". Figure 2 illustrates this process known as **mining**.

The node that validates first is labeled a winner and is awarded cryptocurrency as a prize. There are multiple consensus algorithms being used today in many different blockchains. Proof-of-work and proof-of-stake are the most common ones.

Blockchains have changed over the years. The three main generations of this technology are as follows (Swan, 2015):

- **First Generation:** Satoshi Nakamoto, an unknown person, was responsible for the birth of this generation. Blockchains are considered to belong to this generation if they are similar to the world's first cryptocurrency, bitcoin and they employ the Proof-of-Work (PoW) consensus algorithm to validate transactions;
- **Second Generation:** building on top of the first generation, this one adds the concept of smart contracts and the easy tokenization of assets. However, major problems such as scalability, high network fees and substantial amounts of energy consumption surged in this generation;

Figure 2. How miners validate a blockchain

Blockchain Transaction Validation

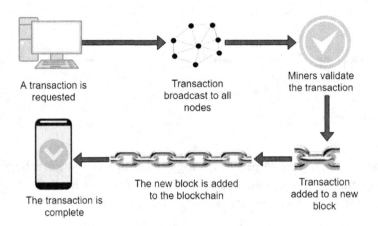

- **Third Generation:** finally, there is a newer, third generation of blockchain: applications beyond currency, economics, and markets. These also attempt to solve some of the problems currently plaguing the second generation of blockchains.

Bitcoin and Ethereum

Two of the most prominent blockchains are Bitcoin (Bitcoin Project, 2018), and Ethereum (Ethereum Foundation, 2018a). Bitcoin represents the first generation of this technology while Ethereum is an example of the second (Buterin, 2013).

A timeline of some of the most important events for Bitcoin and Ethereum (explained later) is presented in Figure 3 (until 2016) and Figure 4 (from 2016 to 2018), using data from (Crane, 2017), (Ethereum Foundation, 2018b), (Ethereum Foundation, 2018c), (Davis, 2015), (Ethereum Community, 2018), (Falkon, 2017), (Bahrynovska, 2017), (Akentiev, 2017), (Zen, 2017) and (Logan, 2018). As it can be seen, bitcoin had a rapid growth in less than a decade. It was first used for a simple pizza purchase, where people started to see some value behind this cryptocurrency and it began to be used across a wide spectrum of applications, ranging from all sectors of activity.

Ethereum, on the other hand, introduced the concept of smart contracts, which was first described by (Szabo, 1996) as "a set of promises, specified in the digital form, including protocols within which the parties perform on these promises". Thus, these are self-enforcing agreements which are expressed in computer code and automatically enforceable (Destefanis, Marchesi, Ortu, & Tonelli, 2018). Trust-less development is therefore possible – the idea that business rules can be coded into a smart contract and rest assured these are enforced by computer code running on the Ethereum blockchain for as long as the network is functional.

In addition, the Ethereum blockchain also allows the development of truly decentralized applications. Ethereum has a neat feature of tokenization: the idea is to use a custom currency which can be exchanged to standard Ether, the Ethereum's master token.

Finally, in Figure 3 and Figure 4, the most relevant and important events in Ethereum are listed.

Note that some of these events are explained throughout this chapter.

Figure 3. Bitcoin and Ethereum timelines part one

Bitcoin		Ethereum
	1996	Nick Szabo pioneered the concept of smart contracts
On January 3rd, the first 50 bitcoins are mined by Satoshi Nakamoto, the pseudonymous inventor of bitcoin	2009	Vitalik Buterin begins his research about cryptocurrency and bitcoin
On October 5th, the first U.S. bitcoin exchange rate is published by New Liberty Standard, the first bitcoin exchange site		
On October 12th, the first known sale of bitcoins in the U.S. takes place		
On May 22nd, two pizzas were purchased with 10,000 bitcoins, making the first known tangible items to be purchased with cryptocurrency	2010	
On November 11th, bitcoin reaches 0.36 USD, the first significant increase in its value: 200 percent in five days		
On February 9th, bitcoin crosses the 1,000 USD mark, a 1000 percent increase in six months	2011	
On June 19th, a raid of Mont Gox, the leading bitcoin exchange at the time, marked the first significant free fall of bitcoin: reaching 0.01 USD at first; then recovering to 15 USD		
On April 1st, bitcoin is valued at 100 USD, then 200 USD	2012	
On May 22nd, bitcoin peaks at a record 1,216.70 USD, not reaching this value until 2016	2013	Late this year, Vitalik Buterin publishes the Ethereum White Paper, where he describes in detail the technical design and rationale for the Ethereum protocol and smart contracts architecture
	2014	This January, Ethereum was formally announced by Vitalik at the North American Bitcoin Conference in Miami, Florida, USA
		Between January and April this year, Vitalik started working with Dr. Gavin Wood and together co-founded Ethereum
		This April, Dr. Gavin published the Ethereum Yellow Paper that would serve as the technical specification for the Ethereum Virtual Machine (EVM)
		This June, the Ethereum Foundation, a non-profit organization responsible for Ethereum development, was founded
	2015	Early this year, an Ethereum Bounty Program was launched, offering BTC (bitcoin) rewards for finding vulnerabilities in any part of the Ethereum software stack
		This April, DEVgrants program was announced, which is a program that offers to fund for contributions both to the Ethereum platform and to projects based on Ethereum
		On July 30th, the Ethereum Frontier network launched, and developers began writing smart contracts and decentralized applications to deploy on the live Ethereum network
	2016	

Figure 4. Bitcoin and Ethereum timelines part two

Bitcoin		Ethereum
	2016	On March 14th, Homestead, the second phase of the Ethereum development, was launched. It featured, among other aspects, many protocol improvements which ultimately speed transactions on the network
		This May, the DAO (Decentralized Autonomous Organization) was a decentralized organization that functioned autonomously, without a central party which allowed anyone with a project to pitch their idea to the community and receives funding from this organization. This marks the first substantial Ethereum project, worth 250 million USD
		On June 17th, a hacker found a loophole in the coding that allowed him to drain funds from the DAO. In the first few hours of the attack, 3.6 million ETH were stolen, the equivalent of 70 million USD at the time
Between April 1st and November 28th, bitcoin rises above 1,000 USD, reaching a new all-time high in June with 1 BTC = a little over 3,000 USD; in September this value reaches 5,000 USD. On November 28, bitcoin hits the impressive 11,000 USD mark	2017	On July 19th, Parity, a popular Ethereum wallet, was first hacked with the hacker stealing 150,000 Ethereum, approximately 30 Million USD at the time
On December 17th, bitcoin reaches a new all-time high: 19,783 USD		On November 7th, Parity was hacked again - about 300 million USD was (and still is) frozen and probably lost forever
		On November 28th, CryptoKitties is the world's first game built on the Ethereum network. Users can collect and breed digital cats called CryptoKitties. The game uses ether (ETH) for all its transactions
Between January 1st and July 16th, after peaking at around 20,000 USD, people were already suspicious of its rapid increase in price and began to quickly sell their bitcoin, which drove its price down to 1 BTC = 5,000 to 7,000 USD in the first 6 months of this year	2018	

Consensus Algorithms

Blockchain security originates from its distribution to many different stakeholders that contain a distinct and dissociated copy of the ledger and is dependent on there being thousands of copies of it stored by independent entities, making it figurately "read-only". To secure itself, it requires agreement algorithms to validate transactions and filter bad blocks which could cause harm to the overall network.

Two of the most used consensus algorithms are:

- **Proof-of-Work (PoW):** the concept goes back decades (Dwork & Moni, 1992). It is used to confirm transactions and to add new blocks to the chain by ensuring a certain amount of work solving a cryptographic puzzle was carried out. Bitcoin is a representative blockchain that applies this strategy (Nakamoto, 2008);

- **Proof-of-Stake (PoS):** the consensus is reached with fewer actors as the creator of a new block is chosen, not arbitrarily, but also considering users wealth, also defined as 'stake'. PPCoin was the first cryptocurrency to adopt this consensus mechanism (King & Nadal, 2012).

Both methods ensure that blocks being processed in a transaction are cryptographically validated. Table 1 (Zheng, Dai, Xie, Wang, & Wang, 2017) briefly illustrates the differences and similarities between these two consensus algorithms.

Participating nodes in most blockchains usually enforce the PoW consensus algorithm, which is highly resource-intensive and consumes a substantial amount of energy. However, other blockchains already implement a mixture of PoW and PoS consensus algorithms as a method of significantly reducing electricity consumption and the number of resources needed to perform this task. For example, in Ethereum version **Metropolis**, in its second phase, **Constantinople**, it will transition from PoW to this mixture of PoW and PoS sometime between 2019 to 2021 with the **Casper** consensus mechanism (Dexter, 2018).

Public, Private and Consortium Blockchains

In addition to the three main blockchain generations, each one also has three subcategories: public, private and consortium. Public is the most common one, predominant in Bitcoin, Ethereum and other blockchains and this is the focus of this chapter. In this subcategory, anyone can freely participate in the network by having an auto-generated address assigned to them. For this reason, public blockchains are described as permissionless. A private blockchain is essentially a controlled list of connected nodes, each having its own set of predetermined permissions which ultimately form a private network: they are defined as permissioned blockchains. Moreover, this category tends to be highly centralized and efficient. The final

Table 1. Typical consensus algorithms comparison

Property	PoW	PoS
Node identity management	Open	Open
Energy Saving	No	Partial
Example	Bitcoin and Ethereum	Peercoin (Peercoin, 2018), Ethereum in a future phase

Table 2. Comparisons among public, consortium and private blockchains (Zheng, Dai, Xie, Wang, & Wang, 2017)

Property	Public blockchain	Consortium blockchain	Private blockchain
Consensus determination	Depends on the algorithm	Selected set of nodes	One organization
Consensus process	Permissionless	Permissioned	Permissioned
Read permission	Public	Could be public or restricted	Could be public or restricted
Efficiency	Nearly impossible to tamper	Could be tampered	Could be tampered
Centralized	No	Partial	Yes

subcategory of blockchains is the consortium. It is highly like the private one, with key differences being the partially centralized nature and the number of nodes connected. Table 2 details the key differences between each blockchain subcategory and introduces new concepts such as consensus determination and process. Consensus determination can be defined by how a specific blockchain subcategory determines consensus (i.e. in Bitcoin and Ethereum they use Proof-of-Work) while consensus process is the type of blockchain used: permissioned or permissionless.

THE PAST AND THE PRESENT

Understanding the past (until January 2018) of blockchain technology is mandatory to fully grasp its potential and its concepts. The present (January to October 2018) is also important for anyone to learn from the current state of this technology. In this section, the authors present multiple subsections with emphasis mainly on the past and present, by presenting first the key blockchain problems, and then exploring the most successful projects built with it and how they tackled these issues. Future predictions are reserved for "The Future" section.

Blockchain and Its Problems

In the previous section, it was explained how a blockchain works, with key concepts such as consensus algorithms, the different types of blockchains available and so forth. However, it currently has multiple major problems that prevent its widespread adoption today such as a substantial electricity consumption, major security issues and the lack of data privacy and protection. In this section, its goals are to analyze the said problems, by looking at past data to understand their current state. This is specifically important, as in the next section "Successful Examples of Blockchain Technology" multiple applications are presented with possible solutions to these issues.

Electricity

Electricity cost is a significant problem that both Ethereum and Bitcoin have been facing since their creation. Both PoW and PoS (see section "Overview of Blockchain Technology") require a massive amount of computation --- a lot more in PoW ---, to achieve a solution for the hashes required to build blocks, due to the fact that nonces (a random, generated number that can only be used once) giving enough leading zeros in a block's hash (to solve and generate it), are very hard to discover. This process is measured by an individual's hash power or hash rate: the number of attempts made per second to generate a block (million hashes per second, or MH/s). Ethereum uses Ethash (Ethereum Foundation, 2018d) and Bitcoin employs HashCash (Hashcash). Both are used exclusively for block generation, but Ethash is solely used with Ethereum, while HashCash was adopted in other cryptocurrencies.

A block is accepted by the network when its participants complete a proof-of-work that must cover all the data in the block. All network miners compete to find the solution for a cryptographic puzzle. The miner that found the right solution and therefore announced it to the network and then receives a cryptocurrency reward, as previously illustrated in Figure 2. Each block is generated at approximately every 10 minutes in Bitcoin, while in Ethereum one is generated every 10 to 20 seconds (Bitcoin Wiki, 2018).

When generating a new block, there is also the concept of difficulty: it is what determines the competitive nature of mining. The harder the difficulty, the harder it is to produce a new block. In Bitcoin, every four years, this value increases twofold, therefore halving the reward to miners; in Ethereum there is a decrease in reward but not as significant (Nakamoto, 2009).

With Bitcoin, the idea, in theory, is simple: the more specialized equipment one has, the more hash power is produced which in return brings more reward. In practice, this has already been proven by centralized mining pools – where a group of individuals share their resources to obtain the most possible profit. For example, the three most important mining pools account for over 50% of Bitcoin's hashing power (Blockchain Luxembourg S.A, 2018a). Ethereum, on the other hand, attempts to prevent this with its memory-hard algorithm Ethash which cannot be brute-forced. On top of this, (Vries, 2018) fully compares different hardware and measures the power use and efficiency of bitcoin mining machines, to conclude that, over time, the Bitcoin network consumes an amount of electricity on par with

Figure 5. The estimated all-time number of tera hashes per second (trillions of hashes per second) the Bitcoin network is performing

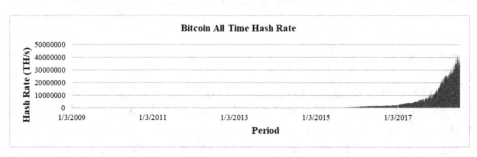

countries such as Ireland. For the near future, he also predicts the Bitcoin network energy consumption will reach alarming levels of 7.67 GW (Gigawatts). With only 200,000 Bitcoin transactions processed per day, it becomes clear Bitcoin has a growing electricity problem.

Figure 5 and Figure 6 show the estimated number of tera hashes (trillions of hashes) per second in both the Bitcoin and Ethereum blockchains. Both figures were generated with data, respectively from (Blockchain Luxembourg S.A, 2018b) and (Etherscan, 2018).

The best way to fully understand the number of electricity blockchains such as Bitcoin and Ethereum consume is by comparing the energy consumption between 1 bitcoin and 100,000 VISA transactions, as seen in Figure 7 - data from (Digiconomist, 2018).

A recent study (Cuthbertson, 2018) predicts Bitcoin will use 0.5% of the world's electricity by the end of 2018.

In conclusion, without electricity, mining in a blockchain is impossible. In Bitcoin, centralized pools exist which try to maximize their profits by sharing resources. With

Figure 6. The estimated all-time number of tera hashes per second (trillions of hashes per second) the Ethereum network is performing

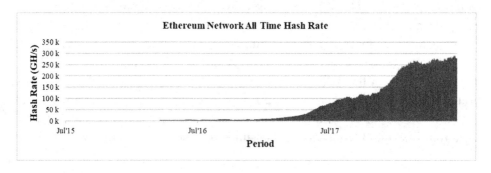

Figure 7. Comparing energy consumption in Kilowatt-hour between one bitcoin transaction and 100 thousand VISA transactions

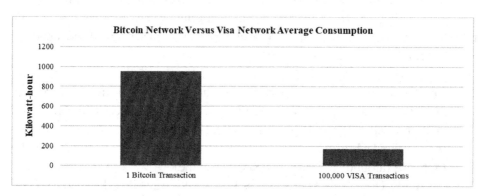

reduced rewards over time for both Bitcoin and Ethereum (although not as significant as Bitcoin), miners may soon look elsewhere to get their reward. Other alternative coins might be considered; however, if the dependency on electricity remains akin to gasoline in cars, the overall cost might be too much to consider remaining profitable in the cryptocurrency business. On top of this, governments are already to block energy access to mining pools (Coppola, 2018). All in all, electricity consumption may prove to be the Achilles kneel of the technology, slowing its adoption growth. It has pointed out that "the only way Bitcoin could reduce its power consumption is through a massive collapse in price" (Weaver, 2018).

Security

Despite the promises of cryptography securing transactions and having a secure, public, and immutable ledger, the reality is that the blockchain is not as secure as one might think. For instance, there are multiple ways to steal cryptocurrency from user's digital wallets. In Bitcoin, this process usually involves exploiting a vulnerability in the user's computer to access his cryptocurrency wallet and transfer these funds to another of the attacker's choosing. To prevent this, a user should have small amounts of possible vulnerable cryptocurrency in hot wallets --- which are connected to the Internet ---, and long-term savings in cold ones which are not connected to the Internet. From the several cold wallets available, arguably the most used are hardware wallets: physical devices that are kept offline with the ability to be plugged into any computer when needed where the user must confirm a transaction by pressing a hardware button (Stellabelle, 2017). This process is theoretically hacker-proof.

In addition, other organizations might capture public trust in their services; ensuring the client deposits their cryptocurrency and therefore they are doing everything they can to keep it secure and free from hackers. On top of that, there are also organizations whose focus is to run an elaborate Ponzi scheme, such as Bitconnect (Mix, 2018). They steal all the deposited cryptocurrency and, after a period, shut down with all the stolen money kept in a given account. There are three major bitcoin heists (Khatwani, 2017):

1. **Mt. Gox:** This Japan-based bitcoin exchange was hacked twice, in June 2011 and 2014. The first time an unknown hacker got access to Mt. Gox's auditor's credentials and transferred a total of 2609 bitcoins. The second time they suffered a breach, with a grand total of 7500,000 bitcoin stolen from the exchange (around 350 Million USD at the time);
2. **BitFloor:** The bitcoin exchange was hacked in 2012 and hackers stole 24,000 BTC (bitcoin);
3. **Poloniex:** Akin to BitFloor and Mt. Gox, this exchange was hacked in 2014, although no exact number of bitcoin stolen was mentioned.

In other newer, popular blockchains such as Ethereum, smart contracts are often supported. These are self-executing agreements between two parties albeit translated into computer code, like a contract between an employer and the employee. They are immutable, decentralized and typically run on a blockchain such as Ethereum. In Ethereum smart contracts, they run on the Ethereum Virtual Machine and can store data which can be used to record information, associations, balances, facts and other information required to implement the logic of real-world contracts.

In addition to the dangers of exploiting known vulnerabilities in an organization's infrastructure, smart contracts are the backbone of all DApps. By being designed to enforce a set of rules automatically, and possibly for a long period of time, many challenges in securing them arise such as a rigorous testing process in their development in addition to predicting and preventing all attack scenarios that might occur years after their creation. On top of this, they are also unchangeable once deployed on the blockchain. The code in smart contracts must, therefore, be thoroughly tested with all the scenarios both short and long-term thought out. Developing smart contracts is also a relatively new process: there is little documentation available, security standards are yet to be robust and best practices are yet to be standardized. Even worse, some high-profile smart contracts hold thousands if not millions of USD in cryptocurrency, making them an easy attack vector for hackers looking to enrich themselves in a moderately easy way.

In Ethereum, there are substantially more high-profile hacks than Bitcoin. The most important ones include Decentralized Autonomous Organization (DAO) and Parity. DAO had no central authority controlling it; operated exclusively using encoded rules in smart contracts - hence, the name autonomous.

Further, the DAO was created at the beginning of May 2016 by a few members of the Ethereum community. As the first of its kind, it was also known as the Genesis DAO and was built with an open-source smart contract on the Ethereum blockchain. The Ethereum community set up an Ethereum Wallet address where anyone could send Ether in exchange for DAO tokens. This was a major success, as the Ethereum community managed to gather 12.7 Ether, or 150 Million USD at the time. Due to Ether's price fluctuation, at some point, the DAO was valued at over 250 Million USD (Falkon, 2017).

In its essence, the DAO was a platform where anyone with a project could pitch their idea to the community directly and receive funding in DAO tokens from it. Further, anyone with DAO tokens could vote on plans and received rewards if the projects turned a profit (Falkon, 2017).

With any major successful project involved, especially with this kind of money involved, hackers are always trying to exploit vulnerabilities and enrich themselves. On June 17, 2016, a hacker found and exploited a loophole which ultimately allowed him to drain funds from the DAO. In the first couple of hours, a grand total of 3.6 million Ether was stolen, or 70 Million USD at that time. After all the damage was done, the attacker withdrew from the hack (Falkon, 2017).

In the exploit, the attacker successfully managed to get the DAO smart contract to give Ether back multiple times to an account before the balance could be updated in the smart contract. However, these funds were subject to a 28-day holding period which prevented the hacker from completing his getaway (Falkon, 2017).

The Ethereum community was split regarding whether the money should be refunded. One side of the community argued the blockchain is immutable, therefore when hacks happen, funds should not be recovered. The other part wanted desperately to recover the lost funds. As a direct result of this, Ethereum was divided into two similar blockchains: Ethereum and Ethereum Classic (Ethereum Classic, 2018). The former is essentially Ethereum but reverted to the point in time just before the DAO hack occurred, so that the money could be recovered. The latter did not revert to a point in time and continued with the DAO lost funds.

In addition to the DAO hack, Parity, an Ethereum wallet, became infamous in 2017 for its clear lack of security. There were two huge vulnerabilities that resulted in the loss of millions of USD in funds:

Part 1: An unknown hacker stole from three accounts a grand total of approximately 32 million USD by exposing a smart contract vulnerability (Pearson, 2017);
Part 2: A person by the GitHub handle @devops199 exploited another vulnerability in the smart contract mentioned above to successfully freeze 300 million USD, most certainly until the end of time (Akentiev, 2017).

Security is certainly one of the most difficult issues to tackle in blockchain technology. In this section, it was covered the different hacks that occurred in blockchain technology in the past, including the most important attacks on the Ethereum Wallet Parity and the DAO. One must understand what attacks were made in the past, in addition, to realize the key focus that must be made on security, to better develop secure blockchain applications in the future.

Data Privacy and Protection

Data is a key element in many businesses. Corporations do not always employ consumer-friendly techniques to protect their valuable data; instead, they may choose to gather it as much, even to influence opinions (Solon & Siddiqui, 2017).

Blockchain technology faces similar problems. Some current concerns are as follows:

- How, if all data is stored publicly, user privacy can be ensured?
- How data can be deleted from the blockchain if it is immutable, especially when a user might request data deletion?
- How blockchain technology can comply with special data protection regulation such as the General Data Protection Regulation (GDPR), already enforceable by the European Union, and the focus of this chapter, albeit several others could have been mentioned as well?

The GDPR is the European Union privacy law that was approved in 2016 and has been enforceable since May 28th, 2018. It also applies to organizations that have offices registered in the EU which process or monitor personal data of EU citizens. This law also has some clear boundaries on what should be considered personal or not: "personal data means any information relating to an identified or identifiable natural person ('data subject'); an identifiable natural person is one who can be identified, directly or indirectly, in particular by reference to an identifier such as a name, an identification number, location data, an online identifier or to one or more factors specific to the physical, physiological, genetic, mental, economic, cultural or social identity of that natural person" (European Union, 2016).

Data subjects, or people using good and services from organizations in the EU, have, under the GDPR, some rights (European Union, 2016):

1. **Right to Data Access:** If a data subject requests to view his data, the organization where this was requested must provide a fully detailed and free transcript of the data collected about him, in addition, to explicitly state in what ways is this information used;

2. **Right to Rectification:** Data subjects have the right to obtain without undue delay the rectification of inaccurate information regarding him or her;

3. **Right to Erasure:** This right ensures that if the data subject wants his personal data deleted, it must be accepted and promptly the data deleted;

4. **Right to Data Portability:** The right for a data subject to receive his personal data in a commonly-used machine-readable format such as JSON or XML. As an example, if the data subject wants to stop having a given service provided by company A and instead purchases this to company B, company A must provide in machine-readable formats the individual's data to company B.

Other important GDPR aspects include privacy by design principles (European Union, 2016) and obtaining consent. To obtain consent, organizations under this law must provide their terms of service in a clear, simple language. The data subject must explicitly agree or disagree with these terms. There cannot be fine prints or other hidden ways to automatically agree on the terms of service. Consent can be easily given or withdrawn at any point in time (European Union, 2016)

Furthermore, the penalties for not complying with this law are enormous: at a lower level, "up to €10 million, or 2% of the worldwide annual revenue of the prior financial year, whichever is higher"; at an upper level, "up to €20 million, or 4% of the worldwide annual revenue of the prior financial year, whichever is higher" (European Union, 2016).

There are several blockchain solutions that might be able to comply with the GDPR. These include:

1. **Quorum:** It is a private/permissioned, blockchain based on the "official Go implementation of the Ethereum protocol. Quorum uses a voting-based consensus algorithm and achieves data privacy through the introduction of a new 'private' transaction identifier. One of the design goals of Quorum is to reuse as much existing technology as possible, minimizing the changes required to go-ethereum in order to reduce the effort required to keep in sync with future versions of the public Ethereum codebase" (JPMorgan Chase & Co, 2016). It achieves data privacy "through cryptography and segmentation. Cryptography is applied to the data in transactions, which everyone sees on the blockchain. Segmentation is applied to each node's local state database which contains the contract storage and is only accessible to the node. Only nodes party to private transactions can execute the private contract code associated with the transactions which result in updating the private contract data storage in the local state database. The result is that each node's local state database is only populated with public and private data they are party to" (JPMorgan Chase & Co, 2016);

Figure 8. A possible approach for a user to invoke the GDPR's right to erasure with Ethereum blockchain technology

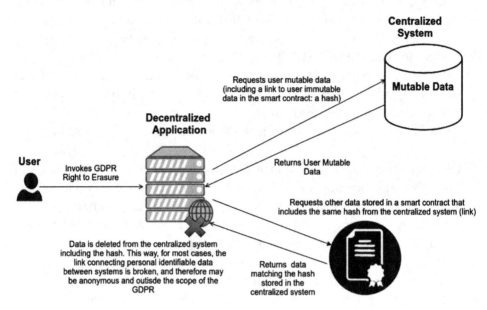

2. **Hawk:** It is a system that uses blockchain-based smart contract, but transactions are encrypted before stored on the blockchain, relying heavily on maintaining data protected (Kosba, Miller, Shi, Wen, & Papamanthou, 2016). Thus, privacy is the main concern. However, although still in active development from 2015, there are no practical uses as of this writing.

In addition to the methods of possibly complying with the GDPR mentioned above, there is one other way: saving mutable data (that is, information that can be changed or deleted such as person's email address) in traditional centralized systems that do not use blockchain technology at all and then proceed to store other data in one or more smart contracts (in the case of Ethereum) where both the smart contracts and the centralized systems have a link between them: a unique hash.

This way, data is safely referenced in the immutable nature of the blockchain, in addition to preserving the right to erasure: once the data subject requests for his data to be deleted, the reference stored in the blockchain is viewed, followed by a query to the centralized system to fetch the right user data. Then, the data is deleted (in the centralized system). Figure 8 better illustrates this idea, when the user invokes this right with Ethereum smart contracts.

The GDPR is an important law in modern history, due to its global stature and principles focused on the end consumer. Moreover, a blockchain, especially a public one, has some key principles such as data immutability that make GDPR compliance difficult.

Successful Examples of Blockchain Technology

Previous significative problems that blockchain technology currently faces today were discussed. Despite these issues, there are several successful examples of applications built with this technology. These range from multiple key sectors of activity, where blockchain technology has been adopted for different purposes.

In this section, some relevant successful blockchain projects in areas besides finance, which t captured the initial applications, are presented.

Health

Currently, health is largely based on electronic health records, which can allow better access to patient data, reducing medical costs and thus gaining the patient's trust. Quickly accessing a comprehensive record of a person's medical history has the potential to provide better diagnostics and treatments, but also some security to clinical treatments. For instance, not knowing that a patient has an allergy to a medication can result in severe consequences. It should be noted that medical errors, due to ignorance of situations like the one mentioned or any other reason, is considered a disease, would rank as the third top cause of death in the United States, in accordance to a recent study (Daniel & Makary, 2016).

However, sensitive data is exchanged between a patient, a physician, and one or more clinics or hospitals.

Estonia is a country with some advancing solutions already developed and others in progress. Electronic health records have been adopted with their integrity ensured by the Keyless Signature Infrastructure (KSI) blockchain. In this section, E-Estonia Healthcare is presented, which is a centralized, digitalized healthcare solution for Estonians with the aim of adding a layer of security and transparency with their own blockchain technology soon.

The last example granted is Medicalchain, a company that recently announced a partnership with Mayo Clinic (Medicalchain, 2018), one of the major health centers in the world.

E-Estonia Healthcare

Estonia is the first country in the European Union to commit to fully embracing blockchain technology in healthcare and every person in Estonia who needed that kind of assistance has an online e-Health record. Sensitive data is "kept completely secure and at the same time accessible to authorized individuals" (E-Estonia, 2018). Estonians are also responsible for the creation of another, yet important blockchain: the KSI blockchain. With it, they are currently testing a system to ensure data integrity with threats to data mitigated (E-Estonia, 2018).

Multiple innovative e-solutions have been created. Estonian health care has two main components:

1. **E-Health Records**: The Electronic Health Record (e-Health Record) is a system available to all Estonian citizens that integrates clinical data from different providers in a record that is accessible to patients. There is a standard format via the e-Patient portal, but each provider can adopt its own system with other formats in use. Authorized professional can access these data as well, and exams results, for instance, can be consulted as soon as they are entered in the system; Despite Estonia leading in digitalized health records storage and accessibility with privacy concerns, they state that their system is still centralized. Soon, they aim to have another version of E-Health Records using their own KSI blockchain to assure the integrity of the whole process;

2. **E-Prescription**: Medical prescriptions are realized through a system that avoids the use of paper, which is unnecessary in the pharmacy too as all data related to the prescription can be consulted by the pharmacist when the patient presents its ID-card.

In summary, with its centralized, digital and secure system, the Estonian government provides its citizens with cutting-edge healthcare and one of the first to truly explore the features of the blockchain to ensure data integrity and a clear access route for system logs.

Medicalchain

Medicalchain is a blockchain project that aims to completely solve many of the problems health care currently faces (Medicalchain, 2018):

1. **Fragmented Health Services:** Legacy systems are predominant, with various data formats and standards which are often vulnerable to attacks;

2. **Patient Data Security:** Electronic health records are stored on centralized databases with a single point of failure. As a result, these are a profitable target for hundreds of hackers worldwide, which employ ransomware techniques to completely disrupt medical services and their patient data;

3. **Record Tampering and Fraud:** Allowing existing medical records to be changed, removed or added ensures an unnecessary risk for the patients by having a record of fake or non-existent conditions. This, therefore, leads to fraud.

Medicalchain has developed a new solution. It adopts what is called an "off-chain storage" where each block contains cryptographic signatures of documents that are remotely stored, and these signatures are used to prove the authenticity of the documents. This kind of storage also allows dealing with regulations that forbid private healthcare data to be stored in other countries (Engelhardt, 2017).

As previously discussed, in section "Overview of Blockchain Technology", Ethereum and Bitcoin blockchains are public blockchains (every transaction made is available in a transparent and immutable manner), that present the issue of privacy in user data, which can be considered as a major drawback in utilizing blockchain technology for medical purposes. However, in Medicalchain, a solution to deal with the security and privacy problems mentioned in section "Blockchain and its Problems" was achieved using a combination of private and public blockchains in addition to other technologies such as a permissioned system to read/write sensitive patient data and a method for patients to grant and revoke access, among others.

Besides Ethereum, Medicalchain uses Hyperledger Fabric, an open-source blockchain platform supported by the Linux Foundation (Linux Fouindation, 2018).

In July 2018, some preliminary uses were planned by Medicalchain for patients of the Groves Medical Group (Ngo, 2018). This pilot experience includes payment with cryptocurrency and, among other functionalities, will improve the overall system. A timeline of Medicalchain is shown in Figure 9, with some past and present events.

The Medicalchain timeline in Figure 9 displays the fast evolution of the company, ranging from a simple startup to one of the industry's leading health experts when using blockchain technology. For this reason, anyone should understand the importance of Medicalchain by analyzing the above timeline.

Education

In most sectors of activity, organizations usually issue some form of document which ensures a person is certified to perform a certain task or is ready for a potential job. Driving licenses and high school diplomas are examples of these documents, that

Figure 9. Medicalchain timeline

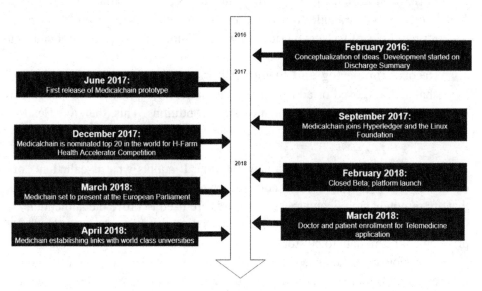

traditionally have been stored in a centralized system, which are prone to attacks and ransomware.

Akin to health care, the education sector faces similar challenges today. In education, important documents such as certificates are often time-consuming and expensive to issue and process. Furthermore, these cannot have its contents altered or even destroyed, but they are highly dependent on institutions' security standards. For this reason, leveraging blockchain technology to issue documents in a tamper-proof, immutable way, have been explored and important documents, such as diplomas, are cryptographically secured and made immutable.

Blockcerts (Blockcerts, 2018a) is the most used and successful example of validating and issuing certificates. It is an open standard which uses blockchain technology to issue credentials. It was created by the developed by MIT's Media Lab and Learning Machine. It integrates "open-source libraries, tools, and mobile apps enabling a decentralized, standards-based, recipient-centric ecosystem, enabling trustless verification through blockchain technologies" (Blockcerts, 2018b).

Blockcerts has three main entities (Blockcerts, 2018b) to ensure privacy and security (see section "Blockchain and its Problems"):

- **Issuer**: Invites the recipient to receive a blockchain credential; uses the address sent from the recipient to send a blockchain credential to him;
- **Recipient**: Accepts and sends the issuer their blockchain address;
- **Verifier**: Checks the blockchain to verify the certificate.

Blockcerts is undoubtedly a successful blockchain project. By being fully open-source, it allows developers and institutions to fully issue credentials powered by all the advantages of the blockchain.

Gaming (E-Sports) and CryptoKitties

With the introduction of the video game Pong back in 1972 by Atari (The Centre for Computing History, 2018), video games became a new form of entertainment for many people worldwide. However, in 1983, this industry crashed massively due to several bad games (Plunkett, 2017). Overall, video gaming eventually recovered with Super Mario Bros in 1985.

In the 1990's, with video games such as Doom, Quake, Half-Life, and Sonic the Hedgehog, there was a clear opportunity for multiplayer experiences. In the 2000's, with Counter-Strike, Halo, Team Fortress 2 the first e-sports tournaments were held (Lopes, 2018). Fast forward to this decade, the biggest e-sports tournaments are held by two corporations, Valve and Riot. The former is responsible for topping the total prize money given to players each year with its signature video game, Dota 2 (E-Sports Earnings, 2018).

Over the past almost five decades, video games have taken new heights in terms of popularity, adoption, and prize money for the competitive scene. Blockchain implementations were the next revolution in this industry and two examples are described in the following subsections: the game CryptoKitties, which allows users to trade, breed and collect unique virtual kittens, and DMarket, a global marketplace where gamers can trade their digital items from multiple video games.

DMarket

The video game industry grows fast every year and this year the total revenue generated is estimated to reach 137.9 Billion USD (Newzoo, 2018). Furthermore, professional gamers earn digital items which can later be traded for money.

In addition, existing technologies are not suited and designed to connect the many existing game platforms together. Players are directly impacted by this with useless gained items despite significant time and effort put into place.

DMarket (DMarket, 2018) is a market based on blockchain technology and open-source Ethereum smart contracts. Users can buy, sell and trade their items from multiple video games such as Dota 2 and Counter-Strike: Global Offensive. Unlike traditional gaming stores, DMarket embraces blockchain technology to store and track user transactions made on the platform. This way, it differentiates itself from other similar platforms by being extremely secure with every transaction publicly available --- and therefore there is a clear lack of privacy --- while combating fraudulent user items and transactions. Most data in DMarket is anonymized, which therefore is outside of the scope of data protection regulations such as the GDPR.

CryptoKitties

CryptoKitties is essentially "a game centered around breedable, collectible, and oh-so-adorable creatures" (CryptoKitties, 2018a). These creatures are cats, each one is unique and owned by a user, and the animal cannot be replicated, taken away or destroyed (CryptoKitties, 2018a).

CryptoKitties is one of the most successful blockchain projects of 2017 and beyond. As a collectible or, more precisely, crypto collectible, it allows anyone to buy, sell, trade CryptoKitties as if it was a traditional collectible, with security and ownership tracking. All of this is anonymized; the user only has to create an Ethereum address to get into action. Even more remarkable is the huge amount of transactions CryptoKitties, soon after launch, was responsible for a large congestion in the Ethereum network, due to its popularity (Wong, 2017). On December 5th, 2017, it was responsible for roughly 25% of the Ethereum network total traffic (CryptoKitties, 2018b).

On top of this, in March 2018, CryptoKitties announced the company had gathered a grand total of 12 million USD in funding. It currently has more than 250 000 users.

CryptoKitties is one of the biggest projects to have ever been made with blockchain technology, more precisely Ethereum. It was one of the first real tests to this network, with its current scalability status being put into question. Most of its data is anonymized, which, in addition to DMarket, is outside of the scope of data protection regulations such as the GDPR.

THE FUTURE

Blockchain technology is already shaping the present with innovative solutions in many sectors of activity. In the past nine years, there have been multiple blockchain generations and each building upon the predecessor with the aim of vastly improving certain aspects such as performance and security. After the second generation, the promise of building complex systems through decentralization became a reality. Each generation has had its fair share of hacks which led to digital assets being lost or stolen.

In the section "Successful Examples of Blockchain Technology", some of the most successful blockchain applications were discussed. One key factor for their success is how they tackle its problems, as seen in a previous section, "Blockchain and its Problems". For instance, Medicalchain combines a mixture of Ethereum and the Linux Foundation's Hyperledger to allow flexibility between user privacy and security, while at the same time having the possibility to comply with data protection regulations such as the GDPR. Cryptokitties and DMarket offer secure and public transactions, albeit anonymously and therefore presenting valid approaches to solve the issue of data protection (by having anonymous data) and security. There are countless more examples not discussed throughout this chapter. The future appears to head into combining the best of current decentralized technologies such as Ethereum or Bitcoin blockchains, in addition to centralized solutions.

Electricity, on the other hand, is the most difficult problem to solve, where only in the next decade or more, could there be more energy-efficient blockchains or newer versions of existing blockchains which allow for blockchain applications to become mainstream. In this section, possible solutions to the problems listed in the section "Blockchain and its Problems" are presented.

Electricity

The main challenge, as described before, is the clear inefficiency of the consensus algorithms, more specifically Proof-of-Work.

According to (Digiconomist, 2018), the amount of U.S. households that could be powered with the electricity consumed to mine bitcoin, the leading cryptocurrency, is **6,662,361**, or simply to put this into another perspective: **32.32** U.S. households can be powered for one day with the electricity required for a single bitcoin transaction. Solving the issue of electricity will not be an easy, straightforward task. Replacing Proof-of-Work with another consensus algorithm such as Proof-of-Stake is the first logical step. By comparing PoW to PoS, it can be concluded that PoS saves more energy and is, therefore, more effective. "Unfortunately, as the mining cost is nearly zero, attacks might come as a consequence" (Zheng, Dai, Xie, Wang, & Wang, 2017). For example, Ethereum is mixing Ethash with Casper in its next version, Metropolis, therefore having a more energy-friendly blockchain (Ethereum Foundation, 2018e).

In addition to PoS and PoW, there are other consensus algorithms which consume far less electricity than these two such as Practical Byzantine Fault Tolerance (PBFT) and Tendermint (Zheng, Dai, Xie, Wang, & Wang, 2017). However, such consensus algorithms are designed only for the permissioned type of blockchains and are not suited as a result for the most predominant category of blockchains: the public one. On top of these, there are others which could be in theory be applied to public blockchains and at the same time solve the critical problem of too much electricity consumption: Proof of Elapsed Time (PoET) uses time as a central aspect with some benefits regarding consumed power and required hardware (Intel Corporation, 2017), and Ripple, a algorithm that subnetworks within the larger network are used, but having been regarded as trustful before (Zheng, Dai, Xie, Wang, & Wang, 2017).

Soon, one of the several consensus algorithms will have to be handpicked and tried to massively reduce the energy fingerprint in the world. Clever solutions to massively reduce energy consumption are needed, and eventually, other consensus algorithms will surge, with little electricity consumption.

Security

Security is another major issue with blockchain technology. In each generation, users usually set up a cold or hot digital wallet to store their bought or earned cryptocurrency. As previously mentioned, one should only have a small amount on hot wallets and their long-term savings in cold wallets.

Financially motivated hackers' probe for known and unknown vulnerabilities in the user's computers, social media accounts or other common attack vectors with the only purpose of stealing cryptocurrency from the user's wallets. Further, in the second generation onwards, smart contracts are significantly difficult to write and cannot be altered once deployed. Therefore, having one or more smart contracts without software bugs, inconsistencies and critical vulnerabilities is an arduous, painful task that few developers achieve.

Furthermore, in recent memory are the many high-profile hacks bitcoin users suffered (as discussed in subsection "Security" under section "Blockchain and its Problems") which resulted in stolen funds from hackers as a direct result of successfully exploiting vulneraries in user's computers or by other attack techniques such as social engineering.

For all these reasons, preventing successful attacks led by financially motivated hackers is the number one priority on pair with fixing electricity consumption.

Keeping cryptocurrency wallets secure from hackers is no easy feat. Handpicking the best possible wallet greatly decreases the chances of a successful attack.

Hardware wallets are by far the safest method of storing cryptocurrency, as they are made of top-grade cryptography which makes them difficult to hack. However, the choice should consider the safest at the time of decision.

Other common-sense steps users should follow to prevent their precious cryptocurrency being stolen are:

Step 1: Never click on suspicious links which can lead to attacker-controlled websites: a technique known as phishing;
Step 2: Keep antivirus and operating system up-to-date;

Step 3: Never transfer cryptocurrency to strange accounts;

Step 4: Use a password manager to safely secure the cryptocurrency wallet;

Step 5: Never give the wallet's private key to anyone;

Step 6: Avoid social engineering attacks;

Step 7: Only buy bitcoin and other cryptocurrencies from reputable exchanges such as Coinbase.

Ethereum revolutionized the world by fully embracing the concept of decentralization through smart contracts. However, developing these is a difficult task for developers. Further, (Tikhomirov, et al., 2018) describe the current security challenges in Ethereum with the most alarming one being the inability to patch smart contracts after deployment.

As discussed, security is one of the leading problems when embracing blockchain technology, in every generation. Funds are stolen via financially-motivated hackers who exploit vulnerabilities in cryptocurrency wallets, user's computers or in smart contracts. To solve this, the authors provided a list of steps anyone should follow for the first generation of blockchains and Ethereum. The authors also believe that in the event, these steps are followed, blockchain technology adoption will rise substantially as a direct consequence of fewer attacks.

Data Privacy and Protection

Another problem blockchain technology faces today is related to privacy and protection, as explained in section "Blockchain and its Problems", subsection "Data Privacy and Protection". Solving data privacy in blockchain technology poses some challenge for the developing community as, by design, its principles are already in violation with data protection regulations.

To comply with strict data protection regulations such as the GDPR, public blockchains keep some data separately and not widely accessible with secure links stored in the blockchain. As blockchain technology matures, there will be more and more solutions that attempt to tackle the difficult issue of privacy in public blockchains such as Ethereum and Bitcoin. However, achieving GDPR compliance for those, without the use of other technologies, is extremely unlikely soon.

In conclusion, the GDPR was not designed for the growing number of applications built using public blockchains such as Ethereum and Bitcoin, as it mandates that organizations must delete data from their users, within a specific timeframe: its right to erasure. This is, as previously discussed, incompatible with the immutable nature of a blockchain. In the future, there are two possible options to solve this problem: one where the EU drafts a version of the GDPR considering its right to erasure and the immutable nature of a blockchain; another where someone develops a privacy solution for public blockchains which can comply with its right to erasure and therefore achieve full GDPR compliance.

CONCLUSION

The first generation of blockchain started in 2009 with a work credited to Satoshi Nakamoto. Since then, the second and third generations surged, with the introduction of smart contracts and a wide application of the technology. At the beginning of this chapter, the core concepts of a blockchain were explained, such as the multiple differences between generations and the most common consensus algorithms in use (Proof-of-Work and Proof-of-Stake) to validate transactions. The key characteristics of different subcategories of blockchain (private, public and consortium) were described, as well as the two most predominant blockchains, Ethereum, and Bitcoin, which are public ones. On top of this, historical perspectives of some events that popularized them were also included.

After an extensive overview of a blockchain, several successful examples of its usage were presented, covering multiple sectors of activity, without neglecting its problems and challenges. These include the massive amounts of electricity consumption, several security concerns with multiple high-profile hacks and the issue of data protection and privacy.

Finally, the future of the technology was examined with the discussion of multiple possible solutions to the problems mentioned. For instance, to drastically diminish the blockchain electricity consumption, a possible approach is to change to a more efficient consensus algorithm. Other possible solutions follow for the other remaining problems.

On a final note, technical and application perspectives were combined in this paper. There are multiple new developments occurring every single day and blockchain can be massively adopted in several key areas following the current trends, and solutions that integrate this technology can become standard.

REFERENCES

Akentiev, A. (2017, November 8). *Parity Multisig Hacked. Again.* Retrieved from https://medium.com/chain-cloud-company-blog/parity-multisig-hack-again-b46771eaa838

Bahrynovska, T. (2017, September 27). *History of Ethereum Security Vulnerabilities, Hacks and their Fixes.* Retrieved from https://applicature.com/blog/history-of-ethereum-security-vulnerabilities-hacks-and-their-fixes

Bitcoin Project. (2018). *Bitcoin is an innovative payment network and a new kind of money.* Retrieved from https://bitcoin.org/en/

Bitcoin Wiki. (2018). *Block.* Retrieved from https://en.bitcoin.it/wiki/Block

Blockcerts. (2018a). *Blockcerts.* Retrieved from https://www.blockcerts.org/

Blockcerts. (2018b). *Blockcerts.* Retrieved from https://www.blockcerts.org/guide/

Blockchain Luxembourg, S. A. (2018a). *Bitcoin Hashrate Distribution.* Retrieved from https://www.blockchain.com/pools

Blockchain Luxembourg, S. A. (2018b). *Hash Rate.* Retrieved from https://www.blockchain.com/charts/hash-rate?timespan=all

Boersma, J. (2016, November 22). *Blockchain technology – how to improve online identity management.* Retrieved from https://www2.deloitte.com/nl/nl/pages/financial-services/articles/4-blockchain-how-to-improve-online-identity-management.html

Buterin, V. (2013). *A Next-Generation Smart Contract and Decentralized Application Platform.* Retrieved from http://blockchainlab.com/pdf/Ethereum_white_paper-a_next_generation_smart_contract_and_decentralized_application_platform-vitalik-buterin.pdf

Cisneros, J. L., Aarestrup, F. M., & Lund, O. (2018). Public Health Surveillance using Decentralized Technologies. *Blockchain in Healthcare Today*, 1-14.

Coppola, F. (2018, May 30). *Bitcoin's Need For Electricity Is Its 'Achilles Heel'.* Retrieved from https://www.forbes.com/sites/francescoppola/2018/05/30/bitcoins-need-for-electricity-is-its-achilles-heel/#688658e72fb1

Crane, J. (2017, December 28). *How Bitcoin Got Here: A (Mostly) Complete Timeline of Bitcoin's Highs and Lows.* Retrieved from http://nymag.com/selectall/2017/12/bitcoin-timeline-bitcoins-record-highs-lows-and-history.html

CryptoKitties. (2018a). *CryptoKitties.* Retrieved from https://www.cryptokitties.co/

CryptoKitties. (2018b). *Key Information.* Retrieved from https://www.cryptokitties.co/technical-details

Cuthbertson, A. (2018, May 16). *Bitcoin will use 0.5% of world's electricity by end of 2018, finds study.* Retrieved from https://www.independent.co.uk/life-style/gadgets-and-tech/news/bitcoin-mining-energy-use-electricity-cryptocurrency-a8353981.html

Daniel, M., & Makary, M. A. (2016). Medical error—the third leading cause of death in the US. *BMJ (Clinical Research Ed.).* PMID:27143499

Davis, W. (2015, April 7). *DEVgrants: Here to Help.* Retrieved from https://blog.ethereum.org/2015/04/07/devgrants-help/

Destefanis, G., Marchesi, M., Ortu, M., & Tonelli, R. (2018, March 20). *1st International Workshop on Blockchain Oriented Software.* Retrieved from https://www.researchgate.net/profile/Giuseppe_Destefanis/publication/323545752_Smart_Contracts_Vulnerabilities_A_Call_for_Blockchain_Software_Engineering/links/5a9bca3d0f7e9be379669bb6/Smart-Contracts-Vulnerabilities-A-Call-for-Blockchain-Software-Enginee

Dexter, S. (2018, August 15). *Ethereum Roadmap Update [2018]: Casper & Sharding Release Date.* Retrieved from https://www.mangoresearch.co/ethereum-roadmap-update/

Digiconomist. (2018). *Comparing Bitcoin's energy consumption to other payment systems.* Retrieved from https://digiconomist.net/bitcoin-energy-consumption

DMarket. (2018). *DMarket Smart Contract.* Retrieved from https://etherscan.io/address/0x2ccbff3a042c68716ed2a2cb0c544a9f1d1935e1#code

Durant, E., & Trachy, A. (2017, October 17). *Digital Diploma debuts at MIT.* Retrieved from https://news.mit.edu/2017/mit-debuts-secure-digital-diploma-using-bitcoin-blockchain-technology-1017

Dwork, C., & Moni, N. (1992). Pricing via Processing or Combatting Junk Mail. In C. Dwork, M. Naor, & E. F. Brickell (Eds.), *Advances in Cryptology --- CRYPTO' 92* (pp. 139–147). Springer Berlin Heidelberg.

E-Estonia. (2018). *Healthcare.* Retrieved from E-Estonia: https://e-estonia.com/solutions/healthcare/e-health-record/

Engelhardt, M. A. (2017). *Hitching healthcare to the chain: An introduction to blockchain technology in the healthcare sector.* Technology Innovation Management Review.

E-Sports Earnings. (2018). *Largest Overall Prize Pools in eSports.* Retrieved from https://www.esportsearnings.com/tournaments

Ethereum Classic. (2018). *Ethereum Classic.* Retrieved from https://ethereumclassic.github.io/

Ethereum Community. (2018). *History of Ethereum.* Retrieved from http://ethdocs.org/en/latest/introduction/history-of-ethereum.html

Ethereum Foundation. (2018a). *Ethereum Blockchain App Platform.* Retrieved from https://www.ethereum.org/

Ethereum Foundation. (2018b). *White Paper.* Retrieved from https://github.com/ethereum/wiki/wiki/White-Paper

Ethereum Foundation. (2018c). *Yellow Paper.* Retrieved from https://github.com/ethereum/yellowpaper

Ethereum Foundation. (2018d). *Ethash.* Retrieved from https://github.com/ethereum/wiki/wiki/Ethash

Ethereum Foundation. (2018e). *Casper Proof of Stake compendium.* Retrieved from https://github.com/ethereum/wiki/wiki/Casper-Proof-of-Stake-compendium

Etherscan. (2018). *Ethereum HashRate Growth Chart.* Retrieved from https://etherscan.io/chart/hashrate

European Union. (2016, April 27). *Regulation (EU) 2016/ 679 of the european parliament and of the council on the protection of natural persons with regard to the processing of personal data and on the free movement of such data.* Retrieved from https://eur-lex.europa.eu/legal-content/EN/TXT/PDF/?uri=CELEX:32016R0679

Eysden, R. A., & Boersma, J. (2016, November 1). *Blockchain technology – speeding up and simplifying cross-border payments.* Retrieved from https://www2.deloitte.com/nl/nl/pages/financial-services/articles/1-blockchain-speeding-up-and-simplifying-cross-border-payments.htm

Falkon, S. (2017, December 24). *The Story of the DAO - Its History and Consequences.* Retrieved from https://medium.com/swlh/the-story-of-the-dao-its-history-and-consequences-71e6a8a551ee

Hashcash. (n.d.). *Hashcash.* Retrieved from http://www.hashcash.org/

Intel Corporation. (2017). *PoET 1.0 Specification.* Retrieved from https://sawtooth.hyperledger.org/docs/core/releases/latest/architecture/poet.html?highlight=proof%20elapsed%20time

JPMorgan Chase & Co. (2016). *Quorum.* Retrieved from https://github.com/jpmorganchase/quorum-docs/blob/master/Quorum%20Whitepaper%20v0.1.pdf

Khatwani, S. (2017, November 11). *Biggest Bitcoin Hacks Ever.* Retrieved from https://coinsutra.com/biggest-bitcoin-hacks

King, S., & Nadal, S. (2012, August 19). *Ppcoin: Peer-to-peer crypto-currency with proof-of-stake.* Retrieved from https://peercoin.net/assets/paper/peercoin-paper.pdf

Kosba, A., Miller, A., Shi, E., Wen, Z., & Papamanthou, C. (2016). *Hawk: The Blockchain Model of Cryptography and Privacy-Preserving Smart Contracts.* Retrieved from https://eprint.iacr.org/2015/675.pdf

Linux Fouindation. (2018). *Hyperledger.* Retrieved from https://www.hyperledger.org/

Logan, S. (2018, May 7). *Ethereum Roadmap Explained.* Retrieved from https://thecryptograph.net/ethereum-roadmap-explained/

Lopes, J. (2018). *eSports History.* Retrieved from https://www.timetoast.com/timelines/esports-history

Medicalchain. (2018). *MedcialChain Whitepaper.* Retrieved from https://medicalchain.com/en/whitepaper/

Medicalchain. (2018, June 18). *Medicalchain Announces Joint Working Agreement with Mayo Clinic.* Retrieved from https://medium.com/medicalchain/medicalchain-announces-joint-working-agreement-with-mayo-clinic-9cfb474dcf0f

Mix. (2018, January 17). *How BitConnect pulled the biggest exit scheme in cryptocurrency.* Retrieved from https://thenextweb.com/hardfork/2018/01/17/bitconnect-bitcoin-scam-cryptocurrency/

Nakamoto, S. (2008, October 31). *Bitcoin: A Peer-to-Peer Electronic Cash System.* Retrieved from https://bitcoin.org/bitcoin.pdf

Nakamoto, S. (2009, January 10). *Bitcoin v0.1 released.* Retrieved from https://satoshi.nakamotoinstitute.org/emails/cryptography/16/

Newzoo. (2018, April). *2018 Global Games Market.* Retrieved from https://newzoo.com/key-numbers/

Ngo, D. (2018, March 8). *UK Groves Medical Group Partners With Medicalchain To Pilot Blockchain Platform.* Retrieved from https://coinjournal.net/uk-groves-medical-group-partners-with-medicalchain-to-pilot-blockchain-platform/

Norry, A. (2017, November 17). *The History of Silk Road: A Tale of Drugs, Extortion & Bitcoin.* Retrieved from https://blockonomi.com/history-of-silk-road/

Pearson, J. (2017, July 19). *'THIS IS NOT A DRILL:' A Hacker Allegedly Stole $32 Million in Ethereum.* Retrieved from Motherboard: https://motherboard.vice.com/en_us/article/zmvkke/this-is-not-a-drill-a-hacker-allegedly-stole-dollar32-million-in-ethereum

Peercoin. (2018). Retrieved from https://peercoin.net/

Plunkett, J. (2017, August 28). *What was the Great Video Game Crash of 1983?* Retrieved from https://www.bugsplat.com/great-video-game-crash-1983

SolonO.SiddiquiS. (2017, October 31). Retrieved from https://www.theguardian.com/technology/2017/oct/30/facebook-russia-fake-accounts-126-million

Stellabelle. (2017). *Cold Wallet Vs. Hot Wallet: What's The Difference?* Retrieved from https://medium.com/@stellabelle/cold-wallet-vs-hot-wallet-whats-the-difference-a00d872aa6b1

Suberg, W. (2015). *Factom's Latest Partnership Takes on US Health-care.* Retrieved from https://cointelegraph.com/news/factoms-latest-partnership-takes-on-us-healthcare

Swan, M. (2015). *Blockchain: Blueprint for a New Economy.* O'Reilly Media.

Szabo, N. (1996). *Smart Contracts: Building Blocks for Digital Markets.* Retrieved from http://www.fon.hum.uva.nl/rob/Courses/InformationInSpeech/CDROM/Literature/LOTwinterschool2006/szabo.best.vwh.net/smart_contracts_2.html

The Centre for Computing History. (2018). *Atari Pong.* Retrieved from http://www.computinghistory.org.uk/det/4007/Atari-PONG/

Tikhomirov, S., Voskresenskaya, E., Ivanitskiy, I., Takhaviev, R., Marchenko, E., & Alexandrov, Y. (2018). SmartCheck: Static Analysis of Ethereum Smart Contracts. *WETSEB'18: WETSEB'18:IEEE/ACM 1st International Workshop on Emerging Trends in Software Engineering for Blockchain*. Retrieved from http://orbilu.uni. lu/bitstream/10993/35862/1/smartcheck-paper.pdf

Vries, A. d. (2018). Bitcoin's Growing Energy Problem. *Joule*, 801-809.

Walport, M. (2016, January). *Distributed ledger technology: beyond block chain, U.K. Government Office Sci., London, U.K., Tech. Rep.* Retrieved from https://cointelegraph.com/news/factoms-latest-partnership-takes-on-us-healthcare

Weaver, N. (2018). Risks of cryptocurrencies. *Communications of the ACM, 61*(6), 20–24. doi:10.1145/3208095

Wong, J. I. (2017, December 4). *The ethereum network is getting jammed up because people are rushing to buy cartoon cats on its blockchain.* Retrieved from https://qz.com/1145833/cryptokitties-is-causing-ethereum-network-congestion/

Yrjölä, S. (2017). Analysis of Blockchain Use Cases in the Citizens Broadband Radio Service Spectrum Sharing Concept. *International Conference on Cognitive Radio Oriented Wireless Networks*, 128-139.

Zen, A. (2017, November 28). *CryptoKitties: The World's First Ethereum Game Launches Today.* Retrieved from https://www.prnewswire.com/news-releases/cryptokitties-the-worlds-first-ethereum-game-launches-today-660494083.html

Zheng, Z., Dai, H.-N., Xie, S., Wang, H., & Wang, H. (2017). An Overview of Blockchain Technology: Architecture, Consensus, and Future Trends. *ResearchGate*, 557-564.

Chapter 3
Digital Social Networking:
Risks and Benefits

Suparna Dhar
RS Software, India

Indranil Bose
Indian Institute of Management, India

Mohammed Naved Khan
Aligarh Muslim University, India

ABSTRACT

Digital social networking (DSN) sites such as Facebook, Twitter, LinkedIn, WhatsApp, Instagram, Pinterest, among many others have garnered millions of users worldwide. It is an instance of information and communication technology that has brought about changes in the way people communicate, interact, and affected human lifestyle and psyche across the world. Some people have become addicted; some see this as beneficial, while others are skeptical about its consequences. This risk-benefit paradox of DSN flummoxes academicians and practitioners alike. This chapter discusses the social and organizational and business risks and benefits of DSN. It goes on to provide a timeline of the evolution of DSN sites, enumeration of typical characteristics of DSN sites, and a systematic comparison of offline and digital social networking. The chapter intends to serve as a cornerstone towards developing a framework for organizational strategy formulation for DSN.

DOI: 10.4018/978-1-5225-7949-6.ch003

INTRODUCTION

Digital social networking (DSN) is one of the biggest disruptive technology implementations of the twenty-first century having far reaching social and economic implications (Hughes, Rowe, Batey, & Lee, 2012). DSN sites such as Facebook, Twitter, LinkedIn, Instagram, WhatsApp and many others have affected human psyche across the world resulting in significant social upheaval (Kane, Alavi, Labianca, & Borgatti, 2014). DSN has changed the way the masses communicate and exchange information. It has affected the way people act and interact as individuals, in groups, in communities and in the context of organizational networks. The speed and scale of DSN adoption have exceeded all previous technology platforms (Chui *et al.*, 2012). Today, DSN platforms permeate geographic boundaries, physical distances have become meaningless enabling users to connect with people having shared interests and activities across the globe. This phenomenon and its potential risks and benefits have caught the attention of academic researchers (Kaplan and Haenlein, 2010).

DSN allows users' self-disclosure. It has increased users' ability to share views and opinions and propagate information, thus elevating the role of common users to social reporters. User gratification, pervasive access and mobile connectivity attributes have boosted DSN adoption (Park, Kee, and Valenzuela, 2009). Such novel networking capabilities of DSN have introduced new dimensions to social networking habits of the masses. People flock to DSN for fulfilling their social, cultural and professional responsibilities (Van Dijck, 2013). The DSN phenomenon has transcended individual use and permeated the domain of business management, introducing unique unprecedented aspects of business information management (Luo, Zhang, & Duan, 2013). It has become an alternate, albeit more powerful channel for communication, interaction and collaboration among business stakeholders (Skeels and Grudin, 2008) as well as for brand promotion activity (Kim and Ko, 2012).

The convenience in social networking and rich interaction facilitated by DSN is also laden with harmful consequences. Extant literature suggests rumor-mongering, privacy breach and health hazards as negative effects of DSN (Sprague, 2011). Social reporting on DSN led to questions regarding content reliability and which propelled the rumor theory (Oh, Agarwal, and Rao, 2013). Unscrupulous expansion of digital social network introduces social and health risks (Forte, Agosto, Dickard, & Magee, 2016; Holland and Tiggemann, 2016). User gratification is linked to DSN addiction (Ryan, Chester, Reece, and Xenos, 2014). DSN has introduced multi-vocality[1] in communication, which has reduced organizational control on information outflow and branding (Huang, Baptista, & Galliers, 2013).

Review of extant literature on DSN showed that a large number of studies have focused on the benefit facet only, there has been very limited research on the DSN risk (Fox and Mooreland, 2015). Organizational business strategy formulation needs to balance the risks and benefits for optimal leveraging of DSN potential. This necessitates a comparative study of DSN risks and benefits. There exists a gap in literature that necessitates expounding of the DSN benefit and risk paradigms in parallel. This chapter is an attempt to address this gap. It makes an endeavor to examine and expound the risk-benefit paradox inflicting DSN and provides a comparative analysis. The present work intends to serve as a cornerstone towards developing a framework for organizational strategy formulation for DSN.

BACKGROUND

To elicit and expound the risks and benefits of DSN, it is imperative to delve into the evolution and characteristics of DSN. This section provides a brief history of DSN evolution and illustrates DSN characteristics in general and in comparison to offline social networking[2] in particular.

In fact, social networking involves interacting with friends and connections and the phenomenon has undergone multitude of changes with the advent of internet technologies. Offline communications, such as face to face interaction and postal mail, were substituted with online communication, such as email. By the second decade of the twenty-first century, DSN emerged. DSN offered users a novel opportunity of self-disclosure (Liu and Brown, 2014). In general websites[3] the content was largely controlled by the host allowing little or no scope for user-generated content while DSN empower the users to generate and manage the content. These sites foster social networking needs of various types of users. The sites tend to display a consistent set of features and technological capabilities; but vary in focus and interest (Boyd and Ellison, 2007). They cater to diverse cultural, emotional and cognitive needs of users.

A Brief History of DSN

The history of DSNs is quite interesting. SixDegrees.com, the pioneer site, started its journey in 1997 but closed after four years of operation. AsianAvenue, which started in 1999, targeted the Asian American community. Some DSN sites targeted specific geographical or linguistic communities such as QQ and WeChat in China, Odnoklassniki in Russia, VKontakte in Eastern Europe, Skyrock in France, LunarStorm in Sweden, Mixi in Japan and Cyworld in Korea. Bebo became popular in distinct geographical pockets including UK, Australia and New Zealand (Boyd and Ellison, 2007; WEFORUM, 2017). Some sites targeted groups with specific religious, ethnic or sexual orientation. Classmates.com focused on users finding and reconnecting with school and college friends. Sites such as Dogster and Catster targeted pet lovers. Orkut started as an English only site but reinvented itself to cater to Portuguese speaking Brazilians. Friendster launched in 2002 and gained popularity but faced technical and networking challenges with a rise in user base. Later, the site reinvented itself as a gaming site and has since gained popularity in the Asia Pacific region. Live Spaces was launched in 2006 for blogging, messaging and photo sharing, but failed to gain adoption.

Sites such as Ryze.com, LinkedIn, Visible Path and Xing focused on professional users. Ryze.com targeted business and technology community in the San Francisco Bay area but did not gain much adoption. LinkedIn gained popularity among the professionals globally. Academia.edu focused on social networking among academic users. While most DSN sites supported bi-directional relationships, sites such as LiveJournal and Twitter supported unidirectional relationships. Flickr, Youtube and Last.FM focused on sharing content such as photos, videos and music respectively. Facebook started as a closed community site for Harvard and later opened up for public use. The site reported more than 2 billion users in 2017. Some sites focused on specific services, such as Waze for connecting drivers and ReferHire for connecting job seekers. Sites such as Epinions, Yelp and ThirdVoice focused on consumer feedback (Edosomwan, Prakasan, Kouame, Watson, & Seymour, 2011; Stephen and Toubia, 2010).

The social networking sites mentioned in this section are a representative sample from hundreds of such sites. This representative sample of DSN platforms illustrates strategic focus, continuous evolution and transformation based on user profile, and technological and networking capabilities. Though sites have emerged, prospered and gained adoption, yet some have perished too. However, in overall terms there has been increasing adoption on DSN in different spheres of life circumventing age, gender, social and economic status, linguistic and ethnic barriers (Bashar, Ahmad, & Wasiq, 2012). Some large organizations too have developed organizational DSN sites such as Beehive and Bluepages at IBM, Town Square at Microsoft, Watercooler at HP, Harmony at SAP, D Street at Deloitte, and People Pages at Accenture (Archambault and Grudin, 2012; Rooksby et al., 2009) to facilitate better networking among employees. In 2012, McKinsey reported that 70 per cent of the organizations used social technologies, and of these 90 per cent reported business benefits (Chui et al., 2012).

DSN Characteristics

DSN is defined as "web based services that enable users to (1) construct a public or semi-public profile within a bounded system, (2) articulate a list of other users with whom they share a connection, and (3) view and traverse their list of connections and those made by others within the system" (Boyd and Ellison, 2007, p. 2). An alternate definition of DSN provided by Kaplan and Haenlein (2010, p. 63) states, "applications that enable users to connect by creating personal information profiles, inviting friends and colleagues to have access to those profiles, and sending e-mails and instant messages between each other".

DSN sites allow users to create personal profiles, articulate their affiliations and list of network connections, express likes, views, and hobbies that are visible to the network (Boyd and Ellison, 2007; Kaplan and Haenlein, 2010). The articulated profiles allow profile discovery by friends and strangers in the network. The sites allow users to search profiles in the network with specific attributes, such as specific interests or resource access. Users can form new connections and form a network of friends and communities. DSN has thus offered general users a global reach. In fact, the ability to search and connect with like-minded users having similar goals, views and interests has facilitated the formation of cohesive connections on DSN (Padula, 2008). A group of people with cohesive connections endows the network with richer community context (Zhang, Yu, Guo, and Wang, 2014). People with common interests form virtual groups to contribute content, collaboratively explore and enhance their competence in specific knowledge areas. It allows free flow of ideas followed by interactive discussions (Remidez and Jones, 2012).

Users can traverse their digital network to locate and befriend 'friends of friends' and thereby expand their network. Such network expansion involves connecting with offline friends, latent ties and forming entirely new connections, often spanning geographic and cultural boundaries (Haythornthwaite, 2002; Shipps and Phillips, 2013). Thus DSN offers an easy and economical means to form and maintain a large social network with large number of ties (Ellison et al., 2007). User self-disclosures on the platform provide insight into the user's interests and views to others who are part of the network. Users having similar interests, views or sharing common characteristics create virtual communities on DSN sites. Virtual communities formed on common interests promote rich interaction which fosters innovation (Ebner, Leimeister, and Krcmar, 2009).

On DSN, users post self-generated textual and multimedia content or share content posted by other users. The sites empower common users to act as social reporters to share information and views in the network that reaches a global audience (Kaplan and Haenlein, 2010). Unique communication protocols, such as, "like" and emoticons featured by DSN platforms expand the horizon of written communication to convey human feelings, decimating the need of language skills (Wallace *et al.*, 2018).

DSN sites present a fairly consistent set of structural and technological features but vary in their focus and hence attract different types of users exhibiting varied behaviors (Lee and Suh, 2013). The sites primarily vary in the extent of profile visibility, and access to connections and profile content. For example, Facebook requires elaboration of user's personal information for profile creation; Twitter preserves users' anonymity (Hughes *et al.*, 2012) thus creating a structural difference between the two platforms. User anonymity shifts focus to the communication content as opposed to the perpetrator of the information, thus reducing social pressure on content creator (Lee and Suh, 2013). Facebook supports bidirectional connections where the connection represents friendship manifested equally on both the nodes. Twitter supports directed connections, with a follower on one end of the connection and a followee on the other end (Hofer and Aubert, 2013). Some DSN sites have specific user focus, serving users from specific ethnocentric groups based on cultural, religious, sexual and language diversity. Some DSN sites have specific content focus, such as video sharing or pet care extending the scope of focused interaction and information sharing.

Comparison Between Digital and Offline Social Networking

Social networking on DSN platforms varies significantly from offline social networking. This section enumerates the key differences between them. The six-degrees of separation phenomenon had shown a small distance between any two individuals through the referral chain (Watts and Strogatz, 1998). With network search and traversal features of DSN, this small world has become even smaller (Fu, Liu, & Wang, 2008). Social stratification of similar individuals increases the probability of two individuals having a minimum referral chain with a common friend, but the awareness of this minimum chain is uncertain in offline scenario (Pool and Kochen, 1979). Identifying the right path in the chain is difficult in offline social networks. Online referral webs have facilitated identification of minimum referral chains (Kautz *et al.*, 1997). Online social networks differ from offline networks in ways the new ties are formed to expand the network boundary and form inter-group ties, and in tie strength in the intra-group network (Suh *et al.*, 2011). DSN technology support and asynchronous communication feature allow individuals network to transcend geographical and temporal boundaries. Table 1 provides a comparison of social networking in offline and digital platforms.

DSN RISK-BENEFIT PARADOX

The risk-benefit paradox of DSN from social, organizational and business perspective based requires elaboration. Figure 1 presents a summary of such risks and benefits.

Table 1. Comparison between offline and digital social networking

Feature	Offline social networking	DSN
Profile and self-disclosure (Boyd and Ellison, 2007; Liu and Brown, 2014)	Profiles of network nodes comprise of formal disclosures, impressions of other nodes and hearsay.	Documented digital profiles are generated by self-disclosure. The profile is augmented by network activity visible in the network.
Anonymity and disguise (Hughes *et al.*, 2012)	Anonymity is mostly not possible. Anonymity may be achieved through collusion or disguise.	Anonymity and disguise in the network is permissible in some DSN platforms.
Trust (Bapna *et al.*, 2017)	The people in the network are known to each other and the relationships are endowed with trust.	Connections reflect offline relationships as well as new relations formed on the platform. New relations with hitherto unknown profiles imbibe lower trust.
Network traversal and discovery (Boyd and Ellison, 2007; Kautz, Selman, & Shah, 1997)	Searching the offline network is tedious and slow. Network traversal mediated by common connections. Identifying the right or shortest path in a chain is difficult in offline social networks.	Digital platform allows easy and instant search facility. Traverse the digital network or directly view the network depending on DSN platform. Online referral webs ease the identification of minimum referral chains.
Context collapse (Vitak, 2012)	Offline synchronous communication with personally connections with limited audience.	A large, distributed, weakly tied virtual network has diversified audience of information shared.
Communication rhythm (Ku, Chu and Tseng, 2013)	Mostly synchronous communication.	Mostly asynchronous communication.
Information diffusion (Guille, Hacid, Favre and Zighed, 2013; Huang *et al.*, 2013; Kaplan and Haenlein, 2010; Luo *et al.*, 2013)	Facilitated by influencers in the network. Opinions and views shared in the network are limited within the network boundary.	Determined by influencers in the network, herd behavior and information cascade. Wide ambit of DSN platforms allows the content to reach a large audience. Increases reach and richness in communication through the digital network. Allows sharing and spreading of information virally.
Network expansion (Ellison *et al.*, 2007; Liben-Nowell and Kleinberg, 2007)	Network expansion is slow and effort intensive process. Networks with limited geographic, demographic and cultural variety. Small networks support strong trust.	Digital social networks are highly dynamic, growing and changing rapidly over time, with the addition of nodes and new interchanges along the edges. Networks permeate geographic, demographic and cultural boundaries. Large networks showing weak solidarity and trust.
Content generation and quality (Boyd and Ellison, 2007, Huang et al., 2013)	Content generation is attributed to people with linguistic, artistic, informational and/ or positional privileges. Supports rich media specific content delivered by experts. Content quality review conducted by specialized critics.	Content generation and sharing is democratized. Supports multimedia content generated or shared by people at large which reduces the content reliability. Allows simultaneous consumption and co-production of rhetorical content.
Content integrity (Oh, Agarwal and Rao, 2013)	Noise may be introduced while content flows through the network, distorting the original message, thus reducing integrity of the message. Originator and propagator of the message may not be identifiable and the message flow in the network is not traceable.	Content shared on digital DSN platforms withstands distortion while flowing through the network, thus maintaining integrity of content. In a named network, the profiles of originator and propagator of the message are known and the message flow is digitally traceable.

Figure 1. Risk and benefits of digital social networking sites

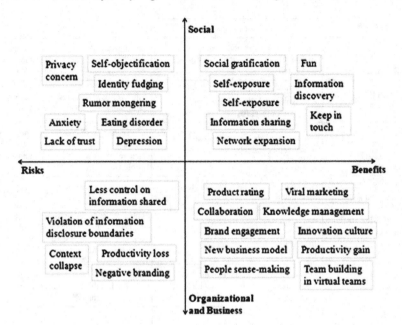

Social Benefits of Digital Social Networks

Social networking involves social norms of reciprocity and trust (Putnam, 2007). Online socializing, self-status seeking, and information exchange motivates the use of digital social networking (Park, Kee, and Valenzuela, 2009). Online social networks facilitate the formation of new ties within the group and across groups to expand the network boundary. Using digital social networking leads to social gratification (Cheung, Chiu, & Lee, 2011). Social relationship influences user engagement in organization's profile pages on digital social networking sites (Men and Tsai, 2013). On the emotional dimension trust, personalization, self-exposure and fun are determinants of using digital social networking (Morris, Teevan and Panovich, 2010). Some users harness their social networks as sources of information and organizational productivity. For example, craft-artists use social networks for information propagation and in return receive "gifts of information" on relevant and beneficial online resources.

Some DSN users access DSN sites multiple times a day and spend significant time for networking (Steinfield, Ellison and Lampe, 2008). DSN intentions include social expectancy, information expectancy, entertainment, and gratification (Park, Kee, and Valenzuela, 2009). Both intrinsic and extrinsic benefit perception drive

DSN use. Intrinsic benefit perceptions on DSN include altruism, obligation, humor, ego, visibility of expertise and feeling of making a unique contribution (Leng et al., 2011). Number of peers and perceived complementarity have strong influence on benefit perception of DSN and motivation to DSN adoption (Lin and Lu, 2011). Coleman (1988) posited human actions are governed by social norms and individual and collective goals. Cheung et al. (2011) study confirmed DSN to be influenced by collective "We-Intention", a subjective norm and compliance in one's social group and social presence.

Extrinsic DSN benefit perception factors include job performance, job satisfaction, organizational commitment and career success of DSN users (Moqbel, Nevo, and Kock, 2013; Seibert et al., 2001). The study by Moqbel et al. (2013) found significant positive effects of DSN use on job performance, job satisfaction and organization commitment, the effect was explained by work-life balance facilitated by DSN as opposed to presenteeism. Location-based social networks allow users to share information on venues visited (Shi and Whinston, 2013), which offers first hand feedback on the venues from experiences shared by friends in the network. Collaborative user-generated content involves richer interaction in the network; the embedded content generates more viewership increasing intensity of interactions in the network (Ransbotham, Kane, & Lurie, 2012).

Computer-mediated interactions show positive effects on community interaction, involvement, and social capital[4] (Hampton and Wellman, 2003). DSN facilitates meeting of likeminded people forming communities of common interest and shared goals, often sharing success stories and solving each other's problems. This improved interaction generates social capital (Hofer and Aubert, 2013). Formation of new ties on DSN leads to formation of large number of ties. DSN allows users to locate and reinvigorate latent ties with past friends and associates, which leads to maintained social capital (Ellison et al., 2007). Weak ties[5] lead to bridging social capital[6] (Putnam, 2000). Weak ties facilitate heterogeneous connections and information diffusion to a large audience which is useful in job searching and knowledge acquisition (Granovetter, 1973). DSNs enable increased interaction and bonding on DSN within a small set of closely knit nodes with strong ties[7]. The increased interaction and information sharing on DSN amongst strong ties enhances trust and leads to bonding social capital[8]. Bonding social capital is associated with access to resources and social support in the network (Wellman, 1988). Strong ties mobilize reciprocity, strong emotional and substantive support, solidarity and access to scarce resources (Williams, 2006). Table 2 provides a summary review of related literature on social impacts of DSN.

Table 2. Summary of related literature on social impact of DSN

Source	Premise of the Study	DSN Benefits
Ellison *et al.* (2007)	Examined the relationship between Facebook and formation and maintenance of social capital through a survey of students.	• Helps generate social capital. • Creates sense of well-being in users experiencing low self-esteem and low life satisfaction
Cheung *et al.*, (2011)	Improved "We-Intention" model (Cheung and Lee, 2010) to include uses and gratification as determinants of DSN intention.	• Improves collaboration and communication • Promotes creativity, collaboration, and sharing knowledge and wisdom • Promotes collective behavior
Hughes *et al.* (2012)	Studied relation between personality and use of DSN. Found DSN use was determined by online socializing and information exchange motivations.	• Improves online socializing and information seeking/exchange
Al-Debei, Al-Lozi, & Papazafeiropoulou (2013)	Examined DSN post-adoption behavior and usage continuance intention. Proposed model extending Theory of Planned Behavior (Ajzen, 1985). Found that value adds on DSN was a key determinant of DSN continuance intention and behavior.	• Offers economic utility • Generates user gratification
Weinberg *et al.*, (2013)	Studied role of collaborative community and expressive individuality in social business context. Argued that the concept of organization is changing – collaborative is gaining prominence complementing organizational structure. Proposed research agenda for future research.	• Facilitates and supports collaborative community • Introduces expressive individuality
Ellison *et al.* (2014)	Studied relationship maintenance behaviors on DSN and its demographic variances and role of social grooming and attention-signaling in determining resource access.	• Improves resource access
Bapna *et al.* (2017)	Did an exploratory research on the association between social ties and economic measure of trust in the context of Facebook.	• Introduces dyadic trust

Organizational and Business Benefits of DSN

Business organizations and governmental bodies use online social networking platforms as a communication channel to maintain customer equity, comprising of brand equity, value equity and relationship equity (Kim and Ko, 2012). Business professionals use DSN to connect and collaborate with their connections including friends in other organizations, colleagues within the organization and external stakeholders (Skeels and Grudin, 2009). In the era of offline communication, information outflow from the organization to public domain was controlled by designated Public Relations Managers. In the era of DSN, information outflow transgresses organizational control, at times the Public Relations Managers become mere observers (Kaplan and Haenlein 2010). All organizational stakeholders are empowered to voice opinions and views and share content either directly on organizations' DSN page or with indirect reference, which has potential impact on organizational branding and reputation.

Digital social networking sites have found widespread use in marketing. Unlike conventional media, DSN offers the ability to generate, share and spread information virally, which is beneficial in marketing (Luo *et al.*, 2013). From the managerial perspective, DSN helps in product rating, customer targeting, product pricing and brand engagement (Dou, Niculescu, & Wu, 2013). DSN allows consumers to exchange information on self-designed customized products and gather network feedback on the individualized product (Hildebrand, Häubl, Herrmann, & Landwehr, 2013). It opens up consumers' access to purchase information and product opinions of other people supporting the brand. It also enables easy access to competitor information thus increasing organizational awareness of competitor products and performance (Lipsman, Mud, Rich and Bruich, 2012).

Organizations use the digital social networking in increasing effectiveness of knowledge sharing and knowledge dissemination. Tacit knowledge displays stickiness, which is difficult to identify, locate, extract and spread (Tsai, 2000). DSN improves organizational ability to locate tacit knowledge and expertise hidden in the resource pool and channelize it to improve the organizational learning process (Rooksby *et al.*, 2009). Online social network platforms encourage people with common interests to form virtual groups to further explore and enhance their competence in specific knowledge areas. It allows free flow of ideas followed by interactive discussions, which fosters exploration and innovation to enhance organizational capability (Remidez and Jones, 2012). DSN alleviates learning process in persons with reduced attention span and attention deficit disorders (Drigas et al., 2014).

DSN facilitates cross-functional innovation by offering a mechanism to share ideas and viewpoints, express concerns, exchange information, and consult experts on a common platform (Huang *et al.*, 2013). Companies engage with end consumers on DSN for product co-creation conversations, consumer feedback, consumer insights and market intelligence. The speed and scale of information exchange create an environment of value co-creation that fosters innovation. Unique collaboration opportunities offered by social technologies dis-intermediates business relationships and helps the formation of new innovative business models (Chui *et al.*, 2012). On DSN the linkage between innovation and productivity is bi-directional - higher innovativeness leads to higher social network productivity and vice-versa (Magnier-Watanabe, Yoshida, & Watanabe, 2010).

DSN offers leverages in areas of project management, human resource management, hiring, organization culture, and so on. Social networking in organizations comprise of formal and informal relationships with employees and other stakeholders, which are determinants of organizational performance and culture (Rooksby *et al.*, 2009). Online DSN introduces a new perspective on people's networking ability and habits. DSN sites improve interaction between employees, specifically in geographically distributed and culturally diversified work environments (Dhar and Bose, 2016). It nurtures an environment of trust and reinforces organizational values and beliefs. DSN helps employees connect with new people, who work closely on a project, even if they do not meet face to face (Remidez and Jones, 2012). Access to user profile and posts help users assess their connections and build a network of trust. Small talk on the platform builds familiarity and rapport, which nurtures the supportive, collaborative and interactive environment. It fosters personal and emotional connect and trust in virtual project teams spread across geographies, time zones and cultural boundaries. Project managers leverage the environment of collaboration and trust to increase stakeholder satisfaction. Table 3 provides a summary review of related literature on business uses of DSN.

Table 3. Summary of related literature on business uses of DSN

Source	Premise of the Study	DSN Benefits
Skeels and Grudin (2009)	Studied the impact of DSN use by professionals in an organization through survey and group interviews. Reported tensions when DSN engagement cuts across social groups or the organization boundary. Found that enterprise level and managerial interest in DSN is high.	• Offers fun, personal socializing/networking • Supports organizational networking and external professional networking • Supports knowledge access, rapport building and people sense-making • Helps build social capital • Benefits productivity
Lovejoy, Waters, and Saxton, (2012)	Examined the organizational use of DSN for user engagement in a study of non-profit organizations. Found organizational use of Twitter as one way communication channel, not maximizing the platform potential in consumer engagement.	• Allows stakeholder engagement
Jussila *et al.* (2014)	Studied online social network usage in the business-to-business sector compared to business-to-consumer sector. Survey analysis showed a significant gap in actual use and perceived DSN potential. Identified mechanisms to help businesst-to-business companies better strategize DSN leverage.	• Enhances communication, interaction, learning and collaboration • Allows innovative products and services, more effective marketing and time to market • Enhance customer collaboration and relationship
Ihm (2015)	Studied organizational ego-networks of non-profit organizations to examine stakeholder-management engagement and stakeholder-stakeholder communication on DSN.	• Improves stakeholder engagement

Social Risks of Digital Social Networking

Individual use of digital social networking carries multitude of risks which includes the psychological impacts of addictive use of these platforms and other direct risks (Ryan *et al.*, 2014). This section enumerates keys risks in DSN use for individuals. This section discusses the social risks of engaging in digital social networking based on literature review.

Online social networks induced users to form new ties, adding hitherto unknown individuals to one's social network based on their unattested digital profiles[9] carrying the risk of forming harmful ties (Forte et al., 2016). Users' lack of awareness and limited understanding of features such as privacy settings and connection grouping features, or unavailability of these features on specific DSN platforms, lead to information proliferation to unintended recipients on DSN. Information shared on DSN dissipates relationship contexts such as family, friends and colleagues. In consequence, unsuspecting DSN users, such as teenagers, become easy victims of cyber-bullying (Wright, 2018).

DSN platform allows general users the capability of self-disclosure in the public domain. Lack of awareness of information disclosure and privacy needs lead to inappropriate information disclosure to unintended recipients (Aggarwal, Gopal, Sankaranarayanan, & Singh, 2012). Malicious intent is manifested as false profiles with fudged and fabricated identity on DSN (Hasib, 2009). The veracity of self-disclosed profile and shared information on DSN needs validation to assure reliability of business insights gained (Park, Huh, Oh, and Han, 2012). However, the traditional measures of trust faltered in the context of online DSN (Bapna, Gupta, Rice, and Sundararajan, 2017).

False profiles and profile-masked content sharing on DSN platforms lead to source ambiguity. Content ambiguity is caused when users post messages on hearsay or forwarded content from other sources without verification. The speed and scale of information exchange on DSN platforms fuels viral circulation of ambiguous content (Oh, Agarwal, and Rao, 2013). Source ambiguity and content ambiguity attributes make DSN a potential rumor-mill. Fast information propagation on DSN could lead to quick spread of rumor, leading to a crisis situation.

DSN use is also associated with physical and psychological disorders (Holland and Tiggemann, 2016). Negative feedback on self-images lowers self-esteem, creates anxiety and depression, and leads to eating disorders. Unique DSN interactions and information exchange can invoke sense of envy with feeling quite distinct from envy generated through offline interaction and information exchange (Wallace et al., 2018). Comparison of self-images with others leads to self-objectification that creates constant anxiety and mental health issues. Comparison with others' activities on DSN induces jealousy, which jeopardizes social relationships. Frequent users of DSN are stressed by peer pressure to constantly keep updated with network activities and anxiety of missing out (Fox and Moreland, 2015). Frequent DSN use increases the risk of agony of dealing with irritating content and cyber-bullying. Table 4 provides a summary literature on risks of DSN.

Organizational and Business Risks of DSN

Organizational use of digital social networking too has its share of risks. One of the major deterrents to organizational adoption of DSN has been a privacy concern (Wisniewski, Islam, Lipford, & Wilson, 2016). Open public information dissemination on digital social networking platforms has the potential to violate organizational information disclosure boundaries (Aggarwal et al., 2012). Unscrupulousness information sharing across context-specific network[10] boundaries leads to undesired information diffusion, allowing information exposure to undesired recipients or groups, resulting in information context collapse[11].

DSN reduces organizational control in communication and introduced multi-vocality (Huang et al., 2013). Decontrolling information outflow to allow multiple people to voice their views and ideas leads to ambiguous and conflicting messages, tarnishing organizational image (Aggarwal *et al.*, 2012). It leads to communication of unverified information and disclosure of confidential or sensitive information, thus incurring loss of business, loss of branding and confusion and discontent among stakeholders. Democratization of information sharing may cause deliberate negative messages from malicious stakeholders. DSN information has the potential to mobilize masses towards collective action, leading to political protests, consumer outrage and social unrest.

Some academicians view DSN to be a waste of valuable time and a productivity killer (Aguenza, Al-Kassem, and Mat Som, 2012; Wilson, 2009). In addition to loss of productive time, addictive use of DSN leads to neuroticism, narcissism, anxiety, depression and other attitude and psychological disorders that have negative effect on performance (Hughes et al., 2012). Some researchers have even questioned the efficacy of DSN in innovation citing that product innovations through DSN involving diverse stakeholders dilute organizational focus and expertise generally associated with product innovation, thus degrading the value of the outcome of the process (Hildebrand et al., 2013).

Speed and scale of information exchange offered by DSN sites introduce risks such as identity theft, reputation damage, intellectual property violation, compromise of privacy (Chui *et al.*, 2012). During 2009 to 2011 timeframe, a major car manufacturer made consecutive large car recalls in the United States due to faulty accelerator pedals. The brand became a target for negative comments in online social networks (Oh, Agrawal and Rao, 2013). This resulted in a dip in overall car sales in the United States and immense negative branding for the manufacturer brand.

Positive brand advocacy from a trusted network of consumers help positive brand reinforcement (Dhar and Bose, 2016). On the other hand, negative feedback causes significant damage to the brand. On DSN, consumers may promote a brand or reinforce competitor brands, either of which impacts organizations' competitive position (Lipsman *et al.*, 2012). Lack of organizational DSN strategy could lead to unforeseen calamities and unwarranted negative branding. When a Red Cross employee accidentally posted a message on beer drinking on organization's Twitter account, it posed a potential threat to Red Cross brand value. Going by their DSN strategy, Red Cross admitted the mistake with humor, which helped the organization avoid the threat (Sprague, 2011). The strategic response resulted in positive branding. The opposite was evident in the case where Domino's Pizza's lack of DSN policy led to an employee posting a YouTube video in 2009. The video reached millions of viewers in a short time, causing the brand a catastrophic damage. Taco Bell was criticized for using Facebook promotions as a cover up. Some organizations scan DSN profile of candidates, their network and activity to evaluate job candidature. However, the unscrupulous use of private information residing in public domain has been interpreted as prying into the candidate's private affairs and it's legitimacy has been questioned (Sprague, 2011).

FUTURE RESEARCH DIRECTIONS

DSNs have increased the availability of data on social networks. They offer improved opportunities to study the basic properties and recurring structural features of social networks (Liben-Nowell and Kleinberg, 2007). Researchers need to study the risks and benefits of sharing profile information, network of connections and content from social and business perspectives. The studies need to encompass the DSN risks and benefits in the context of technological and structural dimensions of digital social networking. For example, a study of possible containment of risk on privacy setting in DSN platform will help researchers determine the effectiveness of privacy settings on organizational application of DSN in the context of marketing activities. There is a need to develop a framework for organizational DSN strategy formulation to minimize the risk paradigm and leverage the benefit paradigm.

Effective use and benefits derived from DSN varies with age, gender, job position, culture, and other demographic parameters (Archambault and Grudin, 2012; Guo, 2015). Researchers need to determine the moderating effects of age, gender and

Table 4. Summary of related literature on risks of DSN

Source	Premise of the Study	DSN Risks
Sprague (2011)	Explored employment related legal issues in context of rising use of DSN. The study offers a set of DSN best practices for employers.	• Introduces possibility of negative branding
Aggarwal et al. (2012)	Studied the efficacy of blogs on product visibility. Explored the consequences of employee negative posts.	• Wields potential to violate organizational information disclosure boundaries • Increases risks of negative branding
Archambault and Grudin (2012)	Conducted a longitudinal study of organizational communication and information-gathering on DSN. Found increase in DSN use. Adoption varied depending on gender, age and position.	• Introduces distraction and reduces productivity • Diffuses information disclosure boundaries
Hildebrand et al. (2013)	Studied effect of network feedback on product self-design process and user satisfaction with self-designed products. The study found negative influence of network feedback on customer satisfaction with self-design products.	• Lowers uniqueness of final self-designs and user satisfaction • Diminishes usage frequency and lowers monetary valuations of the self-designed product
Oh et al. (2013)	Studied efficacy of citizen-driven collective information processing through DSN services in social crises situation. The study covered the citizen reporting to address crisis situation and as potential romor-mill.	• Reduces veracity of information with lack of clarity on information source • Increases anxiety • Allows rumor mongering leading to social crisis situations
Fox and Moreland (2015)	Studied negative psychological and relational experiences of DSN and its affordance. The thematic analysis yielded inappropriate or annoying content, social pressure, privacy concern, self-objectification, and relationship issues and key DSN concerns.	• Allows sharing of inappropriate or annoying content • Causes social pressure to be updated • Diminishes privacy and control • Brings social comparison and jealousy, and relationship tension and conflict
Forte et al. (2016)	Examined the role of DSN in networking between school students and adults. Connecting their findings to literature on homophily[12] and context collapse, the study found that organizational DSN policy supports or inhibits communication in teen-adults.	• Homophily and context collapse on DSN results in awkward and unpleasant interactions • Users become potential victims of predation, exploitation, or harassment on DSN
Holland and Tiggemann (2016)	Did a systematic literature review on DSN use and body image and eating disorders. Found negative network feedback on photo posts on DSN leas to eating disorders.	• Photo sharing and negative network feedback on DSN leads to lower self-esteem, introduces anxiety, depression and eating disorders
Wisniewski et al. (2016)	Studied boundary regulation for privacy preferences on DSN platform design and user behavior. The paper proposed ten boundary types and scales to operationalize them.	• Interpersonal boundary regulation is used to balance the tradeoffs between social interactions in the network and protecting one's privacy on DSN
Wallace et al., (2018)	Studied the relationship between envy and DSN affordances. Proposed a theory on the impact of DSN affordances on envious feelings.	• Invoke envious feelings which lead to depression and lower sense of well-being
Wright (2018)	Examined the moderating effect of parental mediation strategies on the relationship between cyber-bullying victimization and adjustment difficulties.	• Teenagers are susceptible to become victims of cyber-bullying on online DSN platforms

other demographic parameters on the perceived risks and benefits of DSN use. Researchers need to study the risk-benefit paradox on different demographic cohorts so that organizations can align their DSN strategy with demographic cohorts of their stakeholders. The brief history of DSN illustrates the multifarious DSNs in existence. It also depicts the uncertainty of the DSN platform sustainability. Researchers need to understand the optimal employment of DSN platforms and develop models to assess sustainability of DSN platforms.

DSN serves as an effective learning medium for people with lower attention span as seen in the younger generation. Researchers need to study the association between DSN use and productivity to demystify the ensuing debate on whether DSN enhances or diminishes productivity (Archambault and Grudin, 2012; Skeels and Grudin, 2009). DSN risks pertaining to users physical and psychological health leads to anxiety, depression and eating disorders are discussed in academic literature (Holland and Tiggemann, 2016). On the other hand, DSN is attributed to beat loneliness in older generation and feeling of social isolation in new migrants (Damant and Knapp, 2015). This leads to us to question the causal relationship between DSN use and disorders. Researchers need to investigate the cause and effect relationship between DSN use and physical and psychological health. Researchers need to determine the benefits and risks in context of specific DSN platforms and technological and networking features offered therein.

McKinsey estimated that in monetary terms impact of DSN on business communications is likely to be around USD 1 trillion (Chui *et al.*, 2012). However, the risk-benefit paradox of DSN use has left businesses undecided on DSN strategy. There is need to study effective applications of DSN beyond the marketing function. Researchers need to investigate business benefits and risks involved in DSN use in different business functions for policy formulation for effective leveraging of DSN across the organization.

CONCLUSION

It is evident that DSN offers multitudes of risks and benefits on social and organizational business dimensions. The risks and benefits discussed in this chapter are generalized for DSN phenomenon as a whole. Specific feature or specific focused DSN platform may be associated with unique benefits and risks, which need to be explored.

There is need for academic research to unravel DSN intentions and attitudes, expound DSN constructs that determine the risks and benefits and investigate the causal relationship between the risks, benefits and DSN use. There is need to asses optimal employment of DSN platforms and assess sustainability of DSN platforms. The present study intends to provide practitioners with insights into DSN mechanisms and help businesses in making studied managerial decisions at operational management and strategic policies and practices leveraging DSN. From the academic standpoint, the chapter contributes a comprehensive study of extant literature on the topic. It intends to attract academic interest to the risk-benefit paradox of DSN to invigorate further research. The present work intends to serve as a cornerstone in deeper examination of DSN risks and benefits on different dimensions and sub-dimensions towards developing a framework for organizational strategy formulation for DSN.

REFERENCES

Aggarwal, R., Gopal, R., Sankaranarayanan, R., & Singh, P. V. (2012). Blog, Blogger, and the Firm: Can Negative Employee Posts Lead to Positive Outcomes? *Information Systems Research, 23*(2), 306–322. doi:10.1287/isre.1110.0360

Aguenza, B. B., Al-Kassem, A. H., & Mat Som, A. P. (2012). Social Media and Productivity in the Workplace: Challenges and Constraints. *Interdisciplinary Journal of Research in Business, 2*(2), 22–26.

Ajzen, I. (1985). From Intentions to Actions: A Theory of Planned Behavior. In J. Kuhl & J. Beckmann (Eds.), Action Control (pp. 11-39). Springer. doi:10.1007/978-3-642-69746-3_2

Al-Debei, M. M., Al-Lozi, E., & Papazafeiropoulou, A. (2013). Why people keep coming back to Facebook: Explaining and predicting continuance participation from an extended theory of planned behaviour perspective. *Decision Support Systems, 55*(1), 43–45. doi:10.1016/j.dss.2012.12.032

Archambault, A., & Grudin, J. (2012, May). *A Longitudinal Study of Facebook, LinkedIn & Twitter Use*. Paper presented at the SIGCHI Conference on Human Factors in Computing Systems, Austin, TX. 10.1145/2207676.2208671

Bapna, R., Gupta, A., Rice, S., & Sundararajan, A. (2017). Trust And The Strength Of Ties In Online Social Networks: An Exploratory Field Experiment. *Management Information Systems Quarterly, 41*(1), 115–130. doi:10.25300/MISQ/2017/41.1.06

Bashar, A., Ahmad, I., & Wasiq, M. (2012). Effectiveness of Social Media as a Marketing Tool: An Empirical Study. *International Journal of Marketing, Financial Services & Management Research, 1*(11), 88–99.

Boyd, D. M., & Ellison, N. B. (2007). Social Network Sites: Definition, History, and Scholarship. *Journal of Computer-Mediated Communication, 13*(1), 210–230. doi:10.1111/j.1083-6101.2007.00393.x

Butler, B. S. (2001). Membership Size, Communication Activity, and Sustainability: A Resource-Based Model of Online Social Structures. *Information Systems Research, 12*(4), 346–362. doi:10.1287/isre.12.4.346.9703

Cheung, C. M. K., Chiu, P.-Y., & Lee, M. K. O. (2011). Online social networks: Why do students use facebook. *Computers in Human Behavior, 27*(4), 1337–1343. doi:10.1016/j.chb.2010.07.028

Chui, M., Manyika, J., Bughin, J., Dobbs, R., Roxburgh, C., Sarrazin, H., ... Westergren, M. (2012). *The Social Economy: Unlocking Value and Productivity through Social Technologies*. McKinsey Global Institute.

Coleman, J. S. (1988). Social capital in the creation of human capital. *American Journal of Sociology, 94*, S95–S120. doi:10.1086/228943

Damant, J., & Knapp, M. (2015). *What are the likely changes in society and technology which will impact upon the ability of older adults to maintain social (extra-familial) networks of support now, in 2025 and in 2040? Future of ageing: evidence review.* London, UK: Government Office for Science.

Dhar, S., & Bose, I. (2016). Framework for Using New Age Technology to Increase Effectiveness of Project Communication for Outsourced IT Projects Executed from Offshore. In V. Sugumaran, V. Yoon, & M. Shaw (Eds.), *E-Life: Web-Enabled Convergence of Commerce, Work, and Social Life. WEB 2015. Lecture Notes in Business Information Processing* (Vol. 258, pp. 207–211). Cham: Springer. doi:10.1007/978-3-319-45408-5_23

Dou, Y., Niculescu, M. F., & Wu, D. J. (2013). Engineering Optimal Network Effects via Social Media Features and Seeding in Markets for Digital Goods and Services. *Information Systems Research, 24*(1), 164–185. doi:10.1287/isre.1120.0463

Drigas, A. S., Ioannidou, R.-E., Kokkalia, G., & Lytras, M. D. (2014). ICTs, Mobile Learning and Social Media to Enhance Learning for Attention Difficulties. *Journal of Universal Computer Science, 20*(10), 1499–1510.

Ebner, W., Leimeister, J. M., & Krcmar, H. (2009). Community Engineering for Innovations - The Ideas Competition as a method to nurture a Virtual Community for Innovations. *R & D Management, 39*(4), 342–356. doi:10.1111/j.1467-9310.2009.00564.x

Edosomwan, S., Prakasan, S. K., Kouame, M. D., Watson, J., & Seymour, T. (2011). The History of Social Media and its Impact on Business. *The Journal of Applied Management and Entrepreneurship, 16*(3), 79–91.

Ellison, N., Vitak, J., Gray, R., & Lampe, C. (2014). Cultivating Social Resources on Social Network Sites: Facebook Relationship Maintenance Behaviors and Their Role in Social Capital Processes. *Journal of Computer-Mediated Communication, 19*(4), 855–870. doi:10.1111/jcc4.12078

Ellison, N. B., Steinfield, C., & Lampe, C. (2007). The benefits of Facebook "friends:" Social capital and college students' use of online social network sites. *Journal of Computer-Mediated Communication, 12*(4), 1143–1168. doi:10.1111/j.1083-6101.2007.00367.x

Forte, A., Agosto, D., Dickard, M., & Magee, R. (2016, November). *The Strength of Awkward Ties: Online Interactions between High School Students and Adults.* Paper presented at GROUP '16, Sanibel Island, FL.

Fox, J., & Moreland, J. J. (2015). The dark side of social networking sites: An exploration of the relational and psychological stressors associated with Facebook use and affordances. *Computers in Human Behavior, 45*, 168–176. doi:10.1016/j.chb.2014.11.083

Fu, F., Liu, L., & Wang, L. (2008). Empirical analysis of online social networks in the age of Web 2.0. *Physica A, 387*(2-3), 675–684. doi:10.1016/j.physa.2007.10.006

Granovetter, M. (1973). The strength of weak ties. *American Journal of Sociology, 78*(6), 1360–1380. doi:10.1086/225469

Guille, A., Hacid, H., Favre, C., & Zighed, D. A. (2013). Information Diffusion in Online Social Networks: A Survey. *SIGMOD Record, 42*(2), 17-28. doi:10.1145/2503792.2503797

Guo, Y. (2015). Moderating Effects of Gender in the Acceptance of Mobile SNS Based on UTAUT Model. *International Journal of Smart Home, 9*(1), 203–216. doi:10.14257/ijsh.2015.9.1.22

Hampton, K., & Wellman, B. (2003). Neighboring in Netville: How the Internet supports community and social capital in a wired suburb. *City & Community, 2*(4), 277–311. doi:10.1046/j.1535-6841.2003.00057.x

Hasib, A. A. (2009). Threats of online social networks. *International Journal of Computer Science and Network Security, 9*(11), 288–293.

Haythornthwaite, C. (2002). Strong, weak, and latent ties and the impact of new media. *The Information Society, 18*(5), 385–401. doi:10.1080/01972240290108195

Hildebrand, C., Häubl, G., Herrmann, A., & Landwehr, J. R. (2013). When Social Media Can Be Bad for You: Community Feedback Stifles Consumer Creativity and Reduces Satisfaction with Self-Designed Products. *Information Systems Research, 2*(1), 14–29. doi:10.1287/isre.1120.0455

Hofer, M., & Aubert, V. (2013). Perceived bridging and bonding social capital on Twitter: Differentiating between followers and followees. *Computers in Human Behavior, 29*(6), 2134–2142. doi:10.1016/j.chb.2013.04.038

Holland, G., & Tiggemann, M. (2016). A systematic review of the impact of the use of social networking sites on body image and disordered eating outcomes. *Body Image, 17*, 100–110. doi:10.1016/j.bodyim.2016.02.008 PMID:26995158

Huang, J., Baptista, J., & Galliers, R. D. (2013). Reconceptualizing rhetorical practices in organizations: The impact of social media on internal communications. *Information & Management, 50*(2-3), 112–124. doi:10.1016/j.im.2012.11.003

Hughes, D. J., Rowe, M., Batey, M., & Lee, A. (2012). A tale of two sites: Twitter vs. Facebook and the personality predictors of social media usage. *Computers in Human Behavior, 28*(2), 561–569. doi:10.1016/j.chb.2011.11.001

Ihm, J. (2015). Network measures to evaluate stakeholder engagement with nonprofit organizations on social networking sites. *Public Relations Review, 41*(4), 501-503. http://dx.doi.org./10.1016/j.pubrev.2015.06.018

Jussila, J. J., Kärkkäinen, H., & Aramo-Immonen, H. (2014). Social media utilization in business-to-business relationships of technology industry firms. *Computers in Human Behavior, 30*, 606–613. doi:10.1016/j.chb.2013.07.047

Kane, G. C., Alavi, M., Labianca, G., & Borgatti, S. P. (2014). What's Different about Social Media Networks? A Framework and Research Agenda. *Management Information Systems Quarterly, 38*(1), 274–304. doi:10.25300/MISQ/2014/38.1.13

Kaplan, A. M., & Haenlein, M. (2010). Users of the world, unite! The challenges and opportunities of Social Media. *Business Horizons, 53*(1), 59–68. doi:10.1016/j.bushor.2009.09.003

Kautz, H., Selman, B., & Shah, M. (1997). ReferralWeb: Combining social networks and collaborative filtering. *Communications of the ACM, 40*(3), 63–65. doi:10.1145/245108.245123

Kim, A. J., & Ko, E. (2012). Do social media marketing activities enhance customer equity? An empirical study of luxury fashion brand. *Journal of Business Research*, *65*(10), 1480–1486. doi:10.1016/j.jbusres.2011.10.014

Ku, Y. C., Chu, T. H., & Tseng, C. H. (2013). Gratifications for using CMC technologies: A comparison among SNS, IM, and e-mail. *Computers in Human Behavior*, *29*(1), 226–234. doi:10.1016/j.chb.2012.08.009

Lee, J., & Suh, E. (2013, June). *An Empirical Study of the Factors Influencing Use of Social Network Service*. PACIS, Jeju Island, South Korea.

Leng, G. S., Lada, S., Muhammad, M. Z., Ibrahim, A. A. H. A., & Amboala, T. (2011). An Exploration of Social Networking Sites (SNS) Adoption in Malaysia Using Technology Acceptance Model (TAM), Theory of Planned Behavior (TPB) And Intrinsic Motivation. *Journal of Internet Banking and Commerce*, *16*(2).

Liben-Nowell, D., & Kleinberg, J. (2007). The Link-Prediction Problem for Social Networks. *Journal of the American Society, 58*(7), 1019–1031.

Lin, K.-Y., & Lu, H.-P. (2011). Why people use social networking sites: An empirical study integrating network externalities and motivation theory. *Computers in Human Behavior*, *27*(3), 1152–1161. doi:10.1016/j.chb.2010.12.009

Lipsman, A., Mud, G., Rich, M., & Bruich, S. (2012). Beyond the "Like" Button: The Impact of Mere Virtual Presence on Brand Evaluations and Purchase Intentions in Social Media Settings. *Journal of Advertising Research*, *52*(1), 40–52. doi:10.2501/JAR-52-1-040-052

Liu, D., & Brown, B. B. (2014). Self-disclosure on social networking sites, positive feedback, and social capital among Chinese college students. *Computers in Human Behavior*, *38*, 213–219. doi:10.1016/j.chb.2014.06.003

Lochner, K., Kawachi, I., & Kennedy, B. P. (1999). Social capital: A guide to its measurement. *Health & Place*, *5*(4), 259–270. doi:10.1016/S1353-8292(99)00016-7 PMID:10984580

Lovejoy, K., Waters, R. D., & Saxton, G. D. (2012). Engaging stakeholders through Twitter: How nonprofit organizations are getting more out of 140 characters or less. *Public Relations Review*, *38*(2), 313–318. doi:10.1016/j.pubrev.2012.01.005

Luo, X., Zhang, J., & Duan, W. (2013). Social Media and Firm Equity Value. *Information Systems Research*, *24*(1), 146–163. doi:10.1287/isre.1120.0462

Magnier-Watanabe, R., Yoshida, M., & Watanabe, T. (2010). Social network productivity in the use of SNS. *Journal of Knowledge Management, 14*(6), 910–927. doi:10.1108/13673271011084934

Men, L. R., & Tsai, W. H. S. (2013). Beyond Liking or Following: Understanding Public Engagement on Social Networking Sites in China. *Public Relations Review, 39*(1), 13–22. doi:10.1016/j.pubrev.2012.09.013

Moqbel, M., Nevo, S., & Kock, N. (2013). Organizational Members' Use of Social Networking Sites and Job Performance: An Exploratory Study. *Information Technology & People, 26*(3), 240–264. doi:10.1108/ITP-10-2012-0110

Morris, M. R., Teevan, J., & Panovich, K. (2010, April). *What Do People Ask Their Social Networks, and Why*. Paper presented at the SIGCHI Conference on Human Factors in Computing Systems, New York, NY. 10.1145/1753326.1753587

Oh, O., Agrawal, M., & Rao, H. R. (2013). Community Intelligence and Social Media Services: A Rumor Theoretic Analysis of Tweets During Social Crises. *Management Information Systems Quarterly, 3*(2), 407–426. doi:10.25300/MISQ/2013/37.2.05

Padula, G. (2008). Enhancing the innovation performance of firms by balancing cohesiveness and bridging ties. *Long Range Planning, 41*(4), 395–419. doi:10.1016/j.lrp.2008.01.004

Park, N., Kee, K. F., & Valenzuela, S. (2009). Being immersed in social networking environment: Facebook groups, uses and gratifications, and social outcomes. *Cyberpsychology & Behavior, 12*(6), 729–733. doi:10.1089/cpb.2009.0003 PMID:19619037

Park, S.-H., Huh, S.-H., Oh, W., & Han, S. P. (2012). A Social Network-Based Inference Model for Validating Customer Profile Data. *Management Information Systems Quarterly, 36*(4), 1217–1237. doi:10.2307/41703505

Pool, I. D. S., & Kochen, M. (1979). Contacts and Influence. *Social Networks, 1*(1), 5–51. doi:10.1016/0378-8733(78)90011-4

Putnam, R. D. (2000). *Bowling alone: The collapse and revival of American community*. Simon & Schuster Paperbacks.

Putnam, R. D. (2007). E Pluribus Unum: Diversity and Community in the Twenty-first Century The 2006 Johan Skytte Prize Lecture. *Scandinavian Political Studies, 30*(2), 137–174. doi:10.1111/j.1467-9477.2007.00176.x

Ransbotham, S., Kane, G. C., & Lurie, N. (2012). Network Characteristics and the Value of Collaborative User-Generated Content. *Marketing Science, 31*(3), 387–405. doi:10.1287/mksc.1110.0684

Remidez, H., & Jones, N. B. (2012). Developing a Model for Social Media in Project Management Communications. *International Journal of Business and Social Science, 3*(3), 33–36.

Rooksby, J., Baxter, G., Cliff, D., Greenwood, D., Harvey, N., Kahn, A. W., . . . Sommerville, I. (2009). *Social Networking and the Workplace.* Pew Research Center. Retrieved from http://www.lscits.org/pubs/HOReport1b.pdf

Ryan, T., Chester, A., Reece, J., & Xenos, S. (2014). The uses and abuses of Facebook: A review of Facebook addiction. *Journal of Behavioral Addictions, 3*(3), 133–148. doi:10.1556/JBA.3.2014.016 PMID:25317337

Seibert, S. E., Kraimer, M. L., & Liden, R. E. (2001). A Social Capital Theory of Career Success. *Academy of Management Journal, 44*(2), 219–237.

Shi, Z., & Whinston, A. B. (2013). Network Structure and Observational Learning: Evidence from a Location-Based Social Network. *Journal of Management Information Systems, 30*(2), 185–212. doi:10.2753/MIS0742-1222300207

Shipps, B., & Phillips, B. (2013). Social Networks, Interactivity and Satisfaction: Assessing Socio-Technical Behavioral Factors as an Extension to Technology Acceptance. *Journal of Theoretical and Applied Electronic Commerce Research, 8*(1), 35–52. doi:10.4067/S0718-18762013000100004

Skeels, M. M., & Grudin, J. (2009, May). *When social networks cross boundaries: a case study of workplace use of Facebook and LinkedIn.* Paper presented at the ACM 2009 international conference on Supporting group work, Sanibel Island. 10.1145/1531674.1531689

Sprague, R. (2011). Invasion of the social networks: Blurring the line between personal life and the employment relationship. *University of Louisville Law Review, 50*(1), 1–34.

Steinfield, C., Ellison, N. B., & Lampe, C. (2008). Social capital, self-esteem, and use of online social network sites: A longitudinal analysis. *Journal of Applied Developmental Psychology, 29*(6), 434–445. doi:10.1016/j.appdev.2008.07.002

Stephen, A. T., & Toubia, O. (2010). Deriving Value from Social Commerce Networks. *JMR, Journal of Marketing Research, 47*(2), 215–228. doi:10.1509/jmkr.47.2.215

Suh, A., Shin, K., Ahuja, M., & Kim, M. S. (2011). The Influence of Virtuality on Social Networks Within and Across Work Groups: A Multilevel Approach. *Journal of Management Information Systems*, 28(1), 351–386. doi:10.2753/MIS0742-1222280111

Tsai, W. (2000). Social Capital, Strategic Relatedness and the Formation of Intraorganizational Linkages. *Strategic Management Journal*, 21(9), 925–939. doi:10.1002/1097-0266(200009)21:9<925::AID-SMJ129>3.0.CO;2-I

Van Dijck, J. (2013). *The Culture of Connectivity. A Critical History of Social Media*. New York: Oxford University Press. doi:10.1093/acprof:o so/9780199970773.001.0001

Vitak, J. (2012). The Impact of Context Collapse and Privacy on Social Network Site Disclosures. *Journal of Broadcasting & Electronic Media*, 56(4), 451–470. do i:10.1080/08838151.2012.732140

Wallace, L., Warkentin, M., & Benbasat, I. (2018, January). *How Do You Handle It? Developing a Theory of Facebook Affordances and Envy*. Paper presented at the 51st Hawaii International Conference on System Sciences. Retrieved from http://hdl.handle.net/10125/50544

Watts, D. J., & Strogatz, S. H. (1998). Collective dynamics of 'small-world' networks. *Nature*, 393(6684), 440–442. doi:10.1038/30918 PMID:9623998

WEFORUM. (2017). *The world's most popular social networks, mapped*. Retrieved September 29th, 2017 from https://www.weforum.org/agenda/2017/03/most-popular-social-networks-mapped/

Weinberg, B. D., Ruyter, K., Dellarocas, C., Buck, B., & Keeling, D. I. (2013). Destination Social Business: Exploring an Organization's Journey with Social Media, Collaborative Community and Expressive Individuality. *Journal of Interactive Marketing*, 27(4), 299–310. doi:10.1016/j.intmar.2013.09.006

Wellman, B. (1988). Structural Analysis: From Method and Metaphor to Theory and Substance. In B. Wellman & S. D. Berkowitz (Eds.), *Social Structures: A Network Approach* (pp. 19–61). Cambridge, UK: Cambridge University Press.

Williams, D. (2006). On and Off the 'Net: Scales for Social Capital in an Online Era. *Journal of Computer-Mediated Communication*, 11(2), 593–628. doi:10.1111/j.1083-6101.2006.00029.x

Wilson, J. (2009). Social networking: The business case. *Engineering & Technology*, 4(10), 54–56. doi:10.1049/et.2009.1010

Wisniewski, P., Islam, A. K. M. N., Lipford, H. R., & Wilson, D. C. (2016). Framing and Measuring Multi-dimensional Interpersonal Privacy Preferences of Social Networking Site Users. *Communications of the Association for Information Systems*, *38*, 235–258. doi:10.17705/1CAIS.03810

Wright, M. (2018). Cyberbullying Victimization through Social Networking Sites and Adjustment Difficulties: The Role of Parental Mediation. *Journal of the Association for Information Systems*, *19*(2), 113–123. doi:10.17705/jais1.00486

Zhang, D., Yu, Z., Guo, B., & Wang, Z. (2014). Exploiting Personal and Community Context in Mobile Social Networks. In A. Chin & D. Zhang (Eds.), *Mobile Social Networking. Computational Social Sciences*. New York, NY: Springer. doi:10.1007/978-1-4614-8579-7_6

ADDITIONAL READING

Agarwal, R., Gupta, A. K., & Kraut, R. (2008). Editorial Overview—The Interplay Between Digital and Social Networks. *Information Systems Research*, *19*(4), 243–252. doi:10.1287/isre.1080.0200

Borgatti, S. P., & Foster, P. C. (2003). The Network Paradigm in Organizational Research: A Review and Typology. *Journal of Management*, *29*(6), 991–1013. doi:10.1016/S0149-2063(03)00087-4

Ellison, N. B., Lampe, C., & Steinfield, C. (2009). Social Network Sites and Society: Current Trends and Future Possibilities. *Interaction*, *16*(1), 6–9. doi:10.1145/1456202.1456204

Granovetter, M. (1985). Economic Action and Social Structure: The Problem of Embeddedness. *American Journal of Sociology*, *91*(3), 481–510. doi:10.1086/228311

Kane, G. C., & Borgatti, S. P. (2011). Centrality–Is Proficiency Alignment And Workgroup Performance. *Management Information Systems Quarterly*, *35*(4), 1063–1078. doi:10.2307/41409973

Martin, A., & Bavel, R. V. (2013). *Assessing the Benefits of Social Networks for Organizations*. European Commission.

McPherson, M., Smith-Lovin, L., & Cook, J. M. (2001). Birds of a Feather: Homophily in Social Network. *Annual Review of Sociology*, *27*(1), 415–444. doi:10.1146/annurev.soc.27.1.415

UNCP. (2014). *The Brief History of Social Media.* UNCP. Retrieved from http://www2.uncp.edu/home/acurtis/NewMedia/SocialMedia/SocialMediaHistory.html

Yates, D., & Paquette, S. (2011). Emergency knowledge management and social media technologies: A case study of the 2010 Haitian earthquake. *International Journal of Information Management, 31*(1), 6–135. doi:10.1016/j.ijinfomgt.2010.10.001

KEY TERMS AND DEFINITIONS

Digital Social Networking: Social networking through digital networking platforms such as Facebook, LinkedIn, etc.

Information Expectancy: The degree to which a user believes his/her behavior will help him/her attain gains in seeking and exchanging information.

Self-Objectification: Self-objectification is a process wherein individuals perceive themselves as an object to be looked at and evaluated based on their appearance.

Social Expectancy: The degree to which an individual believes his/her behavior will help him/her attain gains in maintaining and enhancing the social relationship.

Social Network: Social relations studied as a network, where individuals or groups are represented as nodes and their relationship and interactions are represented by edges.

Social Networking: Interacting with friends and connections in ones' social network and expanding ones' social network.

User Gratification: Fulfillment of social and psychological motives and goals through purposeful use of media.

ENDNOTES

[1] Univocality refers to single point control of information outflow from the organization to ensure correctness, avoid ambiguity in the messages and the intended meanings. In contrast, multi-vocality fosters a communication culture that loosens control of information outflow and allows voicing of alternative and multiple views.

[2] Offline social networking refers to connection and interaction with friends and associates in absence of online medium.

[3] General websites refer to static websites and sites hosting web applications other than online social platforms.

[4]   "Good-will, fellowship, mutual sympathy and social intercourse among a group of individuals and families who make up a social unit" (Hanifan, 1916, p. 130).

[5]   Weak ties are social network connections that display weak tie strength. Tie strength combination of the amount of time, the emotional intensity, the intimacy (mutual confiding), and the reciprocal services which characterize the tie.

[6]   Bridging social capital denotes the type of social capital formed between weak ties in a social network.

[7]   Strong ties are social network connections that display strong tie strength.

[8]   Bonding social capital denotes the type of social capital formed between strong ties, such as family and close friends in a social network.

[9]   Self-disclosed digital profiles on DSN are not verified, hence lack veracity. Predators and imposters can create false profiles (Forte et al., 2016).

[10]   A context-specific network refers to the social network formed with a specific context, such as an organization or a family.

[11]   Context collapse refers to the large and diversified audiences possible online as opposed to limited groups reachable in face-to-face interactions.

[12]   Homophily is the tendency to bond with similar people.

Chapter 4
The Future of Digital Game-Based Learning (DGBL) in Shaping Intercultural Communication Competency

Ahmed Karam Yousof
Pennsylvania State University, USA

Nahla Abousamra
Indiana University of Pennsylvania, USA

ABSTRACT

Although intercultural communication has long been a vital issue, accelerating globalization and immigration over the past century have increased its importance. Therefore, it is imperative that education and training in intercultural communication are created and continually evaluated for effectiveness. One operative new strategy is the use of digital game-based learning (DGBL) in intercultural communication training. This chapter aims at explaining—from theoretical and practical perspectives—the effectiveness of DGBL to enhance intercultural communication skills. The chapter expounds on the effectiveness of utilizing DGBL as a pedagogical tool in education and training. It then concludes with demonstrating the research results of using HERO I® as an example of the effectiveness of DGBL for cultural competency training. This interconnectedness between theory and practice projects the future of DGBL in shaping intercultural communication competency.

DOI: 10.4018/978-1-5225-7949-6.ch004

INTRODUCTION

Intercultural communication first became an issue when people began traveling and, as a result, were exposed to other cultures. Prior to these interactions, people could not fully assess their own culture, because they did not have the opportunity to compare it to another culture. It is also important to understand intercultural communication because it can be utilized to highlight many communication problems that naturally occur in interactions between people from different backgrounds such as religion, ethnicity, and education (Spencer-Oatey & Franklin, 2009). Although people of different cultures share some basic concepts, they view these concepts from various angles and perspectives, or through their own cultural biases, leading them to behave in a manner which can be considered irrational or unacceptable when compared to what some people from other cultures consider to be the norm (Bakić-Mirić, 2012). Naturally, then, this can create challenges in communicating effectively across different cultures.

Potential problems in intercultural communication include, but are not limited to, inability to appreciate differences, anxiety, stereotyping, prejudice, and racism (Ihtiyar & Ahmad, 2015; Samovar & McDaniel, 2007; Spencer-Oatey & Franklin, 2009). One strategy to avoid such problems is to develop a strong intercultural communication competency (Bakić-Mirić, 2012; Franklin, 2007). To achieve this, most intercultural training programs require participants to attend classes and interact with people from other cultures. An increasingly important educational strategy is to use digital game-based learning (DGBL) to make education and training more engaging and meaningful by using technological tools to facilitate the learning process.

The history of digital games is a central element in considering the relationship between games and communication. Since the beginning of the 21st century, digital gaming has continued to gain popularity and attract new users from all over the world. In 2006, Nintendo was the first company to capitalize on the communicative side of digital games when the company focused on social gaming by producing video games that enabled all family members to play together (Eklund, 2015). Later, digital games were released with multiplayer features, allowing several players to play together from different locations. Currently, the most popular genre of digital games played over the Internet is social gaming (Lee, Choi, Kim, Park, & Gloor, 2013). Today, digital games have become tools that enhance many cultural activities and meaningful communication (Eklund, 2015; Lee et al., 2013). Accordingly, higher levels of interpersonal communication competency have become a requirement for successful video game players, because online video gamers collaborate or compete with other players to achieve a certain goal. Therefore, players from anywhere in the world can virtually mingle with each other, communicate, and share ideas during their gameplay (Taylor, 2008). Given that digital and online games have brought players from all over the world together, this has important consequences for interpersonal as well as intercultural communication. For example, although players may have different languages, backgrounds, and cultures, they can interconnect to play online games.

DGBL is a desired tool in education because it has a positive impact on intercultural education. This chapter aims at elaborating on the educational effectiveness of DGBL in the context of intercultural competency enhancement. A research-based game – HERO I® has been developed by the authors to explain the effectiveness of DGBL in cultural training. The chapter demonstrates the research results behind the use of the game and how they shed light on the relationship between pedagogy and DGBL to form effective training for enhancing intercultural communication competency.

BACKGROUND

The background in this chapter incorporates two essential sections that are related to intercultural communication and digital game-based learning (DGBL) as a potential training tool for enhancing intercultural communication competency. Accordingly, the two main sections that shape the review of the literature are DGBL and pedagogy, and intercultural communication training.

DGBL and Pedagogy

A trend in the literature shows that digital games and learning are discussed from general and specific perspectives. Hence, this section starts with a discussion of the impact that digital games have had, and continue to have, on pedagogy. It then elaborates on the review of the literature about digital game-based learning and intercultural training.

The Impact of Digital Games on Pedagogy in the Classroom

The impact of digital games on learning and education has been significant. According to researchers, the impact of digital games on pedagogy and education includes an impact on learning and assessment (Gee, 2005; Moline, 2010; Prensky, 2011; Smart & Csapo, 2007). Therefore, implementing digital games as a training tool could be an effective strategy to use in intercultural communication training.

Impact Upon Learning

The use of digital games specifically for educational purposes has been examined by many researchers in different fields related to the learners and the learning process. In terms of learners and their use of games, the literature demonstrates that the use of digital games (i.e. video games) can increase learners' enjoyment and engagement during the learning process (Gee, 2005). Learners are also able to gain critical thinking skills and experience-based learning (Gee, 2005; Prensky, 2011). Prensky (2011) found that digital game-based learning is beneficial to students because it focuses on learners' enjoyment and engagement as well as the intermixing of learning and interactivity into a newly digital and entertaining medium. Guerro (2011) concurred with Prensky's claim by stating that sports games, war games, and even games like *Grand Theft Auto* simulate real-world experiences. Through such games, players must think critically and solve problems without realizing they are learning. Guerro (2011) took the example farther by stating that the Massive Multiplayer Online Games (MMOG) genre of videogames has more educational potential because it necessitates that students do more than just sit passively and listen; rather, it promotes critical thinking. As Guerro noted, "These virtual settings anticipate advanced online learning worlds that can be dedicated to distinct subjects, populated by single users and teams, and pedagogically structured for deep and rapid experience-based learning" (p. 12).

Digital games affect the learning process by promoting constructive and critical learning. Gamers develop constructive learning through being placed in actual experiences (emotionally, physically, and intellectually), such as role-playing scenarios/situations (Lebedeva, Makarova & Tatarko 2013). For example, the Massive Multiplayer Online Games (MMOG) genre of video games focuses on the process, rather than the outcomes of learning by encouraging the player to gain the required skills that enable the player to complete the required mission successfully (Chan, 2012). Experiential use of MMOGs necessitates that gamers use communication and analytical skills as they interact with others who are also playing the game. Moline (2010) found that a constructivist-learning environment exists in some digital games, such as *Lineage*. In this game, an apprenticeship relationship is formed whereby the more experienced veteran players will help a new player by demonstrating successful performance and pointing out important contextual aspects. The veteran player will also teach the new player how to handle certain situations and model what kind of person they should become in order to successfully complete the game. Once the new player is self-sufficient, the veteran player allows the player to play on his or her own.

Digital games also promote critical learning that occurs when one experiences the world in new ways and forms new affiliations (Rehm & Leichtenstern, 2012). Games implement critical learning when they allow a learner to build a virtual world rather than only playing within a pre-designed world. This gives the player the opportunity to express him or herself and interact meaningfully with other participants in the virtual environment (Gee, 2005). Because members are distributed throughout the world, they have an expanded network of friends and colleagues and are able to form new affiliations (Walsh, 2010). However, Guerro (2011) warned that such virtual new affiliations may impede critical learning due to distance, group size, and cultural differences. In fact, if successfully created, online game affiliations or virtual communities of practice can be more successful in promoting critical learning than face-to-face communities because they can attract a more diverse and larger group of individuals while overcoming time and space constraints of face-to-face communities (Gee, 2005).

Impact on Assessment

Researchers have also found that digital games have an impact on assessment by increasing a player's performance in exams (Chen, 2010; Gee, 2005). Competitive games, games with animated characters, and MMOGs without animated characters were three major digital game types examined by research in relation to educational assessment. In one study, Moline (2010) examined the impact a physics computer game had on learning, investigating if collaborative and competitive games affected learning and social practice. Two 8th-grade classes served as the control group and three classes served as the experimental group. The experimental group played the physics game *Supercharged* (Moline, 2010). The results showed that the experimental group performed better on exams after playing the game than the group that did not use the game.

Intercultural Communication Training

Intercultural training contexts and the different types of intercultural training are two main perspectives that emerge in the literature about intercultural communication training. The intercultural training section contains the business and school contexts. Also, the various training types are discussed at the end of this section.

Intercultural Communication Training Contexts

Intercultural communication training was not a commonly used term until 1950. It started in a business- training context where different approaches had been used. However, Intercultural training was marginalized within school settings, due to different factors dealing with pedagogical and social contexts.

Business Context

Since 1950, the year that marked the start of intercultural training, business and intercultural communication training took two approaches: the anthropological and socio-cultural approaches. The first anthropological-based intercultural training took place in 1951 when the Foreign Service Institute assigned Edward Hall as the lead trainer of a training program to service officers assigned to work in different countries (Moon, 2008). Foreign Service personnel were considered representatives of the US government in their countries of assignments. Therefore, they would require a variety of specialized cultural training. In reflecting upon this anthropological approach, Hall (1959) was dissatisfied with the outcomes of this training because the program relied upon theoretical anthropological information. In this approach, Hall focused on general information about cultural differences among nations. Perceiving it difficult to understand and irrelevant, the trainees asked Hall to change the training into something pragmatic and goal-oriented. Thus, Hall redesigned his training to move from macro-analysis (i.e. culture in general) to microanalysis (i.e. smaller cultural units, such as tone of voice, gestures, time, and spatial relations) (Moon, 2008). The socio-cultural approach was then created.

The socio-cultural approach entails training on subjective and objective cultural aspects (Rehm & Leichtenstern, 2012). For culture-specific training that mainly explains subjective culture, training was based on explicitly comparative studies of two or more cultures, often originating in management science (Lebedeva et al., 2013). For the implicit or objective culture, training was primarily based on the pioneering work of Edward Hall, focusing on behavioral orientations and communication styles across a variety of national cultures. This type of training also relied upon the contrastive and value-oriented work of Hofstede (1983, 2010). These two scholars dominate the field of intercultural communication training in business and management worldwide (Franklin, 2007). In a study conducted among 261 intercultural trainers, Berardo and Simons (2004) concluded that Hofstede (1983, 2010) and Hall (1959) together attracted 110 out of 170 responses from trainers when they were asked to name cultural models. The studies by Hofstede and Hall supply insights about the values that can be found in society generally, in the family, at school, and in the workplace in a large variety of national cultures (Franklin, 2007).

School Context

Sociological and pedagogical influences have shaped the way intercultural communication training has been delivered at schools. Studies on school-bound interpersonal communication skills have shown that school-based socialization should be examined with respect to the effect of the host culture on the interpersonal skills of students who belong to other cultures (Lebedeva et al., 2013; Scherr, 2007; Wang

& Kulich, 2015). For example, school is not only the place where the hegemony of the dominant culture is played out and transmitted; it also appears in the scene of daily conflicts about culturally legitimate vs. illegitimate behaviors and values demonstrated by students from the host culture and other cultures (Scherr, 2007).

From a sociological perspective, Barbour (2007) mentioned that education in school should have an increased focus on the relationship between national, racial, ethnic, and religious stereotypes and communication. Hence, Scherr (2007) stressed the fact that multicultural education programs should require the implementation of sociological practices, especially in situations where problems related to sensitivity towards cultural differences among students in class are clearly observed. Consequently, Latane and Bibb (2010) found that difficulties in mutual understanding among school students stem from differences among cultures. He explained that problems and conflicts are likely when students from different cultural origins remain innocently caught in the perspectives and domains of their own culture failing and, therefore, are unable to go beyond their own cultural beliefs and certainties. Further, Siegfried (2011) found that the sociological perspective of multicultural education at schools needs to address the socially disadvantaged migrants and minorities, so that students from diverse and different racial, ethnic, and social class groups will be able to experience educational equality.

The pedagogical influence upon intercultural education at schools involves teachers' expectations about their pupils who belong to different cultures (Stuart & Gay, 2010). Unlike US teachers, teachers in Canadian schools are required to be culturally sensitive to the ethnic and religious backgrounds of their pupils, and to take these into account when choosing instructional materials and methods. In US schools, teachers are not required to cater to any cultural differences that may exist among students in class; however, they should be culturally sensitive to their students' unique backgrounds (Scherr, 2007; Stuart & Gay, 2010). Studies of multicultural education suggest that in interactions between teachers and students, cultural stereotypes shape teachers' expectations about the abilities and potentials of students who appear to come from different cultures (Hugh, 2012). In language education, for example, a recent German study showed that teachers tend to attribute linguistic deficits to children with immigrant backgrounds (Hugh, 2012; Scherr, 2007). This phenomenon contributes to the judgment that immigrant children have low linguistic competence (Scherr, 2007).

Types of Intercultural Communication Training

Wang and Kulich (2015) noted four effective types of intercultural training: (a) cognitive, (b) behavioral, (c) experiential, and (d) culturally assimilating training. Cognitive training emphasizes facts about the host culture. It provides information about what sojourners frequently experience in that culture. Typical teaching methods for this type of intercultural training include lectures, group discussions, and presentation of written materials. The drawback of this approach is the small correlation between mastering facts about a certain culture and the trainees' subsequent ability to function effectively in the host culture (Lebedeva et al., 2013; Wang & Kulich, 2015).

Behavioral training is another type of intercultural communication training. This training focuses on the roles of rewards and punishment in a person's life. Typical methods for this type involve asking trainees to visualize what is rewarding and what is punishing for them in their own culture. Trainees would then be asked to compare between their own culture and the host culture through which to note the differences. The major drawback of this approach is the high degree of specificity required and the relatively few trainees who can benefit from such programs (Hugh, 2012; Smart & Csapo, 2007; Wang & Kulich, 2015).

Experiential training urges trainees to participate in intercultural activities that make them able to experience different cultural aspects of the host culture. Typical methods of experiential training include having trainees role-play potentially problematic situations, take part in simulations of other cultures, and take field trips into other cultures. This face-to-face training is extremely costly and time consuming (Smart & Csapo, 2007; Wang & Kulich, 2015).

The last type of intercultural training is a so-called cultural assimilator. It was designed to prepare individuals from one cultural group for interactions with people from another specific cultural group (Cushner & Brislin, 1996). Wang and Kulich (2015) mentioned a variety of culture-specific assimilators that have been developed for different uses, such as preparing French bankers to live and work in Thailand, preparing American adolescents to volunteer in health programs in Honduras, and preparing white and black servicemen to live and work together in the US military. The challenge in using cultural assimilators, according to Wang and Kulich (2015) is that such training is developed for particular audiences and often tailored for specific purposes. Thus, these assimilators are not applicable to the general public. Additionally, an individual needs to have a wide network of colleagues in the field of cross-cultural training to gain access to the cultural-specific assimilators that have been developed by other trainers (Wang & Kulich, 2015).

THE EFFECTIVENESS OF DIGITAL GAME-BASED LEARNING IN INTERCULTURAL COMMUNICATION TRAINING

The Nature of DGBL

The definitions offered to digital game-based learning in empirical and conceptual research have mostly been instrumental. Every definition has covered one of the purposes that DGBL is used for. Therefore, the nature of DGBL has remained equivocal and broad. The purpose of this section of the chapter is to empirically examine the various explanations of DGBL in order to provide a succinct description of the nature of DGBL.

Coffey (2009) has linked DGBL to instruction and described it as an instructional method that incorporates learning materials with the goal of entertaining and engaging learners. This description has partially been challenged by Hamari, Shernoff, Rowe, Coller, Asbell-Clarke, & Edwards (2016) who defined DGBL as an instructional method that has a sole purpose of educating and training. Thus, they perceive DGBL as a form of serious play that is more developed for education rather than entertainment or leisure. This serious play could be achieved by the design of competitive activities that challenge the learners and help them acquire new skills. Similarly, Erhel and Jamet (2013) stated that the activities must have clear learning objectives that promote learning and cognitive skills. However, game-based learning should take place in a virtual environment in order to be considered digital (Erhel & Jamet, 2013)

DGBL has also been associated with learning skills. Kim, Park, and Baek (2009) suggested that gaming and learning skills are overlapping and both are simultaneously used by learners to gain knowledge. In DGBL, learning strategies and gaming strategies are the primary factors behind the high achievements in both learning and gaming. This implies that higher scores in learning and gaming require better problem-solving abilities, which require, in turn, well-chosen strategies for both learning and gaming (Kim, Park, & Baek, 2013).

The learning environment has been another angle through which DGBL was described. Qian and Clark (2016) described digital game-based learning as the environment that incorporates game content and game play. Both have the purpose of enhancing knowledge and skills. Besides, this gaming environment has problem-solving activities that give the learners a sense of achievement. Furthermore, Huang, Huang, and Tschopp (2010) added that DGBL should be a student-centered environment that helps students achieve the learning goals.

Hence, scholars have associated DGBL with different aspects that can be used as a foundation for describing the nature of DGBL in education. DGBL mainly incorporates instructions, learning objectives, learning skills, and learning environment. The collaborative integration of those aspects forms the pillars of DGBL in education. Lack of any one of those pillars may affect the nature of DGBL and therefore result in deficient learning. A game-based lesson that has clear learning objectives, promotes certain learning skills, and takes place in a virtual environment, yet lacks instructions (i.e. the first pillar) may result in learners losing a sense of direction, as they are not knowledgeable about instructions or what to do. Similarly, the lack of learning objectives (i.e. the second pillar) may result in a game-based learning with no specific goal. The absence of the third or fourth pillars, namely learning skills or a virtual environment from DGBL may result in affecting the plausibility of the game-based learning.

The Pedagogical Effectiveness of DGBL

The pedagogical effectiveness of DGBL in intercultural communication training emerges from the variety of pedagogical approaches that have been utilized in the training programs. This section highlights the types of intercultural communication training programs and pedagogical approaches used in these programs. It then elaborates on the effectiveness of DGBL as a pedagogical approach in terms of cost, ease of use, resemblance to life social problems, and experiential learning.

There are different types of cultural training programs and pedagogical approaches. However, they have lacked effectiveness in helping trainees develop authentic and reliable intercultural communication competency. Hiratsuka, Suzuki, and Pusina (2016) identified five necessary levels that need to be included in the pedagogy of intercultural training programs: interpersonal, intragroup, intergroup, organizational/institutional, and community levels. Wang and Kulich (2015) found that the content of most intercultural training programs focuses mainly on the organizational level. Earlier research conducted by Cushner and Brislin (1996) concluded that culture has two sides: (a) the tangible side, or objective culture, and (b) the invisible side, or subjective culture. Building on this seminal work, other scholars have suggested that most of the intercultural training pedagogy focuses on the objective aspect of culture (i.e. food, costume, music, etc.) rather than the subjective ones (i.e., values, social roles, cultural dimensions) (Franklin, 2007; Gražulis & Markuckienė, 2014; Hiratsuka et al., 2016; Velasco, 2015; Wang & Kulich, 2015). In terms of methods of delivery for intercultural training, most intercultural training programs require participants to attend seminars and classes, interact with people from other cultures, and participate in role-plays and simulations. However, Gražulis and Markuckienė (2014) found that many attendees find this type of training difficult due to the required effort and time commitment related to traveling to such face-to-face programs. While intercultural training in a face-to-face setting can be effective, there are costs to participants, such as spending a significant amount of time and money. Currently, there is no solution to this problem, since there are no affordable cultural training programs available for a large number of individuals (Bakić-Mirić, 2012; Gražulis & Markuckienė, 2014; Hiratsuka et al., 2016). Therefore, it is necessary that more effective and practical training pedagogy be created.

DGBL is a cost-effective and convenient training tool that can be utilized to enhance the intercultural communication competency of participants. Not only can DGBL be used as a training tool to teach the subjective and objective aspects of cultures in a way that many people find more engaging than most traditional approaches, they are also cost-effective tools given that participants do not need to be face-to-face during the training session(s). Lewis (2006) estimated that cross-cultural training and consulting services may annually cost up to $ 850,000. This amount includes the cost of the trainer, materials, needs assessment, evaluation, and follow-up sessions. This figure may even go up when a business corporation hires a consulting and training company. For instance, British Petroleum dedicated millions of dollars for cross-cultural training for its employees (Berardo & Simons, 2004) because it operates in 72 countries and has 74,500 employees (Behrisch, 2016). Big corporations do not rely on on-line training for cross-cultural training, because they rely on the trainer's first-hand experience with the culture (Spencer-Oatey & Franklin, 2009). DGBL has enabled people to attain education and training wherever and whenever it is convenient for them, often at a reduced cost. Pioneering universities and corporations, such as Boston University and IBM, have been educating and training students/employees by using online serious games for the past 30 years (Hugh, 2012; Scherr, 2007). These institutions allow participants to pursue the training they need for improving their intercultural communication skills from anywhere in the world, without interrupting their professional and personal lives, and without the travel costs associated with face-to-face training.

Furthermore, ease of use and accessibility are two additional factors that contribute to the effectiveness of DGBL in enhancing intercultural communication skills. For example, video digital games can be used by all age ranges due to the interactivity and visual nature of these games (Gee, 2005; Guerro, 2011; Prensky, 2011). In addition, digital games are accessible to anyone anywhere in the world provided they have Internet access; thus, people from all over the globe are able to virtually share their online experiences regardless of their cultural background, language, or values (Guerro, 2011; Kain, 2015; Lumby, 2014). Although big corporations and governmental institutions can afford the massive cost of cross-cultural training and consultancy, other institutions may not be able to afford it (Behrisch, 2016). The U.S. Immigration and Customs Enforcement Service stated that the number of exchange students who received education and training in U.S. universities amounted to six million students (Zong & Batalova, 2016). Similarly, the number of U.S. students studying abroad in 2015 was 400,000 students (Zong & Batalova, 2016).

For educational institutions to offer proper cross-cultural training to this massive number of students they will need to rely on learning tools with easy accessibility and that have widespread appeal to students. Therefore, using digital games to teach students about intercultural communication might be that effective tool.

DGBL is also effective because it links pedagogy to real-life social problems that are subject to emerge when an individual is placed into a different culture. Thus, students gain the ability—through DGBL—to develop critical thinking and be able to solve such problems. The skills that are used during game play are similar to the skills needed in solving social problems. Jørgensen (2003) proposed that social and learning problems resemble the game missions. They share the same characteristics, which are: givens, goals, and obstacles. They also mentioned that the process used in solving problems during game play is the same process that can be used to solve social problems. According to Jørgensen (2003), the player's initial task is to comprehend the nature of the problem. Second, the player develops a strategy linking comprehensive activity and physical action. In the last phase, the player's mental activity is realized as physical attempts to solve the problems, otherwise known as intentional action. Besides, Barab, Thomas, Dodge, Carteaux, and Tuzun (2005) found that digital games combine reflection and action: two elements that are highly needed to solve real-life social problems. Therefore, Grundy (1988) and Curtis and Lawson (2002) concluded that computer-based adventure games provide a healthy environment that help learners develop, practice, and master general problem-solving skills.

Another effective use of DGBL in enhancing intercultural communication competency involves the experiential cultural learning that can occur during digital game play. Creating one's own knowledge is a fundamental principle of experiential learning. According to Dewey (2007), experience can be described as a continuous interaction between human beings and their environment. Dewey states that the experience is a result of interplay between the present situation and prior experiences. In learning through digital games, as with all learning, the learner constructs his or her own knowledge through a process called scaffolding (Chan, 2012). Scaffolding in digital games occurs when a more knowledgeable entity (e.g. avatar) creates conditions that enable a novice to practice and build skills and knowledge in order to further develop his/her game competence (Molenaar, Sleegers, & Boxtel, 2014). As the novice improves in skill and becomes more self-sufficient, the more knowledgeable entity provides less guidance. Scaffolding is then gradually removed as the novice becomes self-sufficient and no longer requires the extra support. Moline (2010) noted that multiple level-based digital games are a clear example of scaffolding and experiential learning. The gamer—playing a videogame—may use the initial levels to build up more knowledge and learn instructions about the game. Then he/she becomes more autonomous and relies on the skills developed in the easier levels to overcome the more difficult levels (Chan, 2012; Moline, 2010; Salen & Zimmerman, 2003).

Experiential learning has always been an essential framework for the designers of digital learning environments (Lainema, 2003). Experiential learning builds upon the work of Piaget, Lewin, and Dewey (Nielsen-Englyst, 2003). Successful experiential learning combines two important elements that are direct experience and reflective observation. Kolb's (1984) experiential learning model assumes that learning starts with a definite experience. The learner shapes this experience through collection of data and reflective observations about that experience. Then, the stage of abstract conceptualization is triggered when the learner makes generalizations and forms hypotheses about the experience. In the final stage, the learner tests these hypotheses by going through active experimentation of those hypotheses in new conditions and circumstance. Experiential learning is effective as long as feedback is continuous and provides the foundation for a goal-driven action. Accordingly, the concept of experiential learning is a fruitful framework for integration of gameplay and pedagogy (Kiili, 2005).

HERO I® as an Embodiment of the Pedagogical Effectiveness of DGBL in Intercultural Communication Training

In order to examine the effectiveness of DGBL in intercultural communication training, a video game called HERO I® was developed by the authors to educate individuals about cultural differences between the United States and the Middle East, to assess players' unique levels of cultural awareness, and then to teach these differences and/ or areas of limited cultural understanding. This study aims to explore the possibility of using DGBL to deliver intercultural training to U.S. individuals who have never been exposed to Middle Eastern culture. Using the literature pertaining to DGBL, and intercultural communication and competency, this study examines two primary research questions and hypotheses. .

Research Question 1: Does the HERO I® videogame enhance learning of subjective intercultural communication skills?

Hypothesis 1: There is no significant difference between subjects who complete the HERO I® videogame and those who do not in terms of performance on an instrument measuring their subjective intercultural communication skills.

Research Question 2: Does the HERO I® videogame enhance learning of objective intercultural communication skills?

Hypothesis 2: There is no significant difference between subjects who complete the HERO I® videogame and those who do not in terms of performance on an instrument measuring their objective intercultural communication skills.

METHODOLOGY

The study adopted a Posttest-only design. A posttest-only control group design was used as a research method to investigate the research questions that guided this study. A posttest-only control group is a type of experimental design that consists of two or more groups (Fraenkel & Wallen, 2006). A pretest was not required for this design because the two groups were probabilistically equivalent, as both of them were never exposed, or never had a first-hand experience with Middle Eastern culture. These groups were randomly formed. The posttest was given to both groups; however, only one group played the game while the other group just took the posttest and did not play the game. The game—HERO I®—was developed to educate college-age students about the cultural differences between the United States and the Middle East.

Instruments

HERO I® is a first-person simulation game that was developed and used for this study to educate the subjects about Middle Eastern culture. The experiment group, which played the game, completed two levels of the game. By the end of the two levels, the subjects should have been able to recognize, practice, and evaluate objective and subjective cultural aspects of Middle Eastern culture. Level 1 of the game focused on the explicit and tangible aspects of the culture such as outfit, food, and personal space. Level 2 then focused on the implicit and abstract aspects of the culture such as power, collectivism, and social roles.

Both the control and experiment groups took the Intercultural Communication Competency (ICC) posttest. The ICC test contains 20 questions, wherein 10 questions measure the subjective aspects of the Middle Eastern culture and 10 questions measure the objective aspects of the culture. Three demographic questions conclude the posttest. Split-Half Reliability was used to measure the reliability of the instrument. Split-Half Reliability was used in this study because it measures the reliability of the instrument with one administration.

Face validity was implemented for the ICC test validity. An international faculty from the Middle East examined the content of the ICC posttest as well as the game to determine whether it appeared to be related to that which the researcher wished to measure. Also, the Middle Eastern faculty member decided if the items in the posttest were reasonably representative of Middle Eastern culture. The international faculty member was born and raised in Egypt. He had received his education in Egypt and moved to the United States to pursue his post-graduate studies in Computer Science. Although he has become a U.S. permanent resident, he spends three months every year in his home country to reconnect with his macro family still living in Egypt.

Additionally, a pilot study was conducted to verify the reliability and validity of the instruments. Although the size of the pilot sample depended on the actual sample size that would be used in the study, McCuskar and Gunaydin (2015) mentioned that a sample of approximately 30 to 50 people was usually sufficient to identify any major flaws in the ICC posttest. Therefore, the researcher decided that, before starting the actual data collection, a full pilot study would be conducted. Thirty participants—who would not be part of the experiment itself—were identified to play the game and take the posttest as well as the survey included within it. Not only would this pilot sample be used to verify the reliability and validity of the instruments, but it would also help to test the steps of conducting this posttest from start to finish.

Sample

Undergraduate students enrolled in a midsized (i.e., 12,000 undergraduate and graduate students) university in Western Pennsylvania, from different disciplines and majors, were invited to participate in the study. The sample included undergraduate students from the Communications Media, Computer Science, Sociology, Business, and History Departments. The sample did not have any subjects who might have any prior experience living and/or working in the Middle East. There were 78 students in the experiment group and 80 students in the control group for a total of 158 students. In coordination with some of the faculty in the Communications Media, Business, Computer Science, Sociology, and History Departments, e-mails were forwarded to the students within these majors to invite them to participate in the study. In this e-mail, students were asked to visit the Doodle website to sign up for a timeslot.

Of the 372 students (total number of students enrolled in some of the classes in the above-mentioned majors), 254 students signed up for certain timeslots. However, only 158 students showed up throughout the five-day experiment. According to the power analysis that was conducted to decide on the number of subjects needed for the study compared to the target population, the results indicated that 162 subjects ($N = 162$) are needed at a confidence level of 90% (CF = 0.9). Males represented

Table 1. Treatment breakdown

Subject Group	Treatment	Number of Subjects
Experiment Group	HERO I® & ICC Test	78
Control Group	ICC Test	80

61% ($N = 48$) of the total number of the experiment group ($N = 78$). In the control group, males composed 62% ($N = 50$) of the group ($N = 80$). Table 2 demonstrates the gender distribution among groups.

Statistical Analysis

The two research questions utilized unpaired groups in which the subjects were different. For each research question, differences among individuals were measured. In comparing two groups in each question, an individual in one group could not also be a member of the other group. For this reason, the researcher used an independent *t*-test to determine whether there was a statistically significant difference between the means in the two unrelated groups.

In order to determine if the groups had similar variance, the researcher used Levene's test to find out about the homogeneity of the variances. The test for homogeneity of variance provides an F-statistic and a significance value (p-value). If the significance value is greater than 0.05 (i.e., $p > .05$), group variances can be treated as equal. However, if $p < 0.05$, this means that the homogeneity of variance assumption is violated. If so, an adjustment to the degrees of freedom using the Welch-Satterthwaite method will take place.

RESULTS

The data was analyzed using an independent *t*-test. The first research question investigated whether the HERO I® videogame enhanced learning of subjective intercultural communication skills. Analysis of H1 showed that there was a significant difference between the subjects who played the game and those who did not in learning about the abstract concepts of intercultural communication. The subjects who played the game achieved better scores in the ICC test than those who did not play the game. Similarly, Research Question 2 inquired as to the effectiveness of

Table 2. Gender distribution

Gender		Experiment Group	Control Group	Total
Female	#	30	30	60
	%	39%	38%	38%
Male	#	48	50	98
	%	61%	62%	62%
Total	#	78	80	158
	%	100%	100%	100%

playing HERO I® in terms of enhancing the knowledge of the subjects about the tangible and concrete side of the intercultural communication. Like H1, H2 showed that there was a significant difference between the subjects who played the game and those who did not in learning about the objective side of Middle East culture. According to a comparison of the means of the two groups' scores in the ICC test, those who played the game scored higher than the subjects who did not play the game.

Research Question 1: Does the HERO I® videogame enhance learning of subjective intercultural communication skills?

Research Question 1 measured the impact of playing HERO I® on enhancing the subjective side of intercultural communication. Both groups (i.e., control and experiment) took the same test. In order to find out if there was a difference between the two groups, the researcher formed the following null hypothesis:

Null Hypothesis 1: There is no significant difference between subjects who complete the HERO I® videogame and those who do not in terms of performance on an instrument measuring their subjective intercultural communication skills.

An independent t-test was conducted to determine whether there was a difference between the experiment group ($M = 7.14$, $SD = 2.18$) that played the game and the control group ($M = 5.61$, $SD = 1.21$) that did not in terms of the scores the subjects received in the ICC test (Table 3), specifically, the section of the test pertaining to the subjective culture.

Levene's test for equality of variance was significant ($F = 31.98$, $p < 0.05$), so equality of variance could not be assumed (t (df 119.94) $= 5.42$, $p = 0.001$($P < 0.05$)) (Table 4).

Thus, H1 was rejected as there was a significant difference between the subjects who completed the HERO I® videogame and those who did not in terms of performance on the ICC test that measures their subjective intercultural communication skills. By investigating the means, the subjects who played the game ($M = 7.14$) scored higher than those who did not play the game ($M = 5.61$).

Table 3. H1 descriptive statistical information

Class	N	Mean (ICC Test Scores	Std. Deviation	Std. Error Mean
1.00 (Exper.)	78	7.1410	2.18450	.24735
2.00 (Control)	80	5.6125	1.21690	.13605

Table 4. Independent t-test results for H1

							Levene's Test for Equality of Variances		
		F	*Sig.*	*t*	*df*	*Sig. (2-tailed)*	90% Confidence Interval of the Difference		
								Lower	*Upper*
Scores	Equal variances assumed	31.984	.000	5.451	156	.000		.97464	2.08241
	Equal variances not assumed			5.415	119.941	.000		.96960	2.08745

Research Question 2: Does the HERO I® videogame enhance learning of objective intercultural communication skills?

Research Question 2 investigated the impact of playing HERO I® on developing an understanding of the objective culture. In order to find out if there was difference between the two groups, the researcher formed the following null hypothesis:

Null Hypothesis 2: There is no significant difference between subjects who complete the HERO I® videogame and those who do not in terms of performance on an instrument measuring their objective intercultural communication skills.

An independent *t*-test was conducted to determine whether there was a difference between the experiment group ($M = 7.47$, $SD = 2.16$) and the control group ($M = 3.33$, $SD = 2.08$) in terms of the scores the subjects received on the objective culture section of the ICC test (Table 5).

Levene's test for equality of variance ($F = 0.117$, $p > 0.05$) showed that the variability between the scores of the two groups was about the same (t (df $= 158$) $= 12.33$, $p = .001$ ($P < 0.05$)) (Table 6).

Thus, H2 was rejected as there was a significant difference between subjects who completed the HERO I® videogame and those who did not in terms of performance

Table 5. H2 descriptive statistical information

Class	N	Mean (ICC test Score)	Std. Deviation	Std. Error Mean
1.00 (Exper.)	78	7.4750	2.16400	.24194
2.00 (Control)	80	3.3375	2.08031	.23259

Table 6. Independent t-test results for H2

		Levene's Test for Equality of Variances							
		F	Sig.	t	df	Sig. (2-tailed)	Mean Difference	90% Confidence Interval of the Difference	
								Lower	Upper
Scores	Equal variances assumed	.117	.733	12.328	158	.000	4.13750	3.47464	4.80036
	Equal variances not assumed			12.328	157.755	.000	4.13750	3.47464	4.80036

on the ICC test that measured their objective intercultural communication skills. By investigating the means, the subjects who played the game ($M = 7.47$) scored higher than those who did not play the game ($M = 3.33$).

DISCUSSION

The first hypothesis stated that playing HERO I® would have an impact on the subjects in understanding the less tangible aspects of a certain culture, such as values, norms of behavior, and adopted roles. The subjects in the control group scored lower than their counterparts in the experiment group. Such a finding is supported by the literature in terms of the training and cultural capacities of video games.

The findings indicate HERO I®—and hence DGBL—may act as a training tool for intercultural communication that helps the trainees recognize and understand the subjective elements of the host culture. This finding corresponds to the claim made by Smart and Csapo (2007) in that DGBL promotes experience-based learning because they provide learners with opportunities for interaction and involvement through innovative interventions. This finding also supports the claim that digital games are beneficial in addressing cognitive tasks that require utilization of the memory (De Castell, Larios, Jenson, & Smith, 2015). The experiment group demonstrated better cognitive skills in answering the posttest questions pertaining to the less tangible aspects of the host culture after playing the video game. The ability of the subjects—as shown in the score they achieved in the ICC test—to find out about the implicit aspects of the culture through playing HERO I® came in harmony with Prensky's (2011) conclusion that constructivist learning is one of the benefits of playing video games. Additionally, the results complement Walsh's (2010) concept about digital games and the transferability of skills. He stated that video games provide the learners with an interactive learning experience that enables them to transfer the skills they learned into other contexts.

In terms of intercultural communications, HERO I® helped the subjects recognize the abstract aspects of the host culture (i.e., the Middle East). This is a critical and essential finding as Hofstede (2001) mentioned that failure in intercultural communication mostly takes place on the subjective aspect of the culture. HERO I® tackles abstract values such as collectivism, power, and distance (Hofstede, 1983). Such cultural values have been described as vague and confusing aspects of any culture because they may radically vary from one culture to another (Shuping, 2016). By playing HERO I® and then taking the ICC test, the subjects demonstrated a better understanding for such abstract concepts. Hence, HERO I® could be a potential tool to clear out any vagueness or confusion resulting from the values of the host culture. In relation to Kim's (2001) Adaptation Theory, HERO I® as an example of DGBL is expected to be a helpful tool to help travelers understand the communication system in the Middle East. Thus, the video game might be a tool of adaptation and anxiety reduction for those who will play it. This happened when HERO I® assisted the subjects to achieve a refocusing of interactions (Kim, 2001; Lee et al., 2013). In this process, the game is speculated to walk future players through the communication system of the host culture (i.e., the Middle East) and have them be aware of the difference between the host culture and the old culture.

The second hypothesis stated that playing HERO I® enables the subjects in the experiment group to better understand the objective side of the culture than those in the control group. The objective side of the culture has to do with the visible cultural aspects such as food, outfit, and distance (Cushner & Brislin, 1996). A better comprehension of this cultural aspect can be assumed from the significant difference in the scores achieved by the two groups in the ICC test. In light of Bennett's (2003) developmental model of intercultural sensitivity (DMIS), the subjects who played HERO I® reached an advanced ethno-relative stage by being able to integrate the cultural differences into the context of the game. According to Bennett (2003), the ethno-relative stage of integration in intercultural communication is achieved when the individual is able to form his/her cultural knowledge by intertwining different cultural perspectives with none being central. Thus, DGBL might be a tool to help individuals reduce their anxiety when placed in a foreign culture (Franklin, 2007; Lewis, 2006; Lizardo, 2012). This anxiety-reduction strategy will take place when future trainees adopt DGBL and consider it their "cultural dictionary" (Kotthoff, 2007). Thus, the digital game will function as a reference that the individual can refer to every now and then to know about the tangible aspects of the host culture and therefore reduce his/her level of anxiety in communicating with other cultures. Scholars encourage the use of a cultural reference as it improves the intercultural competency of the individuals (Cornes, 2004; Cushner & Brislin, 1996; Gudykunst, 2010; Kotthoff, 2007; Spreckels & Kotthoff, 2007).

Also, this finding emphasizes the importance of experiential learning. The subjects were involved in a cultural assimilator (i.e., HERO I®) and therefore were able to virtually experience different cultural aspects of the host culture (Smart & Csapo, 2007). Although Wang and Kulich (2015) suspected the effectiveness of using cultural assimilators because they were mainly tailored for business needs, the results of the subjects in the experiment group in the ICC test cast doubt upon the aforementioned claim. HERO I® as a cultural assimilator can easily be used by the general public and address their needs. The video game addresses general cultural areas such as food, outfits, and physical interaction. Those aspects are both tangible and generic.

In addition, the results show that HERO I® demonstrates experiential learning by functioning as a scaffolding tool for the subjects. According to Molenaar, Sleegers, and Boxtel (2014), scaffolding in digital games occurs when a more knowledgeable entity (e.g., avatar) creates conditions that allow a novice to practice and build skills and knowledge in order to further develop his/her game competence. The HERO I® design ensures that the subjects are introduced to the input first, and then go through a series of cultural adventures based on their understanding to this input. Scaffolding is clearly demonstrated in HERO I® through the feedback system that allows the subject to go back to the input whenever he/she made any mistake. Additionally, Moline (2010) found that the multiple level-based digital games are a clear example of scaffolding and hence experiential learning. HERO I® satisfies this view as it consists of six levels. The subjects use the initial levels to build up more knowledge and learn instructions about the host culture. Then they become more autonomous and rely on the skills developed in the easier levels to overcome the more difficult levels (Chan, 2012; Moline, 2010; Salen & Zimmerman, 2003).

Implications

The findings imply that digital interactivity is a successful factor in intercultural training. DGBL may provide a successful platform to utilize the required interactivity. This interactivity is demonstrated through the player's attempt to interact with different cultural elements and properly use them within the right context. Because games are based on the concept of the magic circle that is governed by certain rules and behaviors (Salen & Zimmerman, 2003), digital games can easily make use of the magic circle and impose cultural rules and behavior that allow the player to develop intercultural competency. The findings imply that the magic circle may function as a virtual place where players can perform and master objective and subjective elements of the host culture.

The study's findings have also implied that video games that address cultural differences among individuals may have an impact upon reducing the cognitive discomfort that dominates the communication process. So, the study suggests that DGBL may function as a preliminary tool that enables senders and receivers to be introduced to cultural patterns that they might encounter when they exchange information with one another. (Gudykunst, 2005) outlined some concepts related to uncertainty reduction such as information seeking. According to this concept, individuals—when encountering one another for the first time—obtain more information about each other passively through information and/or actively through conversation. The study's findings suggest that DGBL in intercultural communication training may function as a passive tool to ease the cognitive discomfort related to the tangible aspects of the other culture where the other individual comes from. Also, Kotthoff (2007) suggested three stages of communication through which uncertainty avoidance advances: entry, personal, and exit. The authors propose—in light of the research results—that DGBL may functionally enhance and fit in with the personal stage of communication. In this stage, communicators share personal information including lifestyle, attitude, and values. Digital games will thus allow communicators to identify and be introduced to those aspects away from the influences of any social constraints.

The study implies that DGBL is effective and functional on the levels of interpersonal and intercultural communication. Hence, DGBL may positively influence the intercultural competency of a player. In terms of interpersonal communication, the results as reported in the ICC test, after playing the game show, the players demonstrated a better understanding of the dispositional factors of interpersonal communication. Thus, DGBL may function as a productive training tool by which to address abstract aspects of the communication process. Consequently, DGBL is expected to address the learning needs of young students whose visual learning style can help them understand abstract concepts. Moreover, because intercultural communication is an integral part of interpersonal communication, the findings imply that digital games are highly likely a pragmatic training tool by which communicators may identify the differences between the host and guest cultures. Thus, emerging media may work as an interactive point of reference for individuals placed into a different culture. The feedback system attached to digital games helps individuals predict the consequences of not observing the proper cultural codes and the impact upon the communication process across cultures. Also, the findings imply that the players may successfully formulate a cultural schema that helps them raise their awareness about cultural differences. The more the players become aware of such differences, the better they communicate within the host culture.

FUTURE RESEARCH DIRECTIONS

Future research may investigate the role of video game design aspects in affecting the quality of the learning outcomes when DGBL is implemented. Design aspects include, but are not limited to, User Interface (UI), graphics, virtual 3-D representation, and visual and spatial interactivity within virtual reality settings. Those aspects are expected to lead to better results, as they allow more space for physical interactivity. Also, future research is encouraged to focus on the use of commercial and best-selling video games for cultural training purposes.

CONCLUSION

This chapter examined the effectiveness of using DGBL to enhance intercultural communication training. Investigation of empirical research has shown that adopting DGBL to learn more about the host culture may be a good strategy to reduce uncertainty while dealing with the host culture. According to Franklin's (2007) Uncertainty Reduction Theory, individuals experience high levels of uncertainty when they are attempting to ensure effective communication in intercultural encounters. Additionally, scholars have postulated that the level of anxiety and uncertainty depends on the level of communication skills, motivation, and knowledge of general and specific cultural factors that the person demonstrates Franklin, 2007; Gudykunst, 2010; Lewis, 2006; Lizardo, 2012). The literature suggests other strategies to reduce uncertainty and anxiety such as the use of a cultural dictionary, de-individuation, and cultural identity (Cornes, 2004; Cushner & Brislin, 1996; Gudykunst, 2005; Spreckels & Kotthoff, 2007). DGBL were neither tested nor explicitly suggested as a tool for overcoming intercultural anxiety and uncertainty. Thus, the findings of a research study conducted by the authors proposes that playing 3-D video games about cultural differences might be an effective tension-reducing tool. It may promote information-seeking behavior and, therefore, help gamers communicate effectively with the host culture.

The chapter suggests that specifically designed DGBL that tackle cultural differences with the host culture nurtures the ability of "refocusing of interactions." According to Kim (2001), effective communication within the host culture depends on the level of awareness and understanding of the host communication system; hence, that adopting DGBL may help learners accept the host environment and develop an intercultural identity. The chapter also suggests that playing digital games that address the host culture leads to a better understanding of cultural dimensions (Hofstede, 1983) The findings of the aforementioned study by the authors showed that subjects who played the game showed a better understanding of the concepts of collectivism, high-context, power distance, masculinity, and indulgence. Hofstede (2001) and Cushner and Brislin (1996) emphasized that failure in cross-cultural communication tends to be due to the failure in recognizing and handling those dimensions. Thus, DGBL may work as a functional training tool that helps trainees achieve a better understanding of this subjective level of the culture.

REFERENCES

Bakić-Mirić, N. A. (2012). *An integrated approach to intercultural communication.* Newcastle upon Tyne, UK: Cambridge Scholars Publishing.

Barab, S., Thomas, M., Dodge, T., Carteaux, R., & Tuzun, H. (2005). Making learning fun: Quest Atlantis, a game without guns. *Educational Technology Research and Development, 53*(1), 86–107. doi:10.1007/BF02504859

Barbour, S. (2007). *Nationalism, language, Europe.* Oxford, UK: Oxford University Press.

Behrisch, T. B. (2016). Cost and the craving for novelty: Exploring motivations and barriers for cooperative education and exchange students to go abroad. *Asia Pacific Journal of Cooperative Education, 17*(3), 279–294.

Bennett, M. J. (2003). Towards ethnorelativism: A developmental model of intercultural sensitivity. In R. M. Paige (Ed.), *Education for the intercultural experience* (Vol. 2, pp. 17–32). Interculture Press.

Berardo, K., & Simons, G. (2004). *The intercultural profession: Its profile, practices, and challenges.* Retrieved from http://www.sietar-europa.org/about_us/ICP_Survey_Report.pdf

Chan, C. (2012). Exploring an experiential learning project through Kolb's Learning Theory using a qualitative research method. *European Journal of Engineering Education, 37*(4), 405–415. doi:10.1080/03043797.2012.706596

Chen, M. (2010). The effects of game strategy and preference-matching on flow experience and programming performance in game-based learning. *Innovations in Education and Teaching International, 47*(1), 39–52. doi:10.1080/14703290903525838

Coffey, H. (2009). *Digital game-based learning.* Learn NC.

Cornes, A. (2004). *Culture from the inside out.* Intercultural Press.

Curtis, D. D., & Lawson, M. J. (2002). Computer adventure games as problem-solving environments. *International Education Journal, 3*(4), 43–56.

Cushner, K., & Brislin, R. W. (1996). *Intercultural interactions: A practical guide.* Thousand Oaks, CA: Sage.

De Castell, S., Larios, H., Jenson, J., & Smith, D. H. (2015). The role of video game experience in spatial learning and memory. *Journal of Gaming & Virtual Worlds, 7*(1), 21–40. doi:10.1386/jgvw.7.1.21_1

Dewey, J. (2007). *Experience and education.* Simon and Schuster.

Eklund, L. (2015). Playing video games together with others: Differences in gaming with family, friends and strangers. *Journal of Gaming & Virtual Worlds, 7*(3), 259–277. doi:10.1386/jgvw.7.3.259_1

Erhel, S., & Jamet, E. (2013). Digital game-based learning: Impact of instructions and feedback on motivation and learning effectiveness. *Computers & Education, 67*, 156–167. doi:10.1016/j.compedu.2013.02.019

Fraenkel, R. J., & Wallen, E. N. (2006). *How to Design and Evaluate Research in Education.* New York: McGraw-Hill.

Franklin, P. (2007). Differences and difficulties in intercultural management interaction. In H. Kotthoff & Spencer-Oatey (Eds.), Handbook of Intercultural Communication (pp. 263–284). Hal.

Gee, P. (2005). *What digital games have to teach us about learning and literacy.* Palgrave Macmillan.

Gražulis, V., & Markuckienė, E. (2014). Current issues of the development of employee intercultural competency in a work environment (A case-study of small municipalities of Lithuania). *Darbuotojų tarpkultūrinės kompetencijos plėtros aktualijos darbo aplinkoje (Lietuvos mažų savivaldybių atvejo analizė), 2014*(3), 78–89.

Grundy, S. (1988). *The computer and the classroom: Critical perspectives.* Paper presented at the Educational Research: Indigenous or exotic? Annual Conference of the AARE.

Gudykunst, W. B. (2005). *Theorizing about intercultural communication.* Thousand Oaks, CA: Sage.

Gudykunst, W. B. (2010). Cross-cultural comparisons. In D. Cai (Ed.), *Intercultural communication* (2nd ed.; Vol. 1, pp. 213–253). Thousand Oaks, CA: SAGE.

Guerro, H. (2011). Using video-game-based instruction in an EFL program: Understanding the power of videogames in education. *Colombian Applied Linguistics Journal, 13*(1), 55–70.

Hall, E. T. (1959). *The silent language*. Garden City, NY: Doubleday.

Hamari, J., Shernoff, D. J., Rowe, E., Coller, B., Asbell-Clarke, J., & Edwards, T. (2016). Challenging games help students learn: An empirical study on engagement, flow and immersion in game-based learning. *Computers in Human Behavior, 54*, 170–179. doi:10.1016/j.chb.2015.07.045

Hiratsuka, H., Suzuki, H., & Pusina, A. (2016). Explaining the effectiveness of the contrast culture method for managing interpersonal interactions across cultures. *Journal of International Students, 6*(1), 73–92.

Hofstede, G. (1983). Dimensions of national cultures in fifty countries and three regions. In J. B. Deregowski, S. Dziurawiec, & C. Robert (Eds.), *Expectations in cross-cultural psychology* (pp. 335–355). Lisse: Swets & Zeitlinger.

Hofstede, G. (2001). *Culture's consequences: Comparing values, behaviors, institutions, and organizations across nations*. London: Sage.

Huang, W. H., Huang, W. Y., & Tschopp, J. (2010). Sustaining iterative game playing processes in DGBL: The relationship between motivational processing and outcome processing. *Computers & Education, 55*(2), 789–797. doi:10.1016/j.compedu.2010.03.011

Hugh, M. (2012). Ethnographic studies multicultural eduation in classrooms and schools. In J. Banks (Ed.), Handbook of research on multicultural education (pp. 129–144). San Francisco: Jossey-Bass.

Ihtiyar, A., & Ahmad, F. S. (2015). The Role of intercultural communication competence on service reliability and customer satisfaction. *Journal of Economic & Social Studies, 5*(1), 145–168. doi:10.14706/JECOSS11518

Jørgensen, K. (2003, November). Problem Solving: The Essence of Player Action in Computer Games. *DiGRA Conference*.

Kain, E. (2015). The top ten best-selling video games in 2014. *Forbes Magazine*. Retrieved from http://www.forbes.com/sites/erikkain/2015/01/19/the-top-ten-best-selling-video-games-of-2014/

Kiili, K. (2005). Digital game-based learning: Towards an experiential gaming model. *The Internet and Higher Education, 8*(1), 13–24. doi:10.1016/j.iheduc.2004.12.001

Kim, B., Park, H., & Baek, Y. (2009). Not just fun, but serious strategies: Using meta-cognitive strategies in game-based learning. *Computers & Education, 52*(4), 800–810. doi:10.1016/j.compedu.2008.12.004

Kim, Y. Y. (2001). *Becoming Intercultural: An integrative theory of communication and cross-cultural adaptation*. Thousand Oaks, CA: Sage.

Kolb, D. (1984). *Experiential learning: Experience as the source of learning and development*. Prentice Hall.

Kotthoff, H. (2007). Ritual and style across cultures. In H. Kotthoff & H. Spencer-Oatey (Eds.), Handbook of intercultural communication (pp. 173–197). Hal. doi:10.1515/9783110198584.2.173

Lainema, T. (2003). *Enhancing organizational business process perception: Experiences from constructing and applying a dynamic business simulation game* (PhD thesis). Turku School of Economics and Business Administration.

Latane & Bibb. (2010). Dynamic Social Impact: The Creation of Culture by Communication. In D. A. Cai (Ed.), *Intercultural communication* (2nd ed.; Vol. 1, pp. 105–118). Thousand Oaks, CA: SAGE.

Lebedeva, N. M. n. h. r., Makarova, E. e. m. e. u. c., & Tatarko, A. a. h. r. (2013). Increasing intercultural competence and tolerance in multicultural schools: A training program and its effectiveness. *Problems of Education in the 21st Century, 54*, 39–52.

Lee, H. J., Choi, J., Kim, J. W., Park, S. J., & Gloor, P. (2013). Communication, opponents, and clan performance in online games: A social network approach. *Cyberpsychology, Behavior, and Social Networking, 16*(12), 878–883. doi:10.1089/cyber.2011.0522 PMID:23745617

Lewis, R. D. (2006). *When cultures collide: Leading across cultures: A major new edition of the global guide*. Boston: Nicholas Brealey Publishing.

Lizardo, O. (2012). Embodied culture as procedure: Rethinking the link between personal and objective culture. *Collegium, 12*, 70–86.

Lumby, A. (2014). *The 10 best-selling video games of 2014*. Retrieved from The Fiscal Times website: http://www.thefiscaltimes.com/2014/12/12/10-Best-Selling-Games-2014-Why-Big-Studios-Should-Take-Page-Indie-Games

McCusker, K., & Gunaydin, S. (2015). Research using qualitative, quantitative or mixed methods and choice based on the research. *Perfusion, 30*(7), 537-542. doi:10.1177/0267659114559116

Molenaar, I., Sleegers, P., & Boxtel, C. (2014). Metacognitive scaffolding during collaborative learning: A promising combination. *Metacognition and Learning, 9*(3), 309–332. doi:10.100711409-014-9118-y

Moline, T. (2010). Video games as digital learning resources: Implications for teacher-librarians and for researchers. *School Libraries Worldwide, 16*(2), 1–15.

Moon, D. G. (2008). Concepts of "culture.". In M. Asante, Y. Miike, & J. Yin (Eds.), *The global intercultural communication reader* (pp. 11–26). Routledge.

Nielsen-Englyst, L. (2003). Game design for imaginative conceptualisation. *Proceedings of the international workshop on experimantal interactive learning in industrial management,* 149–164.

Prensky, M. (2011). Digital natives, Digital immigrants. *On the Horizon, 9*(5), 1–6. doi:10.1108/10748120110424816

Qian, M., & Clark, K. R. (2016). Game-based learning and 21st century skills: A review of recent research. *Computers in Human Behavior, 63,* 50–58. doi:10.1016/j. chb.2016.05.023

Rehm, M., & Leichtenstern, K. (2012). Gesture-based mobile training of intercultural behavior. *Multimedia Systems, 18*(1), 33–51. doi:10.100700530-011-0239-8

Salen, K., & Zimmerman, A. (2003). *Rules of play: Game design fundamentals.* Chicago: MIT Press.

Samovar, L. A., & McDaniel, E. R. (2007). *Communication between cultures.* Thomson Learning.

Scherr, A. (2007). Schools and cultural difference. In H. Kotthoff & H. Spencer-Oatey (Eds.), Handbook of intercultural communication (pp. 301–321). Hal.

Shuping, X. (2016). How the diversity of values matters in intercultural communication. *Theory and Practice in Language Studies, 6*(9), 1836–1840. doi:10.17507/tpls.0609.16

Siegfried, B. (2011). *Sisyphus, or the limits of education.* Berkeley, CA: University of California Press.

Smart, K. L., & Csapo, N. (2007). Learning by doing: Engaging students through learner-centered activities. *Business Communication Quarterly, 70*(4), 451–457. doi:10.1177/10805699070700040302

Spencer-Oatey, H., & Franklin, P. (2009). *Intercultural interaction: A multidisciplinary approach to intercultural communication. Palgrave* Macmillan. doi:10.1057/9780230244511

Spreckels, J., & Kotthoff, H. (2007). Communicating identity in intercultural communication. In H. Kotthoff & H. Spencer-Oatey (Eds.), Handbook of intercultural communication (pp. 415–439). Hal.

Stuart, H., & Gay, P. (2010). *Questions of Cultural Identity*. London: Sage.

Taylor, T. L. (2008). Becoming a player: networks, structure, and imagined futures. In Beyond Barbie & mortal kombat: new perspectives on gender and gaming (pp. 51–66). MIT Press.

Velasco, D. (2015). Evaluate, analyze, describe (EAD): Confronting underlying issues of racism and other prejudices for effective intercultural communication. *IAFOR Journal of Education*, *3*(2), 82–93. doi:10.22492/ije.3.2.05

Walsh, C. (2010). Systems-based literacy practices: Digital games research, gameplay and design. *Australian Journal of Language and Literacy*, *33*(1), 24–40.

Wang, Y., & Kulich, S. J. (2015). Does context count? Developing and assessing intercultural competence through an interview and model-based domestic course design in China. *International Journal of Intercultural Relations*, *48*, 38–57. doi:10.1016/j.ijintrel.2015.03.013

Zong, J., & Batalova, J. (2016, May 12). *International students in the United States*. Retrieved from http://www.migrationpolicy.org/article/international-students-united-states

KEY TERMS AND DEFINITIONS

Cultural Training: The design and delivery of intercultural activities that make trainees able to experience different cultural aspects of the host culture.

Game Play: Free movement within rigid structure. In game play, free movement stems from the strategies that the player adopts during the game in order to meet the winning condition of the game.

Intercultural Communication: The communication process that happens between individuals or groups of different linguistic and cultural origins. The differences in cultural origins entail differences in language, values, social norms, and perceptions.

Interpersonal Communication: The process people follow within a certain context to exchange information through verbal and non-verbal messages.

Objective Culture: The tangible aspects of culture such as food, costumes and outfits, and even the names people give to things. It is typically found in the form of practices (e.g., ways of talking or walking), objects, and ritual or religious objects (material culture).

Subjective Culture: Any cultural aspect that is not tangible, such as ideology, values, and social roles.

Values: A set of abstract and general principles that guide behavior. Individual values are, in effect, judgments about what is right or wrong and good or bad.

Chapter 5
International Students' Use of Social Media as Information Sources

Samuel Ekundayo
Eastern Institute of Technology, New Zealand

Chris Niyi Arasanmi
Toi Ohomai Institute of Technology, New Zealand

Olayemi Abdulateef Aliyu
Toi Ohomai Institute of Technology, New Zealand

ABSTRACT

International students face tremendous challenges adapting to a new environment. From the pressure to learn a new language, new approach to learning to making new friends, it can sometimes be a daunting and challenging experience for students. In order to cope, they need to access and process large amount of information very quickly, otherwise their mission and purpose of earning foreign certificates might be jeopardized. For this reason, this chapter looks addresses the limited knowledge around the information needs, seeking behavior, and use of international students. This knowledge is important for educators, institutions, and societies to be able to provide the necessary support to help international students cope and adapt to their new environment.

DOI: 10.4018/978-1-5225-7949-6.ch005

INTRODUCTION

Globalization has increased cross-cultural migration and demand for international education. The quest for international education has also increased the numbers of international students travelling to foreign countries to fulfil their aspirations of attaining foreign certificates. Several countries have developed international market policies and strategies intended to enhance their participation in the competitive market of recruiting international students. Over the years, Canada, USA, United Kingdom, Australia and New Zealand have emerged as popular destinations for international students. International students are "Students who have crossed a national or territorial border for the purpose of education and are now enrolled outside their country of origin" (UNESCO, n.d).

International students in a new environment possess different lifestyles, varied norms, religious affiliations and cultural orientations, which in most cases differ to those of their host countries. Because of these noticeable differences, international students face some cultural shocks in their host countries. Apart from the noticeable differences in cultures; students are faced with challenges of adjustment and adaptability to the climatic conditions, pedagogical and learning styles, food and cultural values of their new environment. The problem of adjustment, cultural integration, and acculturative stress are significant issues that international students find extremely challenging to deal with. Acculturation is, adjusting and adapting to the socio-cultural configurations of a new environment.

International students have different information needs and behaviours compared to their counterparts in their host countries (Andrade, 2006; Sin, 2015). While many institutions tend to provide the necessary information students need to adapt and cope in their new environment, what is common practice is that international students struggle to find legal, financial, personal, cultural and transportation and sometimes academic information (Sin, 2015). They engage in various information seeking behaviours to avail themselves of the support they need in their new environment. But information seeking is usually a challenge in a new environment, where international students need lots of information to thrive and adapt (Hamid, Bukhari, Sri, Norman, & Mohamad, 2016).

Social media is proving to have a strong potential and serve as a valuable source of information for international students (Sin & Kim, 2013). As a result, international students use social media for information seeking purposes to gather valuable information which could hasten their acculturation, adjustment and adaptability in the new environment. International students' information needs have not received much attention in the literature, especially with respect to the role of social media (Andrade, 2006; Sin, 2015).

Our goal in this chapter is to investigate the role of social media in the information need, seeking and use of international students in their bid to adjust and adapt to their new environment. We begin by looking at the information needs and information use of international students. Next, we are looking at the information seeking behaviour of international students. Thereafter, we look at social media as a source of information for international students. We also look at the implications for educators, institutions and the society at large. Lastly, we draw some relevant conclusions on the study.

INFORMATION NEEDS, BEHAVIOUR AND USE AMONG INTERNATIONAL STUDENTS

Information behaviour has been defined as how a person or group of persons actively or passively interacts and connects with channels or sources of information, primarily because of purposive intention. Information needs can also be defined as a situation where a person's current knowledge or available information is inadequate to answer unknown questions or help to achieve their individual or collective goals. This issue has been theoretically argued as an antecedent that continually leads to seeking of further information. Information seeking is an everyday life activity where people unconsciously in their normal daily routines obtain information through mass media, meeting new friends, visiting relatives, associates and recently social media.

The information needs and use of International students differ comparably to their counterparts in their host countries (Sin, 2015). To adapt and thrive in their new environment, international students will have to find and process large amount of information. Some studies suggest that international students do not necessarily refer to their host country's sources of information to meet their information needs due to some social issues (Andrade, 2006). Students from host countries have lived in their countries long enough to know where and how to access the support they need, but for international students, this is not the case.

In a study done in a Malaysian university, Safahieh and Singh (2006) found five main categories of information needs of their international students including information about the university and its faculties, information related to their programme of study, information related to their courses, information related to continuing their education after graduation, local information about their host country – Malaysia. Majority of the students point out the school's electronic digital library was useful in addressing some of the needs. It is easy to see why the students accessed the school's library because the study is targeted at the academic needs of the students and in particular, their use of the library. Although some studies found that international students' first priority was to adjust to their academic life and successfully complete their degrees (Andrade, 2006). While every student has academics needs that the library might be able to meet, students from host countries are likely to visit the library less than their foreign counterparts.

In another study, Yi (2007) found that international students have their own information needs and use requirements. Frequently, they need information for improving their academic coursework, library skills and software application usage. Alzougool, Chang, Gomes, and Berry (2013) found the top information needs and use of international students include for academic development and remedial information for which they tend to use a range of online sources including Google and surprisingly Facebook; for pre-arrival information; for health information; for information about entertainment and social activities; information about accommodation; for information to help keep up with their home country and locally. S. Hamid et al. (2016) found the top information needs and use of international students are academic related, financially related, socioculturally related (relating to adjustment, loneliness, religion differences, etc.), health-related. Sin and Kim (2013) found that the five crucial everyday life information needs of international students were finance, health, news of home country, housing and entertainment. Of the five, finance ranked highest. It is to be noted that the study is strictly about everyday life information needs, hence academics was not included.

Some barriers to meeting the information needs of international students include but are not limited to language barrier, internet access problems, unfamiliarity with the library organisation and the mission of the academic library, inability to seek, obtain and evaluation information and their sources, hesitation in approaching library professionals (Safahieh & Singh, 2006).

International Students' Information Grounds and Sharing of Information

Information grounds have been studied as a focus and as an essential component of information behaviour. From an international student perspective, information ground can be defined as a temporary environment created by the behaviour of these students who have come together with a common need and task to perform. When these students come together, the social atmosphere tends to foster these relationships through the spontaneous sharing of information. Based on this definition, information grounds can be categorized into many places like a classroom, libraries, sports centers, restaurants, cafeterias, supermarkets etc. A primary author in this area of research are Fisher, Landry, and Naumer (2007), who proposed the following as dimensions of information grounds: People related, Place related and Information related.

Table 1 presents the characteristics that are associated with international students.

Table 1. Information ground characteristics

Information ground characteristics		
People Related	**Place related**	**Information related**
Size	Activities	Significance
Types	Friendliness	Frequently discussed
familiarity	Comfort	How created/shared
Roles	Location	Topics
Motivation	Privacy	-
-	Ambience	-

Source: Adapted from Fisher et al. (2007)

Also important to international students' information needs and use is information sharing. Traditionally, information sharing has been defined as face to face exchange of data and information from one person called "a sender and the other called "a receiver". Information sharing has a long history in the theoretical explanation of information technology. This information can be shared through formal and informal channels, mainly through social media and another technical searching. With the continuous development of the online platform through social media, it is vital for governments and academic institutions to maximize information sharing with the international students in an online environment.

INFORMATION SEEKING BEHAVIOUR OF INTERNATIONAL STUDENTS

Information seeking behaviour is generally used for a set of actions taken by an individual to express their information needs, seek necessary information, evaluate and select information, and eventually use this information to address or fulfil their information needs (Majid & Kassim, 2000). Information seeking behaviour of an individual or group of people are influenced by a range of factors. As a result, it is crucial to comprehend the reason for which information is needed. There is little research about international students' information seeking behaviour, as there are limited studies on the information seeking behaviour of international students. While a lot of studies has been done on the information seeking behaviour of domestic students (Al-Muomen, Morris, & Maynard, 2012; Barrett, 2012; Bøyum & Aabø, 2015; Brahme, 2010; Dresang, 2005; Kadli & Kumbar, 2013; Nesset, 2008; Orlu, 2016; Sookhtanlo, Mohammadi, & Rezvanfar, 2009) very few studies on their international students' counterpart are available.

Sin and Kim (2013) conducted empirical research on the everyday life of international students' information-seeking behaviour in America. Their results indicated that social networking sites are a major source of everyday information seeking for the international students. Social-demographic profile of the respondents also indicated that the younger students, particularly the undergraduates and students identified with extroverted personalities often use these social networking sites. However, young adults most preferred online news media as their source of information seeking. Traditionally, information need and information used by international students has been performed through non-social media platforms.

In a study done on the information seeking behaviour of international students in London, Ontario, Hakim Silvio (2006), found that the information needs of the students to be more academic in nature and the sources of such information are colleagues, friends, neighbours and relatives. Many of the students are an unawareness of where to find the right information to meet their information needs. Liao, Finn and Lu (2007) compared the information seeking behaviour of domestic and international students and found that most international students' first place to look for information is the internet while domestic students look at library databases first. Jeong (2004) studied Korean international students in the United States and found that the students isolated themselves from mainstream media but instead seek information and fellowship from major Korean organisations in the society, like the church – a phenomenon referred to as "enclave".

From these studies, it is quite clear that the information seeking behaviour of international student differ from their domestic counterparts. As a result, it is important that their information seeking behaviour is well understood so that appropriate and relevant support can be provided to them to address their information needs.

SOCIAL MEDIA AS A SOURCE OF INFORMATION

The rapid advancement and ubiquitous nature of social media have challenged traditional forms of communication and is increasingly changing our lifestyles. Nowadays, communication is technologically mediated. Social media has revolutionised and disrupted communication systems around the globe. As a disruptive technology, it has also presented some opportunities for the society at large. Social media are applications that augment group interactions and shared spaces for collaboration, social connections, and aggregate information exchanges in a web-based environment (Bartlett-Bragg, 2006). They allow the sharing and uploading of a personal profile, photograph, feelings and opinions with friends and contacts. Users create and share information, ideas, personal messages, and other contents with their contacts or communities. Twitter and Instagram lead the pack among the blogging or microblogging technologies. It is noticeable within the social network technology that, Facebook is dominating this class while the YouTube top the chart in the streaming and multimedia file sharing.

The major drivers of social networks adoption are users' perceptions of ease-of-use and usefulness. Online users believe that social networks are useful in their living and lifestyle. Technology notion of usefulness is the degree to which a person believes that using a system would enhance his or her job performance (Davis, 1989). Specifically, users rely on social networks as sources of credible and quality information from their online contacts. Aside from the perception of usefulness, social networks' feature of ease-of-use has significantly lured many to adopt this technology. Perception of ease-of-use connotes the degree to which a person believes that using a system would be free of effort (Davis, 1989). Seemingly, it is effortless to use social media, and it also meets users' needs for collaboration and communication.

Mostly, information seeking behavior entails a set of actions that an individual takes to seek information, evaluate and select information, and finally use this information to satisfy his/her information needs. Various factors may determine the information seeking behaviour of an individual or a group. Therefore, it is desirable to understand the purpose for which information is required. There are several platforms which are used for gathering information. For instance, social media is useful for gathering a range of information, and as a result, an average adult spends a considerable amount of time on social media sites. This confirms that social media is a recognised and acceptable source for information seekers. Social media is used every day for seeking information that is useful to life, well-being, individual's wellness, social esteem and public individuation. An important segment of the social media users is active people and likely to be students of tertiary institutions within the age bracket of 17-25. Young people are quite active and fond of sharing a range of information online. Though it may seem that young people are only socially active, however, it is evident that their social media activities are noticeable on the academic front. Social media among the young people has found its way into the academic arena. Students, as well as academic institutions, have now adopted social media to interact, gather, and share important educational information (Andrade, 2006). Many tertiary institutions across the globe are now frequent users of social media sites to reach and communicate with their current and potential students.

The Role of Social Media in Information Seeking Behaviour of International Students

Although the world wide web and social media have increasingly eased information seeking for international students, the quality of information available on the internet is still questionable and often require some level of expertise (Sin & Kim,

2013). In their investigation into the role of social media in the information seeking behaviour of international students, Hamid et al. (2016) reported three significant roles including social interaction, information source and education advocacy. Other studies also found social media to be widely accepted and used as a source of information by international students (Cox & McLeod, 2014; Suraya Hamid, Waycott, Kurnia, & Chang, 2015; Hendrickson, Rosen, & Aune, 2011). Sin and Kim (2013), in their survey 97% of their sample have used social networking sites to address their everyday life information needs.

Social media sites such as the Facebook can serve students' educational information needs because it has relevant features that enable peer feedback in a social context in line with the constructivist views. Facebook as a tool supports interaction, peer feedback, group participation, and individual collaboration, encourage international students to rely on it for information searches, gathering and sharing. In fact, some international students tend to trust information from their social networks than other forms of media (Andrade, 2006). Social media educational functions encourage the formation of groups, forums and online communities in a way to open spaces for collaborative learning (Chang et al., 2012; Selwyn, 2007). The collaborative learning strategy allows a group of people to interact, generate knowledge and shared current contents. The collaborative learning capabilities of social networking sites allow students to join academic groups related to their schools, departments or classes (Mazman & Usluel, 2010). Social media communication capability of the free flow of communication, student-tutor interaction and feedback and the spread of important notices to the students has come to stay (Kim, Sin, and Yoo-Lee, 2014).

Group participation and the sharing of relevant resources has become a norm in the academic environment. Collaborative and group work are components of the assessment model in the tertiary institutions can be quickly attended to using the social media. With the social media technology affordances, international students could learn the contents more and sort out social and academic problems that are inherent in their daily and academic lives. Seeking information from this SNS source helps students to withstand the academic and social challenges, especially those challenges around the pedagogical and new learning styles of the host countries.

Given the considerable capabilities and affordances of the social media in terms of collaborative online learning and facilitating knowledge construction and the sharing of information and resources (Mazman & Usluel, 2010); international students have the chance to obtain important resources and information that can help resolve their numerous challenges in a perhaps new learning environment. Information gathered through the usage of the social media may help students to adjust and adapt to a new learning style.

Gathering of background information, gleaning others' opinions, and finding solutions or how-to instructions (Kim, Sin, and Yoo-Lee, 2014) may help students to overturn the challenges and stresses they have encountered in the new environment. In line with the context of acculturation and adaptability, international students who have just migrated to a new educational environment could use as acculturation and adaptation tool in academic environments.

Social media encourages social and entertainment information seeking behaviors among the users. Users continuously check for available leisure and entertainment information from their friends and group members. In many instances, specific information about food shops and locations, popular tourism destinations, cinemas and movie theatres, creative tourism, leisure and sporting and food events are made available to members. Participation in this leisure goings-on provides possibilities for enjoyment, leisure, relaxation, connection and relationships, interaction, adaptability and acculturation. Overall, participating in local leisure events, such as food, dance, music, festivals, motor and cultural shows are a robust way by which international students can quickly adjust and adapt to their new environment.

IMPLICATIONS FOR EDUCATORS, INSTITUTIONS AND SOCIETY

The use of social media can potentially support and enhance international students' adjustment and adapt to the pedagogy and teaching style in their new environment (Greenhow, 2011). The affordances of many of the platforms support peer to peer and group sharing of resources. Support from members and peers have the potential to increase interactions and learnability among students (Veletsianos & Navarrete, 2012). This style resonates with student centred learning approach and constructive pedagogy. Apart from its adaptability function; it is a student-centred technology that enhances personal and self-regulated learning. Social media usage has significant educational and pedagogical implications in view of its capabilities if initialized.

Social media usage satisfies the need for the self-regulated and personalized learning environment. It enhances collaboration on academic group tasks which can be shared among members. Using social media for group work enhances students' creativity and knowledge creation. Above all, students will be able to socialise and develop social, communication and interpersonal skills while using the social media. Development of social and interpersonal skills as informal learning may help international students' future and related endeavours in their local environment. Students should proactively engage and use social media for collaborative actions. Academic institutions should encourage international students to explore the deep use of social media as a tool of orientation and integration.

Interaction and communication with new and old friends and family members could help students' positive psychological state, personal well-being and social esteem in their society. Engaging in the social media may address international students' nostalgic feelings and alleviate the pressures from their new settlement. Consequently, institutions and government agencies should maintain a visible presence online because new visitors often search for information that could help them integrate and adapt to the culture of the host country.

CONCLUSION

Social media has become a household name when it comes to information seeking and use around the world. Even though it was initially intended for people to share about their lives and keep up with friends and family all over the world, it has been assessed as a useful tool in addressing the information needs of individuals.

In this study, we have looked at how international students use social media to meet their information needs while trying to adapt to a new environment. A review of the literature has revealed that the primary and perhaps most prioritised information needs of international students are their academics. In addition, they often do not address their information needs the same way domestic students do. They are more likely to create the support they need to address their information needs around their communities and intimate relations. Social media helps them to do that. They can form groups for learning, share a collaborative space to engage their fellow students and look after their own wellbeing while adapting to life in a foreign land.

This information is essential for educators, academic institutions and societies in order to know how to meet the information needs of international students and support them in the bid for them to succeed in their academics.

REFERENCES

Al-Muomen, N., Morris, A., & Maynard, S. (2012). Modelling information-seeking behaviour of graduate students at Kuwait University. *The Journal of Documentation*, *68*(4), 430–459. doi:10.1108/00220411211239057

Alzougool, B., Chang, S., Gomes, C., & Berry, M. (2013). Finding their way around: International students' use of information sources. *Journal of Advanced Management Science*, *1*(1), 43–49. doi:10.12720/joams.1.1.43-49

Andrade, M. S. (2006). International students in English-speaking universities: Adjustment factors. *Journal of Research in International Education*, *5*(2), 131–154. doi:10.1177/1475240906065589

Barrett, P. L. (2012). *Information-seeking processes of fourth grade students using the internet for a school assignment*. Teachers College, Columbia University.

Bøyum, I., & Aabø, S. (2015). The information practices of business PhD students. *New Library World, 116*(3/4), 187–200. doi:10.1108/NLW-06-2014-0073

Brahme, M. E. (2010). *The differences in information seeking behavior between distance and residential doctoral students*. Pepperdine University.

Chang, S., Alzougool, B., Berry, M., Gomes, C., Smith, S., & Reeders, D. (2012). International students in the digital age: Do you know where your students go to for information. *Proceedings of the Australian International Education Conference*.

Cox, D., & McLeod, S. (2014). Social media marketing and communications strategies for school superintendents. *Journal of Educational Administration, 52*(6), 850–868. doi:10.1108/JEA-11-2012-0117

Dresang, E. T. (2005). Access: The information-seeking behavior of youth in the digital environment. *Library Trends, 54*(2), 178–196. doi:10.1353/lib.2006.0015

Fisher, K. E., Landry, C. F., & Naumer, C. (2007). Social spaces, casual interactions, meaningful exchanges:'information ground'characteristics based on the college student experience. *Information Research, 12*(2), 12–12.

Greenhow, C. (2011). Online social networking and learning. *International Journal of Cyber Behavior, Psychology and Learning, 1*(1), 36–50. doi:10.4018/ijcbpl.2011010104

Hakim Silvio, D. (2006). The information needs and information seeking behaviour of immigrant southern Sudanese youth in the city of London, Ontario: An exploratory study. *Library Review, 55*(4), 259–266. doi:10.1108/00242530610660807

Hamid, S., Bukhari, S., Sri, D. R., Norman, A. A., & Mohamad, T. I. (2016). Role of social media in information-seeking behaviour of international students. *Aslib Journal of Information Management, 68*(5), 643–666. doi:10.1108/AJIM-03-2016-0031

Hamid, S., Waycott, J., Kurnia, S., & Chang, S. (2015). Understanding students' perceptions of the benefits of online social networking use for teaching and learning. *The Internet and Higher Education, 26*, 1–9. doi:10.1016/j.iheduc.2015.02.004

Hendrickson, B., Rosen, D., & Aune, R. K. (2011). An analysis of friendship networks, social connectedness, homesickness, and satisfaction levels of international students. *International Journal of Intercultural Relations, 35*(3), 281–295. doi:10.1016/j.ijintrel.2010.08.001

Jeong, W. (2004). Unbreakable ethnic bonds: Information-seeking behavior of Korean graduate students in the United States. *Library & Information Science Research*, *26*(3), 384–400. doi:10.1016/j.lisr.2004.04.001

Kadli, J. H., & Kumbar, B. (2013). *Library Resources, Services and Information Seeking Behaviour in Changing ICT Environment: A Literature Review*. Library Philosophy & Practice.

Kim, K.-S., Sin, S.-C. J., & Yoo-Lee, E. Y. (2014). Undergraduates' Use of Social Media as Information Sources. *College & Research Libraries*, *75*(4), 442–457. doi:10.5860/crl.75.4.442

Liao, Y., Finn, M., & Lu, J. (2007). Information-seeking behavior of international graduate students vs. American graduate students: A user study at Virginia Tech 2005. *College & Research Libraries*, *68*(1), 5–25. doi:10.5860/crl.68.1.5

Majid, S., & Kassim, G. M. (2000). Information-seeking behaviour of international Islamic University Malaysia Law faculty members. *Malaysian Journal of Library and Information Science*, *5*(2), 1–17.

Mazman, S. G., & Usluel, Y. K. (2010). Modeling educational usage of Facebook. *Computers & Education*, *55*(2), 444–453. doi:10.1016/j.compedu.2010.02.008

Nesset, V. (2008). *The information-seeking behaviour of grade-three elementary school students in the context of a class project*. McGill University.

Orlu, A. D. (2016). Information seeking behaviour of masters students: Affective and behavioural dimensions. *Library Philosophy and Practice (e-journal)*, 1-56.

Safahieh, H., & Singh, D. (2006). *Information needs of international students at a Malaysian University*. Academic Press.

Selwyn, N. (2007). Web 2.0 applications as alternative environments for informal learning-a critical review. *Paper for CERI-KERIS International Expert Meeting on ICT and Educational Performance*.

Sin, S.-C. J. (2015). Demographic Differences in International Students' Information Source Uses and Everyday Information Seeking Challenges. *Journal of Academic Librarianship*, *41*(4), 466–474. doi:10.1016/j.acalib.2015.04.003

Sin, S.-C. J., & Kim, K.-S. (2013). International students' everyday life information seeking: The informational value of social networking sites. *Library & Information Science Research*, *35*(2), 107–116. doi:10.1016/j.lisr.2012.11.006

Sookhtanlo, M., Mohammadi, H. M., & Rezvanfar, A. (2009). Library information-seeking behaviour among undergraduate students of agricultural extension and education in Iran. *DESIDOC Journal of Library and Information Technology, 29*(4), 12–20. doi:10.14429/djlit.29.256

UNESCO. (n.d.). *Glossary: International (or internationally mobile) students.* Retrieved 25 July, 2018, from http://uis.unesco.org/node/334686

Veletsianos, G., & Navarrete, C. C. (2012). Online Social Networks as Formal Learning Environments: Learner Experiences and Activities. *International Review of Research in Open and Distance Learning, 13*(1), 144. doi:10.19173/irrodl.v13i1.1078

Yi, Z. (2007). International student perceptions of information needs and use. *Journal of Academic Librarianship, 33*(6), 666–673. doi:10.1016/j.acalib.2007.09.003

Chapter 6
Sexting Behaviors Among Adolescents and Adults:
Prevalence and Correlates Within Romantic Relationships

Samuel E. Ehrenreich
University of Nevada – Reno, USA

Diana J. Meter
Utah State University, USA

Marion K. Underwood
Purdue University, USA

ABSTRACT

Exchanging sexually explicit messages has become an increasingly common form of interaction for both adolescents and adults. Although sexting has been identified as a risk factor for a variety of negative outcomes, this research has generally been conducted without attention to the relationship context of the communicators. This chapter will examine the prevalence of sexting in the context of existing romantic relationships, and how sexting may relate to features of the relationship. The authors will review existing research examining motivations for sexting with romantic partners, pressure to engage in sexting, and associations between sexting and romantic attachment styles and relationship satisfaction. The chapter will conclude with discussion of important future directions for research.

DOI: 10.4018/978-1-5225-7949-6.ch006

INTRODUCTION

With the rapid rise in the number and popularity of digital communication platforms, exchanging sexually explicit messages has become increasingly common (Madigan, Ly, Rash, Van Ouytsel & Temple, 2018). Sexting, which can include exchanging sexually explicit text communication, images, or video, has been associated with a variety of negative outcomes, including risky sexual behaviors (Dake, Price, Maziarz & Ward, 2012; Ševčíková, 2016), social problems such as cyberbullying (Kowalski, Limber & Agatston, 2007), and psychological maladjustment (Brinkley, Ackerman, Ehrenreich & Underwood, 2017; Selkie, Kota, Chan, & Moreno, 2015; Van Ouytsel, Van Gool, Ponnet & Walrave, 2014). However, much of the foundational research examining sexting has focused on the correlates and consequences of engaging in this behavior (Dake et al., 2012; Houck et al., 2013; Klettke, Hallford & Mellor, 2014; Ybarra & Mitchell, 2014), without examining the context in which this behavior occurs. A commonly overlooked context in which sexting occurs is within offline romantic relationships (Döring, 2014, Drouin & Landgraff, 2012). Understanding how sexting occurs within the context of these relationships, and may be impacted by features of these relationships, is an important step in understanding the impact of sexting on psychosocial functioning. The guiding purpose of this chapter is to describe sexting behaviors within the context of romantic relationships, summarizing research on how sexting may relate to features of these relationships and identifying where additional research is needed.

This chapter will begin with a review of the definitions of sexting and prevalence rates of sexting in and out of both adolescents' and adults' romantic relationships. The primary focus will be to review existing research that has examined sexting behaviors within the context of romantic relationships, focusing on motivations for sexting, pressure to engage in sexting, non-consensual sharing of images, and the correlations between sexting and relationship satisfaction and romantic attachment style. Given that research examining sexting with one's romantic partner has primarily been examined in young adult samples, this will represent the majority of the research reviewed. Studies examining sexting within adolescent and later adult relationships will also be presented when available. Research on sexting has also predominantly focused on heterosexual couples. These couples will be the focus of our review, however we will specify when research examining non-heterosexual relationships is presented. The chapter will conclude with future directions for research.

BACKGROUND

Definitions of Sexting

One of the challenges of assessing the prevalence of sexting lies in the varied definitions that are often attributed to the behavior. Sexting can include sexually provocative written communication, explicit images and videos containing provocative, nearly-nude, or nude images, or both text and image messages (Drouin, Vogel, Surbey & Stills, 2013; Galovan, Drouin & McDaniel, 2018). Although these nude or semi-nude images often depict the person sending the message, they can be easily forwarded. Exchanging sexually explicit textual messages seems to be a more common behavior than exchanging semi-nude or nude images, at least among young and older adults (Drouin et al., 2013; Galovan et al., 2018). Because exchanging nude images of minors constitutes child pornography and therefore is a significantly more concerning behavior, examinations of the prevalence of sexting amongst adolescents often focus on exchanging nude or semi-nude images (Lounsbury, Mitchell & Finkelhor, 2011). For the purpose of this review, sexting will refer to both sexually explicit textual and image-based messages, unless otherwise stated. Research findings that look at only textual messages or images will be described as such. Furthermore, sexts can be sent, received, or both, which likely differentially impacts individuals' well-being and relationships (Anastassiou, 2017). Sexting in studies that examine sending *and* receiving sexts will be referred to as "exchanging" sexts; otherwise reviewed results will refer specifically to either sending or receiving sexts.

Prevalence of Sexting

Age Differences in Prevalence of Sexting

Sexting is a relatively common occurrence among adolescents and adults. In a meta-analytic review of sexting behaviors among adolescents (12-17 years of age), 14.8% of adolescents reported sending a sext (either text or images), and 27.4% reported receiving one (Madigan, et al., 2018). Individual studies typically report that more adolescents and young adults receive sexts than send them (Lenhart, 2009; Rice et al., 2014). Despite the view the sexting is primarily an adolescent issue (Angelides, 2013), sexting behaviors among young adults (generally defined as between 18 and 24-26 years old) are even more common, with estimates that between 50% and 60% of young adults exchange text or image-based sexts (Crimmins & Seigfried-Spellar, 2014; Gordon-Messer, Bauermeister, Grodinski & Zimmerman, 2013; Klettke et al.,

2014). Few studies have examined involvement in sexting beyond adolescent and young adult populations, however the few that have indicate that sexting behavior occurs among middle adults as well. One of the few studies that examined age differences in sexting among adults found that sexting (both text and images) was most common among 25-34 year olds (75.8% engaged), but continued to occur later in life: 63.6% of people 35-44 years old sext, and 33% of people 45-60 years old sext (Gámez-Guadix, Alemendros, Borrajo & Calvete, 2015). Sexting also appears to be gaining popularity among adolescents. Madigan et al's (2018) meta-analysis found that research study publication date was a significant predictor of sexting rates, indicating that the prevalence of sexting is increasing over time. Although Madigan et al's (2018) findings suggests that the number of adolescents engaging in sexting is increasing, it does not inform us as to whether sexting behaviors are continuing at this increased rate into adulthood.

Gender Differences in Prevalence of Sexting

Research examining gender differences in the prevalence of sexting among adolescents has had conflicting findings. Some studies have found that adolescent boys and girls send nude or semi-nude images at equal rates (Dake et al., Lenhart, 2009, Rice et al., 2012). Alternatively, other studies have identified a tendency for adolescent boys to send nude or sexual images more frequently (Jonsson, Priebe, Gladh & Svedin, 2014), whereas others have reported that girls are more likely to exchange sexual text or images (Martinez-Prather & Vandiver, 2014; Mitchell, Finkelhor, Jones & Wolak, 2011). In her recent meta-analysis of adolescent sexting behaviors, Madigan et al. (2018) did not find gender differences in sending or receiving sexually explicit images, or the likelihood of either forwarding a sext or having a sext forwarded without consent. Despite the apparent lack of gender differences in the prevalence of sexting, girls report feeling pressured to engage in sexting more than boys, as well as a greater sense of social censure when they do engage in sexting (see Anastassiou, 2017).

Fewer studies have examined gender differences in sexting behavior among young adults, but the results have demonstrated similarly conflicting results. Some comparisons among male and female college students indicate men and women engage in sexting at similar rates (Crimmins et al., 2014), however other studies suggest that men may be more likely to receive images, but no more likely than women to send or abstain from sexting (Gorden-Messer et al., 2013).

Socioeconomic Differences in Prevalence of Sexting

Socioeconomic variables may also relate to the prevalence of sexting. Studies have identified racial and ethnic differences in the prevalence of sexting behaviors, particularly among adolescent samples (Klettke et al., 2014). Black adolescents are more likely to send sexts than Latino (Fleschler-Peskin et al., 2013) and White adolescents (Dake et al., 2012, Rice et al., 2012). There is also evidence that Latino adolescents exchange more sexts than White adolescents (Rice et al., 2018). In contrast, studies of adult sexting behaviors have generally found that White adults sext more than Asian/Pacific Islanders (Gordon-Messer et al., 2013) and non-white individuals (individual ethnic groups were not compared; Benotsch, Snipes, Martin & Bull, 2013). However at least one study has found that African American women report sexting more than White women (Kimberly, Williams, Dawdy & Cruz, 2017). The only study we are aware of that has examined income as a predictor of sexting behaviors found no income differences between sexting profiles among adults (Galovan et al., 2018).

Prevalence of Sexting Within the Context of Romantic Relationships

Although much of the research examining sexting prevalence has focused on rates of sexting behaviors in a vacuum (Drouin, Ross & Tobin, 2015; National Campaign to Prevent Teen and Unplanned Pregnancy & CosmoGirl, 2008; Silva, Teixeira, Vasconcelos-Raposo & Bessa, 2016), sexting often occurs within the context of a romantic relationship (Dir, Coskunpina, Steiner & Cyders, 2013; Döring, 2014). Indeed studies of the prevalence of sexting with a romantic partner indicate that this is a fairly normative aspect of romantic relationships. Between 55-65% of young adults report exchanging sexts within the context of committed relationships (Drouin & Landgraff, 2012; Drouin, Coupe & Temple, 2017). Sixty-three percent of young adults reported sending a textual sext to someone with whom they are in a casual romantic relationship (Drouin, et al., 2013). Sexting with romantic partners also occurs among later adult samples. In a large international sample of adults in romantic relationships (18-85 years old), 28.5% of participants reported sexting with their partner (Galovan et al., 2018).

Although fewer studies have quantitatively explored sexting amongst adolescents in romantic relationships, qualitative studies suggest that adolescents often exchange sexts with a romantic partner (Anastassiou, 2017; Döring, 2014; Lenhart, 2009). In one qualitative study, 21 participants (out of 31; 68%) reported exchanging sexts only within the context of a romantic and/or sexual relationship (Lippman

& Campbell, 2014). These qualitative studies suggest adolescents' sext with their romantic partners similarly to adults in romantic relationships, although further quantitative support is needed.

Methodological Challenges in Measuring Sexting Prevalence

The prevalence of sexting likely depends not only on how sexing is operationally defined (i.e. written texts, explicit images, or both), but also on how sexting is assessed. The vast majority of research on sexting relies on adolescents' and young adults' self-reports. Self-reports for sexting may be especially problematic because social desirability might lead to both under-reporting (due to the desire to avoid admitting to behavior some might find objectionable) or over-reporting (perhaps in a desire to show sexual prowess or pseudo-maturity). Under-reporting might be especially problematic when studying minors, for whom nude photos are considered child pornography (see Judge, 2012; Richards & Calvert, 2009; Zhang, 2010 for reviews of the legal implications of underage sexting). Given that sexting is digital communication, it is possible to use technology to capture the actual content of sexting rather than rely on self-reports (see Brinkley et al., 2017). It is less than encouraging that the one study that used technology to observe exchanging written sexts among adolescents reported a rate of sending or receiving explicit written text messages (approximately 65%) that is higher than that reported in surveys (Brinkley et al., 2017).

CORRELATES AND FEATURES OF SEXTING WITHIN ROMANTIC RELATIONSHIPS

The studies reviewed above indicate that sexting is a relatively common behavior for adults, and likely adolescents, to engage in with their romantic partners. If sexting has become a normative aspect of romantic relationships, it is important to understand how exchanging these messages may relate to other characteristics of romantic relationships. Sexting within romantic relationships likely has an impact on the correlates and outcomes of sexting behaviors. Whereas sexting in general might be associated with a variety of other risky sexual behaviors (Ševčíková, 2016), sexting within the context of an established romantic relationship, particularly a committed romantic relationship, might be associated with more positive features, or at least fewer negative features than sexting outside of established relationships.

Sexting specifically within the context of romantic relationships may relate to features of these relationships, such as relationship satisfaction and the couple's romantic attachment styles. Furthermore, individuals may have specific goals and motivations when exchanging sexts with their romantic partner. Finally, an individual who is sexting within an existing relationship might feel more pressured or coerced to sext with that person in an attempt to preserve the existing relationships. Thus sexting within romantic relationships may actually provide unique opportunities for romantic relationship maintenance, but also imbue additional risk.

In the following sections we will review research examining correlates and features of sexting that may be most salient when sexting within romantic relationships. We will focus on four aspects of romantic relationships: motivations for sexting with romantic partners, pressured or coerced sexting with romantic partners, and associations between sexting and romantic attachment style and relationship satisfaction. These correlates and features will be reviewed because they are highly relevant to romantic relationships and have received the most empirical study.

Motivations for Sexting Behaviors

In general, individuals engage in sexting as relationship maintenance behavior. The most common rationale for sexting among both adolescents and adults is to engage in flirtation and initiate sexual activity (Drouin et al., 2013; Lippman & Campbell, 2014). In addition to flirtation and initiating sex, there were also different motivations for sexting depending on the type of relationship with the texting partner. For adolescents especially, their motivations may be guided by whether they have been sexually active with their partner before or not. Adolescents in sexually active couples report using sexting as a way to initiate sexual behavior, whereas adolescents in couples that have not been sexually active report being motivated to use sexting as a way to engage in sexual behaviors in lieu of physical sexual activity (Lippman & Campbell, 2014).

Among 18- and 19-year-olds, 64% of individuals who reported sending a sext did so because they wanted to make their boyfriend or girlfriend happy (Englander, 2015). Individuals reported being motivated to send sexts as a way to maintain a relationship with a partner who is far away when they were in a committed relationship with that person, compared to when in a casual sexual relationship, or when they were sexting with a cheating partner (Drouin et al., 2013). Alternatively, individuals who sent sexts to a cheating partner were more likely to be motivated to use sexting as a covert means of communicating that would not be discovered by their primary romantic partner, or to send sexts out of boredom (compared to those sexting with committed or casual romantic relationships; Drouin et al., 2013). Individuals' perceptions of the efficacy of sexting may also be a function of their relationship status. People who were in dating, cohabitating, or married relationships had significantly less negative expectancies about how receiving a sext makes people feel compared to those who were single. Participants' positive and negative expectancies about how exchanging sexts will make them and their partner feel in turn predicted their likelihood for engaging in sexting (Dir et al., 2013). Although individuals are motivated to sext with their romantic partners to promote closeness and intimacy (Englander, 2015), additional research is needed to understand how effective sexting is as a means for fulfilling these motivations. For example, focus group studies have highlighted that adolescents' use sexting as a means to promote intimacy and a sense of closeness with their romantic partner (Lippman & Campbell, 2014). However we are not aware of empirical studies that have directly tested if sexting actually promotes intimacy, connection, and closeness within the relationship.

Sexting is also a common way for individuals to flirt with someone with whom they would like to be in a romantic relationship (but are not), or to convey their romantic interest to that person. Both adolescents (Lippman & Campbell, 2014) and college-aged young adults report using sexting as a means to initiate a sexual or romantic relationship (Englander, 2012), suggesting that this may be an important aspect of contemporary relationship initiation. Additional research is needed to understand the efficacy of this strategy, and if relationships that are initiated via sexting follow a different trajectory than those that are not.

Pressured Sexting and Non-Consensual Sharing of Sexts

In addition to having an effect on the consequences of sexting, the context of sexting may also have implications for whether sexts are non-consensually forwarded. For example, among a sample of young adults, those in committed relationships reported being less concerned that their partner would forward sexts (26%) in comparison to those in casual relationships (53%) and those who were in a relationship with a cheating partner (46%). Only 3% of committed partners actually did report forwarding sexts that should have remained private (Drouin et al., 2013). These results suggest that individuals perceive different levels of risk of having sexts forwarded without consent depending on the context of the relationship. Although people are largely concerned about someone forwarding their images, in one study, only 3% of adolescents reported this had happened (Cox Communications, 2009). However among individuals who received threats that sexual images would be released in order to coerce the victim to provide additional pictures, sex, or other favors, 60% knew the person who extorted them, and this person was often a romantic partner (59% of the time). In this study, most victims reporting the incident(s) were women, and most perpetrators were men (Wolak, Finkelhor, Walsh, & Treitman, 2018).

Importantly not all individuals who engage in sexting do so with full consent. In a study of 18-19-year-old college students, 12% of participants reported that they only sexted when they felt pressure to do so. Fifty-eight percent of participants reported that they sometimes felt coerced to sext. In this sample, only 30% of individuals who engaged in sexting felt no pressure to do so (Englander, 2015). In a study of young adult college students, about 20% of participants reported being coerced into sexting via text or image, typically through repeated asking and being made to feel as though they were obligated to (Drouin et al., 2015). In a retrospective study, 75% of participants reported that they knowingly sent sexual images to future perpetrators of extortion, and 70% of these individuals did so because they were in a romantic or sexual relationship they desired to have with the perpetrator, but two thirds of these same individuals said they felt pressured, tricked, threatened, or forced to share the images (Wolak et al., 2018). Taken together, these findings suggest that although sexting within a romantic relationship may be somewhat protective against the risk of nonconsensual sharing of these images (Drouin et al., 2013), coercion to send explicit messages and non-consensual sharing remains present within these relationships (Wolak et al., 2018).

Sexting and Romantic Attachment

Sexting may also relate to individuals' romantic attachment styles. Romantic attachment styles are the relatively stable set of expectations and perceptions people hold for both themselves and their partners in the context of romantic relationships. Individuals are generally characterized by one of three attachment styles. Securely attached people report feeling comfortable becoming close with others and relying on them. Avoidantly attached people report difficulty becoming close with others and are hesitant to demonstrate commitment to a relationship. Anxiously attached individuals generally report not feeling confident in their partner's commitment to relationships and are often concerned that others do not care for them (Simpson, 1990).

Romantic attachment styles may be an important variable to consider when examining sexting within the context of romantic relationships. Among young adults, insecure attachment styles are a predictor of sending sexts to romantic partners (Drouin & Landgraff, 2012). Among college-aged individuals in committed relationships, individuals characterized by an anxious attachment style were more likely to send their partners sexually explicit textual-messages than those with secure attachment styles. Individuals characterized by an avoidant attachment style were more likely to send both textual and picture/video sexts (Drouin & Landgraff, 2012). This relation was moderated by gender; avoidant men were more likely to send both types of messages than avoidant women. In another study, women's anxious and avoidant attachment styles were associated with sending sexts to their romantic partners. Furthermore, women's difficulty regulating their impulses during moments of emotional distress mediated the association between anxious attachment and sexting (Trub & Starks, 2017).

There are several possible explanations for the associations between attachment styles and sexting behavior. Sexting with romantic partners might provide a sense of control in regulating the amount of intimacy that an individual desires within the relationship. Sexting may also provide a means to elicit intimacy and reinforcement from a romantic partner. This may make it an appealing behavior for individuals who require constant reassurance of the partner's interest and commitment to the relationship—behaviors that would characterize an anxious attachment style (Fraley & Shaver, 2000; Hazan & Shaver, 1987), particularly when they are experiencing emotional distress (Trub & Starks, 2017). Conversely—and somewhat contradictorily—the physical and emotional distance that sexting may provide might also make it an appealing behavior for individuals who prefer to limit their expressions of intimacy and commitment within a relationship, behaviors that would characterize an avoidant attachment style (Fraley & Shaver, 2000; Hazan & Shaver, 1987). In this way, sexting may be a useful tool for promoting the goals of these two distinct romantic attachment styles.

Attachment style may also moderate the effects of sexting. Sexting within both committed and casual relationships is associated with a range of positive and negative outcomes for young adults (Drouin et al., 2017). However these outcomes were moderated by attachment avoidance. Individuals who exhibited higher levels of an avoidant attachment style with their romantic partner experienced less positive consequences of sexting, greater discomfort with sexting, and increased worry, regret, and trauma after sending sexual messages. These findings highlight the impact attachment styles that individuals bring to the relationship may have on the consequences of sexting. Individuals with insecure attachment styles are more likely to engage in sexting behaviors, and are also more likely to suffer adverse consequences of sexting.

Although attachment styles appear to be an important correlate of whether individuals' engage in sexting and the outcomes associated with sexting, research has not examined this feature of relationships in adolescent samples. Romantic relationships during adolescence are important developmental activity, allowing individuals to explore this new form of interpersonal relationship (Connolly & McIsaac, 2011). Adolescents use their early romantic relationships as a means for developing the attachment style that will guide their romantic relationships throughout adulthood (Furman, Simon, Shaffer & Bouchey, 2002). Given that romantic attachment styles are still being established in adolescence, the association between sexting and romantic attachment at this age has the potential for long-term impacts on development.

Sexting and Relationship Satisfaction

Sexting within the context of an established relationship may be related to individuals' satisfaction with, and perception of the relationship, with some even suggesting that sexting could be used as a therapeutic tool to promote intimacy and sexual and relationship satisfaction (Parker, Blackburn, Perry & Hawks, 2013). Despite this speculation, findings have been mixed, with little support for this hypothesis emerging. As observed among adolescent samples (Dake et al., 2012), and young adult samples, sexting in romantic relationships predicted increases in physical sexual behavior, however it was unrelated to sexual satisfaction or pleasure (Castañeda, 2017). In another study, adults in romantic relationships who sexted frequently with text and images rated their relationship as more sexually satisfying compared to those who never sexted, or only exchanged textual sexts (Galovan et al., 2018). However, despite the increased sexual satisfaction reported by these groups, these relationships also exhibited a variety of maladaptive features. Frequent text and image sexters reported greater conflict with their partner and exhibited a variety of technology-related relationship problems such as engaging in infidelity behaviors on social media, and *technoference* (e.g. technology interfering with or distracting from face-to-face interactions with their partner).

Beyond sexual satisfaction and behaviors, limited evidence suggests that sexting behaviors promote overall relationship satisfaction. In Galovan et al's (2018) analysis of sexting profiles, there were no differences between non-sexters, or any of the three sexting profiles (text-only, frequent-, and hyper-sexters) in general relationship satisfaction. Similarly, Parker et al., (2013) found that relationship satisfaction was not a significant predictor of ever having sexted with the relationship partner. In one examination of both heterosexual and non-heterosexual relationships, Currin and colleagues (2016) found that sexting behaviors were unrelated to relationship satisfaction for all men, and for non-heterosexual women. Among non-heterosexual women, those who only received sexts (but did not send them) reported reduced relationship satisfaction compared to non-heterosexual women who did not send or receive any sexually explicit messages.

In the only study we are aware of to find a significant positive association between sexting and relationship satisfaction, McDaniel and Drouin (2015) found that exchanging sexually explicit images was positively associated with relationship satisfaction among men in married/cohabitating relationships, but only among women with elevated attachment anxiety. Exchanging sexually explicit textual messages predicted improved relationship satisfaction, but only among men and women who reported high levels of avoidance (McDaniel & Drouin, 2015). These conflicting findings regarding the relation between sexting and relationship satisfaction suggests that sexting may not be an important predictor of individuals' general satisfaction within a relationship.

FUTURE RESEARCH DIRECTIONS

Although existing research provides an important foundation for understanding the role of sexting within romantic relationships, there are still many gaps in the literature. Important directions for future research include further examination of sexting with romantic partners during adolescence and later adulthood, investigating the role of ethnicity in sexting with romantic partners, and the role of sexting at the initiation of relationships.

Sexting With Romantic Partners During Adolescence

One the most important directions for future research is further investigation of sexting within romantic relationships during adolescence. Although the overall prevalence and risks associated with adolescent sexting has received significant research attention, there has been little empirical investigation of adolescents' sexting specifically with their romantic partners. This is a very significant gap in our understanding given the prominence of adolescence in the development of adult romantic relationships. The focus on adolescent sexting without attending to the relationship context may stem from the view of sexting as exclusively a risk behavior, rather than as a feature of normative sexual exploration and behavior. This emphasis on the risks of adolescent sexting is reflected in the frequent examination of adverse outcomes associated with sexting, such as early sexual activity (Dake et al., 2012), unprotected sex (Trub & Starks, 2017), the legal consequences of underage sexting (Judge, 2012), and the publicity of instances of suicide following the non-consensual sharing of nude images (Agomuoh, 2012; Inbar, 2009).

Although all of these risks are quite real, a singular focus on them does not acknowledge the fact that exploring sexuality and romantic relationships are important developmental tasks during adolescence (Sullivan, 1953). Adolescents' motivations for sexting include a desire to be flirty and intimate with their partners (Lenhart, 2009), but they also use sexting as a way to experiment with non-physical forms of sexuality with partners (Lippman & Campbell, 2014). It is possible that adolescents may be motivated to incorporate sexting into their romantic relationships to experiment with a variety of forms of sexual expression. For example, although the number of youth engaging in sexual intercourse before or during high school has remained slightly below 50% since 2000 (Centers for Disease Control and Prevention, 2014), adolescents have actually become more sexually active in a variety of non-intercourse behaviors including mutual masturbation and oral sex (Diamond & Savin-Williams, 2009). It is possible that the increase in sexting among adolescents over time (Madigan et al., 2018) reflects a motivation to experiment with a range of sexual behaviors that do not necessarily entail intercourse.

Sexting may provide a uniquely ideal environment for this type of experimentation, as well as expressing sexual desires, disclosing intimate details to a romantic partner, and expressing love and affection (Drouin et al., 2013; Lippman & Campbell, 2014). However, understanding the role that sexting plays in the development of romantic feelings and expressions will likely require focusing on this behavior within romantic relationships. Further examination of sexting within adolescents' romantic relationships may require viewing these behaviors as facilitating an important development process. Studying sexting from this developmental perspective will likely lead to a more accurate view of sexting, which presents both risks and opportunities for adolescents (Döring, 2014).

Sexting With Romantic Partners During Middle Adulthood

Further research on sexting with romantic partners is needed among middle adult populations as well. The few large-scale studies that have examined sexting among adults beyond college-aged samples has identified that sexting continues into middle and late adulthood (Gámez-Guadix et al., 2015), but there is still a dearth of understanding about how sexting behaviors develop among middle and older adults. Given that sexting entered the popular lexicon in the mid-to-late 2000's (Döring, 2014), adults who engage in sexting in their 40's, 50's, and 60's (Gámez-Guadix et al., 2015) may have incorporated this behavior into their sexual schemas and scripts later in life. The incorporation of this behavior highlights the lifespan perspective of sexuality development, supporting that sexual relationships continue to develop after the early adult years.

Furthermore, sexting in late-adult relationships may have a different impact on romantic relationships than sexting during adolescence or early adulthood. Middle adulthood may be characterized by more stable relationships and more established sexual norms and preferences. Incorporating sexting into relationships with established sexual scripts and norms may mediate or moderate the impact that this behavior has on relationship satisfaction or sexual satisfaction specifically. Perhaps older adults who engage in sexting exhibit more distinct relationship characteristics from their non-sexting, same-aged peers. This and other speculations are ripe for empirical investigation.

Ethnic Differences in Sexting With Romantic Partners

Very little research has examined the role of race and ethnicity in the prevalence of sexting, although the few studies that have been conducted suggest that these variables may indeed relate to involvement in sexting (Kimberly et al., 2017; Klettke et al., 2014; Rice et al., 2012). Despite these initial differences in the overall prevalence rates, we found no research that examined racial or ethnic differences in the prevalence of sexting within the context of a romantic relationships. This lack of research makes it difficult to speculate on whether sexting within romantic relationships might differ across ethnic or racial groups. However racial differences in more traditional dating behaviors have been identified. For example, Black women are much less likely to engage in "hook ups" (as individually defined by each respondent) during college compared to White women, but are equally likely to value committed dating relationships (Kuperberg & Padgett, 2016). Additional research is needed to clarify ethnic and racial differences in sexting behaviors, and understand if race mediates or moderates associations between sexting and features of romantic relationships.

The Role of Sexting During the Initiation of Relationships

Additional research is also needed to understand the role that sexting plays in the initiation of relationships. Both adolescents and young adults reported the desire to initiate a relationship as a motivation for sexting (Englander, 2012; Lippman & Campbell, 2014). Relying on explicit sexual text and images as a way to initiate a romantic relationship (as opposed to discussing shared interests, spending time together, or interacting in more casual ways) may have powerful implications for how relationships develop. Initiating a relationship through sexting may establish the prominence of sexuality within the relationship (relative to other aspects such as romance, intimacy, and self-disclosure). Alternatively, these relationships might suffer from reduced intimacy and self-disclosure compared to relationships that begin in less sexually explicit ways.

This may be particularly true among adolescents who are still learning and integrating sexual scripts into their relationships. If initiating a relationship via sexting does affect the dynamics of romantic relationships from their onset, it could account for some of the associations between sexting and increased sexual activity (Dake et al., 2012; Ševčíková, 2016). Similarly, phone-based dating apps which may facilitate initiating relationships via sexting (e.g. Tinder and Grindr) may follow a unique developmental course compared to more traditionally initiated relationships.

Alternatively, both adolescents and young adults identified using sexting as a means to promote intimacy and a sense of closeness with their romantic partner (Lippman & Campbell, 2014). If sexting is indeed an effective method of promoting intimacy, relationships initiated via sexting might be characterized by higher levels of intimacy and closeness. Further research is needed to disentangle how relationships initiated via sexting may be different from those that are not.

CONCLUSION

The existing research reviewed in this chapter suggests that sexting may best be considered a normative behavior (or at least non-deviant) within the romantic relationships of both adolescents and adults. Two-thirds of adolescents report sexting with their romantic partners (Lippman & Campbell, 2014), and between 55% and 65% of young adults report doing so (Drouin & Landgraff, 2012; Drouin et al., 2017). Almost 30% of adults between 18 and 85 report sending some form of sexually explicit message to their romantic partner (Galovan et al., 2018).

Sexting has generally been viewed by researchers as a risk behavior (see Döring, 2014). Indeed even sexting within the context of romantic relationships is not without risk. Sexting often occurs in the presence of coercive requests (Wolak et al., 2018) is correlated with relationship conflict. Despite these negative correlates however, sexting is also used by romantic partners to facilitate a variety of relationship functions, including to promote intimacy and closeness with their partner (Drouin et al., 2013; Englander, 2015) and may be an important tool for adolescent as they navigate the development of their sexual identity and preferences (Döring, 2014).

Sexting has become a relatively common behavior among adolescents and young adults, and given its increasing prevalence among adolescents over time (Madigan et al., 2018) is unlikely to disappear. These behaviors may have an important influence on romantic and sexual relationships. It is imperative that researchers, clinicians and educators attempt to understand sexting within the context of romantic relationships to better understand both the risks as well as the potential opportunities.

REFERENCES

Agomuoh, F. (2012). Amanda Todd suicide doesn't end cyber torment for ridiculed teen. *International Business Times*. Retrieved from: http://www.ibtimes.com/amanda-todd-suicidedoesnt-end-cyber-torment-ridiculed-teen-846827

Anastassiou, A. (2017). Sexting and young people: A review of the qualitative literature. *Qualitative Report*, *22*, 2231–2239.

Angelides, S. (2013). 'Technology, hormones, and stupidity': The affective politics of teenage sexting. *Sexualities*, *16*(5-6), 665–689. doi:10.1177/1363460713487289

Benotsch, E. G., Snipes, D. J., Martin, A. M., & Bull, S. S. (2013). Sexting, substance use, and sexual risk behavior in young adults. *The Journal of Adolescent Health*, *52*(3), 307–313. doi:10.1016/j.jadohealth.2012.06.011 PMID:23299017

Brinkley, D. Y., Ackerman, R. A., Ehrenreich, S. E., & Underwood, M. K. (2017). Sending and receiving text messages with sexual content: Relations with early sexual activity and borderline personality features in late adolescence. *Computers in Human Behavior*, *70*, 119–130. doi:10.1016/j.chb.2016.12.082 PMID:28824224

Canary, D. J., & Yum, Y. O. (2015). Relationship maintenance strategies. The International Encyclopedia of Interpersonal Communication, 1-9.

Castañeda, D. M. (2017). Sexting and sexuality in romantic relationships among Latina/o emerging adults. *American Journal of Sexuality Education*, *12*(2), 120–135. doi:10.1080/15546128.2017.1298069

Centers for Disease Control and Prevention. (2014). *Youth risk behavior surveillance, 2013*. Washington, DC: Author.

Connolly, J., & McIsaac, C. (2011). Romantic relationships in adolescence. In M. K. Underwood & L. H. Rosen (Eds.), *Social Development: Relationships in infancy, childhood, and adolescence* (pp. 180–206). New York: The Guilford Press.

Cox Communications. (2009). *Teen online and wireless safety survey: Cyberbullying, sexting, and parental controls*. Retrieved June 12, 2018 from http://www.scribd.com/doc/20023365/2009-Cox-Teen-Online-Wireless-Safety-Survey-Cyberbullying-Sexting-and-Parental-Controls

Crimmins, D. M., & Seigfried-Spellar, K. C. (2014). Peer attachment, sexual experiences, and risky online behaviors as predictors of sexting behaviors among undergraduate students. *Computers in Human Behavior*, *32*, 268–275. doi:10.1016/j.chb.2013.12.012

Currin, J. M., Jayne, C. N., Hammer, T. R., Brim, T., & Hubach, R. D. (2016). Explicitly pressing send: Impact of sexting on relationship satisfaction. *The American Journal of Family Therapy*, *44*(3), 143–154. doi:10.1080/01926187.2016.1145086

Dake, J. A., Price, J. H., Maziarz, L., & Ward, B. (2012). Prevalence and correlates of sexting behavior in adolescents. *American Journal of Sexuality Education*, *7*(1), 1–15. doi:10.1080/15546128.2012.650959

Diamond, L., & Savin-Williams, R. (2009). Adolescent sexuality. In R. Lerner & L. Steinberg (Eds.), 3rd ed.; Vol. 1, pp. 479–523). Handbook of adolescent psychology New York: Wiley.

Diamond, L., & Savin-Williams, R. (2011). Sexuality. In B. Brown & M. Prinstein (Eds.), *Encyclopedia of adolescence* (Vol. 2, pp. 314–321). New York: Academic Press. doi:10.1016/B978-0-12-373951-3.00087-9

Dir, A. L., Coskunpinar, A., Steiner, J. L., & Cyders, M. A. (2013). Understanding differences in sexting behaviors across gender, relationship status, and sexual identity, and the role of expectancies in sexting. *Cyberpsychology, Behavior, and Social Networking, 16*(8), 568–574. doi:10.1089/cyber.2012.0545 PMID:23675996

Döring, N. (2014). Consensual sexting among adolescents: Risk prevention through abstinence education or safer sexting? *Cyberpsychology (Brno), 8*(1). doi:10.5817/CP2014-1-9

Drouin, M., Coupe, M., & Temple, J. R. (2017). Is sexting good for your relationship? It depends.... *Computers in Human Behavior, 75*, 749–756. doi:10.1016/j.chb.2017.06.018

Drouin, M., & Landgraff, C. (2012). Texting, sexting, and attachment in college students' romantic relationships. *Computers in Human Behavior, 28*(2), 444–449. doi:10.1016/j.chb.2011.10.015

Drouin, M., Ross, J., & Tobin, E. (2015). Sexting: A new, digital vehicle for intimate partner aggression? *Computers in Human Behavior, 50*, 197–204. doi:10.1016/j.chb.2015.04.001

Drouin, M., Vogel, K. N., Surbey, A., & Stills, J. R. (2013). Let's talk about sexting, baby: Computer-mediated sexual behaviors among young adults. *Computers in Human Behavior, 29*(5), A25–A30. doi:10.1016/j.chb.2012.12.030

Englander, E. (2012). *Low risk associated with most teenage sexting: A study of 617 18-year-olds*. Retrieved on June 6, 2018 from http://vc.bridgew.edu/cgi/viewcontent.cgi?article=1003&context=marc_reports

Englander, E. K. (2015). Coerced sexting and revenge porn among teens. *Bullying. Teen Aggression & Social Media, 1*, 19–21.

Fleschler Peskin, M., Markham, C. M., Addy, R. C., Shegog, R., Thiel, M., & Tortolero, S. R. (2013). Prevalence and patterns of sexting among ethnic minority urban high school students. *Cyberpsychology, Behavior, and Social Networking, 16*(6), 454–459. doi:10.1089/cyber.2012.0452 PMID:23438265

Fraley, R. C., & Shaver, P. R. (2000). Adult romantic attachment: Theoretical developments, emerging controversies, and unanswered questions. *Review of General Psychology, 4*(2), 132–154. doi:10.1037/1089-2680.4.2.132

Furman, W., Simon, V. A., Shaffer, L., & Bouchey, H. A. (2002). Adolescents' working models and styles for relationships with parents, friends, and romantic partners. *Child Development*, *73*(1), 241–255. doi:10.1111/1467-8624.00403 PMID:14717255

Galovan, A. M., Drouin, M., & McDaniel, B. T. (2018). Sexting profiles in the united states and Canada: Implications for individual and relationship well-being. *Computers in Human Behavior*, *79*, 19–29. doi:10.1016/j.chb.2017.10.017

Gámez-Guadix, M., Almendros, C., Borrajo, E., & Calvete, E. (2015). Prevalence and association of sexting and online sexual victimization among Spanish adults. *Sexuality Research & Social Policy*, *12*(2), 145–154. doi:10.100713178-015-0186-9

Gordon-Messer, D., Bauermeister, J. A., Grodzinski, A., & Zimmerman, M. (2013). Sexting among young adults. *The Journal of Adolescent Health*, *52*(3), 301–306. doi:10.1016/j.jadohealth.2012.05.013 PMID:23299018

Hazan, C., & Shaver, P. (1987). Romantic love conceptualized as an attachment process. *Journal of Personality and Social Psychology*, *52*(3), 511–524. doi:10.1037/0022-3514.52.3.511 PMID:3572722

Houck, C. D., Barker, D., Rizzo, C., Hancock, E., Norton, A., & Brown, L. K. (2014). Sexting and sexual behavior in at-risk adolescents. *Pediatrics*, *133*(2), 1–7. doi:10.1542/peds.2013-1157 PMID:24394678

Inbar, M. (2009). 'Sexting' bullying cited in teen's suicide. 13-year-old Hope Witsell hanged herself after topless photos circulated. *MSNBC Today*. Retrieved from: http://today.msnbc.msn.com/id/34236377/ns/today-today_people

Ivankova, N. V., Creswell, J. W., & Stick, S. L. (2006). Using mixed-methods sequential explanatory design: From theory to practice. *Field Methods*, *18*(1), 3–20. doi:10.1177/1525822X05282260

Jonsson, L. S., Priebe, G., Bladh, M., & Svedin, C. G. (2014). Voluntary sexual exposure online among Swedish youth–social background, Internet behavior and psychosocial health. *Computers in Human Behavior*, *30*, 181–190. doi:10.1016/j.chb.2013.08.005

Judge, A. M. (2012). "Sexting" among US adolescents: Psychological and legal perspectives. *Harvard Review of Psychiatry*, *20*(2), 86–96. doi:10.3109/10673229.2012.677360 PMID:22512742

Kimberly, C., Williams, A., Drawdy, D., & Cruz, C. (2017). Brief report: Young adult women, sexting, and risky sexual behaviors. *Journal of Health Disparities Research and Practice, 10,* 1–8.

Klettke, B., Hallford, D. J., & Mellor, D. J. (2014). Sexting prevalence and correlates: A systematic literature review. *Clinical Psychology Review, 34*(1), 44–53. doi:10.1016/j.cpr.2013.10.007 PMID:24370714

Kowalski, R. M., Limber, S. P., & Agatston, P. W. (2007). *Cyberbullying: Bullying in the Digital Age* (1st ed.). Wiley-Blackwell.

Kuperberg, A., & Padgett, J. E. (2016). The role of culture in explaining college students' selection into hookups, dates, and long-term romantic relationships. *Journal of Social and Personal Relationships, 33*(8), 1070–1096. doi:10.1177/0265407515616876

Lenhart, A. (2009). *Teens and sexting, how and why minor teens are sending sexually suggestive nude or nearly nude images via text messaging.* Pew Internet and American Life Project Research. Retrieved June 12, 2018 from http://www.pewinternet.org/Reports/2009/Teens-and-Sexting.aspx

Lippman, J. R., & Campbell, S. W. (2014). Damned if you do, damned if you don't... if you're a girl: Relational and normative contexts of adolescent sexting in the United States. *Journal of Children and Media, 8*(4), 371–386. doi:10.1080/17482798.2014.923009

Lounsbury, K., Mitchel, K. J., & Finkelhor, D. (2011). *The true prevalence of 'sexting'.* University of New Hampshire. Crimes Against Children Research Centre. Retrieved July 6th 2018 from https://scholars.unh.edu/cgi/viewcontent.cgi?referer=https://scholar.google.com/&httpsredir=1&article=1063&context=ccrc

Madigan, S., Ly, A., Rash, C. L., Van Ouytsel, J., & Temple, J. R. (2018). Prevalence of multiple forms of sexting behavior among youth: A systematic review and meta-analysis. *JAMA Pediatrics, 172*(4), 327–335. doi:10.1001/jamapediatrics.2017.5314 PMID:29482215

Martinez-Prather, K., & Vandiver, D. M. (2014). Sexting among teenagers in the United States: A retrospective analysis of identifying motivating factors, potential targets, and the role of a capable guardian. *International Journal of Cyber Criminology, 8,* 21–35.

McDaniel, B. T., & Drouin, M. (2015). Sexting among married couples: Who is doing it, and are they more satisfied? *Cyberpsychology, Behavior, and Social Networking, 18*(11), 628–634. doi:10.1089/cyber.2015.0334 PMID:26484980

Mitchell, K. J., Finkelhor, D., Jones, L. M., & Wolak, J. (2011). Prevalence and characteristics of youth sexting: A national study. *Pediatrics*, *129*, 1–10. PMID:22144706

National Campaign to Prevent Teen and Unplanned Pregnancy & CosmoGirl.com. (2008). *Sex and tech: Results from a survey of teens and young adults*. Retrieved May 14, 2018 from http://www.thenationalcampaign.org/sextech/pdf/sextech_summary. pdf

Parker, T., Blackburn, K., Perry, M., & Hawks, J. (2013). Sexting as an intervention: Relationship satisfaction and motivation considerations. *The American Journal of Family Therapy*, *41*(1), 1–12. doi:10.1080/01926187.2011.635134

Rice, E., Craddock, J., Hemler, M., Rusow, J., Plant, A., Montoya, J., & Kordic, T. (2018). Associations Between Sexting Behaviors and Sexual Behaviors Among Mobile Phone-Owning Teens in Los Angeles. *Child Development*, *89*(1), 110–117. doi:10.1111/cdev.12837 PMID:28556896

Rice, E., Gibbs, J., Winetrobe, H., Rhoades, H., Plant, A., Montoya, J., & Kordic, T. (2014). Sexting and sexual behavior among middle school students. *Pediatrics*, *134*(1), e21–e28. doi:10.1542/peds.2013-2991 PMID:24982103

Rice, E., Rhoades, H., Winetrobe, H., Sanchez, M., Montoya, J., Plant, A., & Kordic, T. (2012). Sexually explicit cell phone messaging associated with sexual risk among adolescents. *Pediatrics*, *130*(4), 667–673. doi:10.1542/peds.2012-0021 PMID:22987882

Richards, R. D., & Calvert, C. (2009). When sex and cell phones collide: Inside the prosecution of a teen sexting case. *Hastings Communication and Entertainment Law Journal*, *32*, 1–39.

Selkie, E. M., Kota, R., Chan, Y. F., & Moreno, M. (2015). Cyberbullying, depression, and problem alcohol use in female college students: A multisite study. *Cyberpsychology, Behavior, and Social Networking*, *18*(2), 79–86. doi:10.1089/cyber.2014.0371 PMID:25684608

Ševčíková, A. (2016). Girls' and boys' experience with teen sexting in early and late adolescence. *Journal of Adolescence*, *51*, 156–162. doi:10.1016/j.adolescence.2016.06.007 PMID:27391169

Silva, R. B., Teixeira, C. M., Vasconcelos-Raposo, J., & Bessa, M. (2016). Sexting: Adaptation of sexual behavior to modern technologies. *Computers in Human Behavior*, *64*, 747–753. doi:10.1016/j.chb.2016.07.036

Simpson, J. A. (1990). Influence of attachment styles on romantic relationships. *Journal of Personality and Social Psychology, 59*(5), 971–980. doi:10.1037/0022-3514.59.5.971

Sullivan, H. S. (1953). *The Interpersonal Theory of Psychiatry.* New York: Norton.

Trub, L., & Starks, T. J. (2017). Insecure attachments: Attachment, emotional regulation, sexting and condomless sex among women in relationships. *Computers in Human Behavior, 71*, 140–147. doi:10.1016/j.chb.2017.01.052

Van Ouytsel, J., Van Gool, E., Ponnet, K., & Walrave, M. (2014). Brief report: The association between adolescents' characteristics and engagement in sexting. *Journal of Adolescence, 37*(8), 1387–1391. doi:10.1016/j.adolescence.2014.10.004 PMID:25448834

Wolak, J., Finkelhor, D., Walsh, W., & Treitman, L. (2018). Sextortion of minors: Characteristics and dynamics. *The Journal of Adolescent Health, 62*(1), 72–79. doi:10.1016/j.jadohealth.2017.08.014 PMID:29055647

Ybarra, M. L., & Mitchell, K. J. (2014). "Sexting" and its relation to sexual activity and sexual risk behavior in a national survey of adolescents. *The Journal of Adolescent Health, 55*(6), 757–764. doi:10.1016/j.jadohealth.2014.07.012 PMID:25266148

Zhang, X. (2010). Charging children with child pornography–Using the legal system to handle the problem of "sexting.". *Computer Law & Security Review, 26*(3), 251–259. doi:10.1016/j.clsr.2010.03.005

Chapter 7
Wearables and Workload

Michael Schwartz
WEAR Lab, USA

Paul Oppold
University of Central Florida, USA

P. A. Hancock
University of Central Florida, USA

ABSTRACT

Prior research has reported that novelty affects the usage cycle of wearable devices. This chapter investigates the effects of sensation seeking, intensity, novelty, gender, and prior experience on the workload experienced during one aspect of using wearable fitness trackers, the device installation process. Contrary to the authors' hypotheses, prior experience, sensation seeking, intensity, and novelty did not significantly affect workload. The findings suggest that males tend to experience less workload during the setup of wearable fitness trackers; however, only for the Basis B1 and only for some aspects of workload. The claims made by prior research may be limited to specific aspects of the wearable fitness tracker use cycle, and more investigation is needed before broader claims can be made.

INTRODUCTION

Wearable fitness trackers are shaping the ways users pursue health and fitness goals, monitor their own wellness, and pursue behavioral changes. However, this impact extends well beyond the wellness and fitness claims made by the marketing materials for these devices. While initially used for the wellness and fitness purposes marketed by the device manufacturers, device usage has extended into very basic

DOI: 10.4018/978-1-5225-7949-6.ch007

medical monitoring capabilities with the addition of heart rate trackers to some devices. Millions of wearable fitness trackers have been sold in recent years and both the performance and capabilities of the technology are improving (Lamkin, 2017). Wearable devices are still adding additional capabilities and features and changing how their users interact with the devices on a daily and weekly basis. However, in order to be effective, wearable fitness trackers must be worn frequently, charged regularly, and have data extracted periodically. Fitness trackers are marketed as distinct products based on provided functionality and are called by different names: activity monitor, wellness band, fitness tracker, or some combination of those terms. The functions each device provides (e.g., pedometer, heart rate) shape what kind of product labels are applied to the device and fitness trackers can include varying functionality based on model and brand. The term 'fitness tracker' will be used in this paper to signify the range of products that are meant to be worn and used to track health and fitness metrics over time. Not all worn fitness trackers include the ability to record heart rate; however, the devices with this functionality can provide basic medical monitoring capabilities which can benefit both patients and doctors (Rudner, McDougall, Sailam, Smith, & Sacchetti, 2016). As discussed in depth later in this chapter, wearable fitness trackers have helped detect the early signs of stroke, pregnancy, rhabdomyolysis, and even aided doctors in saving a patient's life, all of which are use cases not recommended by device manufacturers, not protected by medical malpractice insurers, and not realized by millions of consumers. There are many challenges to overcome before low-cost, consumer-grade devices can be widely adopted for monitoring health, especially in institutional settings. In this chapter, the authors show how difficulties at the individual level can scale to become problematic barriers for organizations that may wish to deploy wearables to monitor the health of their members. To demonstrate one area of difficulty individuals encounter when using a wearable fitness tracker, a study was conducted to focus on individual differences that may impact the wearable device installation process, an area of research that has not been well studied.

BACKGROUND

Wearable technologies have the potential to be incorporated into a variety of healthcare platforms, provided that existing challenges with the devices are overcome in their deployment and utilization. There are currently workload costs, demands on an individual's physical and mental resources, when using wearable devices (e.g., charging, installing, syncing), interface and application issues (e.g., inability to customize the presentation of data), and motivational issues (e.g., abandonment) that are barriers to using wearables at a larger scale (Brandao, 2016). Fitness trackers can provide benefits to the health, fitness, and medical fields through institutional adoption of wearables to serve as event recording devices for at risk or high-risk activity users (Rudner et al., 2016). A low-cost fitness tracker can be used as a discrete, early warning aid before a more expensive medical device is determined to be necessary. Early monitoring via a consumer-grade, wearable device of those within at-risk populations or those performing high risk activities has been observed, in some limited cases, to provide an early diagnosis and refer individuals to medical professionals for a more advanced diagnosis (Shapiro, 2015). However, fitness trackers are not medical devices; they are not regulated by the FDA, held to the same standards in terms of reliability and accuracy, or as expensive. Medical devices have higher sensor fidelity and the capability to provide real-time status. Fitness trackers are capable of passive data collection and provide retrospective analysis of data. The lower costs of fitness trackers compared to medical monitoring equipment is beneficial to people looking to monitor personal health in a limited fashion over time.

People can benefit from the data collected by wearable fitness trackers in both middle and older adulthood (Dogra & Stathokostas, 2012; Sun, Townsend, Okereke, Franco, Hu, & Grodstein, 2010). Older adults are more at risk for suffering from poor health; however, considering older adults as a separate population may be a confounding issue in some health studies. Research into health and wellness can instead consider how being a member of an at-risk population presents difficulties across the lifespan. For example, young and old adults can both have diabetes; however, older adults are more likely to have serious health complications as a result (Fong et al., 2004; Schwartz et al., 2008). Despite the benefits that fitness trackers can bring to an older population (Miyazaki et al., 2015), there is evidence to indicate that age does not play a factor in long-term adoption of wearable devices (Fausset et al., 2013; Shih, Han, Poole, Rosson, & Carroll, 2015). Brandao (2016) demonstrates how individual differences other than age, such as a desire for novelty, contribute to the adoption of a wearable device. Users' behaviors in interacting with such devices change over time as novelty fades and, once novelty is extinguished, abandonment often results. Novelty has been defined as the newness of an innovation according to the perceptions of the person adopting a technology and the authors will use that definition in this study (Wells, Campbell, Valacich, & Featherman, 2010). The use of a wearable device has operational costs, or workload demands, to the user: installation, charging, syncing, and analysis are actions that require time, effort, and resources and increase the cost of operation at both personal and institutional levels. When the novelty of a wearable fitness tracker is gone, some users abandon their devices or engage in disuse of the devices because the workload of continued operation exceeds the perceived value of the fitness tracker. Therefore, novelty is a characteristic of adoption and abandonment.

Workload is defined as the demand on a human operator's resources that occurs when accomplishing a task or set of tasks (Hart, 2006; Hart & Staveland, 1988). The demand, or cost, to meet the requirements of a task may be too high (e.g., stress, fatigue) and result in unsuccessful performance. The NASA Task Load Index (NASA-TLX) was developed to assess the six subjective components of global workload: mental, physical, and temporal demands, frustration, effort, and performance. Since workload costs can vary between individuals and tasks, a weighting system was originally introduced to account for individual differences in the perceived importance of the sources of workload. Raw-TLX (RTLX) is the most common variation of the original NASA-TLX scale. The RTLX eliminates the subscale weighting process and either averages or adds the subscale ratings. (Hart, 2006, p. 906). There is not a consensus on whether the NASA-TLX or the RTLX is better suited for estimating workload (Byers, Bittner, & Hill, 1989; Hendy, Hamilton, & Landry, 1993; Liu & Wickens, 1994). When RTLX scores are collected, analysis of the individual subscales has also demonstrated diagnostic value in determining the type of workload demands imposed by a system; therefore, the authors use the RTLX to ascertain the type of workload incurred by the participants in this study. Workload incurred during the process of maintaining a worn fitness tracker is a frequent drain on the user and the data collected from a wearable device needs to be perceived to provide enough value, in the form of extracted information, to offset that workload. Users also incur financial costs (purchasing devices), risk exposure of their data, experience a reduction in privacy through third party access to their data, and encounter social costs in the involvement of others in their fitness tracker data. Multiple studies have noted that actions as simple as charging a fitness tracker's battery are enough to cause a person to question if continuing to use a wearable device is worth the effort when considered against the potential value of the data being provided by the device (Brandao, 2016; Shih et al, 2015; Lazar, Koehler, Tanenbaum, & Nguyen, 2015). This presents a problem for the implementation of wearables in an institutional setting as users cannot determine if their devices are accurate and cannot make sense of the information provided that is based on the data captured, issues that affect perceived value. At the institutional level, organizations will have to employ people to interpret data for users or train users to be able to interpret their own data. The presence of anomalous data by an untrained, uninformed user may be mistakenly identified as a device malfunction instead of a potentially serious medical condition. If users are not perceiving value and are incurring workload costs in continuing to use wearable technologies, device disuse (charging only) or device abandonment (no charging and no syncing) has been shown to occur (Brandao, 2016). Perceived value is impacted if the workload to charge a device's battery is too high, the workload to sync a device for extraction is too high, the information provided does not match user expectations, the data is not as precise as the user expected, or the user has decided the device is inaccurate or malfunctioning. The regular effort for charging, syncing, installation, and data analysis should not be considered trivial when performed over a long period of time, especially as some maintenance tasks must be performed in daily or weekly increments. In this chapter, the authors will focus on the workload demands of synching a wearable fitness tracker to a smartphone, a process that must occur semi-regularly during the lifecycle of such devices.

The abandonment of a wearable fitness tracker can be caused by one of several factors. Users may discontinue using a device if they achieve a target goal or shift their focus to a different area of health and, thus, need a device with different functionality. Abandonment due to unsuccessful outcomes, such as not perceiving value in the information provided by a device and a user not achieving personal health and fitness goals, is still an issue. Across different age groups, genders, and sample sizes, two studies had over 50% of people discontinue use of their wearable devices by the end of the second week (Fausset et al., 2013; Shih et al, 2015). Participants in both studies reported abandoning their devices due to not perceiving sufficient value in continued use.

Intentions for adoption and the individual differences affecting long term usage of wearable technologies, including early abandonment, eventual abandonment, and predictive variables of abandonment, have been studied (Kaminski, 2011; Rauschnabel, Brem, & Ivens, 2015). Kaminski's (2011) Diffusion of Innovation Theory suggests that there are individual differences between those who adopt a technology early and those who do not. Rauschnabel et al. (2015) examined how personality and perception of value affected participants' awareness of and intention to adopt Google Glass, an augmented reality (AR) head mounted display. The authors found that participants who reported perceiving a high functional benefit in Google Glass were more likely to indicate that they would adopt the technology; however, these beliefs were moderated by an individual's personality as measured by John, Donahue, and Kentle's (1991) Big Five Inventory. Participants who scored high on openness to experience were more likely to be aware of Glass and adopt the technology. Participants who scored high on extraversion indicated that they were more likely to adopt Google Glass, but also answered that they were not more likely to be aware of the device. Intentions to adopt Glass were based on self-reported answers to a proprietary ad hoc scale. Personality data were collected for the current study; however, novelty has been studied more extensively with regard to wearable devices (Brandao, 2016; Fausset et al., 2013; Shih et al, 2015). Sensation seeking comprises novelty and intensity of experience and is considered a personality trait (Arnett, 1994). Therefore, the authors chose to collect data on sensation seeking, novelty, and intensity of experience in addition to personality data. Arnett (1994) found that males tend to score higher than females on a measure of sensation seeking.

As prior research has indicated, personality may be a factor in a person's willingness to adopt and use a novel technology.

Personality and prior experience have been found to be related to NASA-TLX ratings (Matthews et al., 2006; Rose, Murphy, Byard, & Nikzad, 2002; Sohn & Jo, 2003). Hancock (1988, 1989) found gender differences in subjective workload scores. The NASA-TLX has been used to assess the workload demands of using portable consumer electronics (Kuchenbecker & Wang, 2012; Mayser, Piechulla, Weiss, & Konig, 2003). Chalil, Madathil, Koikkara, Gramopadhye, and Greenstein (2011) utilized the NASA-TLX to evaluate the workload requirements of five different interfaces for recording information; several of the devices were commercially available portable electronics.

While prior research has investigated factors that lead to initial adoption of and long-term use of wearable devices, initial perceptions of the technology based on workload incurred during the syncing process still needs to be investigated. There are workload costs to adopting and setting up a new device and these must be studied. To use many commercially-available fitness trackers on the market today, the devices must first have the battery charged and then be paired with a base station, ordinarily via Bluetooth; in late-model wearable fitness trackers the base station is typically a smartphone with a companion mobile application installed. Research has indicated that differences in mobile phone operating systems have contributed to problems in collecting research data, an issue that must be considered when researching wearable devices (Collins, Aldred, Woolley, & Rai, 2015). Additionally, using Bluetooth drains a smartphone's battery, syncing a wearable device to the phone reduces battery and available bandwidth, and older model phones are typically not compatible with wearable devices that are commercially available. These issues increase both the cost and complexity of the overall system to individual users and become serious barriers for institutions that are looking to scale the use of these or similar devices. The financial and temporal costs of even initially syncing multiple devices in an institutional setting, independent of the time required to resync devices, extract data from them, and troubleshoot issues, has been highlighted as an obstacle for institutions seeking to use wearables in research and practice (Collins et al., 2015). For example, in a healthcare setting each client would need to have a compatible phone, preferably running the same version of the same operating system and using the same brand and model of wearable device; this becomes impractical for clients with different needs and preferences. Participants in Brandao's (2016) study indicated that they believe using more than one wearable device at a time requires too much time and too many resources on the part of the end user, which often leads to abandonment.

Issues, Controversies, Problems

A primary focus of wearable device research is the software required to use such electronics; this includes the algorithms for capturing, analyzing, and summarizing feedback as well as the front-end programs, such as mobile applications, that enable user interaction. Three fitness trackers were used in the current study; however, these devices and associated algorithms are not the focus of this chapter. Instead, the authors chose to focus on the human factors considerations (i.e., individual differences) between users and demonstrate interaction commonalities across devices. This is important because our results demonstrate that sensation seeking and its component elements, novelty and intensity of experience, were not significant factors in workload incurred during device set up and these findings were consistent across devices. While the algorithmic accuracy of fitness tracker software is important, computer science, medical, and engineering researchers have made claims about users that are not supported by the results of their studies (Gurrin, Smeaton, Qui, & Doherty, 2013; Zhang, Qiu, Tsai, Hassan, & Alamri, 2017). When the human factors issues of wearable devices are mentioned in scientific articles, the discussion quickly turns from the humans back to algorithms (e.g., machine learning techniques, automatization of tasks). Fulk et al. (2014) points out that the algorithms made by fitness tracker manufacturers are not suitable for people with cognitive and mobility impairments and customized algorithms must be created; fitness tracker algorithms are made for people who are already healthy. Even researchers who have access to patients in healthcare settings will install and set up the wearable devices for participants, thus reducing the human to a black box (Rosenberger et al., 2013; Rosenberger, Buman, Haskell, McConnell, & Carstensen, 2016). While such studies are valuable and needed, successful implementation of wearable health monitoring devices at both individual and institutional levels must take into account the human factors of the users.

Researchers have demonstrated the computational efficiency of proprietary algorithms, but not the understandability of the data presented to patients (Dubey et al., 2017). The ability to understand the results of one's own health data is even more of an issue for people who have sensory impairments (e.g., blindness) or cognitive impairments (e.g., people suffering from dementia). Cao, Chen, Hou, and Brown (2015) note that patient-focused design is lacking in most studies and neglects the needs and constraints of people who may be able to benefit from a wearable health monitoring device (e.g., stroke patients, people suffering from dementia). The authors' study presented in this chapter recruited participants with no known sensory or cognitive impairments, yet many were not able to successfully set up at least one fitness tracker. People living with a sensory or cognitive impairment may have even more difficulty when attempting to start using a wearable health monitoring device. Mezghani, Exposito, Drira, Da Silveira, & Pruski (2015) suggest using a Knowledge-as-a-Service (KaaS) platform to assist physicians and patients with understanding and managing healthcare data collected from wearable sensors. Such ideas are one possible solution to a complex problem; however, implementing technological solutions may result in another layer of abstraction between people and their data, increase the cost of healthcare delivery, and be unaffordable to patients who are unable to work and are already paying a high cost to manage their health.

Synching a wearable device is an additional daily or weekly task, depending on the device, separate from the effort required to extract and make sense of the data collected. An individual user may persevere through episodes of perceived malfunctioning and difficulty and continue to use her device; institutions, however, must decide if charging and syncing multiple devices, extracting and analyzing data, and providing customized insights to multiple users is possible. Each step in the process can be performed at the institutional or individual level. Unless a system is redesigned, workload cannot be avoided, only offloaded. Thus, institutional implementation of wearable devices for research or application is not an issue of scale, but of scales. Several studies have circumvented the issue of syncing wearables by setting devices up for participants (Mercer et al., 2016; Vooijs et al., 2014), providing extensive, customized tutorials that were created by the researchers (Fausset et al., 2013), recruiting participants who self-reported that they were already using fitness trackers (Brandao, 2016; Harrison, Marshall, Bianchi-Berthouze, & Bird, 2015), or omitted the set up process from their reporting, undermining any commentary or findings about installation, adoption, or on related matters (Jefferis et al., 2014; Miyazaki et al., 2015).

Prior research has not used the installation instructions that were provided with the wearable device by the manufacturer; this is a usability issue that has not been addressed. Wearable devices have been shown to require frequent re-installation (resyncing) with a base station, which presents usability and workload issues in the time and effort required to use fitness trackers regularly over time; these issues are relevant to institutions, meaningful to abandonment, and shape the user experience; thus, they are worth investigating (Brandao, 2016; Lazar et al., 2015; Collins et al., 2015). While usability of wearable devices has been investigated by several of the works cited in this paper, the workload of initially synching a wearable fitness tracker has yet to be empirically examined (Pfannenstiel & Chaparro, 2015). Several studies reported in their findings that workload is a key factor in the abandonment of wearable devices, particularly due to charging, installation, resyncing, and data analysis (Lazar et al., 2015). This study focuses on a specific aspect of usage, installation, and involves participants that used wearable devices in the lab, where actual usage with specific devices could be ensured.

MAIN FOCUS OF THE CHAPTER

Studies that reported novelty as a factor in the adoption of wearable devices have also noted the subsequent abandonment of wearables after novelty is extinguished and the cost of workload remains (Brandao, 2016; Fausset et al., 2013; Shih et al, 2015). It remains unclear if novelty is predictive of the amount of workload incurred during the initial installation of wearable devices, when novelty is likely to be high. This study examines the relationship between sensation seeking, novelty, and intensity on participants' experiences with three wearable fitness trackers: Basis B1 (Basis Science, Inc., 2013), Fitbit Flex (Fitbit, Inc., 2014), and Jawbone UP24 (Jawbone, Inc., 2013). Multiple devices were used in this study to follow the methodologies reported in prior research (Brandao, 2016; Fausset et al., 2013; Shih et al, 2015) and to investigate any similarities in the way devices may affect participants. The authors predict participants who score higher on a measure of sensation seeking, novelty, and intensity will report experiencing lower levels of workload while installing a wearable device compared to those who score low on sensation seeking, novelty, and intensity. A defining characteristic of the testing process for new devices are those participants who are not able to complete the installation process in the allotted time, resulting in a maximum score for time and an overall failure to set up the technology as requested. This study examines the differences between participants who completed system set up for all three wearable fitness trackers versus those who were unable to complete set up for at least one fitness tracker. If novelty affects adoption and abandonment, then novelty could be predictive of successful initial installation of wearable devices. This study predicts that there are significant individual differences between the two groups of participants: those who completed installation and those who did not. The authors predict that participants who do not complete the initial installation process in the allotted time will score lower on a measure of sensation seeking, novelty, and intensity and score higher on a measure of workload than those who did manage to successfully complete the initial installation process. Furthermore, the authors predict that males will score higher on sensation seeking, intensity, and novelty, and lower on workload than females and be more likely to complete set up of the wearable devices.

METHOD

Participants

Fifty-eight participants (27 male, 31 female; $M_{age}=19.93$, $SD_{age}=3.07$) were recruited from the undergraduate psychology student population from a university in the Southeast of the United States. The university's online research recruiting platform, Sona, was used for recruiting purposes. Data collection was conducted between March 2015 and November 2016, in a single session per participant, with a two-hour maximum time period.

Measures

Participants completed a paper-based version of a demographics questionnaire made for the current study. Demographic information about age, race, gender and year in school were collected. Participants were predominantly from freshman and sophomore psychology courses, receiving compensation within those courses for research involvement. A survey about prior experience with smartphones, tablets and wearable computers was completed by the participants, which contained items pertaining to motivation to use connected mobile technologies, such as smartphones and tablets, and factors that might influence someone to purchase a wearable computing device. Almost half (48%) of participants reported prior experience with at least one wearable device. Participants completed paper-based versions of the Arnett Inventory of Sensation Seeking (AISS; 16) and the Five Factor Personality Inventory (FFI; Buchanan, Johnson, & Goldberg, 2005). The AISS was chosen by the researchers because the measure comprises collected to utilize the subscales of Novelty and Intensity, whereas the data from the personality measures are not needed for this publication. Paper versions of the NASA Task Load Index (NASA-TLX; Hart, 2006; Hart & Staveland, 1988) and the System Usability Scale (SUS; Brooke, 1996) were used to rate participants' self-reported workload and perceptions of usability for the wearable devices included in this study. The NASA-TLX has been extensively validated (Hart, 2006).

Devices

Three wearable fitness trackers, Basis B1, Fitbit Flex, and Jawbone UP24, were used in this experiment (see Figure 1). These three devices were chosen for investigation because of their popularity in the consumer market (1). All three fitness trackers had companion smartphone apps that operated on the Android mobile OS or Apple's mobile platform, iOS. Basis' B1 required a personal computer to initiate device set

Figure 1. Basis B1

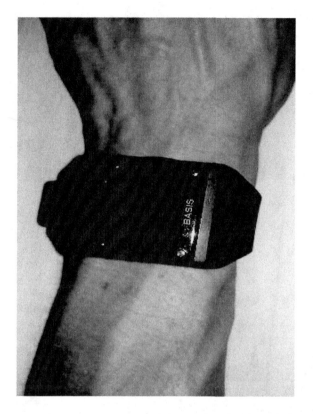

up and participants were allowed to use an HP Spectre x360 running Windows 7 to connect to the Internet in order to complete set up of the Basis. Participants were also provided with printed instructions from each device manufacturer's website and instructed that they could use the set up instructions, if needed, to assist with device set up. Instructions for both Android and iOS phones were given to participants.

Basis B1

The Basis B1 Band is a wristwatch-style fitness tracker with an onboard accelerometer and optical sensor that collects movement, temperature, heart rate, and skin conductance data and an LCD screen for displaying information. Users interact with the device by pressing a button on the wearable, through a smartphone app, or through an online portal. There are very few studies that have included the B1 (Lee, Kim, & Welk, 2014). The B1 is no longer commercially available or supported by the manufacturer (Graziano, 2016).

Figure 2. Fitbit Flex

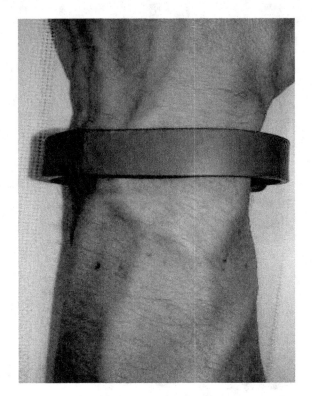

Fitbit Flex

The Fitbit Flex is a wrist-worn bracelet with an onboard accelerometer that tracks movement data. The device contains four LED lights that flash different patterns to indicate the current operation or status. There are no physical buttons on the bracelet and users interact with the Flex by tapping the device or through the smartphone app.

Jawbone UP24

The Jawbone UP24 is a wrist-worn bracelet that tracks movement data via an onboard accelerometer. The device contains one LED that flashes intermittently to indicate the current system status. Users interact with the device by pressing the lone button on the bracelet or through the smartphone app.

Figure 3. Jawbone UP24

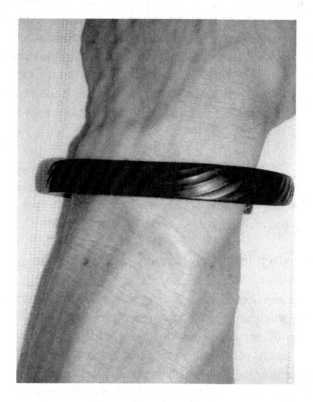

Procedure

After arriving at the lab, reading an informed consent document and indicating agreement to continue with the study, participants filled out a demographics questionnaire, the FFI, and the AISS. After completing the questionnaires, participants interacted with one of three fitness trackers: Jawbone UP24 the Fitbit Flex, or the Basis B1. Participants were instructed to download the smartphone app for each wearable to their phone and set up the device by pairing it with their smartphone. For this study, the authors had participants pair each wearable fitness tracker to their own smartphone to avoid the potential confound of using an unfamiliar phone or mobile operating system. As part of the set up process, participants wore each fitness tracker. Upon completion of interacting with the first wearable, participants rated the device syncing experience by completing the SUS and the NASA-TLX. Participants then interacted with the remaining two devices in the same manner, rating each experience after the interaction was complete. Participants were not being timed to see how quickly each could complete pairing a fitness tracker to their smartphone;

however, participants were only given a maximum of thirty minutes to complete each condition before moving on to rating the fitness tracker and then interacting with the next device. Participants were not informed about a time limit. Device presentation was counterbalanced across participants. The researchers recorded if the participants had trouble pairing a device to a phone and what the solution to the trouble was, if a solution was found. Upon completion of the experimental trials, participants were debriefed and awarded class participation credit as compensation.

Results

All data were analyzed using SPSS 24. Six participants were excluded from analyses due to technical issues with their phones (e.g., battery died); fifty-two participants were included in the final analyses.

Sensation Seeking, Intensity, Novelty, and Workload

A multiple linear regression was calculated to predict workload incurred during system set up based on participants' levels of sensation seeking, intensity of experience, and novelty. A significant regression equation was not found for any of the devices in this study. The results of this study indicate that sensation seeking, intensity, and novelty are not predictive of how much workload a person will incur during initial installation of a wearable fitness tracker. Table 1 provides more detailed results.

Individual Differences Between Finishers and Non-Finishers

Logistic regression was conducted to examine the impact of prior experience, gender, sensation seeking, intensity, and novelty on the likelihood of finishing the process of synching a wearable device with a smartphone. Of the 52 participants included in the final analyses, 22 were not able to complete set up of at least one fitness tracker. Data for all three devices were combined into one condition that was binomially coded to indicate successful or unsuccessful system set up. Prior experience, gender,

Table 1. Multiple regression results of sensation seeking, intensity, and novelty on workload (df = 1,49)

Fitness Tracker	F	p	R^2
Basis B1	1.665	.200	.064
Fitbit Flex	.323	.726	.013
Jawbone UP24	.099	.906	.004

sensation seeking, intensity, and novelty were not found to be statistically significant in predicting successful device set up. The predictor variables did not improve the model fit at a statistically significant level. Table 2 provides more detailed results.

Prior Experience

Correlation analyses were computed to assess the relationship between prior experience with wearable devices and self-reported sensation seeking, intensity, and novelty. No significant correlations were found between prior experience with wearables and novelty, intensity, or sensation seeking. Table 3 provides more detailed results.

Gender

Correlation analyses were computed to assess the relationship between gender and workload for each device set up experience, sensation seeking, intensity, and novelty. Contrary to our hypotheses, no significant correlations were found between gender and novelty, sensation seeking, and workload. The relationship between gender and intensity of experience did achieve significance. Table 4 provides more detailed results.

Table 2. Logistic regression results of gender, prior experience, sensation seeking, intensity, and novelty on device set up

Variable	Score	df	p
Gender	0.41	1	.840
Prior Experience	.778	1	.378
Sensation Seeking	.407	1	.524
Intensity	.146	1	.702
Novelty	.468	1	.494

Table 3. Correlations between prior experience with wearables and sensation seeking, novelty, and intensity (n=52)

Prior Experience	r	p
Sensation Seeking	.148	.295
Novelty	.152	.282
Intensity	.083	.560
Workload	-.102	.473

Table 4. Correlations between gender and sensation seeking, novelty, and intensity (n=52)

Gender	r	p
Sensation Seeking	-.201	.077
Novelty	-.019	.447
Intensity	-.283	.021
Workload (Basis)	.033	.408
Workload (Fitbit)	-.224	.055
Workload (Jawbone)	-.180	.101

NASA-TLX Item Analysis

Raw workload data were collected and analyzed at the item level. Of the six NASA-TLX items that were answered by participants in each of the three fitness tracker conditions, none were significantly predicted by sensation seeking, intensity, or novelty. Only the questions about temporal demand ($r = -.266$, $n = 52$, $p = .028$) and effort ($r = -.258$, $n = 52$, $p = .033$) were significantly correlated with intensity and only for the B1 device, indicating that participants who seek more intense experience incurred less workload during the B1 trials.

Discussion

This research investigated the effect of individual differences in sensation seeking, intensity, and novelty on self-reported workload during initial installation of three wearable fitness trackers. Our findings did not support our hypotheses and contradict prior research claiming that novelty affects the use of wearable devices. If novelty does not play a role in the short-term use of wearables, is this different than the effect it has on long-term use? Is another variable or set of variables a factor in the use, misuse, and abandonment of wearable devices? One possibility is that our study did not consist solely of users who were already using or had used a wearable device; therefore, our users were not self-selected. Also, the authors did not set up the devices for the participants as some prior research has done.

Finishers vs. Non-Finishers

Prior experience with wearable devices was examined to determine the existence of practice effects. Device presentation was counterbalanced to control for practice effects in this study; however, the authors could not control for experience. Prior experience, as self-reported by participants, did not have a significant effect on the probability of completing fitness tracker set up. Almost half of all participants reported having experience with at least one wearable device before participating in this study. An unexpected result was that prior experience with wearables was not significantly correlated with individual levels of sensation seeking, novelty, or intensity. Novelty has been demonstrated to influence the adoption and abandonment of wearable fitness trackers, according to self-reported data; however, Brandao (2016) recruited participants who reported using at least one fitness tracker.

Prior Experience

Prior experience was not significantly correlated with sensation, novelty, or intensity. These findings do not provide support for the claims made by prior research about novelty affecting device adoption and abandonment (Brandao, 2016; Fausset et al., 2013; Shih et al, 2015).

Gender; NASA-TLX Item Analysis

Gender was significantly correlated with intensity of experience, indicating that males tend to seek more intense experiences. This finding supports earlier research (Arnett, 1994). Gender was not significantly correlated with workload, sensation seeking, or novelty. The findings in this study suggest that males tend to experience workload, in terms of effort and temporal demand, when setting up the Basis B1. These results are interesting as the participants did not know they had a time limit. Designers of wearable devices may consider ways to make the device installation process seem less time consuming and effortful.

SOLUTIONS AND RECOMMENDATIONS

Based on statements from the wearables manufacturers, customers that are using their fitness tracker for monitoring heart rate data are using the devices outside of the manufacturer's recommendations. When presented with anomalous data, users have thought that their devices were malfunctioning or thought that their condition was something else, maybe less serious than their actual condition (Shapiro, 2015; CBS News, 2017; Marcus, 2016). Rudner et al. (2016) describes a case study involving a man who was admitted to the emergency room after having a seizure. The doctors noticed that he had arrhythmia but did not know if the condition was chronic or initiated by the seizure; therefore, they did not know whether to perform electrocardioversion or administer an IV as treatment. Electrocardioversion can dislodge blood clots that form due to chronic atrial fibrillation. After consulting the patient's Fitbit Charge HR, doctors noticed that the irregular heartbeat first occurred around the time of the seizure and decided to perform electrocardioversion. The patient was safely treated. Rudner et al.'s (2016) publication is the first recorded case of a wearable fitness tracking device being used to assist doctors in making a diagnosis.

Wearable fitness trackers have been used in individual cases to assist with indicating that someone may need to seek medical attention. Shapiro (2015) explains how a seemingly healthy, young athlete was suffering from rhabdomyolysis, a condition in which muscle breaks down and releases dangerous levels of protein in the body. Rhabdomyolysis can affect multiple organs; the athlete's kidneys, liver, and heart already showed damage by the time doctors were able to diagnose him. The earliest warning sign was an increased heart rate that did not return to baseline levels and was detected and tracked by the boy's smartwatch that had heart rate tracking capability. Rhabdomyolysis can have many causes and can be successfully treated, if detected early enough. Marcus (2016) demonstrates how a Fitbit fitness tracker with heart rate tracking functionality was able to provide the first indication that a woman was pregnant. The woman's average heart rate increased steadily over a period of weeks, as detected by her Fitbit device; she and her husband believed that the fitness tracker was malfunctioning. After unsuccessfully troubleshooting the device, the couple sought advice on the Internet where they discovered that a steadily increasing heart rate could be an indication of pregnancy. The case study described by Marcus indicates how a wearable fitness tracker may be malfunctioning or may be indicating that a more serious condition is present. If a user believes her wearable pedometer is inaccurate, a health or fitness professional may be able to provide insight for anomalous data and provide a context in which health and fitness goals can be accurately framed. Similarly, a medical professional may be able to provide a user of a wearable fitness tracker that has heart rate tracking capability with information about why the device seems to be inaccurate or providing anomalous data.

Wearable fitness trackers, including Fitbits, are not medical devices; they provide limited information and functionality and accuracy vary between models and brands. The case studies presented here demonstrate that a low-fidelity heart rate recording device, such as a fitness tracker that tracks heart rate over time, can assist a clinician in accurately diagnosing a patient and recommending the use of a medical monitoring device or referring to a specialist (Shapiro, 2015; CBS News, 2017; Marcus, 2016). Fitbit, Inc. has released a public statement explaining that Fitbit products are not intended to be used for scientific or medical purposes (Kraft, 2016). However, Rudner et al. (2016) demonstrated how a Fitbit device assisted in a difficult diagnosis that otherwise would not have been identified and treated promptly. Although fitness trackers are not as accurate as medical devices, fitness trackers are more affordable, easier to obtain, and the ability to gather heart rate data over time can have value for patients and doctors.

Users should consult fitness and medical professionals to make the most of their fitness trackers and the data they produce. Accurate interpretation of tracker data for the purposes of meeting health and fitness goals is a key part of reducing abandonment in users, which is a barrier to the integration of wearables into existing healthcare and sports fitness programs. Prior research has indicated that data without perceived value can result in abandoning wearable fitness trackers (Brandao, 2016; Fausset et al., 2013; Shih et al, 2015). As Rudner et al. (2016) and Marcus (2016) demonstrate, data without context is not knowledge and data that do not meet a user's expectations may indicate a medical consultation is needed. Early diagnosis of a medical condition can prevent long term damage, with proper treatment, in some cases (Shapiro, 2015). Wearable fitness trackers that include heart rate tracking over time are now technologically advanced enough to indicate to users that further investigation by a medical professional may be warranted.

Issues With Research

Several issues were encountered while collecting data for this study. Data collection was terminated after Basis Sciences, Inc. recalled the Basis Peak smartwatch. The Peak was not used in this study; however, Basis decided to discontinue providing support to all of its products, including updates to the mobile applications, as of December 31st, 2016. Collins et al. (2015) reported a serious issue with data collection during their study. Android phones had to be rolled back to a previous version of the Android operating system, version 4.4, and system updates were locked out so the phones could not automatically update to the most recent version of the Android software. Preventing a phone from receiving software updates quickly renders it unusable. Collins et al. (2015) suggest a solution involving media streaming devices that run the Android operating system; however, this also has the effect of changing the hardware involved with testing the overall system.

Multiple updates to the mobile applications were made by each device manufacturer during the data collection period for this study. The authors did not compare differences across versions of mobile applications; however, participants experienced problems with installation throughout data collection. A solution to preventing the issue of changes in the mobile application is to involve the device manufacturers in usability studies of rapidly changing technologies. Collins et al. (2015) note how seven of the devices investigated in their study were superseded by newer versions of the hardware within six months of study closure.

FUTURE RESEARCH DIRECTIONS

Having participants use their personal smartphones meant that they were familiar with the cellphone part of the overall wearable device-phone-mobile application system; however, the authors could not control for which phone (Android or iOS) participants had or the version of operating system each phone was running. Future research in this area could more closely control for the hardware and software versions used by participants in order to make more specific recommendations concerning individual and institutional adoption of wearable systems. This study examined workload at an individual level; future research can investigate workload across institutions to empirically determine the costs of scaling wearable fitness trackers for research and practice.

CONCLUSION

This study set out to expand on prior research about the novelty of using wearable fitness trackers by testing the previous findings of overall impact on all parts of device usage. No significant differences were found with regard to the workload incurred during initial device installation as a result of an individual's level of sensation seeking, or novelty seeking, behavior. Prior research did not use installation instructions provided by the manufacturer, measure installation time, or measure the workload of the installation process. While our hypotheses did not replicate the findings from the prior work in regards to novelty, sensation seeking, and intensity, this paper examines in great detail a part of the device usage that was not included in prior research due to constraints on time and resources. The authors investigated the claims made by prior research for installation of a wearable fitness tracker. Brandao (2016) reported that novelty influences adoption and abandonment for wearable devices; however, the authors have demonstrated that novelty does not have a significant effect on the ability to install and begin using a wearable fitness tracker, which is part of the adoption process.

The installation process is a required operation for using wearable fitness trackers, one that has not been scrutinized due to methodological challenges in prior research. Prior research has tested maintenance costs and rates of abandonment, not the workload incurred during initial device installation; however, claims have been made about the effect of novelty across the entire wearable device life cycle. Our results show that the claims made about the effect of novelty on wearable fitness tracker use are limited in scope. If participants had to be excluded from data collection in previous studies due to not being able to start using a wearable device, this issue was not reported; this represents a sampling bias and limits the applicability of their results. If novelty affects long-term adoption and abandonment, the authors have demonstrated that the ability to complete initial system set up of a wearable fitness tracker, when given a maximum time limit of 30 minutes, is unaffected by an individual's level of novelty seeking behavior. One possibility for why our hypotheses were not supported by the results of this study is that prior research has mainly studied people who were able to complete device set up or were already using wearable fitness trackers and, thus, were self-selected into the study. By not including participants that could not complete device set up in their analyses, the claims made by prior research do not extend to the installation of wearable fitness trackers (Brandao, 2016; Shih et al, 2015). Prior experience was examined in this study because previous research has collected data from participants with prior experience (Brandao, 2016). When applied in a healthcare setting, institutions cannot guarantee that users will have prior experience with devices.

We seek to expand on this line of research and hope researchers will replicate our study. While the algorithms and programs made by developers and studied by engineering and computer science researchers are essential to the successful operation of wearable fitness trackers, the devices are purchased, worn, and used by people. A focus on wearable hardware and software is a valuable approach but is one approach to a complex issue. If wearables have tremendous potential benefit in health and fitness domains, a better understanding of the interactions between the variety of available devices and the even more varied users is needed.

ACKNOWLEDGEMENT

The authors wish to thank James Stanley for providing feedback on a draft of this article and Shan Lakhmani for the use of a Basis B1 fitness tracker and for providing feedback on a draft of this article.

This research received no specific grant from any funding agency in the public, commercial, or not-for-profit sectors.

REFERENCES

Arnett, J. (1994). Sensation seeking: A new conceptualization and a new scale. *Personality and Individual Differences*, 16(2), 289–296. doi:10.1016/0191-8869(94)90165-1

Brandao, A. R. D. (2016). *Factors Influencing Long-Term Adoption of Wearable Activity Trackers*. Rochester Institute of Technology.

Brooke, J. (1996). SUS-A quick and dirty usability scale. *Usability Evaluation in Industry, 189*(194), 4-7.

Buchanan, T., Johnson, J. A., & Goldberg, L. R. (2005). Implementing a five-factor personality inventory for use on the internet. *European Journal of Psychological Assessment, 21*(2), 115–127. doi:10.1027/1015-5759.21.2.115

Byers, J. C., Bittner, A. C., & Hill, S. G. (1989). Traditional and raw task load index (TLX) correlations: are paired comparisons necessary? In A. Mital (Ed.), *Advances in Industrial Ergonomics and Safety l* (pp. 481–485). Taylor and Francis.

Cao, Y., Chen, S., Hou, P., & Brown, D. (2015, August). FAST: A fog computing assisted distributed analytics system to monitor fall for stroke mitigation. In *Networking, Architecture and Storage (NAS), 2015 IEEE International Conference on* (pp. 2-11). IEEE.

CBS News. (2017, April 6). Woman says Fitbit helped save her life. *CBS News.* Accessed at http://www.cbsnews.com/news/woman-says-fitbit-helped-save-her-life-blood-clots/

Chalil Madathil, K., Koikkara, R., Gramopadhye, A. K., & Greenstein, J. S. (2011, September). An empirical study of the usability of consenting systems: iPad, Touchscreen and paper-based systems. *Proceedings of the Human Factors and Ergonomics Society Annual Meeting, 55*(1), 813–817. doi:10.1177/1071181311551168

Collins, T., Aldred, S., Woolley, S., & Rai, S. (2015, December). Addressing the Deployment Challenges of Health Monitoring Devices for a Dementia Study. In *Proceedings of the 5th EAI International Conference on Wireless Mobile Communication and Healthcare* (pp. 202-205). ICST (Institute for Computer Sciences, Social-Informatics and Telecommunications Engineering). 10.4108/eai.14-10-2015.2261638

Dogra, S., & Stathokostas, L. (2012). Sedentary behavior and physical activity are independent predictors of successful aging in middle-aged and older adults. *Journal of Aging Research.* PMID:22997579

Dubey, H., Yang, J., Constant, N., Amiri, A. M., Yang, Q., & Makodiya, K. (2015, October). Fog data: Enhancing telehealth big data through fog computing. In *Proceedings of the ASE Big Data & Social Informatics 2015* (p. 14). ACM.

Fausset, C. B., Mitzner, T. L., Price, C. E., Jones, B. D., Fain, B. W., & Rogers, W. A. (2013, September). Older adults' use of and attitudes toward activity monitoring technologies. *Proceedings of the Human Factors and Ergonomics Society Annual Meeting, 57*(1), 1683–1687. doi:10.1177/1541931213571374

Fong, D. S., Aiello, L., Gardner, T. W., King, G. L., Blankenship, G., Cavallerano, J. D., ... Klein, R. (2004). Retinopathy in diabetes. *Diabetes Care, 27*(suppl 1), s84–s87. doi:10.2337/diacare.27.2007.S84 PMID:14693935

Fulk, G. D., Combs, S. A., Danks, K. A., Nirider, C. D., Raja, B., & Reisman, D. S. (2014). Accuracy of 2 activity monitors in detecting steps in people with stroke and traumatic brain injury. *Physical Therapy, 94*(2), 222–229. doi:10.2522/ptj.20120525 PMID:24052577

Graziano, D. (2016, October 25). Basis, ending service Dec. 31, offers B1 fitness watch refunds. *Wearable Tech.* Accessed at https://www.cnet.com/news/basis-b1-band-refunds-service-shuts-down-december-31/

Gurrin, C., Smeaton, A. F., Qiu, Z., & Doherty, A. (2013, November). Exploring the technical challenges of large-scale lifelogging. In *Proceedings of the 4th International SenseCam & Pervasive Imaging Conference* (pp. 68-75). ACM. 10.1145/2526667.2526678

Harrison, D., Marshall, P., Bianchi-Berthouze, N., & Bird, J. (2015, September). Activity tracking: barriers, workarounds and customisation. In *Proceedings of the 2015 ACM International Joint Conference on Pervasive and Ubiquitous Computing* (pp. 617-621). ACM. 10.1145/2750858.2805832

Hart, S. G. (2006, October). NASA-task load index (NASA-TLX); 20 years later. *Proceedings of the Human Factors and Ergonomics Society Annual Meeting, 50*(9), 904–908. doi:10.1177/154193120605000909

Hart, S. G., & Staveland, L. E. (1988). Development of NASA-TLX (Task Load Index): Results of empirical and theoretical research. *Advances in Psychology, 52,* 139–183. doi:10.1016/S0166-4115(08)62386-9

Hendy, K. C., Hamilton, K. M., & Landry, L. N. (1993). Measuring subjective workload: When is one scale better than many? *Human Factors, 35*(4), 579–601. doi:10.1177/001872089303500401

Jefferis, B. J., Sartini, C., Lee, I. M., Choi, M., Amuzu, A., Gutierrez, C., ... Whincup, P. H. (2014). Adherence to physical activity guidelines in older adults, using objectively measured physical activity in a population-based study. *BMC Public Health, 14*(1), 382. doi:10.1186/1471-2458-14-382 PMID:24745369

John, O. P., Donahue, E. M., & Kentle, R. L. (1991). *The big five inventory: Versions 4a and 54, institute of personality and social research.* Berkeley, CA: University of California.

Kaminski, J. (2011). Diffusion of innovation theory. *Canadian Journal of Nursing Informatics*, 6(2), 1–6.

Kraft, A. (2016, Jan 7). Fitbit users sue, claiming heart rate monitor is inaccurate. *CBS News*. Accessed at http://www.cbsnews.com/news/fitbit-users-sue-claiming-heart-rate-monitor-is-inaccurate/

Kuchenbecker, K. J., & Wang, Y. (2012). *HALO: Haptic alerts for low-hanging obstacles in white cane navigation*. Academic Press.

Lamkin, P. (2017, March 3). Fitbit's Dominance Diminishes But Wearable Tech Market Bigger Than Ever. *Forbes*. Accessed at https://www.forbes.com/sites/paullamkin/2017/03/03/fitbits-dominance-diminishes-but-wearable-tech-market-bigger-than-ever/#352076127f4d

Lazar, A., Koehler, C., Tanenbaum, J., & Nguyen, D. H. (2015, September). Why we use and abandon smart devices. In *Proceedings of the 2015 ACM International Joint Conference on Pervasive and Ubiquitous Computing* (pp. 635-646). ACM. 10.1145/2750858.2804288

Lee, J. M., Kim, Y., & Welk, G. J. (2014). Validity of consumer-based physical activity monitors. *Medicine and Science in Sports and Exercise*, 46(9), 1840–1848. doi:10.1249/MSS.0000000000000287 PMID:24777201

Liu, Y., & Wickens, C. D. (1994). Mental workload and cognitive task automaticity: An evaluation of subjective and time estimation metrics. *Ergonomics*, 37(11), 1843–1854. doi:10.1080/00140139408964953 PMID:8001525

Marcus, M. B. (2016, Feb 9). Fitbit fitness tracker detects woman's pregnancy. *CBS News*. Accessed at http://www.cbsnews.com/news/fitbit-fitness-tracker-tells-woman-shes-pregnant/

Matthews, G., Emo, A. K., Funke, G., Zeidner, M., Roberts, R. D., Costa, P. T. Jr, & Schulze, R. (2006). Emotional intelligence, personality, and task-induced stress. *Journal of Experimental Psychology. Applied*, 12(2), 96–107. doi:10.1037/1076-898X.12.2.96 PMID:16802891

Mayser, C., Piechulla, W., Weiss, K. E., & König, W. (2003, May). Driver workload monitoring. In *Proceedings of the Internationale Ergonomie-Konferenz der GfA, ISOES und FEES* (pp. 7-9). Academic Press.

Mercer, K., Giangregorio, L., Schneider, E., Chilana, P., Li, M., & Grindrod, K. (2016). Acceptance of commercially available wearable activity trackers among adults aged over 50 and with chronic illness: A mixed-methods evaluation. *JMIR mHealth and uHealth*, *4*(1), e7. doi:10.2196/mhealth.4225 PMID:26818775

Mezghani, E., Exposito, E., Drira, K., Da Silveira, M., & Pruski, C. (2015). A semantic big data platform for integrating heterogeneous wearable data in healthcare. *Journal of Medical Systems*, *39*(12), 185. doi:10.100710916-015-0344-x PMID:26490143

Miyazaki, R., Kotani, K., Tsuzaki, K., Sakane, N., Yonei, Y., & Ishii, K. (2015). Effects of a year-long pedometer-based walking program on cardiovascular disease risk factors in active older people. *Asia-Pacific Journal of Public Health*, *27*(2), 155–163. doi:10.1177/1010539513506603 PMID:24174388

Pfannenstiel, A., & Chaparro, B. S. (2015, August). An investigation of the usability and desirability of health and fitness-tracking devices. In *International Conference on Human-Computer Interaction* (pp. 473-477). Springer. 10.1007/978-3-319-21383-5_79

Rauschnabel, P. A., Brem, A., & Ivens, B. S. (2015). Who will buy smart glasses? Empirical results of two pre-market-entry studies on the role of personality in individual awareness and intended adoption of Google Glass wearables. *Computers in Human Behavior*, *49*, 635–647. doi:10.1016/j.chb.2015.03.003

Rose, C. L., Murphy, L. B., Byard, L., & Nikzad, K. (2002). The role of the Big Five personality factors in vigilance performance and workload. *European Journal of Personality*, *16*(3), 185–200. doi:10.1002/per.451

Rosenberger, M. E., Buman, M. P., Haskell, W. L., McConnell, M. V., & Carstensen, L. L. (2016). 24 hours of sleep, sedentary behavior, and physical activity with nine wearable devices. *Medicine and Science in Sports and Exercise*, *48*(3), 457–465. doi:10.1249/MSS.0000000000000778 PMID:26484953

Rosenberger, M. E., Haskell, W. L., Albinali, F., Mota, S., Nawyn, J., & Intille, S. (2013). Estimating activity and sedentary behavior from an accelerometer on the hip or wrist. *Medicine and Science in Sports and Exercise*, *45*(5), 964–975. doi:10.1249/MSS.0b013e31827f0d9c PMID:23247702

Rudner, J., McDougall, C., Sailam, V., Smith, M., & Sacchetti, A. (2016). Interrogation of patient smartphone activity tracker to assist arrhythmia management. *Annals of Emergency Medicine*, *68*(3), 292–294. doi:10.1016/j.annemergmed.2016.02.039 PMID:27045694

Schwartz, A. V., Vittinghoff, E., Sellmeyer, D. E., Feingold, K. R., De Rekeneire, N., Strotmeyer, E. S., ... Faulkner, K. A. (2008). Diabetes-related complications, glycemic control, and falls in older adults. *Diabetes Care*, *31*(3), 391–396. doi:10.2337/dc07-1152 PMID:18056893

Shapiro, E. (2015, Sep 22). How an Apple Watch May Have Saved a Teen's Life. *ABC News*. Accessed at http://abcnews.go.com/US/apple-watch-saved-teens-life/story?id=33944550

Shih, P. C., Han, K., Poole, E. S., Rosson, M. B., & Carroll, J. M. (2015). Use and adoption challenges of wearable activity trackers. *IConference 2015 Proceedings*.

Sohn, S. Y., & Jo, Y. K. (2003). A study on the student pilot's mental workload due to personality types of both instructor and student. *Ergonomics*, *46*(15), 1566–1577. doi:10.1080/0014013031000121633 PMID:14668175

Sun, Q., Townsend, M. K., Okereke, O. I., Franco, O. H., Hu, F. B., & Grodstein, F. (2010). Physical activity at midlife in relation to successful survival in women at age 70 years or older. *Archives of Internal Medicine*, *170*(2), 194–201. doi:10.1001/archinternmed.2009.503 PMID:20101015

Varatharajan, R., Manogaran, G., Priyan, M. K., & Sundarasekar, R. (2017). Wearable sensor devices for early detection of Alzheimer disease using dynamic time warping algorithm. *Cluster Computing*, 1–10.

Vooijs, M., Alpay, L. L., Snoeck-Stroband, J. B., Beerthuizen, T., Siemonsma, P. C., Abbink, J. J., ... Rövekamp, T. A. (2014). Validity and usability of low-cost accelerometers for internet-based self-monitoring of physical activity in patients with chronic obstructive pulmonary disease. *Interactive Journal of Medical Research*, *3*(4), e14. doi:10.2196/ijmr.3056 PMID:25347989

Wells, J. D., Campbell, D. E., Valacich, J. S., & Featherman, M. (2010). The effect of perceived novelty on the adoption of information technology innovations: A risk/reward perspective. *Decision Sciences*, *41*(4), 813–843. doi:10.1111/j.1540-5915.2010.00292.x

Zhang, Y., Qiu, M., Tsai, C. W., Hassan, M. M., & Alamri, A. (2017). Health-CPS: Healthcare cyber-physical system assisted by cloud and big data. *IEEE Systems Journal*, *11*(1), 88–95. doi:10.1109/JSYST.2015.2460747

Chapter 8
Who Wants an Automated Vehicle?

David A. Thurlow
York University, Canada

Ben D. Sawyer
Massachusettes Institute of Technology, USA & University of Central Florida, USA

ABSTRACT

New advancements in vehicle automation, electrification, data connectivity, and digital methods of sharing—known collectively as New Mobility—are poised to revolutionize transportation as it is known today. Exactly what results this disruption will lead to, however, remains unknown, as indeed the technologies and their uses are still taking shape amidst myriad interests. The impacts of this shift to New Mobility could be enormous, shaping economies, cities, and the lives of people in them. It is therefore vitally important for public interests to play a strong role in the development and deployment of these technologies. With the current trajectory of these technologies warning of the potential for increased energy use, environmental costs, and social inequity, interests at the community level need to be included and influential as soon as possible.

INTRODUCTION

Driverless cars, it has been widely predicted, are on their way. With advancements in what planners call New Mobility, transportation as it is known today is on the verge of a revolution. While this term has lacked until now a precise industry meaning, it can be best defined as the combination of collective advancements

DOI: 10.4018/978-1-5225-7949-6.ch008

in vehicle automation, electrification, data connectivity, and digital methods of sharing. These advancements have the potential to change how people travel, how businesses operate, and even how cities are developed or reshaped (UITP, 2017). Urban, suburban, and rural communities alike could see their options for mobility improve in a variety of ways, from cost to connections to comfort. With automated vehicles (AVs), we are promised great benefits: an end to traffic gridlock, relaxing free time while traveling, and roads so safe as to render future generations amazed at the thought that humans were ever allowed to drive. At the same time, however, it has become clear that all visions of how such a transportation utopia should work are not necessarily aligned.

Competing versions of New Mobility's future abound. Will people own their own AVs and send them to park themselves, or will they buy rides in automated robotaxis? Will public transit start to offer door-to-door service with municipally-owned driverless vehicles, or will private companies or even co-ops of private AV owners assemble and manage such fleets? If vehicles are connected, what will they be connected to, and who will own the data that flows between them? The key to answering these questions lies in understanding that the results we get will be determined not only by engineering advances, but by the work of various social groups that hold interests in shaping the technologies' uses and outcomes. As this chapter will discuss, who these social groups are, the results they are advocating for, and the potential impacts of their efforts to shape the future of transportation suggest both appealing and alarming possibilities.

New Mobility represents a dramatic and important set of new risks and opportunities, with not only billions of dollars of commercial value at stake, but also the power to dramatically influence the future of jobs, land use, environmental impacts, and human interaction on a grand scale – as well as the safety of millions of human lives (Henaghan, 2018; Lipson and Kurman, 2016). Even if all the engineering challenges are overcome, positive outcomes are not guaranteed, nor is it known what unintended negative effects might result. The implications of new inventions generally require a considerable period of time to be understood (Wiener, 1954), but our experience since the arrival and proliferation of the automobile a century ago assures us that changes in transportation can have far-reaching impacts (Norton, 2011). With so much at stake, it cannot be overstated that transportation stands today at a critical crossroads – the likes of which has not been seen since the original introduction of the automobile.

Given the magnitude of this situation, the current trajectory of New Mobility technologies moving rapidly toward the goals of certain social groups invested in their development demands scrutiny. In this brief window of opportunity before the technologies become established, it is vitally important to carefully examine the imagined futures being presented, the potential broader impacts their realization could bring, and the need for the public to engage and put forth its own ideas for the New Mobility revolution at both the individual and community levels. In this way, without seeking to analyze the viability of vehicle automation or other new transportation technologies, this chapter will explore these issues of impact and engagement through the lens of sociological and scientific research, first by considering the role of social groups in shaping any new technology, then by looking at several examples of groups currently involved in shaping the technologies of New Mobility specifically. These examples will lead into an examination of how certain uses of New Mobility technologies could potentially impact communities. Finally, these concerns will be brought together as an argument for the importance of balancing individual and community perspectives, and for the role communities can and must play in setting their own goals for the future of transportation and advocating for their own interests.

HOW TECHNOLOGIES ARE SHAPED

Seeing the capabilities of mankind advance, many people assume technology is the natural result of human learning – in science, engineering, or math, for example – and that the forms it takes in technological artifacts are for the most part inevitable. From this point of view, technology is seen as always progressing, filling the needs of humans, and in the process shaping society with unstoppable and natural effects. Humans are seen to have little control over the path of technology, and must therefore adapt their lives when technological developments are introduced. Individuals "can't stop progress," it is assumed. In contrast to this perspective, a more nuanced study of such progress reveals how technologies can advance in ways that let them fall short of their potential.

The field of Science and Technology Studies (STS) has shown how technologies take form through the interactions of multiple interests. Society can shape technologies, especially during their early development. Wiebe Bijker, Thomas Hughes, and Trevor Pinch (1987), in their work examining the social construction of technology, explain how social forces can determine the characteristics in technological artifacts. During the process of problem solving that happens during technological development, it is social groups – such as consumers, corporations, or communities – that define the problems to be solved and, in doing so, give meaning to the technology. These relevant social groups, for which a technological artifact represents a shared set of meanings, have different problems with the artifact, each with multiple possible solutions. These solutions represent possible variations for the artifact (Bijker et al., 1987; Kline & Pinch, 1996). Furthermore, when social groups take an interest in a technology, they not only see solutions to their specific problems, but they also

173

form broader visions of desirable futures for the technology. Sheila Jasanoff (2015) identifies these as "sociotechnical imaginaries", which she describes as "collectively held, institutionally stabilized, and publicly performed" (p. 4). Together, these concepts from STS provide a toolkit with which the process of decision-making for the development and implementation of AVs can be better understood, discussed, and influenced.

MANY INTERESTS: GROUPS SHAPING AVs

Who are these social groups who are expressing interest in and visions of the future of automated and connected vehicle technologies? Several examples stand out. Note that, to different groups, such vehicles may represent a very different potential value, and that each group may wield very different means of influence. Understanding this landscape of interest and leverage is helpful for gaining a better view of the direction and scope of these new transportation technologies.

Automobile Manufacturers

While much innovation has in recent years come from new technology startups, major automobile manufacturers have been swift to catch up to, and at times even surpass, the early strides made by their younger competition (Navigant Research, 2018). Advancements in vehicle systems have opened new possibilities for the auto giants. Some, interested in taking a lead role, have taken steps to put forth their own sociotechnical imaginary for the future of vehicle use.

Swedish car maker Volvo is a representative example of the vision, interests, and leverage of an automotive manufacturer. Volvo has been among the leaders of the industry in its efforts to form early partnerships with AV tech and engineering startups, and has also been active in exploring imaginative design possibilities. In 2015 the company began a project dubbed the "Future of Driving" which included concepts for future vehicles that could operate autonomously (Volvo, 2015). One example described on their website, called "Concept 26"[1], visualizes a sleek interior for an imagined automobile that can be operated in three modes: "Drive", "Create", and "Relax". With a retracting steering wheel and reclining seats that operate at the touch of a single button, relief, it seems, may finally be coming to the bored and tired drivers burdened by their stressful task. Alternatively, options for entertainment or work are suggested with a large screen and control panel at hand for occupants. Though the occupant in Volvo's images is alone in his grey-toned, futuristic environment, the vehicle is clearly centered primarily on his comfort.

Figure 1. Design idea for Volvo's "concept 26". Copyright 2015 Volvo Car Corporation

After showing off their modern design, however, Volvo is quick to reassert their support of traditional driving and clarify what they wish to offer with AVs. "Cars have always been a symbol of freedom," a video at the head of the page begins. For Volvo, this means letting their customers drive when they want to, and delegate driving when they want to. By creating a car that allows drivers the "freedom" to choose how they want to use it, the company hopes time that was previously reluctantly spent in the vehicle can transform into a positive experience. "You might actually choose a route that allows you to have *more* time in the car," Volvo suggests.

At the heart of Volvo's vision for the future of driving remains a worldview that is central to the company's own sales model: private ownership. Volvo believes the future will include self-driving technologies, and it is proposing that car designs such as Concept 26 could perform a transitioning role to autonomous driving with which its customers could feel comfortable. In this way Volvo hopes to position itself as a leader in the sales of such cars when the time comes.

Technology Companies

Technology companies such as Google and Apple have expressed a unique vision, backed by specific interests, and unique leverage. Both have made significant investments into vehicle automation research. As might be expected from these iconic companies, their visions of the future are relatively bolder than many others. In 2014, Google (now Alphabet) put forth a prototype that Lipson and Kurman (2016) described as "a shot heard all the way to Detroit" (p. 45), in that it contained no steering wheel or brakes at all. Indeed, such a vehicle projects a very different sociotechnical imaginary from that of Volvo; one in which humans are not only not required, but in fact are *not permitted* to operate a vehicle. Google co-founder Sergey Brin indicated the reasoning behind this includes both the safety benefits of eliminating human drivers and the errors they are prone to making, and the improved accessibility such a design would represent to those who can't drive (Roberts, 2015).

Certainly such innovation does not appear out of line with the company's talents. But like some of the search engine's other endeavors into maps and mobile phones, there may be additional payoff for the company's investment that is perhaps not immediately obvious. One benefit the company would certainly enjoy in a driverless world would be that people, relieved of the burden of driving, could spend more time on their mobile devices using Google's profitable services. As noted by former Google design ethicist Tristan Harris, a top priority for Google and every other online service provider today is to maximise "time-on-site" (Harris, 2017, 18:00). Real life situations such as driving that prevent users from interacting with them are a direct impediment to that goal. *MIT Technology Review* editor Antonio Regalado (2013) likewise points out that freeing the attention of drivers could be worth billions to Google. In a highly competitive attention economy, companies like these which work tirelessly to engineer new ways to keep users attached to their connected devices could see the task of driving as a problem that is keeping vast numbers of potential customers out of reach.

Similarly, both Google and Apple, heavily invested in the collection and use of all kinds of data, could easily see the deployment of automated vehicles as attractive opportunities to expand such work. Also, with 95% of Alphabet's revenue drawn from advertising, the possibility of having direct access to a large captive audience of robotaxi users could be a strong additional reason to invest in promoting a vision and building a reality of shared AV use.

Ride-Hailing Companies

The vision forwarded by ride-hailing companies combines new digital methods of sharing with vehicle automation to usher in a shift from vehicle ownership to ride-buying. Having successfully disrupted the urban taxi industry with new business models, ride-hailing tech companies such as Uber and Lyft have gone on to invest heavily in AV technology and partnerships, while at the same time actively promoting their own vision for the future. In a detailed article published to Medium in September of 2016, Lyft Co-Founder John Zimmer (2016) outlined what he saw as the coming

"Third Transportation Revolution". Most notably, Zimmer claimed in the article that a majority of Lyft rides would take place in AV fleets within five years, going on to predict that private car ownership would "all-but end" in major U.S. cities by the year 2025. The assumption behind this is that, when hiring an AV is cheaper than owning a car, most city-dwellers will opt out of personal vehicles. Citing decreasing percentages of young people who hold driver's licenses, Zimmer declared that for Millennials in particular, car ownership has become less a symbol of freedom and identity, and more like a ball and chain. For the young and the urban, he argued, car payments, parking, refuelling, and repairs are drawbacks that are increasingly seen as unattractive and unnecessary.

This position reflects ideas shared by others that a shift from owning cars to buying rides could profoundly change our physical environments, transforming our lives regardless of whether or not we ever set foot in an AV (SUMC, 2015; Henaghan, 2018). Specifically, many hope that a broad shift to ride-hailing services such as Lyft will bring with it the benefit of significantly reducing the need for parking, thereby freeing spaces currently allocated to parked vehicles to be repurposed in ways that improve cities, communities, and connections (and see Chase, 2016).

Along with such stated benefits, other incentives for ride-hailing champions Lyft and Uber to advocate for AVs are easy to imagine from an economic standpoint. To offer customers on-demand rides from their smartphone, Lyft and Uber have put their Silicon Valley expertise in computer networks to work optimizing connections between vehicles and riders. The human drivers in their systems simply play a functional role of moving the vehicles where they are told. But drivers are a thorn in the side of these companies – they need breaks, demand benefits, and require various incentives to coax them into working in certain areas or at certain times. Like many workers, they are both much less reliable and much more difficult to keep at the ready than a non-human substitute (Latour, 1988). Moreover, these drivers' salaries constitute a full fifty percent of the cost of each ride (Price, 2015). Switching to a business model of acquiring and operating fleets of automated, driverless vehicles – depending on the cost of such a venture – could theoretically enable ride-hailing companies to lower rates for increased ridership, as well as increase their own revenue from each fare. This would be very good news for Lyft and Uber (and their shareholders), neither of which have reportedly made a profit since their inception nearly a decade ago. The potential of vehicle automation to reduce driver costs perhaps explains why they are willing to invest so much into developing the technology.

Automobile manufacturers, although in many ways eager to have a hand in designing and building any such future robotic vehicle fleets, largely remain invested in individual ownership of automobiles as they bring to market new vehicles with advanced automation and connectivity for personal use. Additional comfort, improved safety, and the opportunity to reclaim time spent behind the wheel are commonly touted reasons consumers should want to own these vehicles. But while full automation on all roadways is likely to remain a distant goal in consumer vehicles for years to come, these companies are striving to be well-positioned for both futures: fully-automated ride-hailing for limited urban settings, and semi-automated individual ownership for more flexible uses or rural areas.

Land Developers

Aligning with the vision of ride providers, as well as the interests of auto manufacturers who would be happy to supply them with vehicles, yet another group has begun to see potential value in the increased sharing which New Mobility could enable. Some land developers interested in new urban construction are hoping that alternatives to vehicle ownership can help relieve the dents in their budgets caused by expensive parking. If city ordinances could allow parking minimums to be translated into car-share or ride-hailing accommodations, high-value spaces in dense areas could potentially be used in more valuable ways. Examples of such reasoning can be found far from the urban centers commonly described. Consider Bozeman, Montana, where a 2016 proposal for a new apartment building within the small town's historic downtown area offered to meet parking minimums by including four car-share parking spots, each counting for 5 of the standard spaces required in city codes. In an interview, the developer noted that the practice was already accepted in other communities, and asserted that car-sharing would be routine within five to 10 years. (Dietrich, 2016) This was apparently not a view of the future that all of Bozeman's residents were in agreement with, as the proposal sparked significant public controversy.

In contrast to such visions of densification, land developers with an interest in more expansive greenfield growth are also seeing opportunities in New Mobility. In Florida, the new planned communities of Babcock Ranch and The Villages have both taken steps to boost interest in their low-rise developments with pilot projects that offer access to automated shuttles or taxis to get around (Burns & Scarborough, 2013, and see Stocker & Shaheen, 2018). Although the planned communities do not appear to have eliminated any car infrastructure (the familiar wide roads, curbs, and garages in front of every house remain), the AV services will theoretically enable resident families to make do with only one vehicle instead of several. As the lots in these developments fill up with houses and as test programs of automated shuttles begin moving people slowly along fixed-routes between them, the ultimate impacts on car ownership and use remain to be seen. An alternative possibility is that the addition of automation to personal vehicles, such as Volvo's vision of the future describes, could mean living in low-density neighborhoods or remote city exurbs becomes more attractive to city-dwellers as the pain of long commutes and car-dependency is eased. With the increased demand for their work it might bring, this could be yet another potential sociotechnical imaginary that land developers have reason to support.

Regulatory Groups

At the same time as these commercial interests are charging ahead, various government entities and public interest groups are seeing potential in vehicle automation, electrification, connectivity, and sharing platforms to help them reach their own goals. It is important to note that, while each may be tasked with serving the public good, their specific missions and priorities may differ. At a national level, for example, the United States' federal Department of Transportation (DOT) is tasked with ensuring that the US overall continues to have safe, efficient, modern transportation, and as such the addition of various new transportation technologies supporting improved safety, efficiency, and economic benefits has broadly been made a priority by the organization (DOT, 2018). But these interests can diverge slightly within the DOT's various administrations. The National Highway Traffic Safety Administration (NHTSA), for example, with its focus on safety and security, may not hold the same priorities as the Federal Highway Administration (FHWA), which works to maintain infrastructure, optimize mobility, and encourage innovation. In some ways, FHWA acts as an accelerator toward the deployment of New Mobility technologies through its investments in national highway research (FHWA). NHTSA, in contrast, at times acts more as a force of caution, though most recently quite gently so through its suggestions for voluntary safety approaches (NHTSA, 2017). As a whole, the DOT has been very supportive of the development of new transportation technologies, by both funding research and working to clear the way for private companies to test their products without interference. Of course, this is only one department of one country. Many more federal officials in nations around the globe are also working to clarify their own goals for New Mobility.

At the state and local levels, an even greater number of government branches, public agencies, and special interest groups have likewise taken an interest in the possibilities of New Mobility technologies. Planners seeking to make streets safer, reduce traffic congestion, or decrease vehicle emissions see opportunities to lower accident numbers and improve efficiency and the use of cleaner energies (Henaghan, 2018). Groups focused on social equity are looking to new vehicle technologies to fill gaps that leave those who cannot or do not wish to drive at a disadvantage (and see SUMC, 2016). Indeed, although they may have more limited resources or funding than federal, state, or commercial entities, at the municipal level there is considerable interest growing amongst a wide array of diverse social groups as advocates for the environment, public transit, housing, land use, and many others seek to influence how new transportation technologies are deployed in their communities. As will be discussed next, this can be especially important as the potential impacts of such changes become apparent.

THE IMPACT OF AVs UPON SOCIETY

Many of the possibilities for transportation's future which these and other social groups are calling for appear quite beneficial for companies or consumers. But they can also be seen as problematic, particularly if public interest is defined not just at the level of the individual but at that of communities. While consumers of automated vehicles or rides may see individual benefits through lower prices, better services, or increased amenities, the collective negative impacts of these technologies can add up when costs or downsides are externalized. To better understand how introducing new technologies into transportation could affect society, we will look at four examples of potential areas of impact: vehicle miles traveled, jobs, social equity and privacy, and safety.

Figure 2. Examples of social groups with an interest in shaping the development and use of automated vehicles. The motivation of each group can include multiple and sometimes overlapping interests of differing priorities. When groups at the community level are not involved, however, common community interests risk being underrepresented.

Social groups and their interests in AV technology

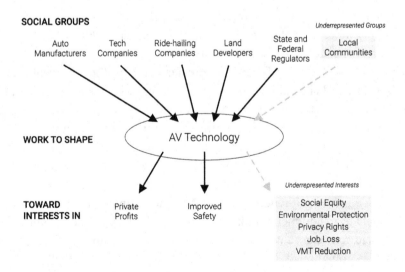

Vehicle Miles Traveled

One key risk of new transportation technologies is that of changing people's vehicle use in ways that could increase the total number of vehicle miles traveled (VMT). This can happen when the number of vehicles goes up, the number of trips increases, or when trips become longer. The increased use of any vehicles correlates to higher energy demands, added road congestion, and a greater footprint for vehicle fleets overall (Puentes & Tomer, 2008), including vehicle construction, maintenance, storage, and ultimately recycling or disposal requirements. Added VMT also brings additional new demand on vehicle infrastructure, which in most of North America today remains publicly funded and free of road pricing (tolls). For most car-centered contemporary cities, improving quality of life for residents involves reducing VMT (Jacobs, 1961). AVs could result in the reverse.

Research on induced travel demand shows that as costs (including monetary expenditures, risk, and discomfort) decrease, vehicle travel increases (Weis & Axhausen, 2009). If the increased comfort and amenities of Volvo's Concept 26 vehicle encourages motorists to spend more time in their vehicles and take more and longer journeys, the result would be increased VMT, congestion, and energy use (not to mention emissions, in all likelihood). Likewise, people who otherwise would have opted for another form of transportation might decide that they would prefer to take their driverless car. Use of mass transportation, cycling, and even walking could be reduced; just as was seen with the introduction of cars a century ago. The occupants in Concept 26, though entertained by screens, would be sitting in worse traffic and pollution than before.

Increased use of ride-hailing services, while potentially reducing parking needs or even improving vehicle occupancy averages, comes with an increased demand for the use of limited public curb space (ITF, 2018). Currently, in dense urban areas, taxis and ride-hailing services frequently pick up and drop off passengers by stopping temporarily at the side of the roadway, frequently blocking a lane of travel (or bike lane) in the process. As this practice increases, traffic flow in popular areas could become worse and worse, with the result resembling the gridlock of a busy airport drop off area.

Also, as above, any shift to vehicle ridesharing by those who would otherwise have used public transit, active transportation, or not have traveled at all constitutes an additional increase in VMT. Some studies have confirmed this pattern (Gehrke, Felix, & Reardon, 2018; NYC DOT, 2018; Schaller, 2018), and indeed that ride-hailing services have already added significantly to VMT in some cities (Schaller, 2017b). Such alternatives to vehicle transportation are likely positioned to be the biggest losers in many of these proposed futures (see UITP, 2017). The fact that they are, in most cases, the more effective way to solve urban transportation problems is unfortunately not enough to ensure they will prevail.

Beyond the additional VMT that could stem from increased use of vehicles by people, both privately-owned AVs and robotaxi fleets have the potential to generate another very significant source of additional VMT: zero-occupancy travel. While an automated taxi is repositioning itself to pick up its next passenger – a practice known as "deadheading" – it is adding to VMT without creating any immediate value. Research has shown that, in a city such as New York, approximately 45 percent of overall miles driven by taxis and ride-hailing vehicles today are unoccupied by passengers (Schaller, 2017a). While opportunities exist to improve this metric, any such gains are likely to pale in comparison to the added deadhead VMT caused by an expansion of ride-hailing services through vehicle automation. Similarly, if privately-owned AVs are able to park themselves after dropping off passengers, or be sent empty to pick up a family member or even cargo, such travel also adds to VMT and contributes to energy use, congestion, and vehicle footprint.

Jobs

Clearly the introduction of fully-automated vehicles would also not be good news for the large number of people currently employed as drivers. In August of 2016, Uber acquired self-driving truck company OTTO with the goal of automating the highway freight transportation industry (Woodall, 2016). Truck driving is one of the most common jobs in North America (Lipson & Kurman, 2016). In the US alone, in addition to 200,000 taxi drivers, there are approximately 1.5 million truck drivers whose jobs could be eliminated if automation efforts are successful (Bureau of Labor Statistics, 2015, 2017).

This is not to say that such a transition would necessarily be instant, nor entirely painful for the groups involved. Overall the trucking industry has faced an ongoing driver shortage for years, and a significant portion of those who do drive trucks today are nearing retirement (Tett, 2018). Some research estimates peak effects of vehicle automation on unemployment at 0.06 - 0.13 percentage points in the U.S., with an average displacement of 350,000-750,000 workers per decade (SAFE, 2018). This is significantly less than the 1.7 million jobs lost per decade in U.S. manufacturing (Groshen, Helper, MacDuffie, & Carson, 2018).

Beyond driving, however, there are still a variety of other positions that could be made expendable in a driverless world. Valets and parking lot attendants, traffic and parking enforcement officers, and driving instructors could all see demand for their services dwindle. Furthermore, with smoother computerized driving there is the potential to minimize wear and tear on roadways, reducing the need for work by road maintenance crews. But perhaps most dramatically, if AV proponents get their wish of eliminating vehicle collisions, entire economic sectors would be impacted. Today's automobile accident industry involves a vast network of ambulances, fire services, hospitals, police, tow-trucks, cleaning crews, forensic photographers, mechanics, auto body repair, insurance assessors, and accident attorneys (Graham, 2007; Lipson & Kurman, 2016). A world with no automobile crashes might ultimately be desirable by everyone, but a transition to that state would likely be difficult for a significant portion of the economy.

Equality and Privacy

In the case of privately-owned automated vehicles, the major benefits implied by many proposed future uses appear likely to remain limited to those who can afford them. It is therefore not difficult to imagine that in such a future there would remain strong divisions between the haves and the have-nots. In this case, any potential for automated vehicles to solve social equity problems for those who are unable to drive themselves would be restricted to only benefit users over a certain economic threshold.

AVs used for ride services could potentially offer more affordable mobility, but that doesn't necessarily mean they would bring a solution to socioeconomic inequity. Those needing to rely on the least expensive option for transportation might find in exchange for a cheap ride, a relatively undesirable robotaxi experience awaits them. In addition to ride-pooling with strangers heading in the same general direction (an option some ride-hailing companies offer today), a rider might find him or herself in a utilitarian, hard-surfaced interior with litter, graffiti, or gum on the seats (Lipson & Kurman, 2016). The car might recognize you when you enter, know your online browsing history, and interrupt you with suggestions for shopping stops along your route. Clearly, in such a scenario there are certain social groups who benefit, and certain groups who give something up.

AVs could indeed become one more source contributing to growing concerns regarding data use. Privacy concerns with AVs could be unique, as not only would their networks see who is riding where and when, but also the cameras they use to see the world would potentially be watching, recording, and transmitting to their networks the activities of everyone they pass. With artificial intelligence that can recognize faces and compile vast amounts of data from multiple sources, it is possible that such a network of moving cameras could comprise a surveillance system on a scale that has never been seen before (Lipson & Kurman, 2016). Such data on people's activities would certainly be of value to many business or government interests, but it would come at the cost of people's privacy (see Rakower, 2011).

Furthermore, such an escalation of data gathering and use brings with it significant new risks. Since the very introduction of computer networks it has been clear that any software, digital network, or data channel can be vulnerable to malicious hacks. Networks can be breached, and software can be tricked into functioning incorrectly (Lipson & Kurman, 2016). Many of the computerized systems required to make AVs function and operate effectively could open them up to new security risks, and data and control that users willingly give up to the machines could end up in the hands of someone else (see NHTSA, 2017).

Because the processes of competition involved in shaping new technologies can lead to certain groups benefiting over others, the results can be both less positive for society overall, and especially detrimental to interests that become marginalized. In many areas of our modern consumer culture, it is clear that externalized costs and consequences can build over time into collective problems such as pollution, resource depletion, and systemic inequality.

Safety

Another set of impacts, perhaps for many the most significant, relate to safety concerns. With non-automated vehicles today, 93% of all traffic accidents are attributed to human error (NHTSA, 2008). Many people see the introduction of AVs as a potential solution to this problem, which globally takes the lives of millions each year and impacts many more. However, it is important to realize that improvements to safety are not actually related directly to the introduction of automated vehicles. Instead, such impacts would only come when we *stop driving today's cars*, which is a very different proposition. AV penetration into the vehicle fleet will be slow; estimates based on adoption of advanced driver assistance systems (ADAS) suggest that under optimal scenarios safety advantages from AVs might arrive between 2040 and 2050 (Litman, 2017; and see Grush & Niles, 2018). The most utopian goals such as the "Vision Zero" of getting to zero automobile accident deaths or injuries, or doing away with traffic signs and signals, will not be possible until all human-driven vehicles are taken off the roads. Such benefits are unlikely to be realized within the lifespan of those who are alive today, if ever. It is therefore important to set expectations regarding the ongoing impacts and limitations of mixed AV and non-AV traffic. New Mobility is a revolution today's population will likely witness, but not see to conclusion.

Amid this intermediate, mixed-vehicle transition, safety could take on the guise of trade-offs. In collision-imminent situations, autonomous systems will make decisions that once fell to humans. Automotive manufacturers, cognizant of the self-preservation instincts of their customers, will need to expressly address this new reality. Each reader should ask themselves, would you buy the vehicle which promises to attempt to save your life at all costs, or the one that will consider the balance of your life against others? Such questions have been explicitly asked in a research setting (Bonnefon, 2016), and results show that while users are in favor of vehicles which make ethically correct choices, they would not like to ride in one themselves. This finding indicates that certain advanced safety systems could face an uphill battle in winning over consumers. If successful, however, ethically programmed vehicles could shift the balance of safety from what it is today, perhaps even to favor specific social groups such as pedestrians, cyclists, small children, or any other group the algorithms chose to prioritize.

Safety further plays into many of the previous concerns. For example, as traveling by car is currently among the riskiest activities in which the general population routinely engages, increases in VMT are generally accompanied by increases in property damage, injury, and fatality. In order to avoid such effects of an increase in VMT due to AVs, it will be necessary for this risk to be offset by the safety gains of New Mobility. However, such changes are likely to be complex and difficult to track. At present, Tesla claims their autopilot technology to be twice as as safe as the average driver (Tesla, 2018, but see Sparrow and Howard, 2017), despite criticism that the technology may be problematic from both a conceptual and design standpoint (Endsley, 2017). Noting that this does not help the above-average driver, one can assume that this product and similar products to come will be most attractive to below-average drivers. In a future where these drivers flock to AV technology, the "average driver" remaining would be significantly better. This confusing scenario is nonetheless a best case scenario. The Dunning Kruger effect (Dunning, 2012) shows that individuals least qualified to perform a task often assume they have superior skills, and so suggests that the individuals that will turn to safer AV technology may in fact be the above-average drivers. Such a future, in which the least qualified remain behind the wheel, is part of what interests insurance companies, safety advocates, and regulatory bodies. This example is only one in a broad array of potential unintended consequences which could accompany the utopian futures automated vehicle proponents suggest (and see Hancock & Parasuraman 1992; Hancock, 2015).

To better research these added safety concerns, new approaches for simulation and experimentation (see Sawyer & Hancock, 2012; Sawyer, Calvo, Finomore, & Hancock, 2015) are being employed to allow industrial and civil engineers, as well as engineering psychologists, to make better predictions of where future pitfalls might lie. With safety, however, as with each of the above concerns, transformative decisions are not determined by the evidence of science, nor the recommendations of engineers, but instead by the amalgamated viewpoints of a variety of influencers (see Wetmore, 2009). Safety in AV systems, whether at the level of the interface in the vehicle, the vehicle on the road, the road network, or the laws that govern it, is not an immutable piece of some inevitable technological advancement. Rather, individuals and social groups will contribute decisions which influence the state of safety, the state of jobs, the number of VMT, and the questions of equality and privacy. Myriad futures are available, but collectively we will only get to realize one.

COMMUNITIES VS. INDIVIDUALS: THE IMPORTANCE OF COMMUNITY INTERESTS

Many of these potential issues for the future of transportation can be seen as various versions of the Tragedy of the Commons, wherein benefit-seeking at the individual level leads to detrimental outcomes for all (Hardin, 1968). This highlights what can be the biggest challenge in involving the voice of the public in the decision-making process, namely that the public itself holds multiple, sometimes conflicting, interests and concerns. As people play multiple roles in their lives, they may belong to multiple relevant social groups. As consumers we may want the cheapest or most convenient form of travel. As parents we may want the safest, or a world of healthy sustainability we can pass on to our children. As taxpayers we may want the most fiscally responsible use of tax dollars, but as employees or business owners we may want whatever boosts our incomes. As drivers we may wish streets to stay clear for our use, but when we park our cars and become pedestrians we may wish streets to be available to us and free of cars. Conflicting viewpoints therefore exist not only between social groups, but between incongruent interests within each person. Focusing on those interests which stem from the community as a whole, therefore, can be a difficult but important challenge.

In this way, the solution to any Tragedy of the Commons is not merely to include the interests of the public, but to include interests at the community level that are often left out or overshadowed by interests at the individual level. For transportation, this might include the safety and enjoyment of shared walkable streets, reducing air pollution, or ensuring equitable mobility for all residents (see UITP, 2017). Each of these can be criteria upon which to evaluate the options for how new transportation technologies are introduced. Any proposed visions for how these technologies can be used in society might therefore be best examined through the lens of community impact by those interested in attaining the most desirable collective results.

This can mean looking beyond short-term interests to long-term benefits and consequences. Where multiple goals conflict, it means taking into consideration the long-term effects of prioritizing one over the other; for example, between goals of a healthy economy on one hand, and a healthy planet on the other. One may be desirable in the short term, the other, in the long term.

As transportation technologies compose a vital layer in the fabric of our actions and interactions within our environment – establishing the parameters of our economic, social, and physical worlds – any consideration of what communities want from them in the long term must also involve thinking about the deeper goals those communities wish to achieve with transportation as a society. It must not only ask how communities wish to move their people and goods, but where, when, and why they are moved at all. Looking at the growing problems of car-oriented society around him in the 1950s, Lewis Mumford (1958) challenged us to consider what transportation is for (suggesting it is not perhaps something that highway engineers ever ask themselves). "To increase the number of cars," he writes, "to enable motorists to go longer distances, to more places, at higher speeds, has become an end in itself" (p. 241). Mumford was frustrated not by a lack of planning, but by a system of planning that had failed to orient itself around human values.

To avoid repeating the same pattern with automated vehicles, those interested in putting AVs to their best use from a community perspective might begin their planning with deeper questions. What kind of world do we want to live in? And what might that world's environment look like? The process of considering these questions must happen early, when sociotechnical imaginaries are being formed.

In this way, bringing forward a true transportation revolution might require shifting to a new mindset, or as Thomas Kuhn described, new paradigms (1962). Instead of focusing on energy use, for example, we might think in terms of sustainability. Although it may be deeply embedded, the current model of unconstrained use of energy and materials could be replaced (Dennis and Urry, 2009). This might mean building an interest in better aligning the cyclic demands on systems, such as by adjusting work schedules to reduce rush hour congestion. Or it could mean, instead of seeking to increase individual travel as a metric for mobility, seeking to reduce unnecessary travel.

Mumford (1958) claimed, in response to his own question, that the purpose of transportation is to move people and things to where they are needed, and to concentrate both in ways that increase choices without the need to travel. In his words, "a good transportation system minimizes unnecessary transportation" (p. 236). This wasn't just about reducing traffic or moving people more efficiently, but providing them with more meaningful movement and better use of their time. "Human purpose", Mumford argued, should govern the choice of a means of transportation (p. 237). Not just faster connections, but better relationships.

Importantly, community-level interests do not necessarily need to compete with interests that benefit individual groups. Making decisions over how new technologies are used is not necessarily a zero-sum game, and therefore including support for community-level interests does not negate the potential for mutually beneficial outcomes. A number of recent collaborations between ride-hailing companies and municipalities provide examples of this, as commercial ride providers have been tasked with supporting connections to transit hubs or even filling in for public transportation services in places that lack them (Schwieterman, Livingston, & Van Der Slot, 2018). The results in many cases have proven to be win-win, as municipalities save money, ride-hailing companies increase their business, and travelers see improved alternatives to private-car use. Clearly, desirable results at the community level may still require compromise. But they do not necessarily require that other interests be excluded.

CHOICES FOR COMMUNITIES: THE NEED FOR COMMUNITY PARTICIPATION

Going a step further, as each social group works to present their own sociotechnical imaginary, it is clear that communities have the power as well to put forth, and advocate for, their own proposed visions of how vehicle automation and connectivity should be used. Understanding that technology can be shaped is ultimately only helpful if followed up with active participation in the efforts that influence what that technology becomes. Engaging in this process requires not only making decisions about desired outcomes, but also actively pushing for the realization of those outcomes. Thus it is necessary to both understand how that process works, and to identify areas where it can be influenced.

Social groups perform a kind of "world-making" when they try to get others to take on their same perspective. They attempt to spread their ideas about which actors and roles are important, as well as what the final sociotechnical imaginary should look like. Michel Callon (1986), well-known for his contributions to STS in Actor-Network Theory, provides us with examples of how this can be done. One is when social groups put forth a spokesman who attributes to an actor an identity, interests, a role to play, or a course of action to follow. Actors of course may resist these roles, but the attribution is necessary to begin an endeavor that may later be achieved. This act of "translation", though not in itself an imperative, can shift the mindsets of other social groups in a way that starts making the paths of the network easier to form.

We see this performed when Volvo puts out videos of models relaxing behind the steering wheel, when Google tells us they are working on problems of safety and accessibility, or when Lyft publishes blog articles about the possibilities of needing fewer parking lots. Although these actions themselves do not make any outcomes a reality, the groups behind them are counting on consumers, lawmakers, and others to support their sociotechnical imaginaries.

In another example, during the early automobile days, certain social groups were relatively successful in convincing others that city streets should be socially reconstructed as motor thoroughfares where cars should take priority, instead of gathering places for residents (Norton, 2011). This idea eventually spread to the politicians and engineers who paved the roads, the pedestrians who stayed out of them, and the police who watched over them. But achieving this was not simply a matter of one social group conveying their interests to the others; it involved a hard fight. As traffic accidents and congestion were originally perceived to be the fault of cars, supporters of the automobile organized together to push the message that these problems were to be seen as issues of regulating human behavior and perfecting road engineering (Norton, 2011).

Ultimately, collaboration and compromise between many voices will be the path toward agreeable and optimal integration of New Mobility technologies. What is good for communities and good for individual social groups can be different, and again, even conflict. At the individual level, the best choice for transport might be a private car, but when everyone takes a private car it increases traffic and creates congestion that negatively impacts the entire community. Potential uses of vehicle automation, electrification, data-connectivity, and digital ride-hailing services could involve many such paradoxes. At a community level, systems of local organization and regional government, working in both private and public forums, must play a leading role in bringing interests together. Such cooperative decision-making enables resources and facilities to be put to use to benefit both suburb and metropolis on a larger scale (Mumford, 1958).

At an individual level, this can occasionally mean concession. "Good public policy favours necessities over luxuries," writes Todd Litman (2009), "and so should favour basic mobility (transport activity considered socially valuable) over less important activity" (p. 213). This might prove challenging to the expectations of today's drivers, who have long benefited from a focus upon individualized and flexible movement (Dennis & Urry, 2009). But although a more libertarian perspective might still be appropriate for many uses of AVs, when it comes to the potential shared consequences and missed opportunities involved, some amount of collaborative planning could bring benefits that prove to be well worth certain sacrifices.

CONCLUSION

Transportation technology is not just another area of consumption. The systems society builds to move people and things affect much more, from the shapes of cities to the social interactions of those within them. Therefore, anyone with an interest in maximizing the benefits and minimizing the negative consequences of a new transportation technology such as vehicle automation must not only pay attention to how that technology could function, but also think in terms of the unintended consequences or deeper long-term impacts it could have. This involves considering the effects of building, operating, and disposing of the technological artifacts involved, as well as thinking a step further to the secondary impacts of integrating them into the social fabric of people's lives.

Given the magnitude of what's at stake, it is simply vital that emerging transportation technologies be steered toward uses which offer the most shared benefits. In shaping vehicle automation, connectivity, electrification, and sharing, we must reconcile our roles as individuals with our roles as community members. If we fail to do so, our transportation systems are in danger of sliding us closer to a dystopia where automation increases vehicle use and congestion, decimates public transit ridership, and only the few see any benefit. Conversely, we now face an incredible opportunity to reduce traffic deaths, make better use of our resources, and improve the mobility options of all people. If communities push toward the future they collectively want with shared interests in mind, they may find that moving toward their goals is only a matter of choice. Communities that wait too long, however, may find that someone else has made these choices for them.

REFERENCES

Bijker, W. E., Hughes, T. P., & Pinch, T. J. (1987). *The social construction of technological systems: New directions in the sociology and history of technology.* MIT Press.

Bonnefon, J. F., Shariff, A., & Rahwan, I. (2016). The social dilemma of autonomous vehicles. *Science, 352*(6293), 1573–1576. doi:10.1126cience.aaf2654 PMID:27339987

Bureau of Labor Statistics, U.S. Department of Labor. (2015, December 17). Taxi drivers and chauffeurs. *Occupational Outlook Handbook.* Retrieved August 8, 2017, from https://www.bls.gov/ooh/transportation-and-material-moving/taxi-drivers-and-chauffeurs.htm

Burns, L. D., Jordan, W. C., & Scarborough, B. A. (2013). Transforming personal mobility. *The Earth Institute, 431,* 432.

Callon, M. (1986). The sociology of an actor-network: The case of the electric vehicle. In M. Callon, A. Rip, & J. Law (Eds.), *Mapping the Dynamics of Science and Technology: Sociology of Science in the Real World* (pp. 19–34). Springer. doi:10.1007/978-1-349-07408-2_2

Chase, R. (2016, August 10). Self-Driving Cars Will Improve Our Cities. If They Don't Ruin Them. *Wired*. Retrieved from https://www.wired.com/2016/08/self-driving-cars-will-improve-our-cities-if-they-dont-ruin-them/

Dennis, K., & Urry, J. (2009). Post-car mobilities. In J. Conley & A. T. McLaren (Eds.), *Car troubles: Critical studies of automobility and auto-mobility* (pp. 235–252). Routledge.

Dietrich, E. (2016, October 12). *Site plan filed for Black-Olive project as neighbors worry about parking*. Retrieved July 18, 2018, from https://www.bozemandailychronicle.com/news/city/site-plan-filed-for-black-olive-project-as-neighbors-worry/article_f7b0d65b-e904-5c86-8031-47b5ea43d3d2.html

Dunning, D. (2011). The Dunning–Kruger effect: On being ignorant of one's own ignorance. In Advances in experimental social psychology (Vol. 44, pp. 247–296). Academic Press.

Endsley, M. R. (2017). Autonomous driving systems: A preliminary naturalistic study of the Tesla Model S. *Journal of Cognitive Engineering and Decision Making*, *11*(3), 225–238. doi:10.1177/1555343417695197

Federal Highway Administration (FHWA). (2003) *Corporate Master Plan for Research and Deployment of Technology & Innovation*. Washington, DC: U.S. Federal Highway Administration. Retrieved from the Library of Congress, https://lccn.loc.gov/2004368060

Gehrke, S., Felix, A., & Reardon, T. (2018). *Fare choices: A survey of ride-hailing passengers in metro Boston*. Metropolitan Area Planning Council Research Brief.

Graham, S., & Thrift, N. (2007). Out of order: Understanding repair and maintenance. *Theory, Culture & Society*, *24*(3), 1–25. doi:10.1177/0263276407075954

Groshen, E. L., Helper, S., MacDuffie, J. P., & Carson, C. (2018, June). *Preparing U.S. workers and employers for an autonomous vehicle future*. Washington, DC: Securing America's Future Energy (SAFE).

Grush, B., & Niles, J. (2018). *The End of Driving: Transportation systems and public policy planning for autonomous vehicles*. Elsevier.

Hancock, P. A. (2015, March). Automobility: The coming use of fully-automated on-road vehicles. In Cognitive methods in situation awareness and decision support (CogSIMA), 2015 IEEE international inter-disciplinary conference (pp. 137-139). IEEE.

Hancock, P. A., & Parasuraman, R. (1992). Human factors and safety in the design of intelligent vehicle-highway systems (IVHS). *Journal of Safety Research, 23*(4), 181–198. doi:10.1016/0022-4375(92)90001-P

Hardin, G. (1968). The tragedy of the commons. *Science, 162*(3859), 1243–1248. doi:10.1126cience.162.3859.1243 PMID:5699198

Harris, S. (Host). (2017, April 4). What is technology doing to us? [Episode 71]. *Waking up with Sam Harris.* Podcast retrieved from https://www.samharris.org/podcast/item/what-is-technology-doing-to-us

Henaghan, J. (2018). *Preparing communities for autonomous vehicles.* American Planning Association. Retrieved from https://www.planning.org/publications/document/9144551/

International Association of Public Transport (UITP). (2017). *Autonomous vehicles: a potential game changer for urban mobility.* Policy brief retrieved from https://www.uitp.org/autonomous-vehicles

International Transport Forum (ITF). (2018). *The shared-use city: managing the curb.* Corporate Partnership Board Report. Retrieved from https://www.itf-oecd.org/sites/default/files/docs/shared-use-city-managing-curb_3.pdf

Jacobs, J. (1961). *The death and life of great American cities.* Vintage Books.

Jasanoff, S. (2015). Future imperfect: Science, technology, and the imaginations of modernity. In S. Jasanoff & S.-H. Kim (Eds.), *Dreamscapes of modernity: Sociotechnical imaginaries and the fabrication of power* (pp. 1–33). University of Chicago Press. doi:10.7208/chicago/9780226276663.003.0001

Kuhn, T. S. (1962). *The structure of scientific revolutions.* Chicago: University of Chicago press.

Latour, B. (1988). Mixing humans and nonhumans together: The sociology of a door-closer. *Social Problems, 35*(3), 298–310. doi:10.2307/800624

Lipson, H., & Kurman, M. (2016). *Driverless: Intelligent cars and the road ahead.* MIT Press.

Litman, T. (2009). Mobility as a positional good: Implications for transport policy and planning. In J. Conley & A. T. McLaren (Eds.), *Car troubles: Critical studies of automobility and auto-mobility* (pp. 199–217). Routledge.

Litman, T. (2017). *Autonomous vehicle implementation predictions.* Victoria, Canada: Victoria Transport Policy Institute.

Mumford, L. (1958). The highway and the city. In L. Mumford (Ed.), *The highway and the city* (pp. 234–246). New York: Harcourt, Brace & World.

National Highway Traffic Safety Administration (NHTSA). (2008). National motor vehicle crash causation survey: Report to congress. *National Highway Traffic Safety Administration technical report DOT HS, 811*, 059.

National Highway Traffic Safety Administration (NHTSA). (2016). *2016 fatal motor vehicle crashes: Overview*. Retrieved from https://crashstats.nhtsa.dot.gov/Api/Public/Publication/812456

National Highway Traffic Safety Administration (NHTSA). (2017). *Automated driving systems 2.0: A vision for safety*. Retrieved from https://www.nhtsa.gov/document/automated-driving-systems-20-voluntary-guidance

Navigant Research. (2018, January 16). *Leaderboard report: Automated driving*. Retrieved from https://www.navigantresearch.com/research/navigant-research-leaderboard-automated-driving-vehicles

New York City Department of Transportation (NYC DOT). (2018, June). *New York City mobility report*. Retrieved from http://www.nyc.gov/html/dot/downloads/pdf/mobility-report-2018-print.pdf

Norton, P. D. (2011). *Fighting traffic: The dawn of the motor age in the American city*. MIT Press.

Price, R. (2015, February 6). Uber drivers keep just 50% of what you pay. *Business Insider UK*. Retrieved from http://uk.businessinsider.com/uber-customer-cost-breakdown-morgan-stanley-2015-2

Puentes, R., & Tomer, A. (2008, December). *The road... less traveled: an analysis of vehicle miles traveled trends in the US*. Brookings Institute. Retrieved from https://rosap.ntl.bts.gov/view/dot/18145

Rakower, L. H. (2011). Blurred line: Zooming in on google street view and the global right to privacy. *Brooklyn Journal of International Law, 37*(1), 317–348.

Regalado, A. (2013, March 5). Is this why Google doesn't want you to drive? *MIT Technology Review*. Retrieved from https://www.technologyreview.com/s/512091/is-this-why-google-doesnt-want-you-to-drive/

Roberts, D. (2015, June 3). Sergey Brin: Here's why Google is making self-driving cars. *Fortune*. Retrieved from http://fortune.com/2015/06/03/google-self-driving-cars/

Sawyer, B. D., Calvo, A. A., Finomore, V. S., & Hancock, P. A. (2015, August). Serendipity in Simulation: Building Environmentally Valid Driving Distraction Evaluations of Google Glass™ and an Android™ Smartphone. In *Proceedings 19th Triennial Congress of the IEA* (*Vol. 9*, p. 14). Academic Press.

Sawyer, B. D., & Hancock, P. A. (2012). Development of a linked simulation network to evaluate intelligent transportation system vehicle to vehicle solutions. *Proceedings of the Human Factors and Ergonomics Society Annual Meeting*, *56*(1), 2316–2320. doi:10.1177/1071181312561487

Schaller, B. (2017a). *Empty seats, full streets: Fixing Manhattan's traffic problem.* Schaller Consulting. Retrieved from http://www.schallerconsult.com/rideservices/ emptyseats.htm

Schaller, B. (2017b). *Unsustainable? The growth of app-based ride services and traffic, travel and the future of New York City.* Schaller Consulting. Retrieved from http://www.schallerconsult.com/rideservices/unsustainable.htm

Schaller, B. (2018, July 25). *The New Automobility: Lyft, Uber and the future of American cities.* Schaller Consulting. Retrieved from http://www.schallerconsult. com/rideservices/automobility.htm

Schwieterman, J. P., Livingston, M., & Van Der Slot, S. (2018, August 1). *Partners in transit: A review of partnerships between transportation network companies and public agencies in the United States.* Chaddick Institute for Metropolitan Development. Retrieved from https://las.depaul.edu/centers-and-institutes/chaddick-institute-for-metropolitan-development/research-and-publications/Pages/default.aspx

Securing America's Future Energy (SAFE). (2018, June). *America's workforce and the self-driving future.* Retrieved from https://avworkforce.secureenergy.org/ wp-content/uploads/2018/06/Americas-Workforce-and-the-Self-Driving-Future_ Realizing-Productivity-Gains-and-Spurring-Economic-Growth.pdf

Shared-Use Mobility Center (SUMC). (2015). *Shared-use mobility reference guide.* Retrieved from http://sharedusemobilitycenter.org/publications/

Shared-Use Mobility Center (SUMC). (2016). *Shared mobility and the transformation of public transit.* Report to the American Public Transportation Association. Retrieved from http://sharedusemobilitycenter.org/publications/

Sparrow, R., & Howard, M. (2017). When human beings are like drunk robots: Driverless vehicles, ethics, and the future of transport. *Transportation Research Part C, Emerging Technologies*, *80*, 206–215. doi:10.1016/j.trc.2017.04.014

Stocker, A., & Shaheen, S. (2018, July). Shared Automated Vehicle (SAV) Pilots and Automated Vehicle Policy in the US: Current and Future Developments. In *Automated Vehicles Symposium 2018* (pp. 131-147). Springer.

Tesla. (2018). *Tesla Autopilot.* Retrieved from https://www.tesla.com/autopilot/

Tett, G. (2018, April 9). A shortage of US truck drivers points to bigger problems. *Financial Times*, p. 11.

U. S. Department of Transportation (DOT). (2018). *Comprehensive Management Plan for Automated Vehicle Initiatives.* Retrieved from https://www.transportation. gov/policy-initiatives/automated-vehicles/usdot-comprehensive-management-plan-automated-vehicle

Volvo. (2015). *Future of driving.* Retrieved from https://www.futureofdriving.com

Weis, C., & Axhausen, K. W. (2009). Induced travel demand: Evidence from a pseudo panel data based structural equations model. *Research in Transportation Economics, 25*(1), 8–18. doi:10.1016/j.retrec.2009.08.007

Wetmore, J. (2009). Implementing Restraint: Automobile safety and the US debate over technological and social fixes. In J. Conley & A. T. McLaren (Eds.), *Car troubles: Critical studies of automobility and auto-mobility* (pp. 111–125). Routledge.

Wiener, N. (1954). *The human use of human beings: Cybernetics and society.* Da Capo Press.

Woodall, B. (2016, August 18). Uber buys self-driving truck startup Otto; teams with Volvo. *Reuters.* Retrieved from https://www.reuters.com/article/us-uber-tech-volvo-otto-idUSKCN10T1TR

Zimmer, J. (2016, September 18). The third transportation revolution: Lyft's vision for the next 10 years and beyond. *Medium.* Retrieved from https://medium.com/@johnzimmer/the-third-transportation-revolution-27860f05fa91

KEY TERMS AND DEFINITIONS

Automated Vehicle (AV): A road vehicle with the ability to complete all driving tasks for some or all portions of a journey without human assistance.

New Mobility: A shift in transportation systems made possible by the emergence and confluence of multiple new transportation technologies, including vehicle automation, electrification, data connectivity, and digital methods of sharing.

Ride-Hailing: A service with which a person can request transportation as it is needed (on-demand), commonly via smartphone app, website, or by telephone.

Social Groups: A set of people for whom a technological artifact represents a shared value or problem.

Sociotechnical Imaginary: A vision for how a technology could be manifested and put into use by social groups, potentially including particular outcomes for these or other social groups.

Tragedy of the Commons: A situation in which the pursuit of individual gain leads to overall collective loss.

Zero-Occupancy: Road travel of an automated vehicle with no persons on board.

ENDNOTE

[1]   Available at https://www.futureofdriving.com/concept26.html

Chapter 9
The Digital Divide and Usability

Lisa Jo Elliott
Pennsylvania State University, USA

ABSTRACT

The digital divide refers to the differences between people who use technology on a regular basis (technology-enabled) and those who do not use technology regularly (technology-disabled). Van Dijk describes three mechanisms that affect the use of technological resources. These are social exclusion, exploitation, and control. In addition to these three mechanisms, the technology itself may exclude potential users through the application design process. The design method used most frequently relies on convenience sampling of current users. The choices that these technology familiar users make in testing lead development teams to interaction design decisions that may exclude novice users. Several theories of technology adoption are reviewed as well as past and potential ways to address the digital divide.

INTRODUCTION

This chapter reviews the literature on the concept of the digital divide from several different viewpoints. Then, the chapter discusses how the digital divide has been affected by industry usability practices when creating technology and applications. The second set of viewpoints are gleaned from leaders in user experience and the experience of the author educating students to enter practice. The chapter synthesizes past approaches to narrow the digital divide from a practical and usability perspective.

DOI: 10.4018/978-1-5225-7949-6.ch009

After reading this chapter, the reader will have a better understanding of the concept of a digital divide, how it is influenced by the application development process, its past and future.

BACKGROUND

The digital divide is a broad term which refers to the differences between people who use technology on a regular basis (Technology Enabled or TE) and those who do not use technology regularly (Technology Disabled or TD). These differences can be in many areas, such as information gained, knowledge, skills, abilities, and opportunities. Technology access refers to having access to a mobile phone that will access the internet through a data plan and/or access to a computer which will access the internet with a browser application. Technology in the digital divide sense refers to the use or non-use of the internet as an information and communications technology. At this point in time, using the internet and technology demands a certain level of proficiency. This proficiency must be learned through using the device(s) over time. Initial use of the device(s) must support a person's current knowledge base and expectations. Therefore, people who use a mobile phone with a data plan for the first time, or connect to the internet for the first time, should encounter a device that minimizes frustrations, is simple for them to use, maximizes their motivation to use and meets with their expectations. We refer to this as having high usability.

Usability refers to the intangible property of an application or device. This property is thought to help or hinder a person's ability to use and learn the application or device. The property of usability is inherent to the application or device through the design choices that the development team makes on behalf of the users. The choices in functionality, features, physical design, and interaction design enables the user to interact with the functional side of the application.

THE DIGITAL DIVIDE

In the previous fifteen years, scholars, educators, social justice advocates, and government officials have become increasingly concerned about the Digital Divide. Van Dijk refines it in terms of their concerns:

The metaphor digital divide suggests a simple divide between two clearly divided groups with a yawning gap between them. Secondly, it suggests that the gap is difficult to bridge. A third misunderstanding might be the impression that the divide is about absolute inequalities, that is between those included and those excluded. A final wrong connotation might be the suggestion that the divide is a static condition while in fact the gaps observed are continually shifting. It is often suggested that the origins of the inequalities referred to lie in the specific problems of getting physical access to digital technology and that achieving such access for all would solve particular problems in the economy and society. (Van Dijk, 2006, p. 222)

Van Dijk (2005, 2006) notes that the inequalities originate with contact with the technology. People seem to either take to it or they do not based on a variety of factors. To compound the issue, Van Dijk suggests that TE individuals use their technological advantage to exclude others (2005). Trolling, restricting access, increasing the cost, or increasing the complexity of the technology effectively discourages TD individuals from adopting additional technology or advancing technologically.

Within developed countries, Technology Enabled citizens (TE) in the dominant group embrace technological approaches to government issues for the time savings and convenience. They continue to vote and support the modernization of local government. Van Dijk (2006) describes factors that influence full technology access. These factors include access characteristics, individual characteristics, and categorical characteristics.

Within these factors, Van Dijk (2006) describes three mechanisms that effect the distribution of information and communication technological resources: social exclusion, exploitation, and control. Van Dijk (2006) describes social exclusion as the dominant group restricting the benefits by keeping the relationships closed. For example, in social networking applications such as LinkedIn, in order to communicate with a particular person, that person must have their privacy settings open or you must know their email address/ have a prior friendship. This setting is part of how the software was developed and the design choices that were made by the development team. The second mechanism, technological exploitation, as described by Van Dijk (2006), is exploitation that happens as the command of technological resources is orchestrated through a coordinated effort. One may see this in action through crowd-sourced funding applications such as GoFundMe. In order for a person to benefit from the donation of others' money, someone must set up an account and page for that person according to the rules of the application. The third mechanism, control, is described by van Dijk (2006) as allocation of economic capital in property and money, social capital in obligations/connections, embodied cultural capital in training/ education, objectified cultural capital in goods, and institutionalized cultural states in educational qualifications. One may see this in action through the exchange of property: Ebay/Amazon/Craigslist; Online Classes; Online Certifications/Badges; Online Knowledge exchanges such as Stack Exchange.

The Pew Research Center conducted a surveyed of over 40,000 individuals in 37 countries between February and May of 2017. They found internet use and smart phone ownership steadily increasing across all countries. In the most developed countries, respondents reported the highest access and ownership rates. Table 1 summarizes the data with the actual percentage reported for 2017 in parentheses.

Many scholars hypothesize that as the divide increases poverty, crime, and despair increases as well for those without technology resources/access. For example, the implementation of an e-service means that there may be another layer of difficulty to pay a parking ticket. To overcome this layer of difficulty, the TD citizen must go to the city library in order to use a public computer with internet access. The journey will cost the citizen an extra bus trip or parking in addition to the time it takes to wait for a public computer to become available and learning to use the new e-service. Some TD citizens may choose not to engage at all in this way and instead use the physical services. Again, they may face other e-challenges such as electronic parking meters that no longer accept cash or a government office which accepts only credit/debit cards.

Fears that the TD citizens will fall further behind has created scenarios such as this one which may result in cities retaining the physical parking ticket payment system. Eventually, the TD citizens learn the new system or face non-payment. Many in social services fear that the increased embrace of government e-services will result in those who are currently marginally disenfranchised sliding deeper into poverty because of small issues (Lee, Lee, & Choi, 2016).

According to Van Dijk (2006; Van Deursen & Van Dijk, 2010), TD citizens struggle with challenges beyond access. They may be economically disadvantaged, may lack a quality education, may have low literacy, may live in a rural location and/ or have a disability. According to Friemel and others (2016) TD citizens struggle with learning how to integrate the technology into their lives and its usefulness, then they struggle with the fear associated with learning, the lack of instruction, lack of cultural support, and a lack of understanding the complexity of the technology

Table 1. Internet use across the world as measured by the Pew 2018 study

Percentage of adults who use the internet or own a smartphone by country (actual percentage)	
80% or more	United States (89), Canada(91), France(87), Germany(87), Netherlands (93), Sweden (92), United Kingdom (88), Spain (87), Australia (93), South Korea (96), Israel (88), Jordan (80), Lebanon (83)
60-79%	Greece(66), Hungary (74), Italy (71), Poland (75), Russia (78%), Japan (76), Vietnam (64), Turkey (76), China (71), Argentina (78), Brazil (70), Chile (78), Columbia (75), Mexico (67), Peru (64), Venezuela (72)
40 – 59%	Philippines (56), Tunisia (44), Nigeria (42), Senegal (46), South Africa (59),
Less than 40%	India (25%), Indonesia (30), Ghana (39), Kenya (39), Tanzania (25)

Source: (Poushter, 2018)

(Friemel, 2016; Van Deursen & Van Dijk, 2014; Vigdor, Ladd, & Martinez, 2014). Of these issues, the access issue is the most objective and well defined. However, when the access issue is resolved additional multi-layered barriers are revealed (Garrett, Brown, Hart-Hester, Hamadain, Dixon, Pierce, & Rudman, 2006).

The Digital Divide

Some barriers are generational and situational. The computer supported cooperative work environment widely introduced in about the 1990s, created the initial Digital Divide. Typewriters were replaced with word processors and then computers. If a person entered the workforce before 1970 and had been promoted to a supervisory position by 1985-1990, it is likely that they were not required to perform some of the manual operations on a computer such as using a word processing application. These workers may be considered 'pre-digital workers'. They simply supervised those who did this sort of work for them or had jobs which did not require a computer. Conversely, individuals whose jobs involved doing the word processing or spread sheet work, or had a white collar job after about 1985-1990 learned how to use the first generations of office computers and then more easily grasped technology as it advanced. The 'pre-digital workers' with sparse work exposure to technology had few peers to exchange information on technology or informal opportunities to learn the technology outside of work.

A similar situation still exists in elementary schools. However, many underprivileged elementary schools are recognizing the disadvantage that the lack of technology imparts to their students and are implementing technology grants. For many individuals entering elementary school, they are issued an internet connected device such as a Chromebook. These individuals may face some of the same financial, physical space, and connectivity challenges in the future but they will have the technological skill to gain the knowledge to address their problems. Then, contrast the entering elementary school students where the school does not issue internet connected devices to each student. These students are at a disadvantage without the constant use of technology. This is one way in which the TE (e. g. students issued Chromebooks) and the TD (e. g. students without technology) continue to be created.

Scholars such as Van Dijk and Leaning are amongst the most cited in the digital divide literature. Van Dijk (2005) champions a multi-layered approach to the factors contributing to the digital divide. Leaning (2017) suggests similar factors but in a three layered approach similar to Maslow's Hierarchy of Needs (Maslow, 1943). In Leaning's (2017) model, an individual must solve the access to the internet problem first (first level), then develop the knowledge, skills, and abilities to be proficient in understanding and use of ICT (second level), at which point the individual may understand ICT well enough to generate content and create benefit from the interaction (third level). Leaning and others believe that it isn't until the third level of use that individuals begin to see benefit from ICT use and integrate it into their lives. Following this model, seniors who used technology as part of their white collar jobs and students who use technology in elementary school have the advantage of being at the third level of having the ability to generate content. The 'pre-digital' workers and those students who did not have technology in elementary school may be at Leaning's first or second level during a critical time in their adulthood.

The Role of User Experience Design in the Digital Divide

While it is important to understand how society creates the divide through existing conditions apart from poverty, the point of this chapter is to discuss how the technology itself may exclude individuals through standard user experience design practices. User experience design and interaction design differ from visual design. While visual design focuses on how an application looks, user experience and interaction design focus on how the application acts and functions (Interaction Design Foundation, 2015). If an application acts in unpredictable or undesirable ways, an individual will not understand how to use it or be motivated to not use it. User experience designers are very busy as the development of new applications increases exponentially each year. These applications become increasingly complex as one builds on prior knowledge of others.

In July 2008, 800 applications (apps) were available in the Apple store for download on an Apple device (Statista, 2018). In September 2008, there were 3,000 available. In November 2009, there were 100,000. In June of 2011, there were 425,000. In June of 2012, there were 650,000. In June of 2014, 1,200,000 apps were available. Then, in June of 2016, 2,000,000 apps were available in the Apple store for download (Statista, 2018). The apps available here are only a portion of the entire app market and a small fraction of what TE individuals may choose to use.

According to Saffer (2010), technology organizations had used 'the genius' design method to create groundbreaking design solutions before the current method of user centered design. This method is similar to the approach used by advertising agencies. A 'genius' design relies on a single person to decide how a product feels, looks, and acts. The character of Don Draper in the series Mad Men exemplifies the 'genius' approach (AMC Network Entertainment, 2010). In this series describing the day to day life of an advertising executive, Don had the last say in what the client saw and bought. He guided the creative process from start to finish. A more modern example would be Steve Jobs. Steve's vision was the ultimate guide for Apple (Fjord, 2011). He decided how each product would look, feel, and act. The 'genius' design method assumes that whatever the designer considers correct is the correct product design decisions. Don Norman discusses the flaws in the genius design approach in his book, The Design of Everyday Things (Norman, 2013). According to Norman, the 'genius' design approach costs organizations time, money, and sometimes lives through a singular viewpoint. Norman, Jakob Nielsen, Jarod Spool, others championed a user centered design approach in which all design decisions were made by testing actual consumers with the different product or application designs under consideration.

Saffer discusses the user centered design approach or UCD (2010). The concept is simple: the future user of the device, not the designer, should make all of the design decisions from the product inception to the final testing before release. This gave rise to the phrase, 'you are not your user', in the usability community. This design approach can be tedious as nearly anyone can find a problem with nearly any product. Development teams felt disenfranchised as their designs are constantly reworked by users who may have had little appreciation for what they were trying to accomplish. As a result, user experience designers became more judicious as to how and when to bring the user into the process. Designers decided that they needed to try methods to popularize the understanding of the importance of their work. Evangelizing the user experience design methodologies became popular with multiple websites and blogs devoted to educating others on the benefits of UCD.

UCD has been a dramatic shift from the genius design perspective. It's not to say that Apple did not also practice UCD, they have a large cadre of designers, researchers, prototypers and other professionals to support this approach and clarify Jobs' work. This approach has created millions of apps that are usable and satisfactory to the vast majority of technology users. As this approach has grown and been adopted across apps, libraries of standard solutions have emerged. This gives the development team a starting point and is a great advance for users as well. No longer are there hundreds of different solutions for how to log into a system. There are only a few solutions and the pre-designed buttons are freely available in the pattern library. TE users know the conventions and have contributed to the development of these designs. Patterns were only tested on users who already knew how to use the system. The TE users were the ones that helped develop the libraries as they were the users on which UCD was conducted. It is not known if the TD users would also naturally interact with the system in these standard ways. Their voices were not part of the conversation. Why?

Most of the technology organizations are central to one area of the United States. The UCD method relies on convenience sampling or the snowball sampling of users. This means that the people who have the opportunity to make the design decisions are those who are easily accessible (i.e. convenient). In the case of snowball sampling, if you knew someone who worked in a technology organization or if you knew someone who had done the user testing for an app, you may be contacted through your friend. Therefore, if you lived within driving distance of Facebook, you were more likely to be involved in user testing for Facebook than if you lived hundreds of miles away. You had special status to make design decisions for Facebook. Your input created the standard library for Facebook as you participated in their user testing.

As a sophisticated user of technology, your choices during the user testing sessions guided the product's development to be increasingly complex. In other words, poorly designed tools that may confuse the user in Excelsior Springs Missouri are not confusing to you, the expert user in Silicon Valley who engages in many of the usability tests (Elliott & Polyakova, 2014). For this reason, the historical use of convenience and snowball sampling in UCD has widened the digital divide. Until recently, this had been the primary design approach.

In the past few years, the use of unmoderated user testing online has gained popularity. Services such as Trymyui (http://www.trymyui.com) and UserZoom (http://www.userzoom.com) allow a person who is not physically located near the technology organization to participate in user testing. The organization specifies the target audience, the tasks, the site, and specifies what they want to know. Groups of users sign up for testing and are selected at random. All users must have access to a smart phone or a computer with a camera. Once the users begin the testing, their devices' camera records their face as they test. Upon completion of the test and the survey questions, the users get paid a small amount. Users who participate must know about these tests which requires a high level of technology skill. This second method of user testing does sample a broader range of users, but all with the same high level of technical expertise.

Technology organizations also use A/B testing. In this methodology, they deploy two or more versions of a design. Users of the application may not be aware that they are using either the A design or the B design of the application. Then, on the applications back end, data is analyzed to see which design led to fewer errors or more engagement. A design or design change is chosen on the basis of actual users of the different designs. Again, users from the TD group are ignored because of a lack of access. The technology organization does not access them and they are unaware of the testing opportunities. This leads to the adoption of sophisticated designs and features that may further restrict access to the TD group.

Another approach to finding and fixing usability problems is participatory design/ group design. This approach can be based on games, focus groups, brainstorming sessions, or group design meetings. As in the other approaches, the user must already have access to the application or be in touch with the development/design team to participate. This approach has the most promise for incorporating TD users during the development process.

UCD is based on prior knowledge of previous iterations of the application/product. This makes the learning curve for new users steeper as each iteration may become more complex than the last in order to incorporate newer features, faster processes, and better integration with other services. As the designs are incorporated into the design library, the design approach is adopted by similar applications to unify the design across platforms enabling the TE to gain speed and fluidity when using different applications on their phone, work and home computers, and reading tablets. This has the potential to disenfranchise the TD, locking them out of multiple platforms until they have learned the standard design. While this does confer advantages once the standard design is learned, there are interactions that are not transparent and so complex that a rare random guess would enable a TD individual to happen upon the right procedure.

Anecdotally, users have reported that many TE users learn from TE friends. One person adopts Snapchat and wants to converse with another user. The first invites the second and shows her/him how to use it. Another way is through operational conditioning. A TE user finds a new app and 'plays with it'. As the user tries new actions (i.e. swiping left or right on a phone) the app reinforces the behavior by going on to the next part of the feature which the user may be trying to access. As the new action is reinforced, the user associates this action with the apps reaction. As the app functions predictably in reaction to a specific user action, the user learns that this action on her/his part causes the app to react in this way. Then, the user who is 'playing with it' has been operationally conditioned to create behaviors that trigger app functionality. Users who are unable to 'play with it' because they lack the background knowledge of how to start may become very frustrated. Hypothetically, if the TD user does not have TE friends, there are few resources outside of the technology itself to help. Library classes, community college classes are available but require attendance. As the technology increases in complexity, the TD user who does not learn the basic functionality faces a steeper learning curve. As Nielsen states,

Technology remains so complicated that many people couldn't use a computer even if they got one for free. Many others can use computers, but don't achieve the modern world's full benefits because most of the available services are too difficult for them to understand. (Nielsen, 2006)

The assumptions in user knowledge fuel increasingly complex technical terminology and complex concepts. For example, as the current discussion on third party applications accessing Facebook data deepens, producers of the Today Show, on the television station CBS, gave a tutorial during their show demonstrating how to change these settings (How to limit Facebook access to third party app data, March 21, 2018). During the tutorial, users are instructed to go through complex menus more than three deep to change these important settings. Traditional wisdom in usability practice recommends that important functions be no less than two clicks deep as users' working memory capacity can be exceeded. This begs the question of user experience practitioners: are standard practices being violated purposefully? In the case of privacy settings, are these settings being hidden from users through increased complexity?

Cayola and Macias (2018) cite forty-three types of user experience design methodologies. Of these, 64% rely on testing users, observing users, or getting feedback from users while using the software or doing the tasks that the software aids or replaces. Some of the methods suggested were based on expert evaluation (14%), and others were based on a standard methodology not involving user or expert evaluation (21%). The majority of these methods assume that the person being tested is TE. For example, during a user test if the user being tested does not know what a log in screen is or why someone would use one, the user test comes to an abrupt end. When championing user centered design methods, Cayola and Macias state effectiveness (percentage of tasks successfully completed), efficiency (the amount of time it took to complete a task), ratings of satisfaction, usefulness, ease of use and ease of learnability. It is the last two measures which contribute most to the digital divide: ease of use and ease of learnability. If prior knowledge of similar applications or the background content knowledge is not present in the users tested it may be impossible for them to provide useful information.

Another view of user experience design methodologies is presented by Peter Morville's User Experience Honeycomb (Wesolko, 2016). The user experience honeycomb describes hypothetical facets of user experience design (Wesolko, 2016). Originally, Peter created the Honeycomb to help educate clients. The Honeycomb states that usefulness, desirability, findability, accessibility, usability, and credibility are all important components. Again, if prior knowledge is not present in the users tested, their ratings would be incomprehensible.

Until recently, creating learnable applications has not been a priority. Technology companies, such as Google, have recognized that their user base is limited to the TE, and that in order to grow, they must make the technology less prohibitive to the TD. Google has led initiatives to narrow the digital divide as they learn that this is a promising area of innovation and growth. As Mangalindan states, "some of today's greatest strides in innovation don't come from Silicon Valley darlings like Apple or Facebook but organizations bent on improving quality of life in developing countries" (Mangalindan, 2014).

Theory and the Digital Divide

Much of the theorizing about what motivates individuals to use technology has been based on TE individuals' choices and current use. At least four primary perspectives on technology use have emerged. Some of the perspectives are based on the attributes that the technology must have to invite adoption such as the Technology Acceptance

Model (Davis, 1989) and Rational Actor Perspective (Bowman, Westerman, & Claus, 2012). The second perspective is based on the idea that technology use is driven by Uses and Gratifications theory (Phua, Jin & Kim, 2017). The third and fourth perspectives are very similar with a focus on the users' intention to adopt the technology as in the UTAUT model (Venkatesh, Thong, Chan, Hu, & Brown, 2011) and the UCTAM model (Abhyankar, 2017).

The Technology Acceptance Model, or TAM, states that individuals choose to use technology based on its usefulness in increasing job performance and its ease of use in terms of effort. Davis states that ease of use precedes usefulness (1989). The Rational Actor Perspective, or RAP, suggests that there is a relationship between goal attainment, cognitive cost and self-efficacy with the relationship between cognitive cost and self-efficacy as inverse (Bowman, Westerman & Claus, 2012). Some individuals find that the application has a large cognitive cost in terms of the number of items to keep track of and the iterative steps required. For example, in some social media applications an individual must know the following items to post a picture and share with her friends: a) the name of the picture, b) where it is located on her device, c) if the picture will exceed the maximum or minimum size requirements, d) who she wants to share the picture with, e) how she wants the picture shared with that person. This is a cognitively complex task. When the cognitive cost exceeds the individual's ability, the goal is not attained and the individual's self-efficacy feelings are affected. As Davis (1989) suggests, ease of use is critical in overcoming the cognitive cost associated with a novice user attaining a goal and feeling more efficacious.

Elliott and Polyakova (2014) found support for the combination of TAM and RAP. There were two types of users in the study- users who had many social network applications that they used hourly and users who had only a few social network applications that they used infrequently. This made two groups: expert users and novice users. Expert users stated usefulness was of primary importance in that they would not use the application if their friends were not on it already. Novice users stated that ease of use was more important than if their friends were already there. During user testing, one tool was very difficult for novice users to operate. The frustration with this tool seemed to override the desire to connect with their friends. The same tool was not difficult for the expert users. Novice users became so frustrated with the tool that they would not use the application in the future regardless of how many friends were already on it. The high cognitive cost of the tool forced them to forego the opportunity the app presented because of the lousiness of use.

A second perspective on how usability is related to the digital divide has been prompted by the uses and gratification theory (Blumler & Katz, 1974). Individuals will select specific social networks based on their goal (use) and the way in which the application fulfills that goal (gratifications). These goals can be informational, social, and/or leisure based (Phua, Jin, & Kim, 2017). An individual will use many different social networks for different goals. For example, she may use SnapChat to talk with her friends and establish social capital among her close peers, but then LinkedIn to talk with office colleagues and arrange for an upcoming conference presentation.

The third perspective, the Unified Theory of Acceptance and Use of Technology (UTAUT) is a way of defining the perception of gains in job performance due to technology adoption or use (Venkatesh, et al., 2011). According the UTAUT model there are four determining factors: performance expectancy, effort expectancy, social influence, and facilitating conditions. Venkatesh and colleagues discuss how users value different things depending on the type of system and the role that the system encompasses in their lives (2011). For example, if the system/application use is required by an employer, the employee will have a different view of the system than a social network app. Venkatesh and colleagues discuss that, before using an app, a user's perceptions and expectations about an app by be anchored to their general understanding of the computer system rather than the specific app or part of a system(2-11). Venkatesh also discusses trust as a belief that the system can do what it is expected to do. Second, there is a belief that the system will act in the best interest of the user. Third, there is a belief that the system will be honest and fulfill the expectations of the user. The UTAUT model suggests that there is an unofficial social contract that the system/app has with the user.

The fourth perspective is the UCTAM by Abhyankar (2017). The User Centered Technology Acceptance Model (UCTAM) validates designs and aims to predict behavioral intention to use. There are many theories of behavioral intention. However, theories addressing the interaction between behavioral intention and the attributes of the technology itself are fairly recent. Abhyankar (2017) provides an excellent overview of the many behavioral intention models and notes that usability is inextricably tied to intent. With this perspective, as experienced users become more involved and intentional, novice users' intentions may be thwarted as the usability alienates them by focusing on the expert users' needs.

Initiatives to Narrow the Digital Divide

These theories suggest that an individuals' intent to use, expectations, goals, and perceptions of the app/system are as complex as the digital divide itself. While the theories are useful in addressing the complexities between motivation, learning, expectations and continual use they are yet to be empirical evidence in supporting why TD individuals do not use technology based on these theories. Consistently, initiatives to narrow the divide have ignored theory and instead focused on creating full access to technology. In itself, it has demonstrated that some TD individuals are able to gain full access and become TE while others do not (Rennie, 2018). Of those TD individuals who transfer to full TE individuals, social networks and entertainment are the primary and most prominent ways that they learned the skills necessary to bridge the divide (Rennie, 2018). Google Fiber and the city of Kansas City have been at the forefront of these efforts to understand why TD individuals do not use technology. Exploring how user centered design methods thwarted their efforts may help.

It was once thought that the barrier to the digital divide was only access to the internet. This was the reason for the introduction of Google Fiber across an entire city with focus on creating 'Fiberhoods' in underserved areas. According to Rachel Merlo, Google Fiber Community Impact Manager, Google chose to introduce home fiber in 2011 in Kansas City because of the pre-existing infrastructure (e. g. lowest cost to install), the collaborative partnerships with the local government, and the city's diversity (Sisson, 2017). Prior to Google Fiber's introduction, one fourth of Kansas Citians reported no broadband access at home and 17% reported not internet at home (Sisson, 2017). Merlo stated that it was an opportunity for Google to "get more folks online and address the digital divide". Google Fiber adopted Kansas City as one of the first U.S. cities to enjoy Google Fiber. The city embraced the opportunity as billboards emerged encouraging Kansas Citians to sign up before the deadline. TE Kansas Citians embraced Google Fiber and signed up.

As few TD citizens signed up for the $300 installation fee and $70 per month for 1 gigabyte per second initial offering, Google Fiber recognized the difference between their assumptions and reality about the Kansas City economy. They started a series of lower speed offerings and partnered with the federal department of Housing and Urban Development to install Fiber in several Kansas City housing projects. According to the most recent American Community Survey in 2016, there was a reported 6% increase in broadband across the Kansas City area where Google Fiber was made available (Sisson, 2017). The Wall Street Journal reported an 11% increase and others reported a 33% increase (Deacon, 2015). Technology volunteers started nonprofit organizations, such as the Free Network Foundation, and local nonprofits such as Connect for Good, and the Digital Inclusion workgroup began to identify factors outside of access (Rogers, 2017; Wohlson, 2012).

Google Fiber and the city governments acknowledged that the true purpose of the project was to engage all citizens. It is unclear if citizens in disadvantaged communities understood what was being offered and why it was important. As Google Fiber company spokesperson, Jenna Wandres stated, "...trying to convince people without internet access of the benefits of getting their homes online... they don't think they need it, they don't see why (Wohlson, 2012)." Kansas City has a typical city population with at least 70% of the students in the public schools without home access (Rogers, 2017). The TE individuals who led the adoption of Google

Fiberhoods failed to fully understand how their target populations may not yet have the intention to adopt because the registration process itself was unusable for them. To the TE individuals, the registration process was transparent and completely usable. It had been tested on people just like them. No one anticipated that Google Fiber would fail based assumptions built in Mountain View, California.

TE households were quick to meet the registration requirements of an online application and credit card registration fee of $10. TD households were not signing up. Google Fiber had overlooked key assumptions (Rothacker, 2015). To address this unanticipated challenge, a substantial door to door effort was made to register the TD neighborhoods by Google Fiber employees and Connect for Good. During the door to door effort, they found that the requirement of a registration fee by credit or debit was a hurdle. TD families justified registration not to be worth the potential benefit. Many of the TD families in Kansas City simply did not use banks. A few bad checks, the lack of cash, and/or a low credit score can restrict your ability to have a bank account (Jacobson, 1995; Sullivan, 2013; Feeney, 2016). Many TD families use payday loan offices which cash an employer's check for a small fee (Jacobson, 1995). Connect for Good recognized this dilemma and applied for small grants for all of the households within these neighborhoods. Then, the neighborhood organizations distributed the grants to the households to purchase prepaid debit cards in order to register (Rothacker, 2015).

This demonstrated a lack of testing the registration process in Kansas City with the TD households. In addition, it demonstrated a lack of understanding the TD users. Purportedly, user testing near headquarters with TE users led to design assumptions based on the convenience sample. After the initial sign up period, additional registration waves failed to yield the promised results in acquiring TD households.

During this time, a Kansas City non-profit organization developed a special digital access website built on the assumption that the TD lacked information on where to find free or low cost computers and Wi-Fi in the Kansas City area. User testing of this application revealed that most TD users who were also part of the homeless community had been provided a smart phone by social services. This phone could access the internet but lacked a data plan. These individuals were not completely TD, but were not yet completely TE users. However, they knew where to look for free Wi-Fi (Spitzer, Stanhope, Scott, Ries, Moore, McKenzie, Allen, Elliott, 2016). The users uniformly stated that the only thing that they used their phones for was to update their social network accounts or to contact others for social gatherings. For example, users stated that they always go to the same fast food restaurant or coffee shop to access the internet. They did not see the need for this application, their friends told them were to find the free Wi-Fi.

Users also seemed to prefer their phones over a computer, but stated that they did some tasks only by computer. They stated that if they didn't have access to the internet through their phones, they would go to the public library and use a public computer. These phones were provided by the state as part of the food stamp and Medicaid programs. People who had these types of phones would use the free Wi-Fi for social networking. They stated that it was difficult for them to keep a job even if they found one and the primary issue for them was the isolation that homelessness brought. They wanted to be connected to family and friends and know where their friends were going to be (Spitzer et al., 2016). This population liked to go to the library not so much for the services, but for the physical presence of other people and the safety and normality of the library. If they had problems with the computers, they liked talking to one of the librarians for the human contact (Spitzer et al., 2016).

SOLUTIONS AND RECOMMENDATIONS

Other communities have noted this important social component and its potential to narrow the digital divide in a way that the theories on user experience have not. Several other studies have outlined how the use of a community tech center has integrated access and education to address the problems of knowledge, skills, and abilities (Goncalves, Oliveira, & Cruz-Jesus, 2018; Tirado-Morueta, Aguaded-Gomez & Hernando-Gomez, 2018; Suwana, 2017; Nishijima, Ivanauskas & Sarti, 2017; Mumporeze & Prieler, 2017). Wamuyu (2017) and colleagues discuss this approach in Kenya. While Wamuyu discusses internet cafes or cyber cafes and their usefulness in bringing the community together, she also discusses the problems of who owns the technology in a literal and figurative sense. The ownership issue brought additional challenges to the researchers that were unanticipated.

Rennie (2018) also discusses the ownership challenge in Australian Aboriginal communities. In this study, computers and internet access were installed at community centers and in homes. Rennie and colleagues found that that community members treated the technology as a valued resource instead of a commodity. One person chose to keep the cords to the computer on their person when not home to prevent others from unauthorized access to the devices. Others restricted access in other ways through rules as to how and when others could use their computer and their internet. They reasoned that these rules were necessary to prevent others from engaging in dangerous activities with their computers and then a fear that they would be responsible for others' damage. This perception of the internet as a dangerous place is supported by the general fear of computers as dangerous as suggested by UTAUT (Venkatesh et al., 2011).

Leaning (2017) concludes that the access barrier is difficult to remove permanently without addressing financial inequalities. VanDeursen and Van Dijk (2014) note that even when the access barrier is lifted, the technical, content, informational, communication, content creation, and strategic skills must also be in place for the technology to be useful.

Once a country or a locality has reached the 80% threshold, most experts deem that the digital divide has been closed. According to Morozov (2012), 80% is the access rate that determines if there is or is not a digital divide. As Table 1 demonstrates, many developed countries meet or exceed that threshold. However, the idea of a cyber-utopianism (Morozov, 2012), where the disenfranchised enjoy equality across all social and economic classes, is unlikely to come to fruition. For TE individuals, the learning curve seems to have peaked. For TE individuals, their TD status becomes more difficult to overcome as technology advances. As Curran states, "despite significant investment and numerous attempts digital technologies have not eradicated or ameliorated social inequalities but have instead become a vehicle by which such inequalities are further entrenched and reinforced. This is the opposite of what many early advocates of digital media had predicted (as cited in Leaning, 2017, p. 109)." Leaning (2017) reports, TD individuals will choose not to engage in technological activities which could improve their socioeconomic status dramatically. Ultimately, understanding how the digital-divide contributes to social inequality is important, but its complexity suggests that the digital-divide may be the most useful by measuring future inequality between and within social groups (Leaning, 2017).

FUTURE RESEARCH DIRECTIONS

The digital divide is an important construct describing opportunity loss or opportunity gain associated with the use of internet enabled devices on a regular basis. As these devices become embedded in our everyday lives, their use becomes required. Those individuals who do not understand and make use of technology will become increasingly disadvantaged. Prior efforts to address this divide by distributing resources to those without technology have demonstrated that the reasons for the Digital divide go beyond access. These reasons include prior knowledge, motivation, cultural support, and technological skill. Free access, classes, and inexpensive computers are embraced by current technology users but seem to have done little to remediate the Digital divide. While the theories of UTAUT (Venkatesh et al., 2011), UCTAM (Abhyankar, 2017), Uses and Gratifications (Phua, Jin & Kim, 2017), TAM (Davis, 1989) and RAP (Bowman, Westerman & Clause, 2012) are useful in describing TE users' adoption and current use of technology, still little is empirically known about non-adoption and how to bridge the Digital divide. This is an area for future research as these theories could be extended and combined to provide a more comprehensive view of technology use.

CONCLUSION

The Digital divide is also a usability issue as application design methods are focused on current technology users. Future design methods which seek to understand a broad category of current and future technology users would help development teams extend their user base and create better applications for us all. In addition, further research is needed to explore what contributes to technology usefulness, ease of use, learnability, the motivation to use technology, and the satisfaction derived from different types of use to attain different goals. Research may help us to understand why the digital-divide exists and if there is a future possibility to abolish it.

REFERENCES

Abhyankar, K. (2017). *Enhancing engineering education using mobile augmented devices* (Dissertation). Retrieved from Wright State University Dissertation #1767: https://corescholar.libraries.wright.edu/etd_all/1767/

AMC Network Entertainment. (2010). *Mad Men*. Retrieved September 28, 2018 from https://www.amc.com/shows/mad-men

Blumler, J. G., & Katz, E. (1974). *The uses of mass communications: Current perspectives on gratifications research.* Beverly Hills, CA: Sage Publications, Inc.

Bowman, N. D., Westerman, D. K., & Claus, C. J. (2012). How demanding is social media: Understanding social media diets as a function of perceived costs and benefits–A rational actor perspective. *Computers in Human Behavior, 28*(6), 2298–2305. doi:10.1016/j.chb.2012.06.037

Cayola, L., & Macías, J. A. (2018). Systematic guidance on usability methods in user-centered software development. *Information and Software Technology, 97*, 163–175. doi:10.1016/j.infsof.2018.01.010

Davis, F. D. (1989). Perceived usefulness, perceived ease of use, and user acceptance of information technology. *Management Information Systems Quarterly, 13*(3), 319–340. doi:10.2307/249008

Deacon, A. (2015). *The truth about Google Fiber and the Digital Divide in Kansas City*. Retrieved July 20, 2018 from http://www.kcdigitaldrive.org/article/the-truth-about-google-fiber-and-the-digital-divide-in-kansas-city/

Elliott, L. J., & Polyakova, V. (2014). Beyond Facebook: The generalization of social networking site measures. *Computers in Human Behavior, 33*, 163–170. doi:10.1016/j.chb.2014.01.023

Feeney, L. (2016). *Why the poor face a higher cost of banking*. Retrieved September 26, 2018 from https://www.pbs.org/newshour/nation/why-the-poor-face-a-higher-cost-of-banking

Fjord, C. L. (2011). *The design genius of Steve Jobs*. Retrieved July 29, 2018 from https://gigaom.com/2011/10/06/christian-lindholm-on-steve-jobs/

Friemel, T. N. (2016). The digital divide has grown old: Determinants of a digital divide among seniors. *New Media & Society, 18*(2), 313–331. doi:10.1177/1461444814538648

Garrett, P., Brown, C. A., Hart-Hester, S., Hamadain, E., Dixon, C., Pierce, W., & Rudman, W. J. (2006). Identifying barriers to the adoption of new technology in rural hospitals: A case report. *Perspectives in Health Information Management, 3*(9), 1–11. PMID:18066367

Goncalves, G., Oliveira, T., & Cruz-Jesus, F. (2018). Understanding individual-level digital divide: Evidence of an African country. *Computers in Human Behavior, 87*, 276–291. doi:10.1016/j.chb.2018.05.039

Interaction Design Foundation. (2015). *What is the difference between interaction design and UX design?* Retrieved September 28, 2018 from https://www.interaction-design.org/literature/article/what-is-the-difference-between-interaction-design-and-ux-design

Jacobson, L. (1995). *Bank failure: The financial marginalization of the poor*. Retrieved September 26, 2018 http://prospect.org/article/bank-failure-financial-marginalization-poor

Leaning, M. (2017). *Media and information literacy: An integrated approach for the 21st century*. Cambridge, MA: Chandos Publishing. doi:10.1016/B978-0-08-100170-7.00001-9

Lee, H., Lee, S. H., & Choi, J. A. (2016). Redefining digital poverty: A study on target changes of the digital divide survey for disabilities, low-income and elders. *Journal of Digital Convergence, 14*(3), 1–12. doi:10.14400/JDC.2016.14.3.1

Mangalindan, J. P. (2014). *How third-world tech can help the U.S.* Retrieved July 22, 2018 from http://fortune.com/2014/09/12/how-third-world-tech-can-help-the-u-s/

Maslow, A. H. (1943). A theory of human motivation. *Psychological Review, 50*(4), 370–396. doi:10.1037/h0054346

Morozov, E. (2012). *The net delusion: The dark side of internet freedom.* Public Affairs.

Mumporeze, N., & Prieler, M. (2017). Gender digital divide in Rwanda: A qualitative analysis of socioeconomic factors. *Telematics and Informatics, 34*(7), 1285–1293. doi:10.1016/j.tele.2017.05.014

Nielsen, J. (2006). *Digital divide: The 3 stages.* Retrieved July 20, 2018 from https://www.nngroup.com/articles/digital-divide-the-three-stages/

Nishijima, M., Ivanauskas, T. M., & Sarti, F. M. (2017). Evolution and determinants of digital divide in Brazil (2005–2013). *Telecommunications Policy, 41*(1), 12–24. doi:10.1016/j.telpol.2016.10.004

Norman, D. (2013). *The design of everyday things: Revised and expanded edition.* Philadelphia, PA: Basic Books.

Phua, J., Jin, S. V., & Kim, J. J. (2017). Uses and gratifications of social networking sites for bridging and bonding social capital: A comparison of Facebook, Twitter, Instagram, and Snapchat. *Computers in Human Behavior, 72*, 115–122. doi:10.1016/j.chb.2017.02.041

Poushter, J., Bishop, C., & Chwe, H. (2018). Social media use continues to rise in developing countries but plateaus across developed ones. *Global Attitudes and Trends.* Retrieved July 22, 2018 from http://www.pewglobal.org/2018/06/19/social-media-use-continues-to-rise-in-developing-countries-but-plateaus-across-developed-ones/

Rennie, E. (2018). Policy experiments and the digital divide: Understanding the context of internet adoption in remote Aboriginal communities. In M. Dezuanni, M. Foth, K. Mallan, & H. Hughes (Eds.), *Digital Participation through Social Living Labs* (pp. 299–313). Cambridge, MA: Chandos Publishing. doi:10.1016/B978-0-08-102059-3.00016-2

Rogers, K. (2017). *Kansas City was first to embrace Google Fiber, now Its broadband future Is 'TBD'.* Retrieved July 20, 2018 from https://motherboard.vice.com/en_us/article/xwwmp3/kansas-city-was-first-to-embrace-google-fiber-now-its-broadband-future-is-tbd

Rothacker, R. (2015). *Google Fiber: Kansas City offers Charlotte 'Digital Divide' lessons*. Retrieved July 22, 2018 from https://www.thecharlotteobserver.com/news/business/article13806530.html

Saffer, D. (2010). *Designing for interaction* (2nd ed.). San Francisco, CA: New Riders Book.

Sisson, P. (2017). *Kansas City wants to be the city of the future; Has Google helped it get there?* Retrieved July 20, 2018 from https://www.curbed.com/2017/1/17/14298148/kansas-city-google-fiber-tech-hub

Spitzer, B., Stanhope, J., Scott, M., Ries, T., Moore, M., McKenzie, B., . . . Elliott, L. J. (2016). *Digital Inclusion App User Testing*. Paper presented to Code for Kansas City, Kansas City, MO.

Statista. (2018). *Number of available apps in the Apple App Store from July 2008 to January 2017*. Retrieved September 23, 2018 from https://www.statista.com/statistics/263795/number-of-available-apps-in-the-apple-app-store/#0

Sullivan, B. (2013). Poverty in America: Millions of families too broke for bank accounts. *NBC News*. Retrieved September 26, 2018 from https://www.nbcnews.com/feature/in-plain-sight/poverty-america-millions-families-too-broke-bank-accounts-v17840373

Suwana, F., & Lily. (2017). Empowering Indonesian women through building digital media literacy. *Kasetsart Journal of Social Sciences*, *38*(3), 212–217. doi:10.1016/j.kjss.2016.10.004

Tirado-Morueta, R., Aguaded-Gómez, J. I., & Hernando-Gómez, Á. (in press). The socio-demographic divide in Internet usage moderated by digital literacy support. *Technology in Society*.

Van Deursen, A. J. A. M., & Van Dijk, J. A. G. M. (2010). Measuring internet skills. *International Journal of Human-Computer Interaction*, *26*(10), 891–916. doi:10.1080/10447318.2010.496338

Van Deursen, A. J. A. M., & Van Dijk, J. A. G. M. (2014). The digital divide shifts to differences in usage. *New Media & Society*, *16*(3), 507–526. doi:10.1177/1461444813487959

Van Dijk, J. A. (2005). *The deepening divide: Inequality in the information society*. Thousand Oaks, CA: Sage Publications.

Van Dijk, J. A. (2006). Digital divide research, achievements and shortcomings. *Poetics, 34*(4-5), 221–235. doi:10.1016/j.poetic.2006.05.004

Venkatesh, V., Thong, J. Y., Chan, F. K., Hu, P. J. H., & Brown, S. A. (2011). Extending the two-stage information systems continuance model: Incorporating UTAUT predictors and the role of context. *Information Systems Journal, 21*(6), 527–555. doi:10.1111/j.1365-2575.2011.00373.x

Vigdor, J. L., Ladd, H. F., & Martinez, E. (2014). Scaling the digital divide: Home computer technology and student achievement. *Economic Inquiry, 52*(3), 1103–1119. doi:10.1111/ecin.12089

Wamuyu, P. K. (2017). Bridging the digital divide among low income urban communities leveraging use of community technology centers. *Telematics and Informatics, 34*(8), 1709–1720. doi:10.1016/j.tele.2017.08.004

Wesolko, D. (2016). *Peter Morville's user experience honeycomb.* Retrieved September 26, 2018 from https://medium.com/@danewesolko/peter-morvilles-user-experience-honeycomb-904c383b6886

Wohlsen, M. (2012). *Google Fiber splits along Kansas City's digital divide.* Retrieved July 22, 2018, from https://www.wired.com/2012/09/google-fiber-digital-divide

Chapter 10
Design the Technological Society for an Aging Population

Anne Collins McLaughlin
North Carolina State University, USA

Makenzie Pryor
North Carolina State University, USA

Jing Feng
North Carolina State University, USA

ABSTRACT

Inclusivity of design for an aging population will be one of the most critical problems to address in the near and far future. With advancing age comes new needs, goals, and unique issues – all of which may be ameliorated through well-designed systems and technologies. But what does it mean to be "well-designed"? In this chapter, the authors discuss the background research supporting design principles that take into account age-related changes in cognition, movement, and behavior. These are then applied in a worked example of a "car of the future," partly constructed with current technologies, but also imagining near and far future advances. They conclude with a discussion of how to employ these principles in practice, both when designing new and cutting-edge technologies from the ground-up and revising systems and technologies already in place.

DOI: 10.4018/978-1-5225-7949-6.ch010

INTRODUCTION

An Aging World Population

The need for usable designs for older adults is not new, but it is becoming an increasingly pressing concern. In the U.S., the number of persons over sixty-five will double by 2060. Percentage-wise, their impact on future society will be even larger: fewer children being born combined with increased longevity will make the 'pyramid' of age groups a 'pillar' for the first time in human history (United States Census Bureau, 2018). Again, by 2060, the number of older adults will rise from 15% of the population to 24% (Population Reference Bureau, 2016). The distribution of older persons will not be even - currently and in the future, rural areas will have a disproportionate amount of older residents (Population Reference Bureau, 2016). While the current and near future cohorts of older adults will be the most well-educated the world has seen, they will also likely be working for longer in jobs that require adapting to the use of new technology (Population Reference Bureau, 2016).

At the individual level there will be a diversity of housing in the future, with some older adults living alone or with a spouse, others in group homes and independent care facilities, and others in facilities that provide high levels of care. Projections are for a 75% rise in the need for nursing home care (Population Reference Bureau, 2016). Many of these older persons will be facing age-related changes while also serving as the caretaker of another - adding to their physical and mental burden. It is likely no surprise that, when asked how they would prefer to live, most older adults desire independence: independence of daily activity, independance with transportation, and independance to engage socially (Blieszner & Roberto, 2012; Hillcoat-Nallétamby, 2014). It should be the goal of system and technology design to support their desire for independence, health, and their economic livelihoods.

Multiple research centers are focused on successful aging with the help of technology and aging with a disability. These include the Institute for People and Technology at the Georgia Institute of Technology, Atlanta, GA (iPaT), the multi-institution Center for Research and Education on Aging and Technology Enhancement ("CREATE overview", 2018), and the Center on Aging at the University of Iowa, to name a few. These researchers and others have made advances across a spectrum of issues connected to aging, from the privacy expectations older persons have of new technologies (Caine, Šabanović, & Carter, 2012), to seamless connections between older adults and their families or caregivers (Liu, Stroulia, Nikolaidis, Miguel-Cruz, & Rios Rincon, 2016), to "technology coaches" that can provide just-in-time training and feedback for older adults using new helpful technologies (Rogers, Essa, & Fisk, 2007).

In sum, the time is coming when older adults will comprise a larger and larger segment of society. Developing technologies that can help this age cohort live independently, maintain social relationships, and develop their legacies is an important achievement that will improve lives, but also society as a whole.

BACKGROUND

A Time of Capability and Limitation: Three Principles of Inclusivity

Aging is not lost youth but a new stage of opportunity and strength. (Betty Friedan)

It's common to see aging discussed as a 'problem,' or solely in terms of disability, dependance, and frailty. These stereotypes can be seen in language such as "the elderly" or worse, "the frail elderly." It is important to frame inclusivity of design for older adults in terms of their *capabilities* as well as potential limitations, both situated within a wide range of individual differences. This introduces the first principle of inclusive thinking about age: change across the lifespan is related to aging, not determined by it. As the old saying goes, "age is just a number," and while it may be a number that predicts potential declines, those declines are not universal.

The second principle of inclusivity is to consider age-related changes as part of a human system, not stand alone "facts" about age. The changes that can occur with aging span more than physical and cognitive decline, including changes to desired social interactions, goals, and knowledge. For example, one of the most accepted theories of social aging is socioemotional selectivity theory (Carstensen, Isaacowitz, & Charles, 1999), the idea that as people reach the end of any life-stage, they tend to seek closer connections to others whom they already know rather than new connections with strangers. Connected to this preference is another for positive emotional states (Mather & Carstensen, 2005), where there is a tendency to seek out positive emotions over negative ones in media, relationships, and daily experiences. With this comes an interesting memory bias - older adults show better memory for positive stimuli than for negative ones (Mather & Carstensen, 2005). They also tend to devote more attention to positive stimuli, such as an approachable face compared to an angry one, while younger people show the opposite tendency (Mather and Carstensen, 2003; Isaacowitz et al., 2006). There are numerous reviews of these effects (e.g., Carstensen, Mikels, & Mather, 2006), but the take-home message is that social desires and emotional motivations must be taken into account when designing for older adults, and that in some cases designs built for a younger audience will be diametrically opposed to older adult tendencies and desires. Following guidelines for older adult friendly design that considers vision and hearing can only achieve so much - each product is part of a larger system, and considering the entirety of the system will be crucial to supporting successful aging.

The last principle of design inclusivity is not to treat older adults as a monolith. Though older persons may have predictable age-related change as a *group,* each person is an individual on their own trajectory of the lifecourse. Heterogeneity of cognitive ability increases with age (Ardila, 2007). A sample of persons over age 65 will show a wide range of cognitive and physical ability, while a sample of twenty-year olds will be much narrower. Hertzog et al. published a paper showing this variability of change across the lifespan and detailing the many factors that moderate and mediate age-related declines in ability (2008). Life factors that predicted higher preservation of cognitive ability included: living a socially engaged life, physical activity, positive attitudes/beliefs, and a lack of chronic psychological stress. However, as these factors were mostly correlational, it is difficult to say whether they contributed to a later or shallower decline in fluid ability or whether they were the result of a person destined to have a later or shallower decline in ability. The conclusions Hertzog, et al. drew from these data were that each person has a zone of proximal development across the lifespan. Actions and inactions, environment and biology, all alter the course of an individual's' cognitive ability within that zone. Nurturing the factors that correlate with a higher trajectory should be the goal of systems designed for older adults.

Establishing that older adults are not a monolith is another way of noting that stereotypes of aging should not be applied in design. In addition to being incorrect, stereotypes can also impact performance. For example, older adults to show worse performance on memory tests when they believe they are being stereotyped for their age (Hess, Auman, Colcombe, & Rahhal, 2003). Table 1 provides a short list of stereotypes of older adults' paired with the evidence that not only are they not true, in some cases older adults' trend in the opposite direction.

ADOPTION AND USE OF TECHNOLOGY

Old people are just regular people who happen to be old. (Ceridwen Dovey, 2015)

Though there are principles of designing for older adults as a whole, it is useful to situate those data within illustrative anecdotes. These narratives were collected in the literature via studies of technology adoption and technology disuse. They are useful in that they are reminders than 1) each older person is an individual, with rational desires and means of achieving those desires and 2) that technologies meant to ameliorate age-related declines in sensation, cognition, and movement must also be perceived as more beneficial than current alternatives. As Melenhorst, et al.

Table 1. Stereotypes of aging and their refutation

Stereotypes of Aging	Evidence against Stereotype
Cognition is in decline	Knowledge and similar abilities continue to increase into much older ages (Horn & Cattell, 1967)
Older adults are slow	Simple reaction time is little impacted by age, though choice reaction time does tend to slow
Older adults are lonely and depressed	Adults over 65 show lower rates of depression than adults at any other life stage (Hasin, Goodwin, Stinson, & Grant, 2005)
Older adults cannot learn new things	There are many types of learning unimpacted by age (Giraudeau et al., 2014) and studies showing older adults might just take longer to learn (Scialfa, Jenkins, Hamaluk, & Skaloud, 2000; Ho & Scialfa, 2002)
Older adults do not want to use new technology	Older adults are adopting new technologies (Anderson & Perrin, 2017), provided they perceive a benefit for the change (Melenhorst, Rogers, & Bouwhuis, 2006; Mitzner, et al., 2014)
Older adults are not competitive	Older adults value accomplishment and challenge in their leisure activities (Tyree & McLaughlin, 2016)
Older adults are not creative	Older adults solve some problems more efficiently than younger adults and tailor strategies to fit the problem (Blanchard-Fields, 2007)

wrote, "...the expectation of benefit is imperative to motivate innovation: People need an incentive to consider expending effort to make a change. The lack of benefit is sufficient to prevent people from trying something new" (2006). For example, regarding the use of hearing aids:

I visited my daughter and she said 'mom do you realize that sometimes when you had your back to them they were talking to you and you didn't hear them' ...and that really hit me...when it comes to being present for those that you love and when there's a hearing aid makes a difference... you wear the hearing aids, no matter how sensitive you are about it.

For many, even such a long-standing technology as a hearing aid comes with a cost:

I'm working with a senior who has lost her hearing aid three times ...she thinks they look ugly, so she puts them in Kleenex... and of course, the staff come in they clear away the Kleenex... so we actually made a box for her to put her hearing aids in and decorated and kind of celebrated it rather than trying to hide it, and now it's part of the conversation... she 'll laugh about it now.

These anecdotes are important to understanding why or why not older adults adopt new technologies. A well accepted model for predicting technology adoption is the Technology Adoption Model (TAM) (Davis, 1989), which has seen several iterations since its original inception (e.g., Venkatesh & Davis, 2000; Venkatesh, Morris, Davis, & Davis, 2003; Venkatesh & Bala, 2008). In TAM, the most important predictors of adoption are perceived usefulness of the technology and perceived ease of use. In 2010, Mitzner et al. added nuance to the idea of perceived usefulness in a large scale study of a diverse group of older adults. In their findings, older persons were already likely to use diverse forms of technology, going against many stereotypes of aging (Mitzner et al., 2010). Further, they broke down the idea of perceived usefulness into parts: older adults sought convenience, support for activities, and specific features from new technologies (Mitzner et al., 2010). In sum, benefits dominated cost when older adults are considering technology adoption, echoing earlier findings by Melenhorst, et al. (2006). Lack of benefit can be a strong demotivator for learning and use. For example, when considering adding a computer to the home, one narrative from an older user was:

Well, having inherited this machine which sits on our desk, up in our den, I've asked myself many times, and my wife, 'What are we going to do with it now that we've got it?' We're not interested in playing games on the wretched thing. The Internet doesn't interest me too much because, you know, there's the problems of the thing, and I'd hate to get involved in that. There may be the odd occasion when I'd want to look something up on the Internet.... As for personal records and financial activities and whatever, I mean it's on the back of a notebook. [That] is all I need.

In sum, designers should consider what benefit a new product or changed product gives to an older user beyond what is currently available. If the benefit is not clear, the technology is unlikely to be adopted.

A MISMATCH OF DESIGNER AND END USER

Usable, safe, and enjoyable design is hard to accomplish. Creating designs that are usable, safe, and enjoyable for others unlike oneself is even more challenging. This was an impetus to create the field human factors, back when engineering needs ruled design. For example, according to efficient engineering principles, the controls and displays in early aviation were arranged according to the most efficient wiring and location of mechanical parts (Fitts & Jones, 1947a; Fitts & Jones, 1947b). It did not take long for it to become obvious that this was a poor way to arrange controls that would be used by a human (Fitts & Jones, 1947b). This same lesson has been re-learned repeatedly throughout the decades - the most widely shown example being the rows and rows of identical switches neatly arranged in an unusable (especially in an emergency) nuclear power plant control room from the 1970s (Malone et al., 1980).

There can still be a mismatch between the expectations and knowledge in the mind of the designer and that of the end user. The principle applied in human factors research is to "know the user," and to do that, scientists and practitioners employ many tools. These include a needs analysis, where data is collected on what the user desires to accomplish (Lindgaard et al., 2006), and usability testing, where a user interacts with mock-ups or prototypes to show how they interpret the controls and displays (Nielsen, 1994). Unfortunately, these simple steps are often skipped in the design process and, even when they are included, there can be little consideration of including older users in these studies. As was mentioned earlier, heterogeneity of ability increases with age, and thus a sample of older persons is needed to truly test any new technology.

One avenue is to help the designers better understand their end users by literally experiencing their world (and experiencing the new technology similarly). This has been done by creating "aging suits" that mimic the age-related sensory changes faced by many older adults. For example, as will be discussed in detail further in this chapter, older adults can experience a yellowing of the lens of the eye, changing their perception of other colors, and this can be mimicked with yellow glasses. Joint mobility may be impaired by arthritis, and the suit can be made so that joint movements are limited (albeit without the pain associated with arthritis). Much like personas (Aquino, Vilela, & Filgueiras, 2005), these suits help designers focus on and better understand the needs of their users through the first stages of the design process.

Aging suits have been used in the design of automobiles to accommodate older drivers, but there are two important caveats that should go along with use of this method: 1) It is not a substitute for user testing with actual older users and 2) Thus far, these suits are limited to helping designers experience the physical changes that can come with age, but not the cognitive ones (e.g., the limits of attention and spatial cognition).

In sum, designing products that work well for older adults is a worthy goal, but this goal must be pursued with good methods, tools, and testing of representative users. The first step in a user-centered design process is to "know the user." Older users are a wide spectrum of individuals, each with their own needs and abilities. The following section summarizes the literature on age-related change as it relates to designing for an older population. By understanding age-related change in general, designers can match this knowledge with the individual differences they will see in their own users. This knowledge, combined with human factors methods such as task analysis, prototyping, and iterative design with usability testing, will support older adult independence and personal growth far into the future.

REVIEW OF AGE-RELATED CHANGE IN ABILITY

Cognition

Changes in cognition are less visibly apparent than changes to senses like vision or hearing, which are often accompanied by aids such as glasses or hearing aids support the senses. But cognition can be supported by well-planned designs. Designers can take into account the abilities that are preserved with age and keep in mind the abilities that are not to create systems that are less cognitively demanding for all users.

Age-Related Changes in Cognition

Memory decline is a common age-related concern. However, the extent of memory decline can vary between individuals. Memory decline can also combine with other age-related problems, in the case of an older person with many medications to manage different health conditions who must remember when to take each medication every day, sometimes multiple times a day. In this example, the older person relies on two types of memory which tend to decline with age: recall of episodic memory, retrieval of information about past experiences (Nyberg, Bäckman, Erngrund, Olofsson, & Nilsson, 1996), and prospective memory, remembering an event in the future (Schnitzspahn, Stahl, Zeintl, Kaller, & Kliegel, 2013).

Fluid intelligence, which describes the ability to process new information and interact with it, also tends to decline with age (Horn & Cattell, 1967; Bugg, Zook, DeLosh, Davalos, & Davis, 2006). Components of executive function also decline with age, such as interference resistance (Wecker, Kramer, Wisniewski, Delis, & Kaplan, 2000) and some measures of problem-solving (Cornelius & Caspi, 1987). Older adults also tend to perform worse on complex attentional tasks such as those that assess divided attention or task-switching (Verhaeghen & Cerella, 2002).

Preserved Cognition

Crystalized intelligence, which is based on acquired knowledge and skills, remains stable with age and may even improve (Horn & Cattell, 1967). An example is language ability, which is well-practiced throughout life, and includes vocabulary growth with age (Hartshorne & Germine, 2015). Additionally, some types of problem-solving which rely on acquired knowledge and experience, such as that seen in older chess players who matched the problem-solving abilities of younger players (Charness, 1981). A review of problem-solving and aging literature also found that when everyday problem-solving is measured based on diversity of solutions, older adults also perform as well as younger adults (Mienaltowski, 2013). Procedural memory, like remembering how to ride a bicycle, also tends to remain stable with age (Churchill, Stanis, Press, Kushelev, & Greenough, 2003).

In general, cognitive abilities that are based on experience tend to remain consistent or even improve with age. Designs for older adults that make use of the user's previous experiences can benefit older users.

Vision

From augmented reality advertisements such as the Pepsi MAX Unbelievable Bus Shelter, which showed bus shelter patrons a live video feed of the area around the shelter augmented by unbelievable things like flying saucers, to heads-up displays (HUDs) that display information to drivers in vehicles, developers are finding new applications and new ways to reach more users. However, as these technologies are implemented in more ways, considerations must be made for how people with different visual abilities interact with them.

As mentioned earlier in this chapter, the aging population is growing, and will only continue to increase (Population Reference Bureau, 2016). Changes to vision are normal parts of the aging process and can impact many aspects of everyday life. These changes include acuity (Gittings & Fozard, 1986), contrast sensitivity (Elliot, 1987), and sometimes pathological conditions such as cataracts (National Eye Institute, 2018a) and glaucoma (National Eye Institute, 2018b). However, there are abilities connected to vision that may not change with age, such as the visual search of an area for an attentionally-attractive cue and visual search by experts within the area of their expertise. These preserved capabilities can be capitalized on by designers.

Age-Related Visual Limitations

One common age-related change is in visual acuity, specifically presbyopia (farsightedness). Presbyopia occurs as the lens in the eye loses elasticity. Decreased lens elasticity leads to decreased ability to focus, which can result in a need for bifocal glasses or contact lenses. Another common visual change can come from cataracts, the clouding of the lens. The growth and removal of cataracts can cause changes in vision due to the clouding and due to the removal and replacement of the clouded lens. A less well-known but still common age-related change is to contrast sensitivity, which affects vision in lower lighting conditions and in lower contrast environments, such as at night or in glare or fog. Last, the lens in the eye tends to yellow as it loses flexibility, changing perception of colors (particularly distinguishing between blues and greens).

These common visual impairments can change interactions with multiple technologies, from smartphone use to e-book readers, to the text on buttons for electronics such as media players and remote controls. Keeping track of glasses, learning to use accessibility software, and other solutions all add a layer of cognitive load and time commitment to what should be simple tasks. These impairments may change daily behaviors, such as avoiding driving at night, or other activities in low lighting conditions.

Other age-related visual limitations are related to changes in cognition, rather than physical changes to the eye. For example, visual processing speed often slows with age, where an older person needs more time to detect and respond to visual stimuli. Slowed visual processing has been linked to more issues for older adults with detecting a change in the environment (Costello, Madden, Mitroff, & Whiting, 2010), though it is worth stating that younger adults are also poor at change detection (Rensink, 2005). This potential for slowed processing shows up in studies of visual search, where older adults tend to locate targets more slowly in a cluttered field, and are more affected by clutter (i.e., number of distractors) than younger adults (Feng, Craik, Levine, Moreno, Naglie, & Choi, 2017; McPhee, Scialfa, Dennis, Ho, & Caird, 2004).

Preserved Visual Capabilities

When designing for age-related changes in vision, it is as important to note what is preserved as it is what may change to greater or lesser degrees. Preserved visual ability can be leveraged to create interfaces and designs that work for people across the lifespan. Many of these preserved visual capabilities crossover with preserved cognitive abilities.

Pre-attentive visual search is the search for a single characteristic appearing in a set (Treisman & Gelade, 1980). It is called pre-attentive because it requires little to no processing or attention to notice the characteristic. Visual characteristics shown to be pre-attentive include: color, size, shape, intersection, and curvature (Wolfe & Horowitz, 2014; Figure 1).

Interfaces and displays can use these characteristics to make important information or controls "pop out" from the background for users across the lifespan (Burton-Danner, Owsley, & Jackson, 2001; Müller-Oehring, Shulte, Rohlfing, Pfefferbaum, & Sullivan, 2013).

A second preserved visual/cognitive ability is knowledge-based visual search. A knowledge-based visual search is guided by prior experience or knowledge, such as a radiologist might use with an x-ray, an architect might use on a blueprint, or a layperson might use with a well-known remote control. Looking for the targets in these kinds of searches does not differ for older persons, meaning that a design that takes advantage of transfer of previous experience and knowledge can be easily used. For example, a simple convention can be a number pad on a phone or keyboard.

227

Figure 1. Example of a visual search task by shape. The square "pops out" of the display with little to no attentional processing required

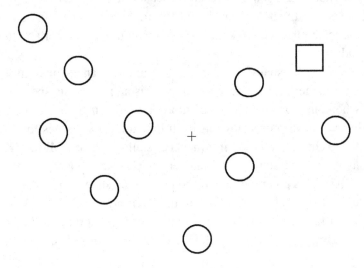

Numbers are organized in a three-by-three square, with "1" at the top left, and "0" in a separate row at the bottom. A virtual keypad or interface that also uses this convention makes it easier for a user to find a particular number.

Similar to the use of previous knowledge in visual search, previous knowledge can help those who have experienced age-related changes in vision. For example, though decreased contrast sensitivity impairs reading, it does not impair the reading of "high expectation" words (Mitzner & Rogers, 2006). When older adults were show words they expected to see in a particular context at low contrast, they were able to read them as easily as younger adults. Thus, the use of more common language and expected verbiage can help to overcome age-related declines in reading - this may be especially applicable for road signs.

Hearing

Age-Related Changes in Hearing

Age-related changes in hearing are often related to other age-related issues like cardiovascular disease or noise exposure (Agrawal, Platz, & Niparko, 2008). For example, older adults who were exposed to loud concerts, heavy machinery, or gunshots (e.g., hunters) tend to show much greater hearing impairments than older adults who were not exposed. However, in general, the type of hearing loss associated with age is predictable: people lose access to the highest and lowest tones on the spectrum of sound. Although there have been great improvements in audio technology, it is important to note that many electronic methods of transferring sound (cell phones, recordings, compressed audio, computerized voices) operate across a range that includes the tones frequently lost as people age.

Auditory displays are increasingly common, with the use of GPS navigation systems, smart speakers in the home, and personal voice assistants (e.g., Siri). In a 2011 review, Nees and Walker specified that auditory displays need three crucial qualities: detectability, discriminability, and identifiability. To be detectable, the sounds or voice must be loud enough to be heard, but not so loud as to damage, strain, or annoy the older user. For example, one study found loud alarms to startle the user to the point that they would make inaccurate decisions (Blumenthal, Noto, Fox, & Franklin, 2006). To be discriminable, the signals or sounds must be different enough from each other to stand out. For a voice to be discriminable, the words must be clear and differentiable, but suited to the language they are spoken in (e.g., in the English language, speakers pronounce "have to" as "hafta" in some cases: I hafta fish vs. I have two fish). Last, the auditory display must be identifiable. This requirement is a bridge between the importance of hearing and cognition. For example, if a GPS is giving commands, are the sentences in an order that facilitates interpretation (Baldwin, 2012)? Do the words make sense in sentences and are those sentences simple and clear? Just as with the preserved visual abilities, such as reading high expectancy words, older adults are best able to hear high expectancy audio (Stewart & Wingfield, 2009). This is not to say that information needs to be "dumbed down" for older adults, or that auditory interfaces need to use "elderspeak". Not only has elderspeak been shown to negatively impact older adults (Williams, Herman, Gajweski, & Wilson, 2010), but many studies have found that improvements in auditory displays for older adults also improves the performance of younger adults (Baldwin, 2012).

Preserved Hearing

As previously discussed, language abilities are preserved with aging, and can even improve as in the case of vocabulary expansion. Although changes to hearing will occur due to environmental conditions and due to aging, language abilities remain consistent as long as older adults are able to hear. Although hearing ability changes with age, the frequencies that are lost tend to be higher pitches and lower pitches, outside the range of the human voice (Brant & Fozard, 1990; Liu & Yan, 2007). Speech comprehension and language ability are often maintained in aging, but other factors can make comprehension more difficult for older adults, such as background noise or multitasking (Tun, Williams, Small, & Hafter, 2012).

Systems should take care to minimize distraction, multitasking, and noise to best support older adults' preserved hearing and language abilities. Changes in hearing can also be supported by devices such as hearing aids. Systems that involve auditory information, or equipment such as headphones, should consider designs that can accommodate hearing aids.

Movement/Haptics

Age-Related Changes in Movement and Touch

Control of movements changes with age at both a fine and a gross level. Fine motor control, such as texting or using cell phones with small screens, often decreases in age. A common solution to this is to provide older adults with larger buttons can support older users. As previously discussed, reaction time also tends to decrease in older adults (Deary & Der, 2005; Ratcliff, Spieler, & McKoon, 2000ref), along with decrease in processing speed (Salthouse, 1996). This can also lead to slower initiation of movements compared to younger adults (Ketcham & Stelmach, 2004).

Balance ability also decreases with age due to general changes in sensory ability, such as decrease in visual processing speed (Owsley & McGwin, 2004) and changes to movement control (Konrad, Girardi, & Helfert, 1999). Changes to balance can increase fall risks in older adults, which can lead to serious injury. Interventions to assist with balance are being explored, including technologies like virtual reality. A recent meta-analysis that examined fall risk in older adults using virtual reality games as an intervention found that older adults who used a virtual reality game showed improvements on balance measures and fear of falling compared to older adults with no intervention (Neri et al., 2017).

Tactile perception is impacted by changes in the skin that occur with aging. Detecting types of material based on the surface sensation was reduced in older adults compared to younger adults (Norman et al., 2016), and older adults required higher thresholds for vibration detection (Stuart, Turman, Shaw, Walsh, & Nguyen, 2003; Amaied, Vargiolu, Bergheau, & Zahouani, 2015). These changes can impact the use of technologies that involve tactile feedback. For instance, a recent study assessed the usefulness of a vibrotactile wristband to communicate when a road was safe for pedestrian crossing, and found that the wristband was useful for reducing the number of unsafe crossing decisions made by both younger and older adults (Cœugnet et al., 2017). However, while the study found that older adults experienced less collisions in a simulator while using the wristband than when not, the study also found that participants in all age groups only responded correctly to the wristband about half the time (Cœugnet et al., 2017). Although the vibrations may not have been high enough for detection even for younger adults, this raises important questions for using haptic feedback for older adults. How perceptible is the haptic feedback to an older person, and how much would the wristband have to vibrate to be detectable for an older person at all times given the differences in detection that occur with age? This wristband is an example of a device that could help older adults, but must be tested with older users.

Preserved Movement Control and Touch

Some touch sensitivity is preserved in the fingertips, such as vibration detection (Stuart, Turman, Shaw, Walsh, & Nguyen, 2003). Additionally, planned movements to targets remain consistent with age, even when targets are small (Rogers, Fisk, McLaughlin, & Pak, 2005).

In summary, there are a number of age-related changes in ability. Younger persons also have individual differences in ability and design for older adults means considering a wider spectrum of ability along with more variability present in the population. Benton Underwood (1974) called individual differences a "crucible for testing theory," meaning that, once a theory of cognition were posited, finding people of various ability levels and observing how those levels did or did not conform to the predictions of the theory would be a true test of the limits of that theory. The same is true of application - a usable design for younger adults can be tested in the "crucible" of age-related differences in ability to see where the design falls short and where the principles of design hold true for older users. An understanding of the basic sensory and cognitive changes that tend to come with age should promote the best applications of design principles for an older user population.

SOLUTIONS AND RECOMMENDATIONS: CAR OF THE FUTURE

Mobility is one of the most desired components of successful aging, playing a part in older adults' functional lives, social lives, and is often a key to maintaining independence. Loss of mobility reduces an older adult's access to physician visits, seeing friends, and active engagement in employment and volunteering, thus consequently leads to impaired feeling of autonomy, prestige, and self-esteem (Ellaway et al., 2003; Steg, 2005).

In the United States, mobility in all but the largest cities requires access to a car, given the lack of alternative transportation means. In an analysis of the adequacy of public transit service for 241 metropolitan areas with a population of 65,000 or more (DeGood, 2011), in the year of 2000, more than 11.5 million older adults in the US experience deficiency in the access to public transit service. During the year of this analysis, it was projected that more than 15.5 million older adults in the US would have poor access to public transit in 15 years and this number would likely continue to grow until well beyond 2030 given the increasing aging population. As the primary method of transportation for many adults (Dobbs et al., 2002), being able to drive a car not only means mobility but is also a symbol of personal freedom and independence (Dickerson et al., 2007).

Thus, one critical issue that will impact science, technology, and future society will be allowing the large percentage of older adults to maintain their mobility (Rosenbloom, 2009). There are many potential avenues to pursue, from public transportation, to the rideshare economy, but this chapter provide a vision of a future much like today, with individuals owning and using vehicles for personal transportation. The worked example details the current, upcoming, and far future advances expected in personal automobiles. Even in this single technology, designers must consider all aspects of age-related changes in vision, hearing, cognition, and movement. After all, automobiles provide transportation but also communication, entertainment, navigation, new and cutting edge technologies such as heads-up displays, automation, and haptic feedback. Each of these technologies requires an understanding of age-related change, but also an understanding (and testing) of how the technologies and users interact as a system. Last, the chapter highlights how designers may take advantage of the capabilities that tend to be preserved or even grow at older ages.

Automobile Communication/Entertainment Technologies

New technologies in vehicles are being added to create a safer and more enjoyable driving experience. For example, auditory interfaces can make interacting with an in-vehicle radio or music player safer than using physical controls. However, considerations must be made for older adults using these technologies.

The Benefits of Usable Systems for Older Drivers

With more than 40 million older drivers on the road and growing, they are powerful segment of the population (Federal Highway Administration, 2016). Even as far back as 2003, studies reported almost 90% of older Americans used personal vehicles (Collia et al., 2003). Older adults are not more likely to be in an automobile crash per capita than younger adults, however older drivers do experience higher crash risks per 100 million miles driven (Tefft, 2017). Unfortunately, accident statistics do support this group as one that, if they are in an accident, they are more likely to be severely hurt or killed (Centers for Disease Control and Prevention, 2017; Li, Braver, & Chen, 2003). Thus, the common issues of unexpected events and driver distraction need to be addressed specific to the older population.

As mentioned in the section on technology adoption, the stereotype of older adults avoiding new technologies is unsupported. Older adults appreciate in-car systems similarly to younger adults. A report from the AARP found that older drivers reported seeking technological features when buying new cars, and this includes communication and entertainment technologies (Preddy, 2015). Sixty percent of older adults report using a cell phone while driving (Hill et al., 2017; Brubaker, 2017). It is likely these are high functioning drivers: cell phone use was predicted by the older driver being "younger old", driving frequently, maintaining employment, and rating their own driving skill as high (Hill et al., 2017).

Age-Related Usability Issues With In-Car Communication Technologies

As mentioned before, the issues of in-car communication and entertainment systems are not unique to older users, but their negative effects may be exacerbated for older drivers. All of the age-related sensory changes apply to use of these technologies, from visual search and focus on a displayed map or phone screen to interacting with "hands free" auditory interfaces, to the need to remember wake words and the syntax needed for voice interaction with these systems. Another example could be in attempting to quickly read text on an in-vehicle display while driving, which for an older adult may require switching between glasses or shifting the view on bifocal or trifocal glasses (Meyer, 2009). These new technologies may also cause distractions if they are poorly designed, which can create more problems for older adults (Meyer, 2009).

Virtual Reality Simulation and Training

As noted in the literature review of age-related change, many of the preserved skills and abilities for older adults are related to prior experience and learning. Allowing exposure and experience to novel technologies in a safe environment may be helpful to all users, but particularly older users interested in adopting a new technology. Two promising technologies that will allow a simulated experience with automobile displays and controls are virtual and augmented/mixed realities.

The Benefits of Virtual Reality for Older Adults

Virtual reality (VR) offers a way to experience different environments or activities that would otherwise be inaccessible or difficult to accomplish. For instance, in the workplace, VR can be a helpful training tool to familiarize workers with a process before they attempt to use complex or dangerous equipment. In private settings, VR can be an engaging way to play games, or can facilitate therapeutic uses like virtual visits to calming locations or with other people. VR has also been used in rehabilitation therapies with older adults with balance or mobility issues (Neri et al., 2017; Seo et al., 2016; and Rendon et al., 2012).

In the *Car of the Future* example, a use for VR could be in training older persons to interact safely with new car features. A recent app called CarTech VR360 attempts to do just that by providing ways for users to test new features before actually driving a vehicle (National Safety Council, 2017). Driving simulators could also provide a safe way to assess driving performance in older drivers, as opposed to using real vehicles in real traffic (Karthaus & Falkenstein, 2016).

Age-Related Usability Issues for Older VR Users

AR systems may pose challenges for older adults, and because of this, may isolate or exclude older workers if their workplaces adopt these systems. For instance, although most VR headset systems are usable with glasses, the comfort of using such a system with glasses will vary by VR headset, individual, and glasses. Additionally, older adults are more likely to suffer from simulator sickness than younger adults. The controls for these systems can also be confusing, especially if a user is unable to view the controls while wearing the VR headset.

However, VR training and interfaces for older adults are areas historically under-researched. A systematic review in 2016 reported that the studies available were not of high quality and potentially biased toward finding a positive effect on older adult heath via virtual reality (Miller et al., 2016). On top of this potential lack of evidence for VR effectiveness, there is little information on the overall usability and interface design of VR for an older user population. As it is well known that non-VR interfaces should be designed to consider age-related differences, the same research and attention will need to be given to VR interfaces. Some of the most likely issues include: motion sickness, attentional tunneling, and visual perception.

Motion sickness is more common in older adults, and can impact use of technologies. For example, older adults are susceptible to simulator sickness (Brooks et al., 2010) and therefore often drop out of driving simulation studies (Matas, Nettelbeck, & Burns, 2015). Though improvements in virtual reality are allowing a closer match of on-screen motion to actual motion, which will reduce some forms of simulator sickness, the disconnect between personal and screen motion cannot be overcome with technologies that do not involve stimulation of the vestibular system (e.g., simulators that use centrifugal force to mimic the motions being witnessed on-screen). A slow introduction of the simulator experience may ameliorate the sickness response for older adults (Mackrous, Lavalliere, & Teasdale, 2014), and use of motion cues during the experience may support faster recover (Keshavarz, Ramkhalawansingh, Haycock, Shahab, & Campos, 2018)

As discussed in the section on age-related changes in cognition, the attentional system tends to change with age, often meaning events in the visual periphery go unnoticed (Ball, Owsley, & Beard, 1990). VR often depends on a heads-up display, which has the advantage of being able to locate information anywhere in the visual field. However, designers often choose to locate displays in the periphery. Also, although attention is typically paired with focal vision, this is not necessarily the case: when displays are closely clustered, even with one overlaid on the other, either display may go unnoticed if attention is directed to the other display (Neisser & Becklen, 1975; Lewis & Neider, 2016; Crawford & Neal, 2006). The catch-22 for designers may also be that, along with a reduction in attention in general, older persons may experience a reduction in attentional control, meaning that unhelpful or uninformative portions of the display may grab their attention away from the more important task at hand (Hasher & Zacks, 1988). This is true for people of all ages (e.g, the buzz of a text message during driving), but may be exacerbated at older ages. A potential, though relatively unexplored, solution may be to incorporate other modalities than vision in displays expected to require inhibition of information (Guerreiro, Murphy, & Van Gerven, 2010).

Haptic Feedback

Like auditory technology, tactile feedback is a way to provide drivers with information that doesn't conflict with the task of driving. For example, it can be safer to provide drivers with navigation information through haptic feedback rather than visual feedback, which can cause distraction from the road and unsafe conditions for the driver.

Visual processing and physical reaction time are both abilities that tend to decrease with age, but when driving, these abilities are important for keeping the driver safe. One solution is to provide the driver with more information, but there is also a danger of presenting information that conflicts with the task of driving. Haptic feedback presents an opportunity to provide that additional information to drivers in a way that does not disrupt the visual aspects of driving. For instance, haptic feedback can be used to alert a driver to an upcoming hazard, or to cue the driver to make an upcoming turn.

Older adults require a higher threshold of vibration to detect compared to younger adults (Stuart, Turman, Shaw, Walsh, & Nguyen, 2003). As with the case of the wristband meant to help pedestrians make safer street-crossing decisions, proposed uses for vibration feedback in a vehicle are often based on safety. However, if these signals are not detectable to older adults, or even less likely to be detected by older adults, then they are not appropriately safe. A study has been done assessing the impact of vibrotactile cues during navigation on working memory (Eisert & Baldwin, 2014), but no studies have yet examined the impact with older adults.

In sum, VR may be a promising way to introduce new automobile experiences and interfaces to older users. Future designs should explore the size and colors of the VR display, and ways to increase comprehension and visibility (e.g., contrast between the display and the background). Overall, the research on designing these VR experiences and interfaces is lacking. Basic findings from cognitive psychology and research on ameliorating age-related differences through good human factors may be of help, but the field of VR will require its own explorations.

Augmented and Mixed Reality Inside the CAR: Heads-Up Displays

Augmented and mixed reality (AR and MR respectively) are similar to VR in that they display virtual information, but both AR and MR also show information overlaid on the real environment. AR presents virtual information alongside real information, such as how cartoon creatures are displayed in the player's environment in the AR game *Pokemon Go*. These elements are visibly present, but do not interact with objects in the environment (for example, one cannot pick up a character in *Pokemon Go* from the ground and place it on a table). MR integrates information from the real world with the virtual information, enabling users to do things like place a virtual cup on a real table, and then move around the room while the virtual cup remains in place.

One example of an application for AR or MR inside of a vehicle is a heads-up display, or HUD. Many new vehicles are being released with a HUD, and consumers can purchase small devices that will project a HUD onto any vehicle's windshield. These HUDs can display information to drivers such as navigational directions or current speed. HUDs can also provide opportunities for augmented reality in driving situations, such as highlighting features to draw attention to potential hazards. However, the same caveats apply as were mentioned in the section on virtual reality regarding age-related changes in visual attention and inattentional blindness.

Figure 2. Example of an envisioned AR/MR in-vehicle display. Dashboard information is shown as a heads-up display (HUD) using augmented reality. Navigational information is shown as an overlay on the environment in mixed reality

The Benefits of AR/MR for Older Drivers

One method of using AR or MR inside of a vehicle has been mentioned already in the HUD section of this chapter: displaying navigation information over the road through the HUD on the windshield, rather than on a separate map display that requires a driver to look away from the road. HUDs may also provide a chance to mediate some of the age-related changes that occur in vision, such as by highlighting crucial details that could be easily missed, or artificially increasing contrast in lower light conditions. Figure 2 provides a visualization of how this might look in a car as part of a navigational display.

Age-related Usability Issues for Older Adult AR Users

Many of the usability issues for AR, particularly in automobiles, are the same for younger and older drivers. For example, visual clutter harms driving performance across age groups (Ho, Scialfa, Caird, & Graw, 2001). Because the production cost of adding an AR/MR display element is less than a physical control or display, it may be tempting to include more options than can be interpreted or operated. Keeping AR/MR displays simple and easy to use is important across age groups.

Existing HUD systems are often on small displays. Given the prevalence of presbyopia, designs for older adults often include larger text sizes to make print easier to read. In HUDS, this creates a problem, as the display should not cover important information on the road, but tiny print is difficult to read for older adults. A related problem is that displays remain a consistent color, which may not be legible depending on the background on the other side of the windshield. The lack of contrast and the small display could cause problems for older adults attempting to read a street name using this navigation system. McLaughlin, Matalenas, and Gandy Coleman provided an overview of design issues specific to older adults and AR/MR (2018).

CONCLUSION

Older persons are a large percentage of the world population and this percentage is continuing to grow, making their health and well-being a crucial issue impacting science, technology, society, and the future. There are many changes that older adults experience, from the sensory to the cognitive. However, technological advances provide an opportunity to support older adults experiencing these changes. This chapter highlights some existing technologies, from VR to haptic feedback systems, and considers possible applications to assist older drivers, along with challenges for older adults using these technologies that must be considered in the design process. Human factors psychology, along with sub-fields of usability, HCI, UX, and user-centered design, will be critical for utilizing these technologies and helping older persons maintain vibrant, meaningful lives in a technological society.

REFERENCES

Agrawal, Y., Platz, E. A., & Niparko, J. K. (2008). Prevalence of hearing loss and differences by demographic characteristics among US adults: Data from the National Health and Nutrition Examination Survey, 1999-2004. *Archives of Internal Medicine*, *168*(14), 1522–1530. doi:10.1001/archinte.168.14.1522 PMID:18663164

Amaied, E., Vargiolu, R., Bergheau, J. M., & Zahouani, H. (2015). Aging effect on tactile perception: Experimental and modelling studies. *Wear*, 323–333, 715–724. doi:10.1016/j.wear.2015.02.030

Anderson, M., & Perrin, A. (2017, May 17). *Tech adoption climbs among older adults*. Retrieved from http://www.pewinternet.org/2017/05/17/tech-adoption-climbs-among-older-adults/

Aquino, P. T., Vilela, L., & Filgueiras, L. (2005). User modeling with personas. *Proceedings of the 2005 Latin American Conference on Human-Computer Interaction*, 277-281. doi:0.1145/1111360.1111388

Ardila, A. (2007). Normal aging increases cognitive heterogeneity: Analysis of dispersion in WAIS-III scores across age. *Archives of Clinical Neuropsychology*, *22*(8), 1003–1011. doi:10.1016/j.acn.2007.08.004 PMID:17904332

Baldwin, C. L. (2012). *Auditory Cognition and Human Performance: Research and Applications*. Boca Raton, FL: CRC Press. doi:10.1201/b11578

Baldwin, C. L., & May, J. F. (2011). Loudness interacts with semantics in auditory warnings to near impact rear-end collisions. *Transportation Research Part F: Traffic Psychology and Behaviour*, *14*(1), 36–42. doi:10.1016/j.trf.2010.09.004

Ball, K., Owsley, C., & Beard, B. (1990). Clinical visual perimetry underestimates peripheral field problems in older adults. *Clinical Vision Sciences*, *5*, 113–125.

Blanchard-Fields, F. (2007). Everyday problem solving and emotion: An adult developmental perspective. *Current Directions in Psychological Science*, *16*(1), 26–31. doi:10.1111/j.1467-8721.2007.00469.x

Blieszner, R., & Roberto, K. (2012). Partners and Friends in Adulthood. In S. K. Whitbourne & M. J. Sliwinski (Eds.), *The Wiley-Blackwell Handbook of Adulthood and Aging* (pp. 381–398). Oxford, UK: Blackwell Publishing Ltd. doi:10.1002/9781118392966.ch19

Blumenthal, T. D., Noto, J. V., Fox, M. A., & Franklin, J. C. (2006). Background noise decreases both prepulse elicitation and inhibition of acoustic startle blink responding. *Biological Psychology*, *72*(2), 173–179. doi:10.1016/j.biopsycho.2005.10.001 PMID:16303226

Brant, L. J., & Fozard, J. L. (1990). Age changes in pure-tone hearing thresholds in a longitudinal study of normal human aging. *The Journal of the Acoustical Society of America*, *88*(2), 813–820. doi:10.1121/1.399731 PMID:2212307

Brooks, J. O., Goodenough, R. R., Crisler, M. C., Klein, N. D., Alley, R. L., Koon, B. L., ... Willis, R. F. (2010). Simulator sickness during driving simulation studies. *Accident; Analysis and Prevention*, *42*(3), 788–796. doi:10.1016/j.aap.2009.04.013 PMID:20380904

Brubaker, M. (2017, April 21). *Survey: nearly 60 percent of seniors use cell phones while driving*. Retrieved from https://health.ucsd.edu/news/releases/Pages/2017-04-21-60-percent-of-seniors-use-cell-phones-while-driving.aspx

Bugg, J. M., Zook, N. A., DeLosh, E. L., Davalos, D. B., & Davis, H. P. (2006). Age differences in fluid intelligence: Contributions of general slowing and frontal decline. *Brain and Cognition, 62*(1), 9–16. doi:10.1016/j.bandc.2006.02.006 PMID:16603300

Burton-Danner, K., Owsley, C., & Jackson, G. R. (2001). Aging and feature search: The effect of search area. *Experimental Aging Research, 27*(1), 1–18. doi:10.1080/036107301750046115 PMID:11205526

Caine, K. E., Šabanović, S., & Carter, M. E. (2012). The Effect of Monitoring by Cameras and Robots on the Privacy Enhancing Behaviors of Older Adults. *Proceedings of the 7th ACM/IEEE International Conference on Human Robot Interaction (HRI),* 343 – 350. 10.1145/2157689.2157807

Carstensen, L. L., Isaacowitz, D. M., & Charles, S. T. (1999). Taking time seriously: A theory of socioemotional selectivity. *The American Psychologist, 54*(3), 165–181. doi:10.1037/0003-066X.54.3.165 PMID:10199217

Carstensen, L. L., Mikels, J. A., & Mather, M. (2006). Aging and the intersection of cognition, motivation, and emotion. In J.E. Birren, K.W. Shaie, R.P. Abeles, M. Gatz, & T.A. Salthouse (Eds.), Handbook of the Psychology of Aging (6th ed.; pp. 343-362). Academic Press. doi:10.1016/B978-012101264-9/50018-5

Centers for Disease Control and Prevention. (2017, November 30). *Older Adult Safety.* Retrieved from https://www.cdc.gov/motorvehiclesafety/older_adult_drivers/index.html

Charness, N. (1981). Aging and skilled problem solving. *Journal of Experimental Psychology. General, 110*(1), 21–38. doi:10.1037/0096-3445.110.1.21 PMID:6453184

Churchill, J. D., Stanis, J. J., Press, C., Kushelev, M., & Greenough, W. T. (2003). Is procedural memory relatively spared from age effects? *Neurobiology of Aging, 24*(6), 883–892. doi:10.1016/S0197-4580(02)00194-X PMID:12927770

Cœugnet, S., Dommes, A., Panëels, S., Chevalier, A., Vienne, F., Dang, N. T., & Anastassova, M. (2017). A vibrotactile wristband to help older pedestrians make safer street-crossing decisions. *Accident; Analysis and Prevention, 109,* 1–9. doi:10.1016/j.aap.2017.09.024 PMID:28987612

Cornelius, S. W., & Caspi, A. (1987). Everyday problem solving in adulthood and old age. *Psychology and Aging, 2*(2), 144–153. doi:10.1037/0882-7974.2.2.144 PMID:3268204

Costello, M. C., Madden, D. J., Mitroff, S. R., & Whiting, W. L. (2010). Age-related decline of visual processing components in change detection. *Psychology and Aging, 25*(2), 35–368. doi:10.1037/a0017625 PMID:20545420

Crawford, J., & Neal, A. (2006). A review of the perceptual and cognitive issues associated with the use of head-up displays in commercial aviation. *The International Journal of Aviation Psychology, 16*(1), 1–19. doi:10.120715327108ijap1601_1

CREATE Overview. (2018). Retrieved August 9, 2018 from http://www.create-center.org/

Davis, F. D. (1989). Perceived usefulness, perceived ease of use and user acceptance of information technology. *Management Information Systems Quarterly, 13*(3), 319–339. doi:10.2307/249008

Deary, I. J., & Der, G. (2005). Reaction time, age, and cognitive ability: Longitudinal findings from age 16 to 63 years in representative population samples. *Neuropsychology, Development, and Cognition. Section B, Aging, Neuropsychology and Cognition, 12*(2), 187–215. doi:10.1080/13825580590969235

DeGood, K. (2011). *Aging in place, stuck without options: fixing the mobility crisis threatening the baby boom generation.* Retrieved from http://t4america.org/maps-tools/seniorsmobilitycrisis2011/

Dickerson, A., Molnar, L. J., Eby, D. W., Adler, G., Bedard, M., Berg-Weger, M., ... Trujillo, L. (2007). Transportation and aging: A research agenda for advancing safe mobility. *The Gerontologist, 47*(5), 578–590. doi:10.1093/geront/47.5.578 PMID:17989400

Dobbs, B. M., Carr, D. B., & Morris, J. C. (2002). Evaluation and management of the driver with dementia. *The Neurologist, 8*(2), 61–70. doi:10.1097/00127893-200203000-00001 PMID:12803692

Dovey, C. (2015, October 1). *What old age is really like.* Retrieved from https://www.newyorker.com/culture/cultural-comment/what-old-age-is-really-like

Eisert, J. L., & Baldwin, C. L. (2014). Driving by the seat of your pants: A vibrotactile navigation study. *Proceedings of the Human Factors and Ergonomics Society Annual Meeting, 58*(1), 2033–2037. doi:10.1177/1541931214581424

Ellaway, A., Macintyre, S., Hiscock, R., & Kearns, A. (2003). In the driving seat: Psychosocial benefits from private motor vehicle transport compared to public transport. *Transportation Research Part F: Traffic Psychology and Behaviour, 6*(3), 217–231. doi:10.1016/S1369-8478(03)00027-5

Elliot, D. B. (1987). Contrast sensitivity decline with ageing: A neural or optical phenomenon? *Ophthalmic & Physiological Optics, 7*(4). doi:10.1111/j.1475-1313.1987.tb00771.x PMID:3454919

Federal Highway Administration, Department of Transportation (US). (2016, September). *Highway Statistics 2015*. Retrieved from https://www.fhwa.dot.gov/policyinformation/statistics/2015/dl20.cfm

Feng, J., Craik, F. I. M., Levine, B., Moreno, S., Naglie, G., & Choi, H. (2017). Differential age-related changes in attention across an extended visual field. *European Journal of Ageing, 14*(2), 167–177. doi:10.100710433-016-0399-7 PMID:28804400

Fitts, P. M., & Jones, R. E. (1947a). *Analysis of factors contributing to 460 "pilot error" experiences in operating aircraft controls* (Report No. TSEAA-694-12). Dayton, OH: Aero Medical Laboratory, Air Materiel Command, U.S. Air Force.

Fitts, P. M., & Jones, R. E. (1947b). *Psychological aspects of instrument display. Analysis of 270 "pilot-error" experiences in reading and interpreting aircraft instruments* (Report No. TSEAA-694-12A). Dayton, OH: Aero Medical Laboratory, Air Materiel Command, U.S. Air Force.

Giraudeau, C., Musielak, C., Hervé, C., Seren, D., Chasseigne, G., & Mullet, E. (2014). Aging, functional learning, and inhibition. *Experimental Aging Research, 42*(4), 329–347. doi:10.1080/0361073X.2016.1191850 PMID:27410242

Gittings, N. S., & Fozard, J. L. (1986). Age related changes in visual acuity. *Experimental Gerontology, 21*(4-5), 423–433. doi:10.1016/0531-5565(86)90047-1 PMID:3493168

Guerreiro, M. J., Murphy, D. R., & Van Gerven, P. W. (2010). The role of sensory modality in age-related distraction: A critical review and a renewed view. *Psychological Bulletin, 136*(6), 975–1022. doi:10.1037/a0020731 PMID:21038938

Hartshorne, J. K., & Germine, L. T. (2015). When does cognitive functioning peak? The asynchronous rise and fall of different cognitive abilities across the lifespan. *Psychological Science, 26*(4), 433–443. doi:10.1177/0956797614567339 PMID:25770099

Hasher, L., & Zacks, R. T. (1988). Working memory, comprehension, and aging: A review and a new view. In G. H. Bower (Ed.), *The psychology of learning and motivation: Advances in research and theory* (pp. 193–225). San Diego, CA: Academic Press.

Hasin, D. S., Goodwin, R. D., Stinson, F. S., & Grant, B. F. (2005). Epidemiology of major depressive disorder: Results from the National Epidemiologic Survey on Alcoholism and Related Conditions. *Archives of General Psychiatry, 62*(10), 1097–1106. doi:10.1001/archpsyc.62.10.1097 PMID:16203955

Hertzog, C., Kramer, A. F., Wilson, R. S., & Lindenberger, U. (2008). Enrichment effects on adult cognitive development: Can the functional capacity of older adults be preserved and enhanced? *Psychological Science in the Public Interest, 9*(1), 1–65. doi:10.1111/j.1539-6053.2009.01034.x PMID:26162004

Hess, T. M., Auman, C., Colcombe, S. J., & Rahhal, T. A. (2003). The impact of stereotype threat on age differences in memory performance. *The Journals of Gerontology: Series B, 58*(1), 3–P11. doi:10.1093/geronb/58.1.P3 PMID:12496296

Hill, L. L., Baird, S., Al-wahab, U., Larocca, J., Chukwueke, J., Engelberg, J. K., Engler, A.-M., Jahns, J., & Rybar, J. (2017, September). *Mobile usage distracted driving behaviors and beliefs among older adults in the U.S.* Washington, DC: AAA Foundation for Traffic Safety.

Hillcoat-Nallétamby, S. (2014). The meaning of "independence" for older people in different residential settings. *The Journals of Gerontology: Series B, 69*(3), 419–430. doi:10.1093/geronb/gbu008 PMID:24578371

Ho, G., & Scialfa, C. T. (2002). Age, skill transfer, and conjunction search. *The Journals of Gerontology: Series B, 57*(3), 277–P287. doi:10.1093/geronb/57.3.P277 PMID:11983739

Ho, G., Scialfa, C. T., Caird, J. K., & Graw, T. (2001). Visual search for traffic signs: The effects of clutter, luminance, and aging. *Human Factors, 43*(2), 194–207. doi:10.1518/001872001775900922 PMID:11592661

Horn, J. L., & Cattell, R. B. (1967). Age differences in fluid and crystallized intelligence. *Acta Psychologica, 26*, 107–129. doi:10.1016/0001-6918(67)90011-X PMID:6037305

Isaacowitz, D. M., Wadlinger, H. A., Goren, D., & Wilson, H. R. (2006). Is there an age-related positivity effect in visual attention? A comparison of two methodologies. *Emotion (Washington, D.C.), 6*(3), 511–516. doi:10.1037/1528-3542.6.3.511 PMID:16938091

Keshavarz, B., Ramkhalawansingh, R., Haycock, B., Shahab, S., & Campos, J. L. (2018). Comparing simulator sickness in younger and older adults during simulated driving under different multisensory conditions. *Transportation Research Part F: Traffic Psychology and Behaviour, 54*, 47–62. doi:10.1016/j.trf.2018.01.007

Ketcham, C. J., & Stelmach, G. E. (2004). Movement control in the older adult. In R. W. Pew & S. B. Van Hemel (Eds.), *Technology for Adaptive Aging* (pp. 64–92). Washington, DC: National Academies Press.

Khosravi, P., Rezvani, A., & Wiewiora, A. (2016). The impact of technology on older adults' social isolation. *Computers in Human Behavior, 63*, 594–603. doi:10.1016/j.chb.2016.05.092

Konrad, H. R., Girardi, M., & Helfert, R. (1999). Balance and aging. *Laryngoscope, 109*(9), 1454–1460. doi:10.1097/00005537-199909000-00019 PMID:10499055

LeRouge, C., Van Slyke, C., Seale, D., & Wright, K. (2014). Baby boomers' adoption of consumer health technologies: Survey on readiness and barriers. *Journal of Medical Internet Research, 16*(9), e200. doi:10.2196/jmir.3049 PMID:25199475

Lewis, J. E., & Neider, M. B. (2016). Through the Google Glass: The impact of heads-up displays on visual attention. *Cognitive Research, 1*(1), 13. doi:10.118641235-016-0015-6 PMID:28180164

Li, G., Braver, E. R., & Chen, L.-H. (2003). Fragility versus excessive crash involvement as determinants of high death rates per vehicle-mile of travel among older drivers. *Accident; Analysis and Prevention, 35*(2), 227–235. doi:10.1016/S0001-4575(01)00107-5 PMID:12504143

Lindgaard, G., Dillon, R., Trbovich, P., White, R., Rernandes, G., Lundahl, S., & Pinnamaneni, A. (2006). User needs analysis and requirements engineering: Theory and practice. *Interacting with Computers, 18*(1), 47–70. doi:10.1016/j.intcom.2005.06.003

Liu, L., Stroulia, E., Nikolaidis, I., Miguel-Cruz, A., & Rios Rincon, A. (2016). Smart homes and home health monitoring technologies for older adults: A systematic review. *International Journal of Medical Informatics, 91*, 44–59. doi:10.1016/j.ijmedinf.2016.04.007 PMID:27185508

Liu, X. Z., & Yan, D. (2007). Ageing and hearing loss. *The Journal of Pathology, 211*(2), 188–197. doi:10.1002/path.2102 PMID:17200945

Mackrous, I., Lavalliere, M., & Teasdale, N. (2014). Adaptation to simulator sickness in older drivers following multiple sessions in a driving simulator. *Gerontechnology (Valkenswaard)*, *12*(2), 101–111. doi:10.4017/gt.2013.12.2.004.00

Malone, T. B., Kirkpatrick, M., Mallory, K., Eike, D., Johnson, J. F., & Walker, R. W. (1980). *Human factors evaluation of control room design and operator performance at Three Mile Island -2* (Technical Report NUREG/CR-1270). Retrieved from https://tmi2kml.inl.gov/

Matas, N. A., Nettelbeck, T., & Burns, N. R. (2015). Dropout during a driving simulator study: A survival analysis. *Journal of Safety Research*, *55*, 159–169. doi:10.1016/j.jsr.2015.08.004 PMID:26683559

Mather, M., & Carstensen, L. L. (2003). Aging and attentional biases for emotional faces. *Psychological Science*, *14*(5), 409–415. doi:10.1111/1467-9280.01455 PMID:12930469

Mather, M., & Carstensen, L. L. (2005). Aging and motivated cognition: The positivity effect in attention and memory. *Trends in Cognitive Sciences*, *9*(10), 496–502. doi:10.1016/j.tics.2005.08.005 PMID:16154382

McLaughlin, A. C., Matalenas, L. A., & Gandy Coleman, M. (2018). Design of human centered augmented reality for managing chronic health conditions. In R. Pak & A. C. McLaughlin (Eds.), *Aging, Technology, and Health* (pp. 261–196). Cambridge, MA: Elsevier. doi:10.1016/B978-0-12-811272-4.00011-7

McPhee, L. C., Scialfa, C. T., Dennis, W. M., Ho, G., & Caird, J. K. (2004). Age difference in visual search for traffic signs during a simulated conversation. *Human Factors*, *46*(4), 674–685. doi:10.1518/hfes.46.4.674.56817 PMID:15709329

Melenhorst, A. S., Rogers, W. A., & Bouwhuis, D. G. (2006). Older adults' motivated choice for technological innovation: Evidence for benefit-driven selectivity. *Psychology and Aging*, *21*(1), 190–195. doi:10.1037/0882-7974.21.1.190 PMID:16594804

Merriman, N. A., Ondřej, J., Rybicki, A., Roudaia, E., O'Sullivan, C., & Newell, F. N. (2016). Crowded environments reduce spatial memory in older but not younger adults. *Psychological Research*, *82*(2), 407–428. doi:10.100700426-016-0819-5 PMID:27783147

Meyer, J. (2009). Designing in-vehicle technologies for older adults. *The Bridge*, *39*(1), 21–26.

Mienaltowski, A. (2013). Everyday problem solving across the adult life span: Solution diversity and efficacy. *Annals of the New York Academy of Sciences, 1235*(1), 75–85. doi:10.1111/j.1749-6632.2011.06207.x PMID:22023569

Miller, K. J., Adair, B. S., Pearce, A. J., Said, C. M., Ozanne, E., & Morris, M. M. (2014). Effectiveness and feasibility of virtual reality and gaming system use at home by older adults for enabling physical activity to improve health-related domains: A systematic review. *Age and Ageing, 43*(2), 188–195. doi:10.1093/ageing/aft194 PMID:24351549

Mitzner, T. L., Boron, J. B., Fausset, C. B., Adams, A. E., Charness, N., Czaja, S. J., ... Sharit, J. (2010). Older adults talk technology: Technology usage and attitudes. *Computers in Human Behavior, 26*(6), 1710–1721. doi:10.1016/j.chb.2010.06.020 PMID:20967133

Mitzner, T. L., Chen, T. L., Kemp, C. C., & Rogers, W. A. (2014). Identifying the potential for robotics to assist older adults in different living environments. *International Journal of Social Robotics, 6*(2), 213–227. doi:10.100712369-013-0218-7 PMID:24729800

Mitzner, T. L., & Rogers, W. A. (2006). Reading in the dark: Effects of age and contrast on reading speed and comprehension. *Human Factors, 48*(2), 229–240. doi:10.1518/001872006777724372 PMID:16884045

Müller-Oehring, E. M., Schulte, T., Rohlfing, T., Pfefferbaum, A., & Sullivan, E. V. (2013). Visual search and the aging brain: Discerning the effects of age-related brain volume shrinkage on alertness, feature binding, and attentional control. *Neuropsychology, 27*(1), 48–59. doi:10.1037/a0030921 PMID:23356596

National Eye Institute. (2018a). *Cataracts*. Retrieved August 20, 2018 from https://www.nei.nih.gov/eyedata/cataract

National Eye Institute. (2018b). *Glaucoma, open-angle*. Retrieved August 20, 2018 from https://www.nei.nih.gov/eyedata/glaucoma

National Safety Council. (2017). *CarTech VR360* [Smartphone app]. Retrieved August 9, 2018 from https://appadvice.com/app/cartech-vr360/1200913564

Nees, M. A., & Walker, B. N. (2011). Auditory displays for in-vehicle technologies. *Review of Human Factors and Ergonomics, 7*(1), 58–99. doi:10.1177/1557234X11410396

Neisser, U., & Becklen, R. (1975). Selective looking: Attending to visually specified events. *Cognitive Psychology, 7*(4), 480–494. doi:10.1016/0010-0285(75)90019-5

Neri, S. G. R., Cardoso, J. R., Cruz, L., Lima, R. M., de Oliveira, R. J., Iversen, M. D., & Carregaro, R. L. (2017). Do virtual reality games improve mobility skills and balance measurements in community-dwelling older adults? Systematic review and meta-analysis. *Clinical Rehabilitation, 31*(10), 1292–1304. doi:10.1177/0269215517694677 PMID:28933612

Nielsen, J. (1994). *Usability Engineering.* San Diego, CA: Academic Press Inc.

Nyberg, L., Bäckman, L., Erngrund, K., Olofsson, U., & Nilsson, L.-G. (1996). Age differences in episodic memory, semantic memory, and priming: Relationships to demographic, intellectual, and biological factors. *The Journals of Gerontology: Series B, 51B*(4), 234–P240. doi:10.1093/geronb/51B.4.P234 PMID:8673644

Owsley, C., & McGwin, G. Jr. (2004). Association between visual attention and mobility in older adults. *Journal of the American Geriatrics Society, 52*(11), 1901–1906. doi:10.1111/j.1532-5415.2004.52516.x PMID:15507069

Population Reference Bureau. (2016, January 13). *Factsheet: Aging in the United States.* Retrieved from https://www.prb.org/aging-unitedstates-fact-sheet/

Preddy, M. (2014, April). *Automakers rediscover and create for boomers.* Retrieved from https://www.aarp.org/auto/trends-lifestyle/info-2015/car-buying-for-older-drivers.html

Ratcliff, R., Spieler, D., & McKoon, G. (2000). Explicitly modeling the effects of aging on response time. *Psychonomic Bulletin & Review, 7*(1), 1–25. doi:10.3758/BF03210723 PMID:10780018

Rendon, A. A., Lohman, E. B., Thorpe, D., Johnson, E. G., Medina, E., & Bradley, B. (2012). The effect of virtual reality gaming on dynamic balance in older adults. *Age and Ageing, 41*(4), 549–552. doi:10.1093/ageing/afs053 PMID:22672915

Rensink, R. A. (2005). Change blindness. In L. Itti, G. Ress, & J. K. Tsotsos (Eds.), *Neurobiology of Attention* (pp. 76–81). Cambridge, MA: Academic Press. doi:10.1016/B978-012375731-9/50017-3

Rogers, W. A., Essa, I. A., & Fisk, A. D. (2007). Designing a technology coach. *Ergonomics in Design, 15*(Summer), 17–23. doi:10.1177/106480460701500303 PMID:22545001

Rogers, W. A., Fisk, A. D., McLaughlin, A. C., & Pak, R. (2005). Touch a screen or turn a knob: Choosing the best device for the job. *Human Factors*, *47*(2), 271–288. doi:10.1518/0018720054679452 PMID:16170938

Rosenbloom, S. (2009). Meeting transportation needs in an aging-friendly community. *Journal of the American Society on Aging*, *33*(2), 33–43.

Salthouse, T. A. (1996). The processing-speed theory of adult age differences in cognition. *Psychological Review*, *103*(3), 403–428. doi:10.1037/0033-295X.103.3.403 PMID:8759042

Scialfa, C. T., Jenkins, L., Hamaluk, E., & Skaloud, P. (2000). Aging and the development of automaticity in conjunction search. *The Journals of Gerontology. Series B, Psychological Sciences and Social Sciences*, *55B*(1), 27–P46. PMID:10728122

Seo, N. J., Kumar, J. A., Hur, P., Crocher, V., Motawar, B., & Lakshminarayanan, K. (2016). Usability evaluation of low-cost virtual reality hand and arm rehabilitation games. *Journal of Rehabilitation Research and Development*, *53*(3), 321–334. doi:10.1682/JRRD.2015.03.0045 PMID:27271199

Siniscarco, M. T., Love-Williams, C., & Burnett-Wolle, S. (2017). Video conferencing: An intervention for emotional loneliness in long-term care. *Activities, Adaptation and Aging*, *41*(4), 316–329. doi:10.1080/01924788.2017.1326763

Steg, L. (2005). Car use: Lust and must. Instrumental, symbolic and affective motives for car use. *Transportation Research Part A, Policy and Practice*, *39*(2-3), 147–162. doi:10.1016/j.tra.2004.07.001

Stewart, R., & Wingfield, A. (2009). Hearing loss and cognitive effort in older adults' report accuracy for verbal materials. *Journal of the American Academy of Audiology*, *20*(2), 147–154. doi:10.3766/jaaa.20.2.7 PMID:19927677

Stuart, M., Turman, A. B., Shaw, J., Walsh, N., & Hguyen, V. (2003). Effects of aging on vibration detection thresholds at various body regions. *BMC Geriatrics*, *3*(1), 1. doi:10.1186/1471-2318-3-1 PMID:12600276

Tefft, B. C. (2017). Rates of motor vehicle crashes, injuries and deaths in relation to driver age, United States, 2014-2015. *AAA Foundation for Traffic Safety*. Retrieved from http://aaafoundation.org/rates-motor-vehicle-crashes-injuries-deaths-relation-driver-age-united-states-2014-2015/

Treisman, A. M., & Gelade, G. (1980). A feature-integration theory of attention. *Cognitive Psychology, 12*(1), 97–136. doi:10.1016/0010-0285(80)90005-5 PMID:7351125

Tsai, H. H., & Tsai, Y. F. (2011). Changes in depressive symptoms, social support, and loneliness over 1 year after a minimum 3-month videoconference program for older nursing home residents. *Journal of Medical Internet Research, 13*(4), e93. doi:10.2196/jmir.1678 PMID:22086660

Tun, P. A., Williams, V. A., Small, B. J., Hafter, E. R. (2012). The effects of aging on auditory processing and cognition. *American Journal of Audiology, 21*(2), 344-350. doi:(2012/12-0030 doi:10.1044/1059-0889

Tyree, G. M., & McLaughlin, A. C. (2016). Older adult engagement in activities: All motivations are not created equal. *Proceedings of the Human Factors and Ergonomics Society Annual Meeting, 56*(1), 135–139. doi:10.1177/1071181312561005

Underwood, B. J. (1974). *Individual differences as a crucible in theory construction.* A distinguished scientific contribution award address presented at the annual meeting of the American Psychological Association, New Orleans, LA.

United States Census Bureau. (2018, March 13). *From pyramid to pillar: A century of change, population of the U.S.* Retrieved from https://www.census.gov/library/visualizations/2018/comm/century-of-change.html

Venkatesh, V., & Bala, H. (2008). Technology Acceptance Model 3 and a research agenda on interventions. *Decision Sciences, 39*(2), 273–315. doi:10.1111/j.1540-5915.2008.00192.x

Venkatesh, V., & Davis, F. D. (2000). A theoretical extension of the technology acceptance model: Four longitudinal field studies. *Management Science, 46*(2), 186–204. doi:10.1287/mnsc.46.2.186.11926

Venkatesh, V., Morris, M. G., Davis, G. B., & Davis, F. D. (2003). User acceptance of information technology: Toward a unified view. *Management Information Systems Quarterly, 27*(3), 425–478. doi:10.2307/30036540

Verhaeghen, P., & Cerella, J. (2002). Aging, executive control, and attention: A review of meta-analyses. *Neuroscience and Biobehavioral Reviews, 26*(7), 849–857. doi:10.1016/S0149-7634(02)00071-4 PMID:12470697

Williams, K. N., Herman, R., Gajweski, B., & Wilson, K. (2010). Elderspeak communication: Impact on dementia care. *American Journal of Alzheimer's Disease and Other Dementias*, 24(1), 11–20. doi:10.1177/1533317508318472 PMID:18591210

Wolfe, J. M., & Horowitz, T. S. (2014). What attributes guide the deployment of visual attention and how do they do it? *Nature Reviews. Neuroscience*, 5(6), 495–501. doi:10.1038/nrn1411 PMID:15152199

KEY TERMS AND DEFINITIONS

Augmented Reality: Presents virtual information alongside real information.
Haptic Feedback: Feedback given through sense of touch, such as vibrations.
Heads-Up Display: A display that presents information in the user's visual field during a task, so they are not required to look at a separate display.
Human Factors: The study of how humans interact with systems.
Mixed Reality: Integrates virtual information with the real world.
Usability: The ease of use of a system or device.
Virtual Reality: An experience of auditory and visual information, and sometimes other sensory modalities, presented in such a way to immerse the user in a virtual environment.

Chapter 11
Thanatology and Human Factors:
Current Research and Future Directions

Alexis R. Neigel
University of Central Florida, USA

Gabriella M. Hancock
California State University – Long Beach, USA

ABSTRACT

The chapter discusses the ergonomic and human factors issues surrounding life and death in terms of 21st century design. In this chapter, the authors describe how current limitations in technologies that are specifically designed to be lethal afford greater pain and suffering than necessary. As human factors is a science dedicated to improving the quality of life, it is necessary to critically examine the end-of-life domain, which is an area of research that has been largely neglected by ergonomic practitioners. By providing an overview of the current research in several area including euthanasia, remotely executed lethal operations, and fully autonomous military robots, the authors demonstrate the need to consider morality and ethics in the design process.

INTRODUCTION

Technology and death have been intimately linked throughout human history, and this well-established relationship is evolving with the technological sophistication of the 21st century. Technology can serve to extend life, but it can also strive to

DOI: 10.4018/978-1-5225-7949-6.ch011

abruptly end it, either intentionally or unintentionally, by design. Thus, end-of-life human factors poses unique challenges for scientists which we address herein. In the present chapter, we discuss the current relationship between thanatology and human factors, as well as the directions for future research at the intersection of these two fields.

Thanatology is the scientific study of death and its associated practices (Meagher & Balk, 2013). Thanatologists, by training, explore the historical contexts of death and end-of-life practices through a sociocultural, psychological, and political lens (Fonseca & Testoni, 2011). Researchers in thanatology also focus on how individuals across various cultures cope with the inevitable end of life (Fonseca & Testoni, 2011). While ancient civilizations and religions have been intrigued by death and the process of dying for centuries, the formalized study of the death system and end-of-life progression are only in their fifth decade of interdisciplinary investigation (Fonseca & Testoni, 2011). As the field of thanatology is relatively small, it has received limited attention in the field of human factors; however, the field's key issues are of course of significant interest to human factors specialists which provides the impetus for the present chapter.

Thanatological issues are typically discussed within the field of human factors as outcomes that should be prevented. Within the context of human factors, practitioners prioritize human safety, and seek to improve training protocols to reduce loss of life from preventable incidents in myriad tasks and environments. However, death is the inevitable outcome of life, and human factors researchers have largely neglected the role that technology can - and arguably should - play as it pertains to the process of death and dying. Furthermore, there is little cohesive discussion regarding the design and implementation of technologies devised with the specific goal of ending life, nor the impact of these technologies on the human psyche.

In this chapter, we tackle difficult ethical issues and questions of morality related to life and living, as well as the antithesis, death and dying. For instance, we provide an overview and discussion of technology involved in physician-assisted death, with a focus on euthanasia and physician-assisted suicide technologies. We also examine the deployment of semi-autonomous and fully-autonomous systems specifically programmed to mete out death with little oversight, such as weaponized unmanned aerial vehicles (e.g., drones) and armed military robots.

In each of these sections, we discuss the morality surrounding the current usage of "thanatology technologies," and the broader societal implications of such controversial systems. We pose several questions worthy of more in-depth reflection, such as: how do these technologies shape our societal beliefs about death and dying? And how would any efforts to further develop such death-dealing technologies be considered morally 'right' and in keeping with human factors' core value as a science to improve the quality of life? Finally, we present a brief discussion to help guide practitioners formulate their own ethical stances with regard to the development and use of such lethal technologies.

BACKGROUND

The objective of this chapter is to facilitate critical thinking related to the technologies that we develop as engineers, scientists, and human factors professionals, and examine how human-machine systems have and will influence the process of death and dying. We encourage readers to question how these technologies may potentially be abused in the ending of life, and if the benefits afforded by these technologies truly outweigh the moral and pragmatic costs. Ultimately, we hope this chapter pushes the field to consider the role of human factors toward the end of the lifespan as this time of life is important, poses unique challenges for promoting the quality of life, and affords exciting possibilities for novel technological solutions.

By remaining cognizant of the human factor in all phases of technological development, undue pain and suffering in the ending of life may be prevented. As laudable as it is to extend life to the greatest possible extent with technological assistance, the process of dying is inevitable and human factors is uniquely situated as a discipline to improve the quality of life until the very end. If the focus of research on these topics remains relatively neglected, we run the risk of misaligning ourselves with the higher goal of human factors: to improve the quality of life (and its inexorable conclusion) through human-centric design.

MAIN FOCUS OF THE CHAPTER

In the following discussion of end-of-life procedures, we find ourselves wading through a very difficult and precarious ethical quagmire. Societies, and the individuals who comprise them, seem to have no moral scruples with supporting the principles of palliative and hospice care (Burdette, Hill & Moulton, 2005; Yun et al., 2011). Indeed, the World Health Organization epitomizes this position, forwarding a global initiative to promote affordable and accessible palliative care as a key means of improving overall health, well-being, and quality of life (Sepúlveda, Marlin, Yoshida & Ullrich, 2002). Such a moral stance seems readily justifiable as hospice and palliative care seek to ease the natural transition from life to death with emphases on comfort and pain management, preservation of dignity, and maximizing the quality of life for as long as possible (Bruera & Hui, 2010). Intriguingly, these values tend to be neglected within the end-of-life and human factors' purview. We begin this chapter with an overview of the human factors associated with human euthanasia and death-by-military robot. We use these as detailed case studies to champion a need for the integration of death and dying into modern human factors course curricula. Finally, we conclude with a discussion of the implications of this education on practitioners, and provide the major issues to be considered when formulating one's own opinion on the ethics of forwarding such systems for widespread use.

Intentional Death-Dealing Technologies: Human Factors Issues in Euthanasia

When discussing end-of-life procedures, wherein humans willfully instigate the life-to-death transition in themselves or others (such as physician-assisted death), opposing viewpoints about the morality of such practices have been raging since quite literally the dawn of humanity (Papadimitriou, Skiadas, Mavrantonis, Polimeropoulos, Papadimitriou & Papacostas, 2007) and show no signs of abating (Levin, Bradley & Duffy, 2018; Porter & Warburton, 2018). We must acknowledge that for the sake of clarity and focus this discussion will be limited to a selective subset of the myriad ethical issues surrounding end-of-life procedures. Such a restricted range of concentration is due to the fact that each constituent factor is so far-reaching and incredibly complex that entire literatures have been devoted to them, such as right-to-life (Feinberg, 1978), right-to-die (Humphry & Wickett, 1986; Genuis, Genuis & Chang, 1994), and the capital punishment debate (and see Tabak & Lane, 1989; Haines, 1996; Lynch, 2002). Special emphases will consequently be placed on the ergonomic issues of individual differences, valid and reliable assessment, and education on these death-delivering procedures.

We progress then knowing that we do so with a fragmentary understanding of the scope and depth of the issues surrounding the human factors associated with thanatology. We must continue despite these limitations, however, given the significant physical, cognitive, emotional, and spiritual ramifications for all system-stakeholders including patients, patients' families, caregivers, and physicians.

It must first be noted that while there exists extensive written works regarding the philosophical and moral considerations surrounding these practices in the literatures on law, ethics, medicine, and religion, there is relatively little empirical research on the psychological and ergonomic underpinnings of end-of-life procedures for unique reasons that we shall briefly discuss here. As a result, we must acknowledge that our discussion of these phenomena is consequently limited, but will present what is available as pertaining to ergonomic interests.

With regard to euthanasia and physician-assisted suicide (PAS), these procedures are generally only applicable (where legal) to terminally ill patients (Foley, 1997), with few exceptions (Pereira, 2011). Recruitment of this population provides a number of unique research challenges including: the patient being too ill to participate, attrition due to subsequent medical decline or death, clinical decisions regarding the appropriateness of broaching the subject, discharge from the recruitment facility due to medical condition, objections on behalf of patients' families and/or attending physicians, and language barriers (Wilson et al., 2000). Consequently, the few available studies comprise a limited and perhaps unrepresentative sample of the larger population of terminally ill individuals contemplating and/or requesting an end-of-life procedure. Research on the attitudes and behaviors of physicians with regard to these practices are therefore relatively more prevalent. However, results from these studies must be considered carefully given the reluctance of medical professionals to admit to, let alone elaborate upon, their participation in said procedures. The consequences for such candor can leave them significantly vulnerable to charges of professional misconduct, jeopardize the retention of their medical license, and potentially invite criminal or civil prosecution (Emanuel, Daniels, Fairclough & Clarridge, 1998). Therefore, one must critically scrutinize results from these studies in terms of 1) their generalizability to all medical professionals who could perform end-of-life procedures (i.e., other doctors, nurses, etc.) and 2) the potential underestimation of the frequency of requests for and occurrence of PAS (Meier, Emmons, Wallenstein, Quill, Morrison & Cassel, 1998).

Physician-Assisted Death: Types and Definitions

Physician-assisted death (PAD) is an umbrella term encapsulating many different types of end-of-life procedures. Generally, it refers to any procedure or treatment that is administered or withheld with the explicit intent of ending a patient's life, with or without the patient's consent (Varadarajan, Freeman & Parmar, 2016; and see Willems, Groenewoud, & van der Wal, 1999). It is critical to first establish the difference between the different types of physician-assisted death and their subsets. Far beyond splitting hairs, these operational definitions determine whether or not a procedure is legal within a particular jurisdiction, and whether or not it is considered ethical by various oversight and professional organizations germane to our discussion of morality. The four types of physician-assisted death include: ending of life without explicit request, terminal sedation, euthanasia, and physician-assisted suicide (Varadarajan et al., 2016). Prevailing attitudes, however, argue that physician-assisted death can only occur with consent (Materstvedt et al., 2003).

Consequently, ending of life without explicit request is not discussed in depth here, and emphasis is devoted to only those procedures that bring about the end of life (i.e., euthanasia and physician-assisted suicide).

Euthanasia represents "an interaction between a patient and a physician in which the physician behaves in a way that is intended...to lead to the death of the patient, for the patient's own sake" (Daskal, 2018, p. 23). Ethicists, lawmakers, and professional organizations have established distinctions between different kinds of euthanasia with regard to process and consent to safeguard patient autonomy and supervise physicians' ethical conduct.

Active euthanasia involves willful interference in the course of natural events, taking concrete steps to hasten a patient's death (Walton, 1976). An example of active euthanasia would be the injection of drugs in such a dosage that would result in death. Quickly, as well, the distinction must be made between active euthanasia and terminal sedation. Terminal sedation involves the non-lethal administration of sedative medication to ease intolerable suffering during the final days (Materstvedt et al., 2003), while active euthanasia would involve the administration of medication with the specific intention of ending the patient's life (Meier et al., 1998). Terminal sedation is therefore perceived as a legitimate palliative treatment option ethically in keeping with the Hippocratic Oath to relieve suffering (Müller-Busch, Oduncu, Woskanjan & Klaschik, 2004; Cowan & Walsh, 2001), while support for active euthanasia periodically fluctuates in both public opinion and in specific medical communities (Braverman, Marcus, Wakim, Mercuirio & Kopf, 2017; Goligher et al., 2017; Emanuel et al., 2016).

Passive euthanasia, in contrast, is the conscious abstention of providing some intervention that is sustaining or could potentially sustain the patient's ebbing life in the face of terminal decline (Walton, 1976). An example of passive euthanasia would be the removal of a feeding tube in a patient who is in a persistent vegetative state. While some experts have contended that there is a prodigious ethical difference between an active versus passive course of action under the laws governing medical practice (McLachlan, 2008), others contend that there can be no such passive option given that patient consent must be obtained and is therefore active by definition in all cases (Materstvedt et al., 2003).

Beyond this distinction of process (i.e., whether an intervention was carried out or withheld) is the other critical issue of consent: did the patient specifically request this course of action knowing that it would result in their death? Again, drawing these distinctions is fundamental to our discussion of the ethics surrounding the human-technology interaction at the heart of these procedures.

Non-voluntary euthanasia occurs when a medical doctor administers medication (or some other intervention) with the intention of ending the life of a non-competent patient who is unable to give consent (Emanuel et al., 2016). Examples of such non-competent patients would include severely ill newborn children, and patients with highly advanced neurodegenerative diseases that compromise effective cognition and decision-making, such as Alzheimer's disease. The Groningen Protocol, a legal and medical framework informing the non-voluntary euthanasia of terminally ill children (younger than 12 years of age), was established in the Netherlands in 2004 (Verhagen & Sauer, 2005). While it is still technically illegal to euthanize anyone below the age of twelve, the Dutch public prosecutor will refrain from filing charges against any doctor who performs such a procedure so long as he or she strictly adheres to all four requirements of the protocol (Verhagen & Sauer, 2005). The conditions which must be met to qualify for exemption from prosecution in non-voluntary euthanasia include: 1) the child is experiencing hopeless and unbearable suffering, 2) the physician must proceed with the full informed consent of the child's parents, 3) medical consultation with other qualified medical colleagues must have taken place, and 4) the termination must be performed with the utmost care (Verhagen, Sol, Brouwer & Sauer, 2005). The Netherlands is the only country with decriminalized non-voluntary euthanasia, and again only under very specific circumstances.

Involuntary euthanasia occurs when a person, typically a physician, administers either medication or another form of intervention with the intent of ending the life of a mentally competent patient, without their consent (Emanuel et al., 2016). Given this critical lack of consent, involuntary euthanasia inhabits a judicial purgatory in the countries where euthanasia is legal and is typically handled on a case-by-case basis; determining whether the involvement should be criminalized or should constitute homicide (whether willful or negligent). Professional medical organizations, however, unequivocally consider involuntary euthanasia to be misconduct and a breach of the Hippocratic Oath as it violates patient autonomy (American Medical Association, n.d.).

Perhaps the most famous example of involuntary euthanasia would be the regicide of George V. In January 1936, King George V lay dying a prolonged death from bronchitis at Sandringham House. Ostensibly, to bring peace to both the suffering king and his family, the royal physician, Betrand Dawson, hastened the monarch's passing with a lethal combination of morphine and cocaine (Ramsay, 1994). Dawson did not seem to suffer legally or professionally because of his actions. He was never prosecuted, was made a viscount only six months after euthanizing the king, and went on to serve as a royal physician to the two subsequent monarchs of the United Kingdom. His medical peers, however, vehemently excoriated him forever afterward (Ramsay, 1994). Passive, non-voluntary euthanasia is legal in Albania provided three or more family members provide their consent to the procedure (Anonymous, 2011). No country, province, or municipality in the world considers active non-voluntary euthanasia legal; although, again, provided compliance with the Groningen Protocol, it is decriminalized in the Netherlands (Verhagen & Sauer, 2005).

Voluntary active euthanasia occurs when an individual (again, typically a medical doctor) administers medication with the intention of ending the life of a mentally competent patient at that terminally ill individual's explicit request (Watts & Howell, 1992; Emanuel et al., 2016). Perhaps the most well-known example of this sort would be the active voluntary euthanasia of Thomas Youk. In 1998, due to his advanced stage of amyotrophic lateral sclerosis, Thomas Youk gave his full informed consent for a physician, Dr. Jack Kevorkian, to inject him with a lethal dose of medication (Charatan, 1999). While Kevorkian had previously supervised physician-assisted suicide and was never successfully prosecuted (Cassel & Meier, 1990), it was this instance of voluntary active euthanasia that saw him convicted of second-degree murder for which he served over eight years in prison (Charatan, 1999). As we shall see in the section on user-centered design of thanatological systems, it was the use of technology in this case that apparently made all the legal difference.

Physician-assisted suicide occurs when a medical doctor prescribes and provides the patient with medication at their explicit request, with the understanding that the patient will then self-administer that medication with the intention of ending their own life (Emanuel et al., 2016). Such a practice is therefore wholly distinct from euthanasia in that all choices are made and positive actions taken by the patient, whereas the physician merely provides the means and oversees the process.

In practice, euthanasia and PAS are both extremely rare (Emanuel, 2017). In jurisdictions where such practices are legal, cases where euthanasia and PAS are cited as cause of death account from anywhere between 0.3% and 4.6% of all deaths (Emanuel et al., 2016). However, given increases in support and strides in legalization throughout the world in the past decade, the prevalence of these instances is growing (Emanuel et al., 2016).

It is true that there have been impressive strides in the quantity, quality, and accessibility of palliative medicine, especially in the last twenty years (Clark, 2007). Moreover, as palliative treatment ameliorates and physicians become increasingly trained in end-of-life care, requests for euthanasia and PAS are more likely to decline (Emanuel, Fairclough & Emanuel, 2000; Emanuel et al., 2000). These trends notwithstanding, there remains a small yet persistent minority of terminally ill people who desire a physician's active or passive assistance to end their life (Wilson et al., 2000), and a small yet persistent minority of doctors and nurses willing to help them (Braverman et al., 2017; Meier et al., 1998; Emanuel, Fairclough, Daniels & Clarridge, 1996; Asch, 1996). Consequently, these end-of-life systems and procedures affect thousands of individuals worldwide every year (Varadarajan et al., 2016; CNN Library, 2018), and the issues will only become more prevalent as the world's elderly population continues to grow (NIH, 2016; Benson, 1999). As a result, there are significant issues that must be addressed to ensure (in as much as possible) the well-being of the patient over the course of their remaining life and during the end-of-life procedure. We will address how human factors can inform these critical issues following our discussion of specific euthanasia and PAS systems.

Safeguards on Euthanasia Thanatological Systems

To prevent misuse or abuse of these systems, the legal and medical communities in which they operate have established certain safeguards. Conditions which must be met in order to qualify for such end-of-life procedures include: "(1) the patient must be terminally ill; (2) the patient must be competent and initiate and repeatedly request euthanasia or PAS; (3) the patient must be experiencing severe pain and/or suffering; and (4) the patient must be evaluated by another physician, who may be a psychiatrist" (Emanuel et al., 1998, p. 507). Some jurisdictions also mandate a waiting period to ensure that the request is in fact in keeping with the patient's resolve (Ganzini & Dobscha, 2004). Therefore, in the marked majority of jurisdictions, the system cannot initiate legally without patients' informed consent and consensus amongst medical professionals.

Secondary safeguards, while not legally required, are sometimes incorporated at the discretion of the attending physician. Some examples of these secondary considerations include the exhaustion of all other palliative care and pain management treatments, and the informed consent and support of the patient's family (De Lima, Woodruff, Pettus, Downing, Buitrago, Munyoro, Venkateswaran, Bhatnagar & Radbruch, 2017; Emanuel et al., 1998). While both these primary and secondary measures seem like appropriate guidelines for navigating the problematic moral maze of euthanasia and PAS, a limited but troubling series of studies suggest that such safeguards are routinely ignored (Pereira, 2011; Emanuel et al., 1998).

Procedures and Devices: User-Centered Design in Physician-Assisted Thanatology

The most common method of physician-assisted suicide appears to be the ingestion of a lethal dose of medication in pill form (Meier et al., 1998). In this procedure, the patient must initiate and repeat their request for an end-of-life procedure. The primary physician will then write a prescription for this fatal dose, and a waiting period must typically pass before its availability (Meier et al., 1998). Based on observational reports from such procedures in the Netherlands, these drugs are most often either barbiturates or a combination of barbiturates and a curare derivative (Willems, Goenewoud & van der Wal, 1999; Groenewoud, van der Heide, Onwuteaka-Philipsen, Willems, van der Maas & van der Wal, 2000). Barbiturate options are preferred over opioids and benzodiazepines as they function more quickly and reliably (Willems, Goenewoud & van der Wal, 1999). Death thereupon results from respiratory depression (Sadock & Sadock, 2008).

While lethal injection is more common in euthanasia (Emanuel et al., 1998), certain automated systems were developed for its use in PAS. Here, a case study approach is adopted focusing on the career of Jacob (Jack) Kevorkian, a famous right-to-die advocate. He oversaw the assisted suicide of over 130 individuals, and in these efforts incorporated many human factors principles herein specified (e.g., automation, user-centered design, universal usability, etc.). The examples of his practices and devices therefore lends context to the user-centered design of thanatological technologies and the specific outcomes of such efforts.

With his medical knowledge and experience, Kevorkian (a retired pathologist), designed and constructed an apparatus called the Thanatron (Caplan & Arp, 2014), which given its Greek roots roughly translates to "the death machine". This device is a metal appliance with series of metal struts and hooks from which to suspend vials of euthanasia drugs, an intravenous line connecting these fluids to the patients' bloodstream, and a timing mechanism to start and stop the fluids' flow with the objective of producing death by lethal injection. Using this system, Kevorkian would insert an intravenous needle into the patient's arm, instigate a saline drip, and provide the patient with a switch (Kevorkian, 1991). Kevorkian's active involvement would end at this point in the procedure. The patient would then choose if and when to relieve the pressure on said switch. Once the pressure is released, the machine would cut off the supply of saline and begin the administration of thiopental, a powerful barbiturate that depresses central nervous system activity (Kevorkian, 1991). This influx of the powerful sedative would render the patient unconscious. The Thanatron would then wait sixty seconds before automatically releasing a lethal dose of potassium chloride, a drug that induces cardiac arrest in sufficiently high doses (Caplan & Arp, 2014). The administration of muscle relaxants would prevent convulsions following the stoppage of the heart (Varadarajan, Freeman & Parmar, 2016). Kevorkian (1991) estimated an average time-to-death using this protocol at two minutes.

Despite several attempts, Kevorkian was never successfully prosecuted for his role in physician-assisted suicide using this procedure and device. It would seem that its crude yet effective automation protected him from conviction. It was only in the case of Thomas Youk's death by euthanasia, wherein Kevorkian depressed the plunger of the needle himself, where the state of Michigan found him morally and legally culpable (Charatan, 1999).

Following the loss of his medical license and associated prescription privileges, Kevorkian no longer had access to the drugs used in the Thanatron. As a result, he designed an alternative device, known as the Mercitron (or mercy machine), whose purpose is to cause death via carbon monoxide poisoning (Nicol & Wylie, 2005). The patient dons a tightly fitting gas mask over his or her nose and mouth. The mask is fed via a plastic tube by a metal tank containing carbon monoxide, a highly toxic gas that compromises the body's ability to transport oxygen to vital organs and tissues (Omaye, 2002). In consideration of the differential levels of disability in his patients, and to promote universal usability, Kevorkian engineered the system so that a clothespin, applying pressure to the line, impedes the free flow of gas (Varadarajan, Freeman & Parmar, 2016). Patients, essentially regardless of physical strength or dexterity, can remove the clothespin and inhale the poisonous gas. Muscle relaxants, again, were administered in an effort to keep the patient calm throughout the process (Varadarajan et al., 2016). Death would result from oxygen deprivation in roughly ten minutes (Nicol & Wylie, 2005).

Philip Nitschke, a physician and founder of the pro-euthanasia organization Exit International, designed an assisted suicide device known as the Deliverance Machine for the brief period in the 1990s when end-of-life procedures were legal in the Northern Territory of Australia (Street & Kissane, 2000). When compared to Kevorkian's protocols, this machine integrated human-computer interaction to secure informed consent and resolve to a higher degree. The Deliverance Machine consists of a laptop computer and software platform connected to an accompanying case of euthanasia drugs (specifically Nembutal) by an intravenous line (Street & Kissane, 2000). The patient self-administers these drugs by interacting with the software. The programs asks the person three questions relating to their awareness and consent that progression through the protocol will result in their death. If the patient clicks on 'yes' all three times, the fatal dose is released (Exit International, n.d.).

As with any other human-machine system, there are significant design and operational issues with these euthanasia and PAS systems (Emanuel, 2017). Groenewoud and colleagues (2000) categorized these concerns into technical issues, complications, and problems with completion. While all three of these problems were relatively rare (affecting less than 10% of patients), they nevertheless impact dozens of cases each, which can be indicative of wider prevalence within the practice (Groenewoud, van der Heide, Onwuteaka-Philipsen, Willems, van der Maas & van der Wal, 2000). Technical problems stem from the administration of the medication, such as difficulty swallowing the pill(s), and difficulty in finding a vein in which to insert the catheter (Groenewoud et al., 2000). Complications arise from individual differences in the metabolism of drugs and pharmacokinetics, such as spasms, nausea, cyanosis, and regurgitation of the medication (Groenewoud et al., 2000; Emanuel et al., 2016). Finally, problems with completion involve issues relating to the lethal effectiveness of the procedure. Such difficulties include instances of the patient regaining consciousness prior to death, and time-to-death exceeding duration projections (Groenewoud et al., 2000). While median time between ingestion/injection and death is typically 25 minutes, and roughly two-thirds of patients die within 90 minutes, time-to-death can range up to 4 days or more (Emanuel et al., 2016).

The condition of unendurable pain is pivotal to the safeguards governing the approval or denial of end-of-life procedures. In this context, pain is considered to have both physical and psychological dimensions (Foley, 1997). The concept of pain, however, has been historically difficult to operationalize and assess. It is a subjective experience that can only semi-reliably be assessed via imperfect self-report measures (Jensen & Karoly, 1992; Herr, Coyne, McCaffery, Manworren & Merkel, 2011). There is no objective test to determine levels of physical pain conclusively (Borsook, Becerra & Hargreaves, 2011). Moreover, given their expertise is in physiological rather than psychological functioning, physicians are particularly ill-suited to appraise non-physical suffering (Back, Wallace, Starks & Pearlman, 1996). Human factors practitioners can therefore improve upon the psychometric instruments of self-report geared toward assessing the psychological constructs driving requests for end-of-life procedures. Developing increasingly valid and reliable pain scales would assist physicians with their diagnoses and treatment recommendations, and consequently would be beneficial for all medical patients. However, terminal patients may benefit disproportionately from such efforts, given the prevalence and severity of pain associated with their conditions.

Scales that are intended to measure the psychological constructs informing decision-making about end-of-life procedures (i.e., pain, anxiety, etc.) should also take special care to accurately assess how these levels change over time. Chochinov, Tataryn, Clinch, and Dudgeon (1999) measured the will to live in terminally ill patients in palliative care. While the will to live appeared stable over time, the average maximum changes in will to live were considerable; and the prominent factor driving these changes was variable over time (Chochinov et al., 1999). Human factors professionals can then help to develop protocols that protect patient autonomy and informed consent by improving the assessment methods used to determine if the request for physician-assisted death is genuine and resolute.

Semi-Autonomous Death: Is Distancing the Human Operator Psychologically Better?

When we consider automating the process of putting an individual to death, we must also consider the effect of such technology on the human operator. Physical distance is not moral distance. Hence, it is unlikely that distancing the Warfighter or drone operator will provide any psychological benefit, nor does this distance change the suffering of the dying. Such claims can be made when we investigate the literature on the modern unmanned aerial vehicle (UAVs) and remotely piloted aircraft (RPAs, or "drones") operations.

In an effort to avoid the loss of life due to warfare, many militaries have weaponized UAVs and drones, which have been deployed to perform surveillance tasks and neutralize enemy threats (Jenks, 2017). Drone strikes, which are authorized in the United States under 2001 Presidential Directives, utilize 'kill lists' of known, profiled individuals, and pre-defined threat categories to end life (Kearns, 2017; Niva, 2013; Shah, 2014). However, this technology can harm innocent civilians through system malfunctions and poor survellienace design, which in turn impacts the situational awareness of the human operator (Foreman, Favaró, Saleh, & Johnson, 2015). In one study, Foreman and colleagues (2015) point out several software "blind spots" involved in military and civilian aviation, suggesting that accident analysis is a missed "learning opportunity" in terms of accident prevention (p. 101). What this means for human factors and ergonomics practitioners is that we are aware of thanatological design issues and we are doing nothing to prevent them. Such refusal or inability to address these issues is ultimately incongruous with the goals of human factors as a discipline focused on improving the quality of life. Thus, we encourage readers to critically consider such design "blind spots" in an effort to improve unnecessary suffering and death in military operations for neglecting them has serious consequences.

For example, in 2012, Momina Bibi was killed in a drone strike while gardening with her two grandchildren in Waziristan (McVeigh, 2013; Stowers, Leyva, Hancock, & Hancock, 2016). In a separate report by Amnesty International (2013), hundreds of civilians have been killed by drone strikes in Pakistan alone, including many children (Boone, 2013). And the trajectory of warfare is on an increasingly autonomous path, which has been extremely concerning for the public, both nationally and internationally in recent years (Jenks, 2017; Warrior, 2015).

While it is arguable that drone operation perhaps saves more lives than it takes, as military personnel do not necessarily have to deploy to war zones to pilot these aircraft, it is also the case that even distanced killing can impact the human psyche. As pointed out by Brandon Bryant, a former drone operator, "artillery doesn't see the results of their actions. It's really more intimate for us, because we see everything" (Warrior, 2015, p. 99). In some cases, this involves drone operators watching allied Soldiers die because they have limited communications with troops and no means of warning them (Warrior, 2015).

Accordingly, 4.3% of United States Air Force drone operators demonstrated moderate to severe post-traumatic stress disorder (PTSD) symptoms (Chappelle, Goodman, Reardon, & Thompson, 2014a). Chappelle and colleagues (2014a) indicated that this prevalence rate of PTSD is lower than military personnel returning from deployment, but higher than incidence rates reported in electronic medical records. In two studies of remotely piloted aircraft (RPA) operators in the United States Air Force, over half of respondents were stressed or extremely stressed

(Chapelle, McDonald, Prince, Goodman, Ray-Sannerud, & Thompson, 2014b; Chapelle, Salinas, & McDonald, 2011), many respondents displayed significant emotional distress (Chapelle, McDonald, Thompson, & Swearengen, 2012), and there were many reports of sleep disturbance (Armour & Ross, 2017). Thus, it is arguable whether the benefits of UAV technologies truly outweigh the psychological and physiological suffering placed on drone operators (Asaro, 2013). It is rather simple and avoidant to automate death-delivering systems, and it is much more difficult to consider the redesign of a system focused on eliminating others. Consequently, human factors and ergonomics practitioners need to consider an alternative to UAV operations and dramatically improve the safeguards and decision aids that prevent civilian casualties.

Fully-Automated Killing Machines: Military Robots

In 21st century warfare, multipurpose robots have helped human Warfighters by assisting with surveillance and reconnaissance (e.g., drones), constructing and maintaining effective situation awareness (Phillips & Jentsch, 2017), and safely disposing of explosive ordinance (Sharkey, 2007). However, fully automated systems have now been deployed in combat theaters to identify and kill military targets independent of human input (Royakkers & van Est, 2015). While once thought only possible in the realm of science fiction, such fully-autonomous weaponized systems are already currently in use by militaries around the world. For example, the American Navy's Phalanx Close-In Weapons System (CIWS) assimilates data and make decisions to launch missiles completely autonomously (Lin, Bekey & Abney, 2009); and fully-autonomous robots act as border guards in both South Korea and Israel (Sharkey, 2007).

Normally, the question at the heart of armed, automated military robots is whether or not it is ethical to deploy them as they are capable of violent and harmful actions and can function independent of human supervision (Royakkers & Olsthoorn, 2018; Stowers, Leyva, Hancock & Hancock, 2016). Strawser (2010), however, claims that it would be morally unethical to refrain from using such systems as they offer protection from harm and fatal injury to human troops. Furthermore, armed military robots arguably have the capacity to minimize combat duration and, as a result, human casualties as "not only would robots expand the battlespace over difficult, larger areas of terrain, but they also represent a significant force-multiplier – each effectively doing the work of many human soldiers, while immune to sleep deprivation, fatigue, low morale, perceptual and communication challenges in the 'fog of war', and other performance-hindering conditions" that impede human soldiers (Lin, Bekey & Abney, 2009, pg. 49).

Once implemented, their behavior in theater (and hence in novel circumstances) would ideally be governed by a mathematically-driven decision-making mechanism structured on internationally recognized laws of war (Arkin, 2009; 2010; Royakkers & van Est, 2015). Such an artificial conscience, however, would certainly not function perfectly in every situation (Arkin, 2009; Lin et al., 2009). Instead, such a mechanism attempts to serve the same function as remote operation in the case of semi-autonomous drones: to put distance between the human operator and the consequences of their actions. Cummings (2006) rightly points out that such a scenario allows for a diminished sense of accountability and responsibility on behalf of the human, but – as we saw with drone use – does little to mitigate the harmful psychological effects on human Warfighters and those who design these systems.

SOLUTIONS AND RECOMMENDATIONS

If we do not want technology to harm or exercise lethal force without morality, then we must consider this in technological design as human factors professionals (Stowers et al., 2016). Through poor ergonomic design and gross negligence of human well-being, human factors can inadvertently but very effectively kill. Thus, we urge practitioners to be diligent in their critical consideration of the ethical and moral implications inherent to the systems they design (Hancock, 2009). In this vein, the purpose of this chapter is not to condemn technology, but rather to encourage a more systematic examination of the morals and ethics underlying intentionally lethal systems, and to showcase the need for greater education on life and death practices from a design perspective.

As the debates rage on as to the ethics of euthanasia and physician-assisted death, drones and armed autonomous military robots, there are multiple avenues for intervention on behalf of the human factors practitioner to influence the consideration and design of such systems. Indeed, as these systems involve stakeholders who are suffering both physically and psychologically, there seems to be a moral imperative for human factors - as a discipline that seeks to improve the quality of life - to address them. Such contributions should include enhancing education, improving training for physicians, improving the assessment of various factors affecting the decision to end one's life, and, most controversially, using one's expertise to advocate for either abandoning or refining such systems' design and procedures.

The Need for Greater Education and Training in End-of-Life Human Factors

Greater education about euthanasia and physician-assisted death (as a last resort), as well as lethal technologies like drones and military robots, is desperately needed for patients, operators, and users. For example, only 30% of medical schools dedicated an entire course to end-of-life care in their curricula, the majority preferring to integrate these issues into a required rotation (Van Aalst-Cohen, Riggs & Byock, 2008). Even as residents, physicians deal with very few dying patients and have little opportunity to develop their knowledge and skills relating to end-of-life care (Hill, 1995). Such lack of knowledge is of great concern as 1) physicians' preferences regarding palliative care and physician-assisted death have a significant influence on their patients' selected course of action (Ganzini, Fenn, Lee, Heintz & Bloom, 1996), and 2) a large percentage of patients rescind their requests for PAS following an intervention that comprehensively explains palliative care options (Ganzini, Nelson, Schmidt, Kraemer, Delorit & Lee, 2000). In terms of technical performance of the procedures, the Royal Dutch Association of Pharmacy has established and regularly updates practical guidelines governing the use and preparation of drugs for the purposes of euthanasia (Groenewoud et al., 2000). These are guidelines, however, as opposed to mandates. Research in the Netherlands and the United States reveals that there is great variability in the drugs and dosages used in end-of-life procedures (Drickamer, Lee & Ganzini, 1997; Emanuel et al., 1998), which can be also extended to capital punishment procedures.

Human factors practitioners therefore have the opportunity to develop, customize, and assess educational materials to convey these options and treatments to system stakeholders. Using our understanding of individual differences, ergonomists can individuate the technological systems designed to impart this knowledge to medical students during their training, and physicians and patients who are most closely affected by end-of-life issues (Hancock, Hancock & Warm, 2009). To have the greatest impact, we consequently suggest targeting oncologists and their patients (Emanuel, 2002). Adequately trained physicians can then impart their knowledge to their patients, who are consequently better equipped to make decisions concerning their comprehensive end-of-life care treatments. Patients can perhaps then preserve their autonomy through this wider range of options, leaving physician-assisted death as a last resort (Emanuel, 2017).

If a human factors practitioner is morally opposed to the practice of physician-assisted death, their efforts would best be devoted to 1) educating the general public, physicians, and patients about palliative care, 2) aiding the aforementioned assessments of pain and suffering, and 3) designing and evaluating medical systems relating to hospice and end-of-life care. Human factors practitioners who support physician-assisted death can and are encouraged to engage in these pursuits as well. It is legally and ethically difficult, however, to take the next step of evaluating and re-designing such systems to be more effective, particularly given the lack of medical expertise. Institutional Review Boards would no doubt preclude such academic efforts.

In a similar vein, the need for a holistic medical education can serve to benefit individuals suffering from PTSD linked to drone operations. As signs and symptoms of PTSD manifest differently in drone operators, one direction for future research will be to better detect these symptoms and appropriately treat these issues, and quite possibly update the Diagnostic and Statistics Manual to include 'non-traditional' occupational hallmarks of PTSD. Furthermore, greater access to trained medical personnel who can detect and treat this form of PTSD will significantly improve the quantity and quality of care for RPA operators. The areas of telehealth and telecare are ripe for human factors-based improvement and usability. Finally, limiting drones, other RPAs, and military robots to surveillance and ordinance disposal may significantly reduce the prevalence of PTSD and suffering in this occupation. While this would not eliminate the viewing of death from afar, it would reduce the psychological burden of killing, and thereby decrease the presence of PTSD within these operators.

Arguably, the most impactful way to make a difference in terms of the thanatology technologies we design and create is to provide a greater education on such a topic, which is what we have strived to do in the present chapter. Given that end-of-life technologies are rarely included in modern human factors textbooks, we provide an overview of the importance of these issues in terms of euthanasia, drone operation, and military robots. An education and introduction to such topics can significantly improve practitioner awareness and be integrated into the design of technologies going forward.

Constructing Personal Ethical Frameworks

In this final section, we put forth three key issues for consideration when practitioners attempt to formulate or revisit their own personal opinions about whether to design, implement, evaluate or maintain thanatological systems. Certain controversial avenues of research have from time to time employed the precautionary principle: restrict or cease further investigation until a more detailed assessment of potential catastrophic outcomes can be performed by the field writ large (Lin et al., 2009). With regard to physician-assisted death, drone operations, and lethal military robots, human factors practitioners do not have the luxury of such an ethical moratorium. Death and dying are everyday realities for those in the medical profession, and militaries throughout the world are of the opinion that the benefits of deploying effective yet imperfect semi- and fully-autonomous lethal systems outweigh the current ethical concerns.

Research consequently proceeds at pace in each of these endeavors. The ethical question therefore shifts from purely: is it ethical to develop such systems (as they are already in place) to is it ethical to redesign, refine, implement, and advocate for such thanatological systems?

The first recommendation, therefore, in the process of building beliefs as to the morality of lethal human-machine systems would be to examine one's own conscience in light of the issues raised here. Practitioners should 1) delve into the literatures of medicine, law, and human factors, 2) examine historical case studies, and 3) stay abreast of current events and developments with the implementation of such systems to determine the extent to which they are personally comfortable with supporting the efficacy of human-machine systems specifically designed to kill. Practitioners should also be aware of how their attitudes might change due to contextual parameters, such as lethal systems for mercy killings (i.e., PAD) versus armed conflict (Lin et al., 2009); and distinctions within these subgroups, such as deploying armed autonomous systems to neutralize enemy forces more effectively (i.e., targeted strikes) versus deploying them in an effort to save friendly forces more effectively (i.e., ordinance disposal; Sharkey, 2007).

The second recommendation would be to ask oneself the extent to which one would be willing to assume responsibility for the intended and unintended actions of these lethal systems. The general public labors under the false belief that highly autonomous systems (i.e., robots) are only capable of performing pre-specified actions that humans have programmed into their operating system. However, given the unprecedented programming that informs current algorithms guiding robots' behavior – which necessitates input from multiple human programmers – as well as the capacity of such systems to learn from experience without re-programming - robots' behavior is just as, if not more, unpredictable than that of humans (Lin et al., 2009). Such complexity has led to novel, emergent behaviors (Kurzweil, 2005). While such complexity is a testament to humans' achievement in design and engineering, it is a disconcerting development when discussing autonomous systems that can wield lethal weapons.

One proposed solution to this issue is to mandate that a portion of a robot's programming should include mandates and directives to preclude any immoral behaviors, Arkin's (2009) ethical governor or Asimov's (1942) laws of robotics, for example. Many researchers advocate for embedding ethics within robots and artificial intelligence systems (Vanderelst & Winfield, 2018); however, the concept of morality is often context-specific and highly culturally dependent (Stowers et al., 2016). It is no wonder then that it is difficult to generate and implement guidelines for ethical behavior in robots when humans often disagree on what is or is not ethical. Such a state of affairs is readily observable in the disparate approval rates for the practices and systems herein presented: euthanasia, physician-assisted suicide, drone operations, and use of military robots. Moreover, even if a consensus can be reached about moral codes of conduct (e.g., the Geneva Convention), people and the systems they design have purposefully or inadvertently violated them in extreme situations such as warfare (Lin et al., 2009). Additional alternatives are to either limit the use of robots all together, or train robots to be ethical by instructing and reinforcing related constructs such as honesty and fairness (Sharkey, 2017). Such efforts to program and train robots to be 'good', however, have been minimally successful – and only then in severely restricted application domains (Sharkey, 2017). Again, as a result, human factors practitioners should consider whether they are willing to assume responsibility for the intended and unintended outcomes of autonomous systems whose ability to learn affords emergent behaviors.

The final recommendation would be for the practitioner to determine their opinion on the feasibility of effectively imposing and enforcing strictures on such thanatological systems. For instance, are the existing safeguards concerning euthanasia sufficient to prevent abuse or misuse of the systems? Are the oversight and regulatory mechanisms governing semi-autonomous drone use comprehensive enough to effectively minimize collateral damage associated with such systems? Are there inclusive, exhaustive, and satisfactory operational and regulatory guidelines in place to justify the use of fully autonomous systems that are capable of exercising lethal force? If the human factors professional believes so, or to an acceptable degree, the practitioner can focus their efforts on actively working with such systems. If not, or to an unacceptable degree, the practitioner has the option to help redress such shortcomings. For example, the researcher can help in the human-centered effort to impose limitations on the most autonomous systems (Hancock, 2017) or establish a standardized chain of responsibility in the case of thanatological systems' malfunction or failure (Sharkey, 2007).

CONCLUSION

Human factors is uniquely poised as a discipline that can facilitate extending or ending life. With this capacity comes great responsibility to ensure that such knowledge is wielded in such a way as to align with the larger goals of the field and the personal morals of the individual practitioner. This ethical question is simple to answer when designing human-machine systems for use in most performance domains; safety, and by extension the preservation of life, is always of paramount importance to the designer. However, in pursuits where the overarching goal of the system is to extinguish life such as euthanasia, semi-automated (i.e., drones) and fully-automated lethal systems (i.e., robots), there are no easy answers about the use and design of such technologies. It is up to the conscience of the individual practitioner to determine if and to what degree they feel morally comfortable in designing, evaluating, and operating thanatological technologies. As a discipline, however, we must confront these issues head-on given that such practices proceed without our input every day, throughout the world. Consequently, as a discipline devoted to improving the quality of human life at all of its stages, we must at the very least address these issues in an effort to generate solutions, whether they be the abolition or refinement of such protocols. Our recommendations for such nascent solutions include greater training and education focused specifically on ethical and moral design.

When we consider death in the design process, as is consistent with the field of healthcare human factors, we as practitioners can serve to improve both quantity and quality of life, especially when we learn from the errors in our design (i.e., improving medical care after documented errors that have led to death). When the end user is neglected throughout the design process moral design cannot occur, which leads to deep-seated suffering that is largely preventable. We dare to say that the human factors profession is not truly acting in the interests of humanity if we are not designing technology responsibly. That said, we encourage readers to consider this chapter as a catalyst for critical thinking about the role of human factors in thanatology and the design of purposefully lethal systems.

ACKNOWLEDGMENT

This research received no specific grant from any funding agency in the public, commercial, or not-for-profit sectors.

REFERENCES

American Medical Association. (n.d.). *Euthanasia*. Retrieved from: https://www.ama-assn.org/delivering-care/euthanasia

Anonymous. (2011, May 7). India joins select nations in legalising "passive euthanasia". *The Hindu*. Retrieved from: https://www.thehindu.com/news/national/India-joins-select-nations-in-legalising- quotpassive-euthanasiaquot/article14938022.ece

Arkin, R. C. (2009). *Governing lethal behavior in autonomous robots*. Boca Raton, FL: Taylor and Francis. doi:10.1201/9781420085952

Arkin, R. C. (2010). The case of ethical autonomy in unmanned systems. *Journal of Military Ethics*, 9(4), 332–341. doi:10.1080/15027570.2010.536402

Armour, C., & Ross, J. (2017). The health and well-being of military drone operators and intelligence analysts: A systematic review. *Military Psychology, 29*(2), 83–98. doi:10.1037/mil0000149

Asaro, P. M. (2013). The labor of surveillance and bureaucratized killing: New subjectivities of military drone operators. *Social Semiotics, 23*(2), 196–224. doi:1 0.1080/10350330.2013.777591

Asch, D. A. (1996). The role of critical care nurses in euthanasia and assisted suicide. *The New England Journal of Medicine, 334*(21), 1374–1379. doi:10.1056/ NEJM199605233342106 PMID:8614424

Asimov, I. (1942). Runaround. Astounding Science-Fiction, 29(1), 94-98.

Back, A. L., Wallace, J. I., Starks, H. E., & Pearlman, R. A. (1996). Physician-assisted suicide and euthanasia in Washington State. *Journal of the American Medical Association, 275*(12), 919–925. doi:10.1001/jama.1996.03530360029034 PMID:8598619

Benson, J. M. (1999). End-of-life issues. *Public Opinion Quarterly, 63*(2), 263–277. doi:10.1086/297716

Boone, J. (2013). U.S. drone strikes could be classed as war crimes, says Amnesty International. *The Guardian.* Retrieved from: https://www.theguardian.com/ world/2013/oct/22/amnesty-us-officials-war-crimes-drones

Borshook, D., Becerra, L., & Hargreaves, R. (2011). Biomarkers for chronic pain and analgesia. Part 1: The need, reality, challenges, and solutions. *Discovery Medicine, 11*(58), 197–207. PMID:21447279

Braverman, D. W., Marcus, B. S., Wakim, P. G., Mercurio, M. R., & Kopf, G. S. (2017). Health care professionals' attitudes about physician-assisted death: An analysis of their justifications and the roles of terminology and patient competency. *Journal of Pain and Symptom Management, 54*(4), 538–545. doi:10.1016/j. jpainsymman.2017.07.024 PMID:28716621

Bruera, E., & Hui, D. (2010). Integrating supportive and palliative care in the trajectory of cancer: Establishing goals and models of care. *Journal of Clinical Oncology, 28*(25), 4013–4017. doi:10.1200/JCO.2010.29.5618 PMID:20660825

Burdette, A. M., Hill, T. D., & Moutlon, B. E. (2005). Religion and attitudes toward physician-assisted suicide and terminal palliative care. *Journal for the Scientific Study of Religion, 44*(1), 79–93. doi:10.1111/j.1468-5906.2005.00266.x

Caplan, A., & Arp, R. (2014). *Contemporary debates in bioethics*. Chichester, UK: John Wiley & Sons.

Cassel, C. K., & Meier, D. E. (1990). Morals and moralism in the debate over euthanasia and assisted suicide. *The New England Journal of Medicine, 323*(11), 750–752. doi:10.1056/NEJM199009133231110 PMID:2388673

Chapelle, W., McDonald, K., Prince, L., Goodman, T., Ray-Sannerud, B., & Thompson, W. (2014b). Assessment of occupational burnout in United States Air Force predator/reaper "drone" operators. *Military Psychology, 26*(5-6), 376–385. doi:10.1037/mil0000046

Chapelle, W., McDonald, K., Thompson, B., & Swearengen, J. (2012). *Prevalence of high emotional distress, symptoms of post-traumatic stress disorder in U.S. Air Force active duty remotely piloted aircraft operators* (Technical Report no. AFRL-SA-WP-TR-2013-0002). Wright-Patterson Air Force Base, OH: U.S. Air Force School of Aerospace Medicine.

Chapelle, W., Salinas, A., & McDonald, K. (2011). *Psychological health screening of remotely piloted aircraft (RPA) operators and supporting units. Wright-Patterson Air Force Base, Ohio Department of Neuropsychiatry*. U.S. Air Force School of Aerospace Medicine.

Chappelle, W., Goodman, T., Reardon, L., & Thompson, W. (2014a). An analysis of post traumatic stress symptoms in United States Air Force drone operators. *Journal of Anxiety Disorders, 28*(5), 480–487. doi:10.1016/j.janxdis.2014.05.003 PMID:24907535

Charatan, F. (1999). Dr. Kevorkian found guilty of second degree murder. *British Medical Journal, 318*(7189), 962. PMID:10195955

Chochinov, H. M., Tataryn, D., Clinch, J. J., & Dudgeon, D. (1999). Will to live in the terminally ill. *Lancet, 354*(9181), 816–819. doi:10.1016/S0140-6736(99)80011-7 PMID:10485723

Clark, D. (2007). From margins to centre: A review of the history of palliative care in cancer. *The Lancet Oncology, 8*(5), 430–438. doi:10.1016/S1470-2045(07)70138-9 PMID:17466900

CNN Library. (2018, June 4). *Physician-assisted suicide fast facts*. Retrieved from: https://www.cnn.com/2014/11/26/us/physician-assisted-suicide-fast-facts/index.html

Cowan, J. D., & Walsh, D. (2001). Terminal sedation in palliative medicine – definition and review of the literature. *Supportive Care in Cancer, 9*(6), 403–407. doi:10.1007005200100235 PMID:11585266

Cummings, M. L. (2006). Automation and accountability in decision support system interface design. *Journal of Technology Studies, 32*(1), 23–31. doi:10.21061/jots. v32i1.a.4

Daskal, S. (2018). Support for voluntary euthanasia with no logical slippery slope to non-voluntary euthanasia. *Kennedy Institute of Ethics Journal, 28*(1), 23–48. doi:10.1353/ken.2018.0001 PMID:29628450

De Lima, L., Woodruff, R., Pettus, K., Downing, J., Buitrago, R., Munyoro, E., ... Radbruch, L. (2017). International Association for Hospice and Palliative Care position statement: Euthanasia and physician-assisted suicide. *Journal of Palliative Medicine, 20*(1), 8–14. doi:10.1089/jpm.2016.0290 PMID:27898287

Drickamer, M. A., Lee, M. A., & Ganzini, L. (1997). Practical issues in physician-assisted suicide. *Annals of Internal Medicine, 126*(2), 146–151. doi:10.7326/0003-4819-126-2-199701150-00009 PMID:9005749

Emanuel, E. J. (2002). Euthanasia and physician-assisted suicide: A review of the empirical data from the United States. *Archives of Internal Medicine, 162*(2), 142–152. doi:10.1001/archinte.162.2.142 PMID:11802747

Emanuel, E. J. (2017). Euthanasia and physician-assisted suicide: Focus on the data. *The Medical Journal of Australia, 206*(8), 339–340. doi:10.5694/mja16.00132 PMID:28446107

Emanuel, E. J., Daniels, E. R., Fairclough, D. L., & Clarridge, B. R. (1998). The practice of euthanasia and physician-assisted suicide in the United States: Adherence to proposed safeguards and effects on physicians. *Journal of the American Medical Association, 280*(6), 507–513. doi:10.1001/jama.280.6.507 PMID:9707132

Emanuel, E. J., Fairclough, D., Clarridge, B. C., Blum, D., Bruera, E., Penley, W. C., ... Mayer, R. J. (2000). Attitudes and practices of U.S. oncologists regarding euthanasia and physician-assisted suicide. *Annals of Internal Medicine, 133*(7), 527–532. doi:10.7326/0003-4819-133-7-200010030-00011 PMID:11015165

Emanuel, E. J., Fairclough, D. L., Daniels, E. R., & Clarridge, B. R. (1996). Euthanasia and physician-assisted suicide: Attitudes and experiences of oncology patients, oncologists, and the public. *Lancet, 347*(9018), 1805–1810. doi:10.1016/S0140-6736(96)91621-9 PMID:8667927

Emanuel, E. J., Fairclough, D. L., & Emanuel, L. L. (2000). Attitudes and desires related to euthanasia and physician-assisted suicide among terminally ill patients. *Journal of the American Medical Association, 284*(19), 2460–2468. doi:10.1001/jama.284.19.2460 PMID:11074775

Emanuel, E. J., Onwuteaka-Philipsen, B. D., Urwin, J. W., & Cohen, J. (2016). Attitudes and practices of euthanasia and physician-assisted suicide in the United States, Canada, and Europe. *Journal of the American Medical Association, 316*(1), 79–90. doi:10.1001/jama.2016.8499 PMID:27380345

Exit International. (n.d.). The Deliverance Machine. *Exit International.* Retrieved from: https://exitinternational.net/the-deliverance-machine-invented-by-philip-nitschke/

Feinberg, J. (1978). Voluntary euthanasia and the inalienable right to life. *Philosophy & Public Affairs, 7*(2), 93–123. PMID:11661543

Foley, K. M. (1997). Competent care for the dying instead of physician-assisted suicide. *The New England Journal of Medicine, 336*(1), 54–58. doi:10.1056/NEJM199701023360109 PMID:8970941

Fonseca, L. M., & Testoni, I. (2011). The Emergence of Thanatology and Current Practice in Death Education. *Omega, 64*(2), 157–169. doi:10.2190/OM.64.2.d PMID:22375350

Foreman, V. L., Favaró, F. M., Saleh, J. H., & Johnson, C. W. (2015). Software in military aviation and drone mishaps: Analysis and recommendations for the investigation process. *Reliability Engineering & System Safety, 137*, 101–111. doi:10.1016/j.ress.2015.01.006

Ganzini, L., & Dobscha, S. K. (2004). Clarifying distinctions between contemplating and completing physician-assisted suicide. *The Journal of Clinical Ethics, 15*(2), 119–122. PMID:15481163

Ganzini, L., Fenn, D. S., Lee, M. A., Heintz, R. T., & Bloom, J. D. (1996). Attitudes of Oregon psychiatrists toward physician-assisted suicide. *The American Journal of Psychiatry, 153*(11), 1469–1475. doi:10.1176/ajp.153.11.1469 PMID:8890683

Ganzini, L., Nelson, H. D., Schmidt, T. A., Kraemer, D. F., Delorit, M. A., & Lee, M. A. (2000). Physicians' experiences with the Oregon Death with Dignity Act. *The New England Journal of Medicine, 342*(8), 557–563. doi:10.1056/NEJM200002243420806 PMID:10684915

Genuis, S. J., Genuis, S. K., & Chang, W.-C. (1994). Public attitudes toward the right to die. *Canadian Medical Association Journal, 150*(5), 701–708. PMID:8313289

Goligher, E. C., Ely, E. W., Sulmasy, D. P., Bakker, J., Raphael, J., Volandes, A. E., … Downar, J. (2017). Physician-assisted suicide and euthanasia in the intensive care unit: A dialogue on core ethical issues. *Critical Care Medicine, 45*(2), 149–155. doi:10.1097/CCM.0000000000001818 PMID:28098622

Groenewoud, J. H., van der Heide, A., Onwuteaka-Philipsen, B. D., Willems, D. L., van der Maas, P. J., & van der Wal, G. (2000). Clinical problems with the performance of euthanasia and physician-assisted suicide in the Netherlands. *The New England Journal of Medicine, 342*(8), 551–556. doi:10.1056/NEJM200002243420805 PMID:10684914

Haines, H. H. (1996). *Against capital punishment: The anti-death penalty movement in America, 1972-1994*. New York, NY: Oxford University Press.

Hancock, P. A. (2009). *Mind, machine, and morality*. Aldershot, UK: Ashgate Publishing.

Hancock, P. A. (2017). Imposing limits on autonomous systems. *Ergonomics, 60*(2), 284–291. doi:10.1080/00140139.2016.1190035 PMID:27409152

Hancock, P. A., Hancock, G. M., & Warm, J. S. (2009). Individuation: The N=1 revolution. *Theoretical Issues in Ergonomics Science, 10*(5), 481–488. doi:10.1080/14639220903106387

Herr, K., Coyne, P. J., McCaffery, M., Manworren, R., & Merkel, S. (2011). Pain assessment in the patient unable to self-report: Position statement with clinical practice recommendations. *Pain Management Nursing, 12*(4), 230–250. doi:10.1016/j.pmn.2011.10.002 PMID:22117755

Hill, T. P. (1995). Treating the dying patient: The challenge for medical education. *Archives of Internal Medicine, 155*(12), 1265–1269. doi:10.1001/archinte.1995.00430120036005 PMID:7778956

Humphry, D., & Wickett, A. (1986). *The right to die*. New York, NY: Harper and Row.

Jenks, C. (2017). The gathering swarm: The path to increasingly autonomous weapons systems. *Jurimetrics: The Journal of Law. Science & Technology, 57*(3), 341–359.

Jensen, M. P., & Karoly, P. (1992). Self-report scales and procedures for assessing pain in adults. In D. C. Turk & R. Melzack (Eds.), *Handbook of pain assessment* (pp. 135–151). New York: Guilford Press.

Kearns, O. (2017). Secrecy and absence in the residue of covert drone strikes. *Political Geography*, *57*, 13–23. doi:10.1016/j.polgeo.2016.11.005

Kevorkian, J. (1991). *Prescription—medicine: The goodness of planned death.* Buffalo, NY: Prometheus Books.

Kurzweil, R. (2005). *The singularity is near: When humans transcend biology*. New York, NY: Viking Penguin.

Levin, K., Bradley, G. L., & Duffy, A. (2018). Attitudes toward euthanasia for patients who suffer from physical and mental illness. *Omega*, *0*(0), 1–23. PMID:29357754

Lin, P., Bekey, G., & Abney, K. (2009). Robots in war: Issues of risk and ethics. In Ethics and robotics. AKA Verlag/IOS Press.

Lynch, M. (2002). Capital punishment as moral imperative: Pro-death-penalty discourse on the internet. *Punishment & Society*, *4*(2), 213–236. doi:10.1177/14624740222228554

Materstvedt, L. J., Clark, D., Ellershaw, J., Førde, R., Boeck Gravgaard, A.-M., & Müller-Busch, H. C. (2003). Euthanasia and physician-assisted suicide: A view from an EAPC Ethics Task Force. *Palliative Medicine*, *17*(2), 97–101. doi:10.1191/0269216303pm673oa PMID:12701848

McLachlan, H. V. (2008). The ethics of killing and letting die: Active and passive euthanasia. *Journal of Medical Ethics*, *34*(8), 636–638. doi:10.1136/jme.2007.023382 PMID:18667657

McVeigh, K. (2013). Drone strikes: Tears in Congress as Pakistani family tells of mother's death. *The Guardian*. Retrieved from: https://www.theguardian.com/world/2013/oct/29/pakistan-family-drone-victim-testimony-congress

Meagher, D. K., & Balk, D. E. (Eds.). (2013). *Handbook f thanatology: The essential body of knowledge for the study of death, dying, and bereavement*. New York, NY: Routledge. doi:10.4324/9780203767306

Meier, D. E., Emmons, C.-A., Wallenstein, S., Quill, T., Morrison, R. S., & Cassel, C. K. (1998). A national survey of physician-assisted suicide and euthanasia in the United States. *The New England Journal of Medicine*, *338*(17), 1193–1201. doi:10.1056/NEJM199804233381706 PMID:9554861

Müller-Busch, H. C., Oduncu, F. S., Woskkanjan, S., & Klaschik, E. (2004). Attitudes on euthanasia, physician-assisted suicide and terminal sedation – A survey of the members of the German Association for Palliative Medicine. *Medicine, Health Care, and Philosophy, 7*(3), 333–339. doi:10.100711019-004-9349-9 PMID:15679025

National Institutes of Health. (2016). *World's older population grows dramatically*. Retrieved from: https://www.nih.gov/news-events/news-releases/worlds-older-population-grows-dramatically

Nicol, N., & Wiley, H. (2005). *Between the dying and the dead: Dr. Jack Kevorkian's life and the battle to legalize euthanasia*. Madison, WI: University of Wisconsin Press.

Niva, S. (2013). Disappearing violence: JSOC and the Pentagon's new cartography of networked warfare. *Security Dialogue, 44*(3), 185–202. doi:10.1177/0967010613485869

Omaye, S. (2002). Metabolic modulation of carbon monoxide toxicity. *Toxicology, 180*(2), 139–150. doi:10.1016/S0300-483X(02)00387-6 PMID:12324190

Papadimitriou, J. D., Skiadas, P., Mavrantonis, C. S., Polimeropoulos, V., Papadimitriou, D. J., & Papacostas, K. J. (2007, January). Euthanasia and suicide in antiquity: Viewpoint of the dramatists and philosophers. *Journal of the Royal Society of Medicine, 100*(1), 25–28. doi:10.1177/014107680710000111 PMID:17197683

Pereira, J. (2011). Legalizing euthanasia or assisted suicide: The illusion of safeguards and controls. *Current Oncology (Toronto, Ont.), 18*(2), e38–e45. doi:10.3747/co.v18i2.883 PMID:21505588

Phillips, E. K., & Jentsch, F. G. (2017). Supporting situation awareness through robot-to-human information exchanges under conditions of visuospatial perspective taking. *Journal of Human-Robot Interaction, 6*(3), 92–117. doi:10.5898/JHRI.6.3.Phillips

Porter, K., & Warburton, K. G. (2018). Physicians' views on current legislation around euthanasia and assisted suicide: Results of surveys commissioned by the Royal College of Physicians. *Future Healthcare Journal, 5*(1), 30–34.

Ramsay, J. H. R. (1994). A king, a doctor, and a convenient death. *British Medical Journal, 308*(6941), 1445. doi:10.1136/bmj.308.6941.1445 PMID:11644545

Royakkers, L., & Olsthoorn, P. (2018). Lethal military robots: Who is responsible when things go wrong? In The Changing Scope of Technoethics in Contemporary Society (pp. 106-123). IGI Global.

Royakkers, L., & van Est, R. (2015). A literature review on new robotics: Automation from love to war. *International Journal of Social Robotics*, *7*(5), 549–570. doi:10.100712369-015-0295-x

Sadock, B. J., & Sadock, V. A. (2008). *Kaplan & Sadock's concise textbook of clinical psychiatry*. Philadelphia, PA: Lippincott Williams & Wilkins.

Sepúlveda, C., Marlin, A., Yoshida, T., & Ullrich, A. (2002). Palliative care: The World Health Organization's global perspective. *Journal of Pain and Symptom Management*, *24*(2), 91–96. doi:10.1016/S0885-3924(02)00440-2 PMID:12231124

Shah, N. (2014). A move within the Shadows: Will JSOC's control of drones improve policy? In P. L. Bergen & D. Rothenberg (Eds.), *Drone Wars: Transforming conflict, law and policy* (pp. 160–184). Cambridge, UK: Cambridge University Press. doi:10.1017/CBO9781139198325.012

Sharkey, A. (2017). Can we program or train robots to be good? *Ethics and Information Technology*, 1–13.

Sharkey, N. (2007). Automated killers and the computing profession. *Computer*, *11*, 122–124.

Stowers, K., Leyva, K., Hancock, G. M., & Hancock, P. A. (2016). Life or Death by Robot? *Ergonomics in Design*, *24*(3), 17–22. doi:10.1177/1064804616635811

Strawser, B. J. (2010). Moral predators: The duty to employ uninhabited aerial vehicles. *Journal of Military Ethics*, *9*(4), 342–368. doi:10.1080/15027570.2010.536403

Street, A., & Kissane, D. W. (2000). Dispensing death, desiring death: An exploration of medical roles and patient motivation during the period of legalized euthanasia in Australia. *Omega*, *40*(1), 231–248. doi:10.2190/JB07-5GCR-BH81-J2QN PMID:12578011

Tabak, R. J., & Lane, J. M. (1989). The execution of injustice: A cost and lack-of-benefit analysis of the death penalty. *Loyola of Los Angeles Law Review*, *23*, 59–146.

Van Aalst-Cohen, E. S., Riggs, R., & Byock, I. R. (2008). Palliative care in medical school curricula: A survey of United States medical schools. *Journal of Palliative Medicine*, *11*(9), 1200–1202. doi:10.1089/jpm.2008.0118 PMID:19021481

Vanderelst, D., & Winfield, A. (2018). An architecture for ethical robots inspired by the simulation theory of cognition. *Cognitive Systems Research*, *48*, 56–66. doi:10.1016/j.cogsys.2017.04.002

Varadarajan, R., Freeman, R. A., & Parmar, J. R. (2016). Aid-in-dying practice in Europe and the United States: Legal and ethical perspectives for pharmacy. *Research in Social & Administrative Pharmacy, 12*(6), 1016–1025. doi:10.1016/j.sapharm.2015.11.008 PMID:26711140

Verhagen, A. A., Sol, J. J., Brouwer, O. F., & Sauer, P. J. (2005). Deliberate termination of life in newborns in The Netherlands; Review of all 22 reported cases between 1997 and 2004. *Nederlands Tijdschrift voor Geneeskunde, 149*(4), 183–188. PMID:15702738

Verhagen, E., & Sauer, P. J. J. (2005). The Groningen Protocol – euthanasia in severely ill newborns. *The New England Journal of Medicine, 352*(10), 959–962. doi:10.1056/NEJMp058026 PMID:15758003

Walton, D. (1976). Active and passive euthanasia. *Ethics, 86*(4), 343–349. doi:10.1086/292010 PMID:11662292

Warrior, L. C. (2015). Drones and targeted killing: Costs, accountability, and U.S. civil-military relations. *Orbis, 59*(1), 95–110. doi:10.1016/j.orbis.2014.11.008

Watts, D. T., & Howell, T. (1992). Assisted suicide is not voluntary active euthanasia. *Journal of the American Geriatrics Society, 40*(10), 1043–1046. doi:10.1111/j.1532-5415.1992.tb04484.x PMID:1401679

Willems, D. L., Groenewoud, J. H., & van der Wal, G. (1999). Drugs used in physician-assisted death. *Drugs & Aging, 15*(5), 335–340. doi:10.2165/00002512-199915050-00001 PMID:10600041

Wilson, K. G., Scott, J. F., Graham, I. D., Kozak, J. F., Chater, S., Viola, R. A., ... Curran, D. (2000). Attitudes of terminally ill patients toward euthanasia and physician-assisted suicide. *Archives of Internal Medicine, 160*(16), 2454–2460. doi:10.1001/archinte.160.16.2454 PMID:10979056

Yun, Y. H., Han, K. H., Park, S., Park, B. W., Cho, C.-H., Kim, S., ... Chun, M. (2011). Attitudes of cancer patients, family caregivers, oncologists and members of the general public toward critical interventions at the end of life of terminally ill patients. *Canadian Medical Association Journal, 183*(10), E673–E679. doi:10.1503/cmaj.110020 PMID:21624907

KEY TERMS AND DEFINITIONS

Physician-Assisted Death: Physician-assisted death refers to any procedure or treatment that is administered (or withheld) with the explicit intent of ending a patient's life, with or without the patient's consent.

Remotely Piloted Aircraft: Remotely piloted aircraft, or RPAs, are typically smaller aircraft, like drones, that can be used for defense or surveillance purposes. A trained operator at a distanced location pilots these aircraft. The location of operation is usually quite far from the location of surveillance or defense.

Thanatology: Thanatology is the scientific study of death and the practices associated with it.

Unmanned Aerial Vehicles: Unmanned aerial vehicles, or UAVS, are aircraft primarily used for surveillance and reconnaissance purposes.

Compilation of References

Abhyankar, K. (2017). *Enhancing engineering education using mobile augmented devices* (Dissertation). Retrieved from Wright State University Dissertation #1767: https://corescholar. libraries.wright.edu/etd_all/1767/

Aggarwal, R., Gopal, R., Sankaranarayanan, R., & Singh, P. V. (2012). Blog, Blogger, and the Firm: Can Negative Employee Posts Lead to Positive Outcomes? *Information Systems Research, 23*(2), 306–322. doi:10.1287/isre.1110.0360

Agomuoh, F. (2012). Amanda Todd suicide doesn't end cyber torment for ridiculed teen. *International Business Times*. Retrieved from: http://www.ibtimes.com/amanda-todd-suicidedoesnt-end-cyber-torment-ridiculed-teen-846827

Agrawal, Y., Platz, E. A., & Niparko, J. K. (2008). Prevalence of hearing loss and differences by demographic characteristics among US adults: Data from the National Health and Nutrition Examination Survey, 1999-2004. *Archives of Internal Medicine, 168*(14), 1522–1530. doi:10.1001/archinte.168.14.1522 PMID:18663164

Aguenza, B. B., Al-Kassem, A. H., & Mat Som, A. P. (2012). Social Media and Productivity in the Workplace: Challenges and Constraints. *Interdisciplinary Journal of Research in Business, 2*(2), 22–26.

Ajzen, I. (1985). From Intentions to Actions: A Theory of Planned Behavior. In J. Kuhl & J. Beckmann (Eds.), Action Control (pp. 11-39). Springer. doi:10.1007/978-3-642-69746-3_2

Akentiev, A. (2017, November 8). *Parity Multisig Hacked. Again.* Retrieved from https://medium.com/chain-cloud-company-blog/parity-multisig-hack-again-b46771eaa838

Al-Debei, M. M., Al-Lozi, E., & Papazafeiropoulou, A. (2013). Why people keep coming back to Facebook: Explaining and predicting continuance participation from an extended theory of planned behaviour perspective. *Decision Support Systems, 55*(1), 43–45. doi:10.1016/j.dss.2012.12.032

Al-Muomen, N., Morris, A., & Maynard, S. (2012). Modelling information-seeking behaviour of graduate students at Kuwait University. *The Journal of Documentation, 68*(4), 430–459. doi:10.1108/00220411211239057

Alzougool, B., Chang, S., Gomes, C., & Berry, M. (2013). Finding their way around: International students' use of information sources. *Journal of Advanced Management Science, 1*(1), 43–49. doi:10.12720/joams.1.1.43-49

Amaied, E., Vargiolu, R., Bergheau, J. M., & Zahouani, H. (2015). Aging effect on tactile perception: Experimental and modelling studies. *Wear, 323–333,* 715–724. doi:10.1016/j.wear.2015.02.030

AMC Network Entertainment. (2010). *Mad Men.* Retrieved September 28, 2018 from https://www.amc.com/shows/mad-men

American Medical Association. (n.d.). *Euthanasia.* Retrieved from: https://www.ama-assn.org/delivering-care/euthanasia

Anastassiou, A. (2017). Sexting and young people: A review of the qualitative literature. *Qualitative Report, 22,* 2231–2239.

Anderson, M., & Perrin, A. (2017, May 17). *Tech adoption climbs among older adults.* Retrieved from http://www.pewinternet.org/2017/05/17/tech-adoption-climbs-among-older-adults/

Andrade, M. S. (2006). International students in English-speaking universities: Adjustment factors. *Journal of Research in International Education, 5*(2), 131–154. doi:10.1177/1475240906065589

Angelides, S. (2013). 'Technology, hormones, and stupidity': The affective politics of teenage sexting. *Sexualities, 16*(5-6), 665–689. doi:10.1177/1363460713487289

Anonymous. (2011, May 7). India joins select nations in legalising "passive euthanasia". *The Hindu.* Retrieved from: https://www.thehindu.com/news/national/India-joins-select-nations-in-legalising- quotpassive-euthanasiaquot/article14938022.ece

Aquino, P. T., Vilela, L., & Filgueiras, L. (2005). User modeling with personas. *Proceedings of the 2005 Latin American Conference on Human-Computer Interaction,* 277-281. doi:0.1145/1111360.1111388

Archambault, A., & Grudin, J. (2012, May). *A Longitudinal Study of Facebook, LinkedIn & Twitter Use.* Paper presented at the SIGCHI Conference on Human Factors in Computing Systems, Austin, TX. 10.1145/2207676.2208671

Ardila, A. (2007). Normal aging increases cognitive heterogeneity: Analysis of dispersion in WAIS-III scores across age. *Archives of Clinical Neuropsychology, 22*(8), 1003–1011. doi:10.1016/j.acn.2007.08.004 PMID:17904332

Arkin, R. C. (2009). *Governing lethal behavior in autonomous robots.* Boca Raton, FL: Taylor and Francis. doi:10.1201/9781420085952

Arkin, R. C. (2010). The case of ethical autonomy in unmanned systems. *Journal of Military Ethics, 9*(4), 332–341. doi:10.1080/15027570.2010.536402

Armour, C., & Ross, J. (2017). The health and well-being of military drone operators and intelligence analysts: A systematic review. *Military Psychology, 29*(2), 83–98. doi:10.1037/mil0000149

Arnett, J. (1994). Sensation seeking: A new conceptualization and a new scale. *Personality and Individual Differences, 16*(2), 289–296. doi:10.1016/0191-8869(94)90165-1

Asaro, P. M. (2013). The labor of surveillance and bureaucratized killing: New subjectivities of military drone operators. *Social Semiotics, 23*(2), 196–224. doi:10.1080/10350330.2013.777591

Asch, D. A. (1996). The role of critical care nurses in euthanasia and assisted suicide. *The New England Journal of Medicine, 334*(21), 1374–1379. doi:10.1056/NEJM199605233342106 PMID:8614424

Asimov, I. (1942). Runaround. Astounding Science-Fiction, 29(1), 94-98.

Back, A. L., Wallace, J. I., Starks, H. E., & Pearlman, R. A. (1996). Physician-assisted suicide and euthanasia in Washington State. *Journal of the American Medical Association, 275*(12), 919–925. doi:10.1001/jama.1996.03530360029034 PMID:8598619

Bahrynovska, T. (2017, September 27). *History of Ethereum Security Vulnerabilities, Hacks and their Fixes*. Retrieved from https://applicature.com/blog/history-of-ethereum-security-vulnerabilities-hacks-and-their-fixes

Bakić-Mirić, N. A. (2012). *An integrated approach to intercultural communication*. Newcastle upon Tyne, UK: Cambridge Scholars Publishing.

Baldwin, C. L. (2012). *Auditory Cognition and Human Performance: Research and Applications*. Boca Raton, FL: CRC Press. doi:10.1201/b11578

Baldwin, C. L., & May, J. F. (2011). Loudness interacts with semantics in auditory warnings to near impact rear-end collisions. *Transportation Research Part F: Traffic Psychology and Behaviour, 14*(1), 36–42. doi:10.1016/j.trf.2010.09.004

Ball, K., Owsley, C., & Beard, B. (1990). Clinical visual perimetry underestimates peripheral field problems in older adults. *Clinical Vision Sciences, 5*, 113–125.

Bapna, R., Gupta, A., Rice, S., & Sundararajan, A. (2017). Trust And The Strength Of Ties In Online Social Networks: An Exploratory Field Experiment. *Management Information Systems Quarterly, 41*(1), 115–130. doi:10.25300/MISQ/2017/41.1.06

Barab, S., Thomas, M., Dodge, T., Carteaux, R., & Tuzun, H. (2005). Making learning fun: Quest Atlantis, a game without guns. *Educational Technology Research and Development, 53*(1), 86–107. doi:10.1007/BF02504859

Barbour, S. (2007). *Nationalism, language, Europe*. Oxford, UK: Oxford University Press.

Barrett, P. L. (2012). *Information-seeking processes of fourth grade students using the internet for a school assignment*. Teachers College, Columbia University.

Bashar, A., Ahmad, I., & Wasiq, M. (2012). Effectiveness of Social Media as a Marketing Tool: An Empirical Study. *International Journal of Marketing, Financial Services & Management Research, 1*(11), 88–99.

Behrisch, T. B. (2016). Cost and the craving for novelty: Exploring motivations and barriers for cooperative education and exchange students to go abroad. *Asia Pacific Journal of Cooperative Education, 17*(3), 279–294.

Bennett, M. J. (2003). Towards ethnorelativism: A developmental model of intercultural sensitivity. In R. M. Paige (Ed.), *Education for the intercultural experience* (Vol. 2, pp. 17–32). Interculture Press.

Benotsch, E. G., Snipes, D. J., Martin, A. M., & Bull, S. S. (2013). Sexting, substance use, and sexual risk behavior in young adults. *The Journal of Adolescent Health, 52*(3), 307–313. doi:10.1016/j.jadohealth.2012.06.011 PMID:23299017

Benson, J. M. (1999). End-of-life issues. *Public Opinion Quarterly, 63*(2), 263–277. doi:10.1086/297716

Berardo, K., & Simons, G. (2004). *The intercultural profession: Its profile, practices, and challenges.* Retrieved from http://www.sietar-europa.org/about_us/ICP_Survey_Report.pdf

Bijker, W. E., Hughes, T. P., & Pinch, T. J. (1987). *The social construction of technological systems: New directions in the sociology and history of technology.* MIT Press.

Bitcoin Project. (2018). *Bitcoin is an innovative payment network and a new kind of money.* Retrieved from https://bitcoin.org/en/

Bitcoin Wiki. (2018). *Block.* Retrieved from https://en.bitcoin.it/wiki/Block

Blanchard-Fields, F. (2007). Everyday problem solving and emotion: An adult developmental perspective. *Current Directions in Psychological Science, 16*(1), 26–31. doi:10.1111/j.1467-8721.2007.00469.x

Blieszner, R., & Roberto, K. (2012). Partners and Friends in Adulthood. In S. K. Whitbourne & M. J. Sliwinski (Eds.), *The Wiley-Blackwell Handbook of Adulthood and Aging* (pp. 381–398). Oxford, UK: Blackwell Publishing Ltd. doi:10.1002/9781118392966.ch19

Blockcerts. (2018a). *Blockcerts.* Retrieved from https://www.blockcerts.org/

Blockcerts. (2018b). *Blockcerts.* Retrieved from https://www.blockcerts.org/guide/

Blockchain Luxembourg, S. A. (2018a). *Bitcoin Hashrate Distribution.* Retrieved from https://www.blockchain.com/pools

Blockchain Luxembourg, S. A. (2018b). *Hash Rate.* Retrieved from https://www.blockchain.com/charts/hash-rate?timespan=all

Blumenthal, T. D., Noto, J. V., Fox, M. A., & Franklin, J. C. (2006). Background noise decreases both prepulse elicitation and inhibition of acoustic startle blink responding. *Biological Psychology, 72*(2), 173–179. doi:10.1016/j.biopsycho.2005.10.001 PMID:16303226

Blumler, J. G., & Katz, E. (1974). *The uses of mass communications: Current perspectives on gratifications research.* Beverly Hills, CA: Sage Publications, Inc.

Boersma, J. (2016, November 22). *Blockchain technology – how to improve online identity management.* Retrieved from https://www2.deloitte.com/nl/nl/pages/financial-services/articles/4-blockchain-how-to-improve-online-identity-management.html

Bonnefon, J. F., Shariff, A., & Rahwan, I. (2016). The social dilemma of autonomous vehicles. *Science, 352*(6293), 1573–1576. doi:10.1126cience.aaf2654 PMID:27339987

Boone, J. (2013). U.S. drone strikes could be classed as war crimes, says Amnesty International. *The Guardian.* Retrieved from: https://www.theguardian.com/world/2013/oct/22/amnesty-us-officials-war-crimes-drones

Borshook, D., Becerra, L., & Hargreaves, R. (2011). Biomarkers for chronic pain and analgesia. Part 1: The need, reality, challenges, and solutions. *Discovery Medicine, 11*(58), 197–207. PMID:21447279

Bowman, N. D., Westerman, D. K., & Claus, C. J. (2012). How demanding is social media: Understanding social media diets as a function of perceived costs and benefits–A rational actor perspective. *Computers in Human Behavior, 28*(6), 2298–2305. doi:10.1016/j.chb.2012.06.037

Boyd, D. M., & Ellison, N. B. (2007). Social Network Sites: Definition, History, and Scholarship. *Journal of Computer-Mediated Communication, 13*(1), 210–230. doi:10.1111/j.1083-6101.2007.00393.x

Bøyum, I., & Aabø, S. (2015). The information practices of business PhD students. *New Library World, 116*(3/4), 187–200. doi:10.1108/NLW-06-2014-0073

Brahme, M. E. (2010). *The differences in information seeking behavior between distance and residential doctoral students.* Pepperdine University.

Brandao, A. R. D. (2016). *Factors Influencing Long-Term Adoption of Wearable Activity Trackers.* Rochester Institute of Technology.

Brant, L. J., & Fozard, J. L. (1990). Age changes in pure-tone hearing thresholds in a longitudinal study of normal human aging. *The Journal of the Acoustical Society of America, 88*(2), 813–820. doi:10.1121/1.399731 PMID:2212307

Braverman, D. W., Marcus, B. S., Wakim, P. G., Mercurio, M. R., & Kopf, G. S. (2017). Health care professionals' attitudes about physician-assisted death: An analysis of their justifications and the roles of terminology and patient competency. *Journal of Pain and Symptom Management, 54*(4), 538–545. doi:10.1016/j.jpainsymman.2017.07.024 PMID:28716621

Brettel, M., Friederichsen, N., Keller, M., & Rosenberg, M. (2014). How virtualization, decentralization and network building change the manufacturing landscape: An Industry 4.0 Perspective. *International Journal of Mechanical. Industrial Science and Engineering, 8*(1), 37–44.

Brinkley, D. Y., Ackerman, R. A., Ehrenreich, S. E., & Underwood, M. K. (2017). Sending and receiving text messages with sexual content: Relations with early sexual activity and borderline personality features in late adolescence. *Computers in Human Behavior, 70,* 119–130. doi:10.1016/j.chb.2016.12.082 PMID:28824224

Brooke, J. (1996). SUS-A quick and dirty usability scale. *Usability Evaluation in Industry, 189*(194), 4-7.

Brooks, J. O., Goodenough, R. R., Crisler, M. C., Klein, N. D., Alley, R. L., Koon, B. L., ... Willis, R. F. (2010). Simulator sickness during driving simulation studies. *Accident; Analysis and Prevention, 42*(3), 788–796. doi:10.1016/j.aap.2009.04.013 PMID:20380904

Brubaker, M. (2017, April 21). *Survey: nearly 60 percent of seniors use cell phones while driving.* Retrieved from https://health.ucsd.edu/news/releases/Pages/2017-04-21-60-percent-of-seniors-use-cell-phones-while-driving.aspx

Bruera, E., & Hui, D. (2010). Integrating supportive and palliative care in the trajectory of cancer: Establishing goals and models of care. *Journal of Clinical Oncology, 28*(25), 4013–4017. doi:10.1200/JCO.2010.29.5618 PMID:20660825

Buchanan, T., Johnson, J. A., & Goldberg, L. R. (2005). Implementing a five-factor personality inventory for use on the internet. *European Journal of Psychological Assessment, 21*(2), 115–127. doi:10.1027/1015-5759.21.2.115

Bugg, J. M., Zook, N. A., DeLosh, E. L., Davalos, D. B., & Davis, H. P. (2006). Age differences in fluid intelligence: Contributions of general slowing and frontal decline. *Brain and Cognition, 62*(1), 9–16. doi:10.1016/j.bandc.2006.02.006 PMID:16603300

Burdette, A. M., Hill, T. D., & Moutlon, B. E. (2005). Religion and attitudes toward physician-assisted suicide and terminal palliative care. *Journal for the Scientific Study of Religion, 44*(1), 79–93. doi:10.1111/j.1468-5906.2005.00266.x

Bureau of Labor Statistics, U.S. Department of Labor. (2015, December 17). Taxi drivers and chauffeurs. *Occupational Outlook Handbook.* Retrieved August 8, 2017, from https://www.bls.gov/ooh/transportation-and-material-moving/taxi-drivers-and-chauffeurs.htm

Burns, L. D., Jordan, W. C., & Scarborough, B. A. (2013). Transforming personal mobility. *The Earth Institute, 431,* 432.

Burton-Danner, K., Owsley, C., & Jackson, G. R. (2001). Aging and feature search: The effect of search area. *Experimental Aging Research, 27*(1), 1–18. doi:10.1080/036107301750046115 PMID:11205526

Buterin, V. (2013). *A Next-Generation Smart Contract and Decentralized Application Platform.* Retrieved from http://blockchainlab.com/pdf/Ethereum_white_paper-a_next_generation_smart_contract_and_decentralized_application_platform-vitalik-buterin.pdf

Butler, B. S. (2001). Membership Size, Communication Activity, and Sustainability: A Resource-Based Model of Online Social Structures. *Information Systems Research, 12*(4), 346–362. doi:10.1287/isre.12.4.346.9703

Byers, J. C., Bittner, A. C., & Hill, S. G. (1989). Traditional and raw task load index (TLX) correlations: are paired comparisons necessary? In A. Mital (Ed.), *Advances in Industrial Ergonomics and Safety l* (pp. 481–485). Taylor and Francis.

Caine, K. E., Šabanović, S., & Carter, M. E. (2012). The Effect of Monitoring by Cameras and Robots on the Privacy Enhancing Behaviors of Older Adults. *Proceedings of the 7th ACM/IEEE International Conference on Human Robot Interaction (HRI)*, 343–350. 10.1145/2157689.2157807

Calignano, F., Manfredi, D., Ambrosio, E. P., Biamino, S., Lombardi, M., Atzeni, E., ... Fino, P. (2017). Overview on Additive Manufacturing Technologies. *Proceedings of the IEEE*, *105*(4), 593–612. doi:10.1109/JPROC.2016.2625098

Callon, M. (1986). The sociology of an actor-network: The case of the electric vehicle. In M. Callon, A. Rip, & J. Law (Eds.), *Mapping the Dynamics of Science and Technology: Sociology of Science in the Real World* (pp. 19–34). Springer. doi:10.1007/978-1-349-07408-2_2

Canary, D. J., & Yum, Y. O. (2015). Relationship maintenance strategies. The International Encyclopedia of Interpersonal Communication, 1-9.

Cao, Y., Chen, S., Hou, P., & Brown, D. (2015, August). FAST: A fog computing assisted distributed analytics system to monitor fall for stroke mitigation. In *Networking, Architecture and Storage (NAS), 2015 IEEE International Conference on* (pp. 2-11). IEEE.

Caplan, A., & Arp, R. (2014). *Contemporary debates in bioethics*. Chichester, UK: John Wiley & Sons.

Carstensen, L. L., Mikels, J. A., & Mather, M. (2006). Aging and the intersection of cognition, motivation, and emotion. In J.E. Birren, K.W. Shaie, R.P. Abeles, M. Gatz, & T.A. Salthouse (Eds.), Handbook of the Psychology of Aging (6th ed.; pp. 343-362). Academic Press. doi:10.1016/B978-012101264-9/50018-5

Carstensen, L. L., Isaacowitz, D. M., & Charles, S. T. (1999). Taking time seriously: A theory of socioemotional selectivity. *The American Psychologist*, *54*(3), 165–181. doi:10.1037/0003-066X.54.3.165 PMID:10199217

Cassel, C. K., & Meier, D. E. (1990). Morals and moralism in the debate over euthanasia and assisted suicide. *The New England Journal of Medicine*, *323*(11), 750–752. doi:10.1056/NEJM199009133231110 PMID:2388673

Castañeda, D. M. (2017). Sexting and sexuality in romantic relationships among Latina/o emerging adults. *American Journal of Sexuality Education*, *12*(2), 120–135. doi:10.1080/15546128.2017.1298069

Cayola, L., & Macías, J. A. (2018). Systematic guidance on usability methods in user-centered software development. *Information and Software Technology*, *97*, 163–175. doi:10.1016/j.infsof.2018.01.010

CBS News. (2017, April 6). Woman says Fitbit helped save her life. *CBS News*. Accessed at http://www.cbsnews.com/news/woman-says-fitbit-helped-save-her-life-blood-clots/

Çelen, S., (2017), Sanayi 4.0 ve Simülasyon. *International Journal of 3D Printing Technologies and Digital Industry*, (1), 9-26.

Cellan-Jones. (2014). Retrieved from https://www.bbc.com/news/technology-30290540

Centers for Disease Control and Prevention. (2014). *Youth risk behavior surveillance, 2013.* Washington, DC: Author.

Centers for Disease Control and Prevention. (2017, November 30). *Older Adult Safety.* Retrieved from https://www.cdc.gov/motorvehiclesafety/older_adult_drivers/index.html

Chalil Madathil, K., Koikkara, R., Gramopadhye, A. K., & Greenstein, J. S. (2011, September). An empirical study of the usability of consenting systems: iPad, Touchscreen and paper-based systems. *Proceedings of the Human Factors and Ergonomics Society Annual Meeting, 55*(1), 813–817. doi:10.1177/1071181311551168

Chan, C. (2012). Exploring an experiential learning project through Kolb's Learning Theory using a qualitative research method. *European Journal of Engineering Education, 37*(4), 405–415. doi:10.1080/03043797.2012.706596

Chang, S., Alzougool, B., Berry, M., Gomes, C., Smith, S., & Reeders, D. (2012). International students in the digital age: Do you know where your students go to for information. *Proceedings of the Australian International Education Conference.*

Chapelle, W., McDonald, K., Thompson, B., & Swearengen, J. (2012). *Prevalence of high emotional distress, symptoms of post-traumatic stress disorder in U.S. Air Force active duty remotely piloted aircraft operators* (Technical Report no. AFRL-SA-WP-TR-2013-0002). Wright-Patterson Air Force Base, OH: U.S. Air Force School of Aerospace Medicine.

Chapelle, W., McDonald, K., Prince, L., Goodman, T., Ray-Sannerud, B., & Thompson, W. (2014b). Assessment of occupational burnout in United States Air Force predator/reaper "drone" operators. *Military Psychology, 26*(5-6), 376–385. doi:10.1037/mil0000046

Chapelle, W., Salinas, A., & McDonald, K. (2011). *Psychological health screening of remotely piloted aircraft (RPA) operators and supporting units. Wright-Patterson Air Force Base, Ohio Department of Neuropsychiatry.* U.S. Air Force School of Aerospace Medicine.

Chappelle, W., Goodman, T., Reardon, L., & Thompson, W. (2014a). An analysis of post traumatic stress symptoms in United States Air Force drone operators. *Journal of Anxiety Disorders, 28*(5), 480–487. doi:10.1016/j.janxdis.2014.05.003 PMID:24907535

Charatan, F. (1999). Dr. Kevorkian found guilty of second degree murder. *British Medical Journal, 318*(7189), 962. PMID:10195955

Charness, N. (1981). Aging and skilled problem solving. *Journal of Experimental Psychology. General, 110*(1), 21–38. doi:10.1037/0096-3445.110.1.21 PMID:6453184

Chase, R. (2016, August 10). Self-Driving Cars Will Improve Our Cities. If They Don't Ruin Them. *Wired.* Retrieved from https://www.wired.com/2016/08/self-driving-cars-will-improve-our-cities-if-they-dont-ruin-them/

Chen, M. (2010). The effects of game strategy and preference-matching on flow experience and programming performance in game-based learning. *Innovations in Education and Teaching International, 47*(1), 39–52. doi:10.1080/14703290903525838

Cheung, C. M. K., Chiu, P.-Y., & Lee, M. K. O. (2011). Online social networks: Why do students use facebook. *Computers in Human Behavior, 27*(4), 1337–1343. doi:10.1016/j.chb.2010.07.028

Chochinov, H. M., Tataryn, D., Clinch, J. J., & Dudgeon, D. (1999). Will to live in the terminally ill. *Lancet, 354*(9181), 816–819. doi:10.1016/S0140-6736(99)80011-7 PMID:10485723

Chui, M., Löffler, M., & Roberts, R. (2010), *Internet of Things,* Retrieved from https://www.mckinsey.com/industries/high-tech/our-insights/the-internet-of-things.

Chui, M., Manyika, J., Bughin, J., Dobbs, R., Roxburgh, C., Sarrazin, H., ... Westergren, M. (2012). *The Social Economy: Unlocking Value and Productivity through Social Technologies.* McKinsey Global Institute.

Churchill, J. D., Stanis, J. J., Press, C., Kushelev, M., & Greenough, W. T. (2003). Is procedural memory relatively spared from age effects? *Neurobiology of Aging, 24*(6), 883–892. doi:10.1016/S0197-4580(02)00194-X PMID:12927770

Cisneros, J. L., Aarestrup, F. M., & Lund, O. (2018). Public Health Surveillance using Decentralized Technologies. *Blockchain in Healthcare Today,* 1-14.

Clark, D. (2007). From margins to centre: A review of the history of palliative care in cancer. *The Lancet Oncology, 8*(5), 430–438. doi:10.1016/S1470-2045(07)70138-9 PMID:17466900

CNN Library. (2018, June 4). *Physician-assisted suicide fast facts.* Retrieved from: https://www.cnn.com/2014/11/26/us/physician-assisted-suicide-fast-facts/index.html

Cœugnet, S., Dommes, A., Panëels, S., Chevalier, A., Vienne, F., Dang, N. T., & Anastassova, M. (2017). A vibrotactile wristband to help older pedestrians make safer street-crossing decisions. *Accident; Analysis and Prevention, 109,* 1–9. doi:10.1016/j.aap.2017.09.024 PMID:28987612

Coffey, H. (2009). *Digital game-based learning.* Learn NC.

Coleman, J. S. (1988). Social capital in the creation of human capital. *American Journal of Sociology, 94,* S95–S120. doi:10.1086/228943

Collins, T., Aldred, S., Woolley, S., & Rai, S. (2015, December). Addressing the Deployment Challenges of Health Monitoring Devices for a Dementia Study. In *Proceedings of the 5th EAI International Conference on Wireless Mobile Communication and Healthcare* (pp. 202-205). ICST (Institute for Computer Sciences, Social-Informatics and Telecommunications Engineering). 10.4108/eai.14-10-2015.2261638

Connolly, J., & McIsaac, C. (2011). Romantic relationships in adolescence. In M. K. Underwood & L. H. Rosen (Eds.), *Social Development: Relationships in infancy, childhood, and adolescence* (pp. 180–206). New York: The Guilford Press.

Coppola, F. (2018, May 30). *Bitcoin's Need For Electricity Is Its 'Achilles Heel'*. Retrieved from https://www.forbes.com/sites/francescoppola/2018/05/30/bitcoins-need-for-electricity-is-its-achilles-heel/#688658e72fb1

Cornelius, S. W., & Caspi, A. (1987). Everyday problem solving in adulthood and old age. *Psychology and Aging, 2*(2), 144–153. doi:10.1037/0882-7974.2.2.144 PMID:3268204

Cornes, A. (2004). *Culture from the inside out*. Intercultural Press.

Costello, M. C., Madden, D. J., Mitroff, S. R., & Whiting, W. L. (2010). Age-related decline of visual processing components in change detection. *Psychology and Aging, 25*(2), 35–368. doi:10.1037/a0017625 PMID:20545420

Cowan, J. D., & Walsh, D. (2001). Terminal sedation in palliative medicine – definition and review of the literature. *Supportive Care in Cancer, 9*(6), 403–407. doi:10.1007005200100235 PMID:11585266

Cox Communications. (2009). *Teen online and wireless safety survey: Cyberbullying, sexting, and parental controls*. Retrieved June 12, 2018 from http://www.scribd.com/doc/20023365/2009-Cox-Teen-Online-Wireless-Safety-Survey-Cyberbullying-Sexting-and-Parental-Controls

Cox, D., & McLeod, S. (2014). Social media marketing and communications strategies for school superintendents. *Journal of Educational Administration, 52*(6), 850–868. doi:10.1108/JEA-11-2012-0117

Crane, J. (2017, December 28). *How Bitcoin Got Here: A (Mostly) Complete Timeline of Bitcoin's Highs and Lows*. Retrieved from http://nymag.com/selectall/2017/12/bitcoin-timeline-bitcoins-record-highs-lows-and-history.html

Crawford, J., & Neal, A. (2006). A review of the perceptual and cognitive issues associated with the use of head-up displays in commercial aviation. *The International Journal of Aviation Psychology, 16*(1), 1–19. doi:10.120715327108ijap1601_1

CREATE Overview. (2018). Retrieved August 9, 2018 from http://www.create-center.org/

Crimmins, D. M., & Seigfried-Spellar, K. C. (2014). Peer attachment, sexual experiences, and risky online behaviors as predictors of sexting behaviors among undergraduate students. *Computers in Human Behavior, 32*, 268–275. doi:10.1016/j.chb.2013.12.012

CryptoKitties. (2018a). *CryptoKitties*. Retrieved from https://www.cryptokitties.co/

CryptoKitties. (2018b). *Key Information*. Retrieved from https://www.cryptokitties.co/technical-details

Cummings, M. L. (2006). Automation and accountability in decision support system interface design. *Journal of Technology Studies, 32*(1), 23–31. doi:10.21061/jots.v32i1.a.4

Currin, J. M., Jayne, C. N., Hammer, T. R., Brim, T., & Hubach, R. D. (2016). Explicitly pressing send: Impact of sexting on relationship satisfaction. *The American Journal of Family Therapy*, *44*(3), 143–154. doi:10.1080/01926187.2016.1145086

Curtis, D. D., & Lawson, M. J. (2002). Computer adventure games as problem-solving environments. *International Education Journal*, *3*(4), 43–56.

Cushner, K., & Brislin, R. W. (1996). *Intercultural interactions: A practical guide*. Thousand Oaks, CA: Sage.

Cuthbertson, A. (2018, May 16). *Bitcoin will use 0.5% of world's electricity by end of 2018, finds study*. Retrieved from https://www.independent.co.uk/life-style/gadgets-and-tech/news/bitcoin-mining-energy-use-electricity-cryptocurrency-a8353981.html

Dake, J. A., Price, J. H., Maziarz, L., & Ward, B. (2012). Prevalence and correlates of sexting behavior in adolescents. *American Journal of Sexuality Education*, *7*(1), 1–15. doi:10.1080/15546128.2012.650959

Damant, J., & Knapp, M. (2015). *What are the likely changes in society and technology which will impact upon the ability of older adults to maintain social (extra-familial) networks of support now, in 2025 and in 2040? Future of ageing: evidence review*. London, UK: Government Office for Science.

Daniel, M., & Makary, M. A. (2016). Medical error—the third leading cause of death in the US. *BMJ (Clinical Research Ed.)*. PMID:27143499

Daskal, S. (2018). Support for voluntary euthanasia with no logical slippery slope to non-voluntary euthanasia. *Kennedy Institute of Ethics Journal*, *28*(1), 23–48. doi:10.1353/ken.2018.0001 PMID:29628450

Davis, W. (2015, April 7). *DEVgrants: Here to Help*. Retrieved from https://blog.ethereum.org/2015/04/07/devgrants-help/

Davis, F. D. (1989). Perceived usefulness, perceived ease of use, and user acceptance of information technology. *Management Information Systems Quarterly*, *13*(3), 319–340. doi:10.2307/249008

De Castell, S., Larios, H., Jenson, J., & Smith, D. H. (2015). The role of video game experience in spatial learning and memory. *Journal of Gaming & Virtual Worlds*, *7*(1), 21–40. doi:10.1386/jgvw.7.1.21_1

De Lima, L., Woodruff, R., Pettus, K., Downing, J., Buitrago, R., Munyoro, E., ... Radbruch, L. (2017). International Association for Hospice and Palliative Care position statement: Euthanasia and physician-assisted suicide. *Journal of Palliative Medicine*, *20*(1), 8–14. doi:10.1089/jpm.2016.0290 PMID:27898287

Deacon, A. (2015). *The truth about Google Fiber and the Digital Divide in Kansas City*. Retrieved July 20, 2018 from http://www.kcdigitaldrive.org/article/the-truth-about-google-fiber-and-the-digital-divide-in-kansas-city/

Deary, I. J., & Der, G. (2005). Reaction time, age, and cognitive ability: Longitudinal findings from age 16 to 63 years in representative population samples. *Neuropsychology, Development, and Cognition. Section B, Aging, Neuropsychology and Cognition, 12*(2), 187–215. doi:10.1080/13825580590969235

DeGood, K. (2011). *Aging in place, stuck without options: fixing the mobility crisis threatening the baby boom generation.* Retrieved from http://t4america.org/maps-tools/seniorsmobilitycrisis2011/

Dennis, K., & Urry, J. (2009). Post-car mobilities. In J. Conley & A. T. McLaren (Eds.), *Car troubles: Critical studies of automobility and auto-mobility* (pp. 235–252). Routledge.

Destefanis, G., Marchesi, M., Ortu, M., & Tonelli, R. (2018, March 20). *1st International Workshop on Blockchain Oriented Software.* Retrieved from https://www.researchgate.net/profile/Giuseppe_Destefanis/publication/323545752_Smart_Contracts_Vulnerabilities_A_Call_for_Blockchain_Software_Engineering/links/5a9bca3d0f7e9be379669bb6/Smart-Contracts-Vulnerabilities-A-Call-for-Blockchain-Software-Enginee

Dewey, J. (2007). *Experience and education.* Simon and Schuster.

Dexter, S. (2018, August 15). *Ethereum Roadmap Update [2018]: Casper & Sharding Release Date.* Retrieved from https://www.mangoresearch.co/ethereum-roadmap-update/

Dhar, S., & Bose, I. (2016). Framework for Using New Age Technology to Increase Effectiveness of Project Communication for Outsourced IT Projects Executed from Offshore. In V. Sugumaran, V. Yoon, & M. Shaw (Eds.), *E-Life: Web-Enabled Convergence of Commerce, Work, and Social Life. WEB 2015. Lecture Notes in Business Information Processing* (Vol. 258, pp. 207–211). Cham: Springer. doi:10.1007/978-3-319-45408-5_23

Diamond, L., & Savin-Williams, R. (2009). Adolescent sexuality. In R. Lerner & L. Steinberg (Eds.), 3rd ed.; Vol. 1, pp. 479–523). Handbook of adolescent psychology New York: Wiley.

Diamond, L., & Savin-Williams, R. (2011). Sexuality. In B. Brown & M. Prinstein (Eds.), *Encyclopedia of adolescence* (Vol. 2, pp. 314–321). New York: Academic Press. doi:10.1016/B978-0-12-373951-3.00087-9

Dickerson, A., Molnar, L. J., Eby, D. W., Adler, G., Bedard, M., Berg-Weger, M., ... Trujillo, L. (2007). Transportation and aging: A research agenda for advancing safe mobility. *The Gerontologist, 47*(5), 578–590. doi:10.1093/geront/47.5.578 PMID:17989400

Dietrich, E. (2016, October 12). *Site plan filed for Black-Olive project as neighbors worry about parking.* Retrieved July 18, 2018, from https://www.bozemandailychronicle.com/news/city/site-plan-filed-for-black-olive-project-as-neighbors-worry/article_f7b0d65b-e904-5c86-8031-47b5ea43d3d2.html

Digiconomist. (2018). *Comparing Bitcoin's energy consumption to other payment systems.* Retrieved from https://digiconomist.net/bitcoin-energy-consumption

Dir, A. L., Coskunpinar, A., Steiner, J. L., & Cyders, M. A. (2013). Understanding differences in sexting behaviors across gender, relationship status, and sexual identity, and the role of expectancies in sexting. *Cyberpsychology, Behavior, and Social Networking, 16*(8), 568–574. doi:10.1089/cyber.2012.0545 PMID:23675996

DMarket. (2018). *DMarket Smart Contract.* Retrieved from https://etherscan.io/address/0x2ccb ff3a042c68716ed2a2cb0c544a9f1d1935e1#code

Dobbs, B. M., Carr, D. B., & Morris, J. C. (2002). Evaluation and management of the driver with dementia. *The Neurologist, 8*(2), 61–70. doi:10.1097/00127893-200203000-00001 PMID:12803692

Dogra, S., & Stathokostas, L. (2012). Sedentary behavior and physical activity are independent predictors of successful aging in middle-aged and older adults. *Journal of Aging Research.* PMID:22997579

Döring, N. (2014). Consensual sexting among adolescents: Risk prevention through abstinence education or safer sexting? *Cyberpsychology (Brno), 8*(1). doi:10.5817/CP2014-1-9

Dou, Y., Niculescu, M. F., & Wu, D. J. (2013). Engineering Optimal Network Effects via Social Media Features and Seeding in Markets for Digital Goods and Services. *Information Systems Research, 24*(1), 164–185. doi:10.1287/isre.1120.0463

Dovey, C. (2015, October 1). *What old age is really like.* Retrieved from https://www.newyorker.com/culture/cultural-comment/what-old-age-is-really-like

Dresang, E. T. (2005). Access: The information-seeking behavior of youth in the digital environment. *Library Trends, 54*(2), 178–196. doi:10.1353/lib.2006.0015

Drickamer, M. A., Lee, M. A., & Ganzini, L. (1997). Practical issues in physician-assisted suicide. *Annals of Internal Medicine, 126*(2), 146–151. doi:10.7326/0003-4819-126-2-199701150-00009 PMID:9005749

Drigas, A. S., Ioannidou, R.-E., Kokkalia, G., & Lytras, M. D. (2014). ICTs, Mobile Learning and Social Media to Enhance Learning for Attention Difficulties. *Journal of Universal Computer Science, 20*(10), 1499–1510.

Drouin, M., Coupe, M., & Temple, J. R. (2017). Is sexting good for your relationship? It depends.... *Computers in Human Behavior, 75*, 749–756. doi:10.1016/j.chb.2017.06.018

Drouin, M., & Landgraff, C. (2012). Texting, sexting, and attachment in college students' romantic relationships. *Computers in Human Behavior, 28*(2), 444–449. doi:10.1016/j.chb.2011.10.015

Drouin, M., Ross, J., & Tobin, E. (2015). Sexting: A new, digital vehicle for intimate partner aggression? *Computers in Human Behavior, 50*, 197–204. doi:10.1016/j.chb.2015.04.001

Drouin, M., Vogel, K. N., Surbey, A., & Stills, J. R. (2013). Let's talk about sexting, baby: Computer-mediated sexual behaviors among young adults. *Computers in Human Behavior, 29*(5), A25–A30. doi:10.1016/j.chb.2012.12.030

Dubey, H., Yang, J., Constant, N., Amiri, A. M., Yang, Q., & Makodiya, K. (2015, October). Fog data: Enhancing telehealth big data through fog computing. In *Proceedings of the ASE Big Data & Social Informatics 2015* (p. 14). ACM.

Dunning, D. (2011). The Dunning–Kruger effect: On being ignorant of one's own ignorance. In Advances in experimental social psychology (Vol. 44, pp. 247–296). Academic Press.

Durant, E., & Trachy, A. (2017, October 17). *Digital Diploma debuts at MIT*. Retrieved from https://news.mit.edu/2017/mit-debuts-secure-digital-diploma-using-bitcoin-blockchain-technology-1017

Dwork, C., & Moni, N. (1992). Pricing via Processing or Combatting Junk Mail. In C. Dwork, M. Naor, & E. F. Brickell (Eds.), *Advances in Cryptology --- CRYPTO' 92* (pp. 139–147). Springer Berlin Heidelberg.

Ebner, W., Leimeister, J. M., & Krcmar, H. (2009). Community Engineering for Innovations - The Ideas Competition as a method to nurture a Virtual Community for Innovations. *R & D Management, 39*(4), 342–356. doi:10.1111/j.1467-9310.2009.00564.x

Edosomwan, S., Prakasan, S. K., Kouame, M. D., Watson, J., & Seymour, T. (2011). The History of Social Media and its Impact on Business. *The Journal of Applied Management and Entrepreneurship, 16*(3), 79–91.

E-Estonia. (2018). *Healthcare*. Retrieved from E-Estonia: https://e-estonia.com/solutions/healthcare/e-health-record/

EğerE. (n.d.). Retrieved from http://www.endustri40.com/endustri-4-0-ile-birlikte-gelecek-10-yeni-meslek/

Eisert, J. L., & Baldwin, C. L. (2014). Driving by the seat of your pants: A vibrotactile navigation study. *Proceedings of the Human Factors and Ergonomics Society Annual Meeting, 58*(1), 2033–2037. doi:10.1177/1541931214581424

Eklund, L. (2015). Playing video games together with others: Differences in gaming with family, friends and strangers. *Journal of Gaming & Virtual Worlds, 7*(3), 259–277. doi:10.1386/jgvw.7.3.259_1

Ellaway, A., Macintyre, S., Hiscock, R., & Kearns, A. (2003). In the driving seat: Psychosocial benefits from private motor vehicle transport compared to public transport. *Transportation Research Part F: Traffic Psychology and Behaviour, 6*(3), 217–231. doi:10.1016/S1369-8478(03)00027-5

Elliot, D. B. (1987). Contrast sensitivity decline with ageing: A neural or optical phenomenon? *Ophthalmic & Physiological Optics, 7*(4). doi:10.1111/j.1475-1313.1987.tb00771.x PMID:3454919

Elliott, L. J., & Polyakova, V. (2014). Beyond Facebook: The generalization of social networking site measures. *Computers in Human Behavior, 33*, 163–170. doi:10.1016/j.chb.2014.01.023

Ellison, N. B., Steinfield, C., & Lampe, C. (2007). The benefits of Facebook "friends:" Social capital and college students' use of online social network sites. *Journal of Computer-Mediated Communication, 12*(4), 1143–1168. doi:10.1111/j.1083-6101.2007.00367.x

Ellison, N., Vitak, J., Gray, R., & Lampe, C. (2014). Cultivating Social Resources on Social Network Sites: Facebook Relationship Maintenance Behaviors and Their Role in Social Capital Processes. *Journal of Computer-Mediated Communication, 19*(4), 855–870. doi:10.1111/jcc4.12078

Emanuel, E. J. (2002). Euthanasia and physician-assisted suicide: A review of the empirical data from the United States. *Archives of Internal Medicine, 162*(2), 142–152. doi:10.1001/archinte.162.2.142 PMID:11802747

Emanuel, E. J. (2017). Euthanasia and physician-assisted suicide: Focus on the data. *The Medical Journal of Australia, 206*(8), 339–340. doi:10.5694/mja16.00132 PMID:28446107

Emanuel, E. J., Daniels, E. R., Fairclough, D. L., & Clarridge, B. R. (1998). The practice of euthanasia and physician-assisted suicide in the United States: Adherence to proposed safeguards and effects on physicians. *Journal of the American Medical Association, 280*(6), 507–513. doi:10.1001/jama.280.6.507 PMID:9707132

Emanuel, E. J., Fairclough, D. L., Daniels, E. R., & Clarridge, B. R. (1996). Euthanasia and physician-assisted suicide: Attitudes and experiences of oncology patients, oncologists, and the public. *Lancet, 347*(9018), 1805–1810. doi:10.1016/S0140-6736(96)91621-9 PMID:8667927

Emanuel, E. J., Fairclough, D. L., & Emanuel, L. L. (2000). Attitudes and desires related to euthanasia and physician-assisted suicide among terminally ill patients. *Journal of the American Medical Association, 284*(19), 2460–2468. doi:10.1001/jama.284.19.2460 PMID:11074775

Emanuel, E. J., Fairclough, D., Clarridge, B. C., Blum, D., Bruera, E., Penley, W. C., ... Mayer, R. J. (2000). Attitudes and practices of U.S. oncologists regarding euthanasia and physician-assisted suicide. *Annals of Internal Medicine, 133*(7), 527–532. doi:10.7326/0003-4819-133-7-200010030-00011 PMID:11015165

Emanuel, E. J., Onwuteaka-Philipsen, B. D., Urwin, J. W., & Cohen, J. (2016). Attitudes and practices of euthanasia and physician-assisted suicide in the United States, Canada, and Europe. *Journal of the American Medical Association, 316*(1), 79–90. doi:10.1001/jama.2016.8499 PMID:27380345

Endsley, M. R. (2017). Autonomous driving systems: A preliminary naturalistic study of the Tesla Model S. *Journal of Cognitive Engineering and Decision Making, 11*(3), 225–238. doi:10.1177/1555343417695197

Engelhardt, M. A. (2017). *Hitching healthcare to the chain: An introduction to blockchain technology in the healthcare sector*. Technology Innovation Management Review.

Englander, E. (2012). *Low risk associated with most teenage sexting: A study of 617 18-year-olds*. Retrieved on June 6, 2018 from http://vc.bridgew.edu/cgi/viewcontent.cgi?article=1003&context=marc_reports

Englander, E. K. (2015). Coerced sexting and revenge porn among teens. *Bullying. Teen Aggression & Social Media, 1*, 19–21.

Erhel, S., & Jamet, E. (2013). Digital game-based learning: Impact of instructions and feedback on motivation and learning effectiveness. *Computers & Education, 67*, 156–167. doi:10.1016/j.compedu.2013.02.019

Ervural, B. C., & Ervural, B. (2018). Overview of Cyber Security in the Industry 4.0 Era. In Industry 4.0: Managing The Digital Transformation (pp. 267-284). Springer.

E-Sports Earnings. (2018). *Largest Overall Prize Pools in eSports.* Retrieved from https://www.esportsearnings.com/tournaments

Ethereum Classic. (2018). *Ethereum Classic.* Retrieved from https://ethereumclassic.github.io/

Ethereum Community. (2018). *History of Ethereum.* Retrieved from http://ethdocs.org/en/latest/introduction/history-of-ethereum.html

Ethereum Foundation. (2018a). *Ethereum Blockchain App Platform.* Retrieved from https://www.ethereum.org/

Ethereum Foundation. (2018b). *White Paper.* Retrieved from https://github.com/ethereum/wiki/wiki/White-Paper

Ethereum Foundation. (2018c). *Yellow Paper.* Retrieved from https://github.com/ethereum/yellowpaper

Ethereum Foundation. (2018d). *Ethash.* Retrieved from https://github.com/ethereum/wiki/wiki/Ethash

Ethereum Foundation. (2018e). *Casper Proof of Stake compendium.* Retrieved from https://github.com/ethereum/wiki/wiki/Casper-Proof-of-Stake-compendium

Etherscan. (2018). *Ethereum HashRate Growth Chart.* Retrieved from https://etherscan.io/chart/hashrate

European Union. (2016, April 27). *Regulation (EU) 2016/ 679 of the european parliament and of the council on the protection of natural persons with regard to the processing of personal data and on the free movement of such data.* Retrieved from https://eur-lex.europa.eu/legal-content/EN/TXT/PDF/?uri=CELEX:32016R0679

Exit International. (n.d.). The Deliverance Machine. *Exit International.* Retrieved from: https://exitinternational.net/the-deliverance-machine-invented-by-philip-nitschke/

Eysden, R. A., & Boersma, J. (2016, November 1). *Blockchain technology – speeding up and simplifying cross-border payments.* Retrieved from https://www2.deloitte.com/nl/nl/pages/financial-services/articles/1-blockchain-speeding-up-and-simplifying-cross-border-payments.htm

Falkon, S. (2017, December 24). *The Story of the DAO - Its History and Consequences.* Retrieved from https://medium.com/swlh/the-story-of-the-dao-its-history-and-consequences-71e6a8a551ee

Faller, C., & Feldmüller, D. (2015). Industry 4.0 learning factory for regional SMEs. *Procedia CIRP*, *32*, 88–91. doi:10.1016/j.procir.2015.02.117

Fausset, C. B., Mitzner, T. L., Price, C. E., Jones, B. D., Fain, B. W., & Rogers, W. A. (2013, September). Older adults' use of and attitudes toward activity monitoring technologies. *Proceedings of the Human Factors and Ergonomics Society Annual Meeting*, *57*(1), 1683–1687. doi:10.1177/1541931213571374

Federal Highway Administration (FHWA). (2003) *Corporate Master Plan for Research and Deployment of Technology & Innovation*. Washington, DC: U.S. Federal Highway Administration. Retrieved from the Library of Congress, https://lccn.loc.gov/2004368060

Federal Highway Administration, Department of Transportation (US). (2016, September). *Highway Statistics 2015*. Retrieved from https://www.fhwa.dot.gov/policyinformation/statistics/2015/dl20.cfm

Federal Trade Commission. (2011). *About identity theft*. Retrieved from http://www.ftc.gov/bcp/edu/microsites/idtheft/consumers/about-identity-theft.html

Feeney, L. (2016). *Why the poor face a higher cost of banking*. Retrieved September 26, 2018 from https://www.pbs.org/newshour/nation/why-the-poor-face-a-higher-cost-of-banking

Feinberg, J. (1978). Voluntary euthanasia and the inalienable right to life. *Philosophy & Public Affairs*, *7*(2), 93–123. PMID:11661543

Feldmann, H. (2013). Technological unemployment in industrial countries. *Journal of Evolutionary Economics*, *23*(5), 1099–1126. doi:10.100700191-013-0308-6

Feng, J., Craik, F. I. M., Levine, B., Moreno, S., Naglie, G., & Choi, H. (2017). Differential age-related changes in attention across an extended visual field. *European Journal of Ageing*, *14*(2), 167–177. doi:10.100710433-016-0399-7 PMID:28804400

Fisher, K. E., Landry, C. F., & Naumer, C. (2007). Social spaces, casual interactions, meaningful exchanges: 'information ground' characteristics based on the college student experience. *Information Research*, *12*(2), 12–12.

Fitts, P. M., & Jones, R. E. (1947a). *Analysis of factors contributing to 460 "pilot error" experiences in operating aircraft controls* (Report No. TSEAA-694-12). Dayton, OH: Aero Medical Laboratory, Air Materiel Command, U.S. Air Force.

Fitts, P. M., & Jones, R. E. (1947b). *Psychological aspects of instrument display. Analysis of 270 "pilot-error" experiences in reading and interpreting aircraft instruments* (Report No. TSEAA-694-12A). Dayton, OH: Aero Medical Laboratory, Air Materiel Command, U.S. Air Force.

Fjord, C. L. (2011). *The design genius of Steve Jobs*. Retrieved July 29, 2018 from https://gigaom.com/2011/10/06/christian-lindholm-on-steve-jobs/

Fleschler Peskin, M., Markham, C. M., Addy, R. C., Shegog, R., Thiel, M., & Tortolero, S. R. (2013). Prevalence and patterns of sexting among ethnic minority urban high school students. *Cyberpsychology, Behavior, and Social Networking, 16*(6), 454–459. doi:10.1089/cyber.2012.0452 PMID:23438265

Foley, K. M. (1997). Competent care for the dying instead of physician-assisted suicide. *The New England Journal of Medicine, 336*(1), 54–58. doi:10.1056/NEJM199701023360109 PMID:8970941

Fong, D. S., Aiello, L., Gardner, T. W., King, G. L., Blankenship, G., Cavallerano, J. D., ... Klein, R. (2004). Retinopathy in diabetes. *Diabetes Care, 27*(suppl 1), s84–s87. doi:10.2337/diacare.27.2007.S84 PMID:14693935

Fonseca, L. M., & Testoni, I. (2011). The Emergence of Thanatology and Current Practice in Death Education. *Omega, 64*(2), 157–169. doi:10.2190/OM.64.2.d PMID:22375350

Foreman, V. L., Favaró, F. M., Saleh, J. H., & Johnson, C. W. (2015). Software in military aviation and drone mishaps: Analysis and recommendations for the investigation process. *Reliability Engineering & System Safety, 137*, 101–111. doi:10.1016/j.ress.2015.01.006

Forte, A., Agosto, D., Dickard, M., & Magee, R. (2016, November). *The Strength of Awkward Ties: Online Interactions between High School Students and Adults.* Paper presented at GROUP '16, Sanibel Island, FL.

Fox, J., & Moreland, J. J. (2015). The dark side of social networking sites: An exploration of the relational and psychological stressors associated with Facebook use and affordances. *Computers in Human Behavior, 45*, 168–176. doi:10.1016/j.chb.2014.11.083

Fraenkel, R. J., & Wallen, E. N. (2006). *How to Design and Evaluate Research in Education.* New York: McGraw-Hill.

Fraley, R. C., & Shaver, P. R. (2000). Adult romantic attachment: Theoretical developments, emerging controversies, and unanswered questions. *Review of General Psychology, 4*(2), 132–154. doi:10.1037/1089-2680.4.2.132

Franklin, P. (2007). Differences and difficulties in intercultural management interaction. In H. Kotthoff & Spencer-Oatey (Eds.), Handbook of Intercultural Communication (pp. 263–284). Hal.

Frey, C. B., & Osborne, M. A. (2017). The future of employment: How susceptible are jobs to computerisation? *Technological Forecasting and Social Change, 114*, 254–280. doi:10.1016/j.techfore.2016.08.019

Friemel, T. N. (2016). The digital divide has grown old: Determinants of a digital divide among seniors. *New Media & Society, 18*(2), 313–331. doi:10.1177/1461444814538648

Fu, F., Liu, L., & Wang, L. (2008). Empirical analysis of online social networks in the age of Web 2.0. *Physica A, 387*(2-3), 675–684. doi:10.1016/j.physa.2007.10.006

Fujii, T., Guo, T., & Kamoshida, A. (2018, August). A Consideration of Service Strategy of Japanese Electric Manufacturers to Realize Super Smart Society (SOCIETY 5.0). In *International Conference on Knowledge Management in Organizations* (pp. 634-645). Springer. 10.1007/978-3-319-95204-8_53

Fulk, G. D., Combs, S. A., Danks, K. A., Nirider, C. D., Raja, B., & Reisman, D. S. (2014). Accuracy of 2 activity monitors in detecting steps in people with stroke and traumatic brain injury. *Physical Therapy*, *94*(2), 222–229. doi:10.2522/ptj.20120525 PMID:24052577

Furman, W., Simon, V. A., Shaffer, L., & Bouchey, H. A. (2002). Adolescents' working models and styles for relationships with parents, friends, and romantic partners. *Child Development*, *73*(1), 241–255. doi:10.1111/1467-8624.00403 PMID:14717255

Galovan, A. M., Drouin, M., & McDaniel, B. T. (2018). Sexting profiles in the united states and Canada: Implications for individual and relationship well-being. *Computers in Human Behavior*, *79*, 19–29. doi:10.1016/j.chb.2017.10.017

Gámez-Guadix, M., Almendros, C., Borrajo, E., & Calvete, E. (2015). Prevalence and association of sexting and online sexual victimization among Spanish adults. *Sexuality Research & Social Policy*, *12*(2), 145–154. doi:10.100713178-015-0186-9

Ganzini, L., & Dobscha, S. K. (2004). Clarifying distinctions between contemplating and completing physician-assisted suicide. *The Journal of Clinical Ethics*, *15*(2), 119–122. PMID:15481163

Ganzini, L., Fenn, D. S., Lee, M. A., Heintz, R. T., & Bloom, J. D. (1996). Attitudes of Oregon psychiatrists toward physician-assisted suicide. *The American Journal of Psychiatry*, *153*(11), 1469–1475. doi:10.1176/ajp.153.11.1469 PMID:8890683

Ganzini, L., Nelson, H. D., Schmidt, T. A., Kraemer, D. F., Delorit, M. A., & Lee, M. A. (2000). Physicians' experiences with the Oregon Death with Dignity Act. *The New England Journal of Medicine*, *342*(8), 557–563. doi:10.1056/NEJM200002243420806 PMID:10684915

Garrett, P., Brown, C. A., Hart-Hester, S., Hamadain, E., Dixon, C., Pierce, W., & Rudman, W. J. (2006). Identifying barriers to the adoption of new technology in rural hospitals: A case report. *Perspectives in Health Information Management*, *3*(9), 1–11. PMID:18066367

Gee, P. (2005). *What digital games have to teach us about learning and literacy*. Palgrave Macmillan.

Gehrke, S., Felix, A., & Reardon, T. (2018). *Fare choices: A survey of ride-hailing passengers in metro Boston*. Metropolitan Area Planning Council Research Brief.

Geissbauer, R., Vedso, J., & Schrauf, S. (2015). *Industry 4.0: Building the digital enterprise*. Retrieved from https://www.pwc.com/gx/en/industries/industry-4.0.html

Genuis, S. J., Genuis, S. K., & Chang, W.-C. (1994). Public attitudes toward the right to die. *Canadian Medical Association Journal*, *150*(5), 701–708. PMID:8313289

Gerbert, P., Lorenz, M., Rüßmann, M., Waldner, M., Justus, J., Engel, P., & Harnisch, M. (2015). *Industry 4.0: The future of productivity and growth in manufacturing industries.* Boston Consulting Group. Retrieved from https://www.bcg.com/publications/2015/engineered_products_project_business_industry_4_future_productivity_growth_manufacturing_industries.aspx

Gilchrist, A. (2016). Introducing Industry 4.0. In: Industry 4.0. Apress.

Giraudeau, C., Musielak, C., Hervé, C., Seren, D., Chasseigne, G., & Mullet, E. (2014). Aging, functional learning, and inhibition. *Experimental Aging Research, 42*(4), 329–347. doi:10.1080/0361073X.2016.1191850 PMID:27410242

Gittings, N. S., & Fozard, J. L. (1986). Age related changes in visual acuity. *Experimental Gerontology, 21*(4-5), 423–433. doi:10.1016/0531-5565(86)90047-1 PMID:3493168

Givehchi, O., & Jasperneite, J. (2013). Industrial automation services as part of the Cloud: First experiences. *Proceedings of the Jahreskolloquium Kommunikation in der Automation–KommA.*

Goligher, E. C., Ely, E. W., Sulmasy, D. P., Bakker, J., Raphael, J., Volandes, A. E., ... Downar, J. (2017). Physician-assisted suicide and euthanasia in the intensive care unit: A dialogue on core ethical issues. *Critical Care Medicine, 45*(2), 149–155. doi:10.1097/CCM.0000000000001818 PMID:28098622

Goncalves, G., Oliveira, T., & Cruz-Jesus, F. (2018). Understanding individual-level digital divide: Evidence of an African country. *Computers in Human Behavior, 87,* 276–291. doi:10.1016/j.chb.2018.05.039

Gordon-Messer, D., Bauermeister, J. A., Grodzinski, A., & Zimmerman, M. (2013). Sexting among young adults. *The Journal of Adolescent Health, 52*(3), 301–306. doi:10.1016/j.jadohealth.2012.05.013 PMID:23299018

Graham, S., & Thrift, N. (2007). Out of order: Understanding repair and maintenance. *Theory, Culture & Society, 24*(3), 1–25. doi:10.1177/0263276407075954

Granovetter, M. (1973). The strength of weak ties. *American Journal of Sociology, 78*(6), 1360–1380. doi:10.1086/225469

Graziano, D. (2016, October 25). Basis, ending service Dec. 31, offers B1 fitness watch refunds. *Wearable Tech.* Accessed at https://www.cnet.com/news/basis-b1-band-refunds-service-shuts-down-december-31/

Gražulis, V., & Markuckienė, E. (2014). Current issues of the development of employee intercultural competency in a work environment (A case-study of small municipalities of Lithuania). *Darbuotojų tarpkultūrinės kompetencijos plėtros aktualijos darbo aplinkoje (Lietuvos mažų savivaldybių atvejo analizė), 2014*(3), 78–89.

Greenhow, C. (2011). Online social networking and learning. *International Journal of Cyber Behavior, Psychology and Learning, 1*(1), 36–50. doi:10.4018/ijcbpl.2011010104

Groenewoud, J. H., van der Heide, A., Onwuteaka-Philipsen, B. D., Willems, D. L., van der Maas, P. J., & van der Wal, G. (2000). Clinical problems with the performance of euthanasia and physician-assisted suicide in the Netherlands. *The New England Journal of Medicine, 342*(8), 551–556. doi:10.1056/NEJM200002243420805 PMID:10684914

Groshen, E. L., Helper, S., MacDuffie, J. P., & Carson, C. (2018, June). *Preparing U.S. workers and employers for an autonomous vehicle future.* Washington, DC: Securing America's Future Energy (SAFE).

Grundy, S. (1988). *The computer and the classroom: Critical perspectives.* Paper presented at the Educational Research: Indigenous or exotic? Annual Conference of the AARE.

Grush, B., & Niles, J. (2018). *The End of Driving: Transportation systems and public policy planning for autonomous vehicles.* Elsevier.

Gudykunst, W. B. (2005). *Theorizing about intercultural communication.* Thousand Oaks, CA: Sage.

Gudykunst, W. B. (2010). Cross-cultural comparisons. In D. Cai (Ed.), *Intercultural communication* (2nd ed.; Vol. 1, pp. 213–253). Thousand Oaks, CA: SAGE.

Guerreiro, M. J., Murphy, D. R., & Van Gerven, P. W. (2010). The role of sensory modality in age-related distraction: A critical review and a renewed view. *Psychological Bulletin, 136*(6), 975–1022. doi:10.1037/a0020731 PMID:21038938

Guerro, H. (2011). Using video-game-based instruction in an EFL program: Understanding the power of videogames in education. *Colombian Applied Linguistics Journal, 13*(1), 55–70.

Guille, A., Hacid, H., Favre, C., & Zighed, D. A. (2013). Information Diffusion in Online Social Networks: A Survey. *SIGMOD Record, 42*(2), 17-28. doi:10.1145/2503792.2503797

Guo, Y. (2015). Moderating Effects of Gender in the Acceptance of Mobile SNS Based on UTAUT Model. *International Journal of Smart Home, 9*(1), 203–216. doi:10.14257/ijsh.2015.9.1.22

Gurrin, C., Smeaton, A. F., Qiu, Z., & Doherty, A. (2013, November). Exploring the technical challenges of large-scale lifelogging. In *Proceedings of the 4th International SenseCam & Pervasive Imaging Conference* (pp. 68-75). ACM. 10.1145/2526667.2526678

Haines, H. H. (1996). *Against capital punishment: The anti-death penalty movement in America, 1972-1994.* New York, NY: Oxford University Press.

Hakim Silvio, D. (2006). The information needs and information seeking behaviour of immigrant southern Sudanese youth in the city of London, Ontario: An exploratory study. *Library Review, 55*(4), 259–266. doi:10.1108/00242530610660807

Hall, E. T. (1959). *The silent language.* Garden City, NY: Doubleday.

Hamari, J., Shernoff, D. J., Rowe, E., Coller, B., Asbell-Clarke, J., & Edwards, T. (2016). Challenging games help students learn: An empirical study on engagement, flow and immersion in game-based learning. *Computers in Human Behavior, 54*, 170–179. doi:10.1016/j.chb.2015.07.045

Hamid, S., Bukhari, S., Sri, D. R., Norman, A. A., & Mohamad, T. I. (2016). Role of social media in information-seeking behaviour of international students. *Aslib Journal of Information Management, 68*(5), 643–666. doi:10.1108/AJIM-03-2016-0031

Hamid, S., Waycott, J., Kurnia, S., & Chang, S. (2015). Understanding students' perceptions of the benefits of online social networking use for teaching and learning. *The Internet and Higher Education, 26,* 1–9. doi:10.1016/j.iheduc.2015.02.004

Hampton, K., & Wellman, B. (2003). Neighboring in Netville: How the Internet supports community and social capital in a wired suburb. *City & Community, 2*(4), 277–311. doi:10.1046/j.1535-6841.2003.00057.x

Hancock, P. A. (2015, March). Automobility: The coming use of fully-automated on-road vehicles. In Cognitive methods in situation awareness and decision support (CogSIMA), 2015 IEEE international inter-disciplinary conference (pp. 137-139). IEEE.

Hancock, P. A. (2009). *Mind, machine, and morality.* Aldershot, UK: Ashgate Publishing.

Hancock, P. A. (2017). Imposing limits on autonomous systems. *Ergonomics, 60*(2), 284–291. doi:10.1080/00140139.2016.1190035 PMID:27409152

Hancock, P. A., Hancock, G. M., & Warm, J. S. (2009). Individuation: The N=1 revolution. *Theoretical Issues in Ergonomics Science, 10*(5), 481–488. doi:10.1080/14639220903106387

Hancock, P. A., & Parasuraman, R. (1992). Human factors and safety in the design of intelligent vehicle-highway systems (IVHS). *Journal of Safety Research, 23*(4), 181–198. doi:10.1016/0022-4375(92)90001-P

Hardin, G. (1968). The tragedy of the commons. *Science, 162*(3859), 1243–1248. doi:10.1126cience.162.3859.1243 PMID:5699198

Harris, S. (Host). (2017, April 4). What is technology doing to us? [Episode 71]. *Waking up with Sam Harris.* Podcast retrieved from https://www.samharris.org/podcast/item/what-is-technology-doing-to-us

Harrison, D., Marshall, P., Bianchi-Berthouze, N., & Bird, J. (2015, September). Activity tracking: barriers, workarounds and customisation. In *Proceedings of the 2015 ACM International Joint Conference on Pervasive and Ubiquitous Computing* (pp. 617-621). ACM. 10.1145/2750858.2805832

Hart, S. G. (2006, October). NASA-task load index (NASA-TLX); 20 years later. *Proceedings of the Human Factors and Ergonomics Society Annual Meeting, 50*(9), 904–908. doi:10.1177/154193120605000909

Hart, S. G., & Staveland, L. E. (1988). Development of NASA-TLX (Task Load Index): Results of empirical and theoretical research. *Advances in Psychology, 52,* 139–183. doi:10.1016/S0166-4115(08)62386-9

Hartshorne, J. K., & Germine, L. T. (2015). When does cognitive functioning peak? The asynchronous rise and fall of different cognitive abilities across the lifespan. *Psychological Science, 26*(4), 433–443. doi:10.1177/0956797614567339 PMID:25770099

Hashcash. (n.d.). *Hashcash.* Retrieved from http://www.hashcash.org/

Hasher, L., & Zacks, R. T. (1988). Working memory, comprehension, and aging: A review and a new view. In G. H. Bower (Ed.), *The psychology of learning and motivation: Advances in research and theory* (pp. 193–225). San Diego, CA: Academic Press.

Hasib, A. A. (2009). Threats of online social networks. *International Journal of Computer Science and Network Security, 9*(11), 288–293.

Hasin, D. S., Goodwin, R. D., Stinson, F. S., & Grant, B. F. (2005). Epidemiology of major depressive disorder: Results from the National Epidemiologic Survey on Alcoholism and Related Conditions. *Archives of General Psychiatry, 62*(10), 1097–1106. doi:10.1001/archpsyc.62.10.1097 PMID:16203955

Haythornthwaite, C. (2002). Strong, weak, and latent ties and the impact of new media. *The Information Society, 18*(5), 385–401. doi:10.1080/01972240290108195

Hazan, C., & Shaver, P. (1987). Romantic love conceptualized as an attachment process. *Journal of Personality and Social Psychology, 52*(3), 511–524. doi:10.1037/0022-3514.52.3.511 PMID:3572722

Henaghan, J. (2018). *Preparing communities for autonomous vehicles.* American Planning Association. Retrieved from https://www.planning.org/publications/document/9144551/

Hendrickson, B., Rosen, D., & Aune, R. K. (2011). An analysis of friendship networks, social connectedness, homesickness, and satisfaction levels of international students. *International Journal of Intercultural Relations, 35*(3), 281–295. doi:10.1016/j.ijintrel.2010.08.001

Hendy, K. C., Hamilton, K. M., & Landry, L. N. (1993). Measuring subjective workload: When is one scale better than many? *Human Factors, 35*(4), 579–601. doi:10.1177/001872089303500401

Heng, S. (2014). *Industry 4.0: Upgrading of Germany's Industrial Capabilities on the Horizon.* Academic Press.

Hermann, M., Pentek, T., & Otto, B. (2016, January). Design principles for industrie 4.0 scenarios. In *System Sciences (HICSS), 2016 49th Hawaii International Conference on* (pp. 3928-3937). IEEE.

Herr, K., Coyne, P. J., McCaffery, M., Manworren, R., & Merkel, S. (2011). Pain assessment in the patient unable to self-report: Position statement with clinical practice recommendations. *Pain Management Nursing, 12*(4), 230–250. doi:10.1016/j.pmn.2011.10.002 PMID:22117755

Hertzog, C., Kramer, A. F., Wilson, R. S., & Lindenberger, U. (2008). Enrichment effects on adult cognitive development: Can the functional capacity of older adults be preserved and enhanced? *Psychological Science in the Public Interest, 9*(1), 1–65. doi:10.1111/j.1539-6053.2009.01034.x PMID:26162004

Hess, T. M., Auman, C., Colcombe, S. J., & Rahhal, T. A. (2003). The impact of stereotype threat on age differences in memory performance. *The Journals of Gerontology: Series B, 58*(1), 3–P11. doi:10.1093/geronb/58.1.P3 PMID:12496296

Hildebrand, C., Häubl, G., Herrmann, A., & Landwehr, J. R. (2013). When Social Media Can Be Bad for You: Community Feedback Stifles Consumer Creativity and Reduces Satisfaction with Self-Designed Products. *Information Systems Research, 2*(1), 14–29. doi:10.1287/isre.1120.0455

Hill, L. L., Baird, S., Al-wahab, U., Larocca, J., Chukwueke, J., Engelberg, J. K., Engler, A.-M., Jahns, J., & Rybar, J. (2017, September). *Mobile usage distracted driving behaviors and beliefs among older adults in the U.S.* Washington, DC: AAA Foundation for Traffic Safety.

Hillcoat-Nallétamby, S. (2014). The meaning of "independence" for older people in different residential settings. *The Journals of Gerontology: Series B, 69*(3), 419–430. doi:10.1093/geronb/gbu008 PMID:24578371

Hill, T. P. (1995). Treating the dying patient: The challenge for medical education. *Archives of Internal Medicine, 155*(12), 1265–1269. doi:10.1001/archinte.1995.00430120036005 PMID:7778956

Hiratsuka, H., Suzuki, H., & Pusina, A. (2016). Explaining the effectiveness of the contrast culture method for managing interpersonal interactions across cultures. *Journal of International Students, 6*(1), 73–92.

Hofer, M., & Aubert, V. (2013). Perceived bridging and bonding social capital on Twitter: Differentiating between followers and followees. *Computers in Human Behavior, 29*(6), 2134–2142. doi:10.1016/j.chb.2013.04.038

Hofstede, G. (1983). Dimensions of national cultures in fifty countries and three regions. In J. B. Deregowski, S. Dziurawiec, & C. Robert (Eds.), *Expectations in cross-cultural psychology* (pp. 335–355). Lisse: Swets & Zeitlinger.

Hofstede, G. (2001). *Culture's consequences: Comparing values, behaviors, institutions, and organizations across nations.* London: Sage.

Ho, G., & Scialfa, C. T. (2002). Age, skill transfer, and conjunction search. *The Journals of Gerontology: Series B, 57*(3), 277–P287. doi:10.1093/geronb/57.3.P277 PMID:11983739

Ho, G., Scialfa, C. T., Caird, J. K., & Graw, T. (2001). Visual search for traffic signs: The effects of clutter, luminance, and aging. *Human Factors, 43*(2), 194–207. doi:10.1518/001872001775900922 PMID:11592661

Holland, G., & Tiggemann, M. (2016). A systematic review of the impact of the use of social networking sites on body image and disordered eating outcomes. *Body Image, 17*, 100–110. doi:10.1016/j.bodyim.2016.02.008 PMID:26995158

Horn, J. L., & Cattell, R. B. (1967). Age differences in fluid and crystallized intelligence. *Acta Psychologica, 26*, 107–129. doi:10.1016/0001-6918(67)90011-X PMID:6037305

Houck, C. D., Barker, D., Rizzo, C., Hancock, E., Norton, A., & Brown, L. K. (2014). Sexting and sexual behavior in at-risk adolescents. *Pediatrics*, *133*(2), 1–7. doi:10.1542/peds.2013-1157 PMID:24394678

Huang, J., Baptista, J., & Galliers, R. D. (2013). Reconceptualizing rhetorical practices in organizations: The impact of social media on internal communications. *Information & Management*, *50*(2-3), 112–124. doi:10.1016/j.im.2012.11.003

Huang, W. H., Huang, W. Y., & Tschopp, J. (2010). Sustaining iterative game playing processes in DGBL: The relationship between motivational processing and outcome processing. *Computers & Education*, *55*(2), 789–797. doi:10.1016/j.compedu.2010.03.011

Hugh, M. (2012). Ethnographic studies multicultural eduation in classrooms and schools. In J. Banks (Ed.), Handbook of research on multicultural education (pp. 129–144). San Francisco: Jossey-Bass.

Hughes, D. J., Rowe, M., Batey, M., & Lee, A. (2012). A tale of two sites: Twitter vs. Facebook and the personality predictors of social media usage. *Computers in Human Behavior*, *28*(2), 561–569. doi:10.1016/j.chb.2011.11.001

Humphry, D., & Wickett, A. (1986). *The right to die*. New York, NY: Harper and Row.

İçerli, M. K. (2007). *Çalışma Ekonomisi*. İstanbul: BETA Yayınevi.

Ihm, J. (2015). Network measures to evaluate stakeholder engagement with nonprofit organizations on social networking sites. *Public Relations Review, 41*(4), 501-503. http://dx.doi.org./10.1016/j.pubrev.2015.06.018

Ihtiyar, A., & Ahmad, F. S. (2015). The Role of intercultural communication competence on service reliability and customer satisfaction. *Journal of Economic & Social Studies, 5*(1), 145–168. doi:10.14706/JECOSS11518

Inbar, M. (2009). 'Sexting' bullying cited in teen's suicide. 13-year-old Hope Witsell hanged herself after topless photos circulated. *MSNBC Today*. Retrieved from: http://today.msnbc.msn.com/id/34236377/ns/today-today_people

Intel Corporation. (2017). *PoET 1.0 Specification*. Retrieved from https://sawtooth.hyperledger.org/docs/core/releases/latest/architecture/poet.html?highlight=proof%20elapsed%20time

Interaction Design Foundation. (2015). *What is the difference between interaction design and UX design?* Retrieved September 28, 2018 from https://www.interaction-design.org/literature/article/what-is-the-difference-between-interaction-design-and-ux-design

International Association of Public Transport (UITP). (2017). *Autonomous vehicles: a potential game changer for urban mobility*. Policy brief retrieved from https://www.uitp.org/autonomous-vehicles

International Transport Forum (ITF). (2018). *The shared-use city: managing the curb*. Corporate Partnership Board Report. Retrieved from https://www.itf-oecd.org/sites/default/files/docs/shared-use-city-managing-curb_3.pdf

Isaacowitz, D. M., Wadlinger, H. A., Goren, D., & Wilson, H. R. (2006). Is there an age-related positivity effect in visual attention? A comparison of two methodologies. *Emotion (Washington, D.C.)*, *6*(3), 511–516. doi:10.1037/1528-3542.6.3.511 PMID:16938091

Ivankova, N. V., Creswell, J. W., & Stick, S. L. (2006). Using mixed-methods sequential explanatory design: From theory to practice. *Field Methods*, *18*(1), 3–20. doi:10.1177/1525822X05282260

Jackman, R., & Roper, S. (1987). Structural unemployment. *Oxford Bulletin of Economics and Statistics*, *49*(1), 9–36. doi:10.1111/j.1468-0084.1987.mp49001002.x

Jacobsen, S. (2010). *The exoskeleton's super technology*. Retrieved from: http://www.raytheon.com/newsroom/technology/rtn08_exoskeleton/

Jacobs, J. (1961). *The death and life of great American cities*. Vintage Books.

Jacobson, L. (1995). *Bank failure: The financial marginalization of the poor*. Retrieved September 26, 2018 http://prospect.org/article/bank-failure-financial-marginalization-poor

Jasanoff, S. (2015). Future imperfect: Science, technology, and the imaginations of modernity. In S. Jasanoff & S.-H. Kim (Eds.), *Dreamscapes of modernity: Sociotechnical imaginaries and the fabrication of power* (pp. 1–33). University of Chicago Press. doi:10.7208/chicago/9780226276663.003.0001

Jefferis, B. J., Sartini, C., Lee, I. M., Choi, M., Amuzu, A., Gutierrez, C., ... Whincup, P. H. (2014). Adherence to physical activity guidelines in older adults, using objectively measured physical activity in a population-based study. *BMC Public Health*, *14*(1), 382. doi:10.1186/1471-2458-14-382 PMID:24745369

Jenks, C. (2017). The gathering swarm: The path to increasingly autonomous weapons systems. *Jurimetrics: The Journal of Law. Science & Technology*, *57*(3), 341–359.

Jensen, M. P., & Karoly, P. (1992). Self-report scales and procedures for assessing pain in adults. In D. C. Turk & R. Melzack (Eds.), *Handbook of pain assessment* (pp. 135–151). New York: Guilford Press.

Jeong, W. (2004). Unbreakable ethnic bonds: Information-seeking behavior of Korean graduate students in the United States. *Library & Information Science Research*, *26*(3), 384–400. doi:10.1016/j.lisr.2004.04.001

John, O. P., Donahue, E. M., & Kentle, R. L. (1991). *The big five inventory: Versions 4a and 54, institute of personality and social research*. Berkeley, CA: University of California.

Jonsson, L. S., Priebe, G., Bladh, M., & Svedin, C. G. (2014). Voluntary sexual exposure online among Swedish youth–social background, Internet behavior and psychosocial health. *Computers in Human Behavior*, *30*, 181–190. doi:10.1016/j.chb.2013.08.005

Jørgensen, K. (2003, November). Problem Solving: The Essence of Player Action in Computer Games. *DiGRA Conference.*

JPMorgan Chase & Co. (2016). *Quorum.* Retrieved from https://github.com/jpmorganchase/quorum-docs/blob/master/Quorum%20Whitepaper%20v0.1.pdf

Judge, A. M. (2012). "Sexting" among US adolescents: Psychological and legal perspectives. *Harvard Review of Psychiatry, 20*(2), 86–96. doi:10.3109/10673229.2012.677360 PMID:22512742

Jussila, J. J., Kärkkäinen, H., & Aramo-Immonen, H. (2014). Social media utilization in business-to-business relationships of technology industry firms. *Computers in Human Behavior, 30,* 606–613. doi:10.1016/j.chb.2013.07.047

Kadli, J. H., & Kumbar, B. (2013). *Library Resources, Services and Information Seeking Behaviour in Changing ICT Environment: A Literature Review.* Library Philosophy & Practice.

Kain, E. (2015). The top ten best-selling video games in 2014. *Forbes Magazine.* Retrieved from http://www.forbes.com/sites/erikkain/2015/01/19/the-top-ten-best-selling-video-games-of-2014/

Kaminski, J. (2011). Diffusion of innovation theory. *Canadian Journal of Nursing Informatics, 6*(2), 1–6.

Kane, G. C., Alavi, M., Labianca, G., & Borgatti, S. P. (2014). What's Different about Social Media Networks? A Framework and Research Agenda. *Management Information Systems Quarterly, 38*(1), 274–304. doi:10.25300/MISQ/2014/38.1.13

Kaplan, A. M., & Haenlein, M. (2010). Users of the world, unite! The challenges and opportunities of Social Media. *Business Horizons, 53*(1), 59–68. doi:10.1016/j.bushor.2009.09.003

Kautz, H., Selman, B., & Shah, M. (1997). ReferralWeb: Combining social networks and collaborative filtering. *Communications of the ACM, 40*(3), 63–65. doi:10.1145/245108.245123

Kearns, O. (2017). Secrecy and absence in the residue of covert drone strikes. *Political Geography, 57,* 13–23. doi:10.1016/j.polgeo.2016.11.005

Keidanren. (2016, April). *Toward realization of the new economy and society.* Japan Business Federation.

Keshavarz, B., Ramkhalawansingh, R., Haycock, B., Shahab, S., & Campos, J. L. (2018). Comparing simulator sickness in younger and older adults during simulated driving under different multisensory conditions. *Transportation Research Part F: Traffic Psychology and Behaviour, 54,* 47–62. doi:10.1016/j.trf.2018.01.007

Ketcham, C. J., & Stelmach, G. E. (2004). Movement control in the older adult. In R. W. Pew & S. B. Van Hemel (Eds.), *Technology for Adaptive Aging* (pp. 64–92). Washington, DC: National Academies Press.

Kevorkian, J. (1991). *Prescription—medicine: The goodness of planned death.* Buffalo, NY: Prometheus Books.

Khatwani, S. (2017, November 11). *Biggest Bitcoin Hacks Ever.* Retrieved from https://coinsutra. com/biggest-bitcoin-hacks

Khosravi, P., Rezvani, A., & Wiewiora, A. (2016). The impact of technology on older adults' social isolation. *Computers in Human Behavior, 63*, 594–603. doi:10.1016/j.chb.2016.05.092

Kiili, K. (2005). Digital game-based learning: Towards an experiential gaming model. *The Internet and Higher Education, 8*(1), 13–24. doi:10.1016/j.iheduc.2004.12.001

Kim, A. J., & Ko, E. (2012). Do social media marketing activities enhance customer equity? An empirical study of luxury fashion brand. *Journal of Business Research, 65*(10), 1480–1486. doi:10.1016/j.jbusres.2011.10.014

Kim, B., Park, H., & Baek, Y. (2009). Not just fun, but serious strategies: Using meta-cognitive strategies in game-based learning. *Computers & Education, 52*(4), 800–810. doi:10.1016/j. compedu.2008.12.004

Kimberly, C., Williams, A., Drawdy, D., & Cruz, C. (2017). Brief report: Young adult women, sexting, and risky sexual behaviors. *Journal of Health Disparities Research and Practice, 10*, 1–8.

Kim, K.-S., Sin, S.-C. J., & Yoo-Lee, E. Y. (2014). Undergraduates' Use of Social Media as Information Sources. *College & Research Libraries, 75*(4), 442–457. doi:10.5860/crl.75.4.442

Kim, Y. Y. (2001). *Becoming Intercultural: An integrative theory of communication and cross-cultural adaptation.* Thousand Oaks, CA: Sage.

King, S., & Nadal, S. (2012, August 19). *Ppcoin: Peer-to-peer crypto-currency with proof-of-stake.* Retrieved from https://peercoin.net/assets/paper/peercoin-paper.pdf

Klettke, B., Hallford, D. J., & Mellor, D. J. (2014). Sexting prevalence and correlates: A systematic literature review. *Clinical Psychology Review, 34*(1), 44–53. doi:10.1016/j.cpr.2013.10.007 PMID:24370714

Koca, K. C. (2018). Sanayi 4.0: Türkiye Açısından Fırsatlar ve Tehditler. *Sosyoekonomi, 26*(36), 245–252. doi:10.17233osyoekonomi.2018.02.15

Koford, B. (2010). *Match.com and Chadwick Martin Bailey 2009 - 2010 studies: recent trends: Online dating.* Retrieved from http://cp.match.com/cppp/media/CMB_Study.pdf

Kolb, D. (1984). *Experiential learning: Experience as the source of learning and development.* Prentice Hall.

Kolberg, D., & Zühlke, D. (2015). Lean automation enabled by industry 4.0 technologies. *IFAC-PapersOnLine, 48*(3), 1870–1875. doi:10.1016/j.ifacol.2015.06.359

Konrad, H. R., Girardi, M., & Helfert, R. (1999). Balance and aging. *Laryngoscope, 109*(9), 1454–1460. doi:10.1097/00005537-199909000-00019 PMID:10499055

Kosba, A., Miller, A., Shi, E., Wen, Z., & Papamanthou, C. (2016). *Hawk: The Blockchain Model of Cryptography and Privacy-Preserving Smart Contracts.* Retrieved from https://eprint.iacr.org/2015/675.pdf

Kotthoff, H. (2007). Ritual and style across cultures. In H. Kotthoff & H. Spencer-Oatey (Eds.), Handbook of intercultural communication (pp. 173–197). Hal. doi:10.1515/9783110198584.2.173

Kowalski, R. M., Limber, S. P., & Agatston, P. W. (2007). *Cyberbullying: Bullying in the Digital Age* (1st ed.). Wiley-Blackwell.

Kraft, A. (2016, Jan 7). Fitbit users sue, claiming heart rate monitor is inaccurate. *CBS News.* Accessed at http://www.cbsnews.com/news/fitbit-users-sue-claiming-heart-rate-monitor-is-inaccurate/

Kuchenbecker, K. J., & Wang, Y. (2012). *HALO: Haptic alerts for low-hanging obstacles in white cane navigation.* Academic Press.

Kuhn, T. S. (1962). *The structure of scientific revolutions.* Chicago: University of Chicago press.

Kuperberg, A., & Padgett, J. E. (2016). The role of culture in explaining college students' selection into hookups, dates, and long-term romantic relationships. *Journal of Social and Personal Relationships, 33*(8), 1070–1096. doi:10.1177/0265407515616876

Kurzweil, R. (2005). *The singularity is near: When humans transcend biology.* New York, NY: Viking Penguin.

Ku, Y. C., Chu, T. H., & Tseng, C. H. (2013). Gratifications for using CMC technologies: A comparison among SNS, IM, and e-mail. *Computers in Human Behavior, 29*(1), 226–234. doi:10.1016/j.chb.2012.08.009

Lainema, T. (2003). *Enhancing organizational business process perception: Experiences from constructing and applying a dynamic business simulation game* (PhD thesis). Turku School of Economics and Business Administration.

Lamkin, P. (2017, March 3). Fitbit's Dominance Diminishes But Wearable Tech Market Bigger Than Ever. *Forbes.* Accessed at https://www.forbes.com/sites/paullamkin/2017/03/03/fitbits-dominance-diminishes-but-wearable-tech-market-bigger-than-ever/#352076127f4d

Latane & Bibb. (2010). Dynamic Social Impact: The Creation of Culture by Communication. In D. A. Cai (Ed.), *Intercultural communication* (2nd ed.; Vol. 1, pp. 105–118). Thousand Oaks, CA: SAGE.

Latour, B. (1988). Mixing humans and nonhumans together: The sociology of a door-closer. *Social Problems, 35*(3), 298–310. doi:10.2307/800624

Lazar, A., Koehler, C., Tanenbaum, J., & Nguyen, D. H. (2015, September). Why we use and abandon smart devices. In *Proceedings of the 2015 ACM International Joint Conference on Pervasive and Ubiquitous Computing* (pp. 635-646). ACM. 10.1145/2750858.2804288

Leaning, M. (2017). *Media and information literacy: An integrated approach for the 21st century.* Cambridge, MA: Chandos Publishing. doi:10.1016/B978-0-08-100170-7.00001-9

Lebedeva, N. M. n. h. r., Makarova, E. e. m. e. u. c., & Tatarko, A. a. h. r. (2013). Increasing intercultural competence and tolerance in multicultural schools: A training program and its effectiveness. *Problems of Education in the 21st Century, 54,* 39–52.

Lee, E. (2008). *Cyber Physical Systems: Design Challenges.* University of California, Berkeley Technical Report No. UCB/EECS-2008-8. Retrieved from http://www.eecs.berkeley.edu/Pubs/TechRpts/2008/EECS-2008-8.html, 2008.

Lee, J., & Suh, E. (2013, June). *An Empirical Study of the Factors Influencing Use of Social Network Service.* PACIS, Jeju Island, South Korea.

Lee, H. J., Choi, J., Kim, J. W., Park, S. J., & Gloor, P. (2013). Communication, opponents, and clan performance in online games: A social network approach. *Cyberpsychology, Behavior, and Social Networking, 16*(12), 878–883. doi:10.1089/cyber.2011.0522 PMID:23745617

Lee, H., Lee, S. H., & Choi, J. A. (2016). Redefining digital poverty: A study on target changes of the digital divide survey for disabilities, low-income and elders. *Journal of Digital Convergence, 14*(3), 1–12. doi:10.14400/JDC.2016.14.3.1

Lee, J. M., Kim, Y., & Welk, G. J. (2014). Validity of consumer-based physical activity monitors. *Medicine and Science in Sports and Exercise, 46*(9), 1840–1848. doi:10.1249/MSS.0000000000000287 PMID:24777201

Lee, J., Bagheri, B., & Kao, H. A. (2015). A cyber-physical systems architecture for industry 4.0-based manufacturing systems. *Manufacturing Letters, 3,* 18–23. doi:10.1016/j.mfglet.2014.12.001

Lee, J., Kao, H. A., & Yang, S. (2014). Service innovation and smart analytics for industry 4.0 and big data environment. *Procedia Cirp, 16,* 3–8. doi:10.1016/j.procir.2014.02.001

Leng, G. S., Lada, S., Muhammad, M. Z., Ibrahim, A. A. H. A., & Amboala, T. (2011). An Exploration of Social Networking Sites (SNS) Adoption in Malaysia Using Technology Acceptance Model (TAM), Theory of Planned Behavior (TPB) And Intrinsic Motivation. *Journal of Internet Banking and Commerce, 16*(2).

Lenhart, A. (2009). *Teens and sexting, how and why minor teens are sending sexually suggestive nude or nearly nude images via text messaging.* Pew Internet and American Life Project Research. Retrieved June 12, 2018 from http://www.pewinternet.org/Reports/2009/Teens-and-Sexting.aspx

LeRouge, C., Van Slyke, C., Seale, D., & Wright, K. (2014). Baby boomers' adoption of consumer health technologies: Survey on readiness and barriers. *Journal of Medical Internet Research, 16*(9), e200. doi:10.2196/jmir.3049 PMID:25199475

Levin, K., Bradley, G. L., & Duffy, A. (2018). Attitudes toward euthanasia for patients who suffer from physical and mental illness. *Omega, 0*(0), 1–23. PMID:29357754

Lewin, T. (2010). *If your kids are awake, they're probably online.* Retrieved from http://www.nytimes.com/2010/01/20/education/20wired.html

Lewis, J. E., & Neider, M. B. (2016). Through the Google Glass: The impact of heads-up displays on visual attention. *Cognitive Research, 1*(1), 13. doi:10.118641235-016-0015-6 PMID:28180164

Lewis, R. D. (2006). *When cultures collide: Leading across cultures: A major new edition of the global guide.* Boston: Nicholas Brealey Publishing.

Liao, Y., Deschamps, F., Loures, E. D. F. R., & Ramos, L. F. P. (2017). Past, present and future of Industry 4.0-a systematic literature review and research agenda proposal. *International Journal of Production Research, 55*(12), 3609–3629. doi:10.1080/00207543.2017.1308576

Liao, Y., Finn, M., & Lu, J. (2007). Information-seeking behavior of international graduate students vs. American graduate students: A user study at Virginia Tech 2005. *College & Research Libraries, 68*(1), 5–25. doi:10.5860/crl.68.1.5

Liben-Nowell, D., & Kleinberg, J. (2007). The Link-Prediction Problem for Social Networks. *Journal of the American Society, 58*(7), 1019–1031.

Li, G., Braver, E. R., & Chen, L.-H. (2003). Fragility versus excessive crash involvement as determinants of high death rates per vehicle-mile of travel among older drivers. *Accident; Analysis and Prevention, 35*(2), 227–235. doi:10.1016/S0001-4575(01)00107-5 PMID:12504143

Li, L. (2018). China's manufacturing locus in 2025: With a comparison of "Made-in-China 2025" and "Industry 4.0". *Technological Forecasting and Social Change, 135,* 66–74. doi:10.1016/j.techfore.2017.05.028

Lilien, D. M. (1982). Sectoral shifts and cyclical unemployment. *Journal of Political Economy, 90*(4), 777–793. doi:10.1086/261088

Lin, P., Bekey, G., & Abney, K. (2009). Robots in war: Issues of risk and ethics. In Ethics and robotics. AKA Verlag/IOS Press.

Lindgaard, G., Dillon, R., Trbovich, P., White, R., Rernandes, G., Lundahl, S., & Pinnamaneni, A. (2006). User needs analysis and requirements engineering: Theory and practice. *Interacting with Computers, 18*(1), 47–70. doi:10.1016/j.intcom.2005.06.003

Lin, K.-Y., & Lu, H.-P. (2011). Why people use social networking sites: An empirical study integrating network externalities and motivation theory. *Computers in Human Behavior, 27*(3), 1152–1161. doi:10.1016/j.chb.2010.12.009

Linux Fouindation. (2018). *Hyperledger.* Retrieved from https://www.hyperledger.org/

Lippman, J. R., & Campbell, S. W. (2014). Damned if you do, damned if you don't… if you're a girl: Relational and normative contexts of adolescent sexting in the United States. *Journal of Children and Media, 8*(4), 371–386. doi:10.1080/17482798.2014.923009

Lipsman, A., Mud, G., Rich, M., & Bruich, S. (2012). Beyond the "Like" Button: The Impact of Mere Virtual Presence on Brand Evaluations and Purchase Intentions in Social Media Settings. *Journal of Advertising Research, 52*(1), 40–52. doi:10.2501/JAR-52-1-040-052

Lipson, H., & Kurman, M. (2016). *Driverless: Intelligent cars and the road ahead.* MIT Press.

Litman, T. (2009). Mobility as a positional good: Implications for transport policy and planning. In J. Conley & A. T. McLaren (Eds.), *Car troubles: Critical studies of automobility and automobility* (pp. 199–217). Routledge.

Litman, T. (2017). *Autonomous vehicle implementation predictions.* Victoria, Canada: Victoria Transport Policy Institute.

Liu, D., & Brown, B. B. (2014). Self-disclosure on social networking sites, positive feedback, and social capital among Chinese college students. *Computers in Human Behavior, 38*, 213–219. doi:10.1016/j.chb.2014.06.003

Liu, L., Stroulia, E., Nikolaidis, I., Miguel-Cruz, A., & Rios Rincon, A. (2016). Smart homes and home health monitoring technologies for older adults: A systematic review. *International Journal of Medical Informatics, 91*, 44–59. doi:10.1016/j.ijmedinf.2016.04.007 PMID:27185508

Liu, X. Z., & Yan, D. (2007). Ageing and hearing loss. *The Journal of Pathology, 211*(2), 188–197. doi:10.1002/path.2102 PMID:17200945

Liu, Y., & Wickens, C. D. (1994). Mental workload and cognitive task automaticity: An evaluation of subjective and time estimation metrics. *Ergonomics, 37*(11), 1843–1854. doi:10.1080/00140139408964953 PMID:8001525

Lizardo, O. (2012). Embodied culture as procedure: Rethinking the link between personal and objective culture. *Collegium, 12*, 70–86.

Lochner, K., Kawachi, I., & Kennedy, B. P. (1999). Social capital: A guide to its measurement. *Health & Place, 5*(4), 259–270. doi:10.1016/S1353-8292(99)00016-7 PMID:10984580

Logan, S. (2018, May 7). *Ethereum Roadmap Explained.* Retrieved from https://thecryptograph.net/ethereum-roadmap-explained/

Lopes, J. (2018). *eSports History.* Retrieved from https://www.timetoast.com/timelines/esports-history

Lorenz, M., Küpper, D., Rüßmann, M., Heidemann, A., & Bause, A. (2016). *Time to Accelerate in the Race Toward Industry 4.0.* Retrieved from: https://www.bcgperspectives.com/content/articles/lean-manufacturing-operations-time-accelerate-race-toward-industry-4/

Lounsbury, K., Mitchel, K. J., & Finkelhor, D. (2011). *The true prevalence of 'sexting'.* University of New Hampshire. Crimes Against Children Research Centre. Retrieved July 6th 2018 from https://scholars.unh.edu/cgi/viewcontent.cgi?referer=https://scholar.google.com/&httpsredir=1&article=1063&context=ccrc

Lovejoy, K., Waters, R. D., & Saxton, G. D. (2012). Engaging stakeholders through Twitter: How nonprofit organizations are getting more out of 140 characters or less. *Public Relations Review, 38*(2), 313–318. doi:10.1016/j.pubrev.2012.01.005

LuethK. L. (2015). Retrieved from https://iot-analytics.com/top-5-new-industrial-iot-jobs/

Lukač, D. (2015, November). The fourth ICT-based industrial revolution" Industry 4.0"—HMI and the case of CAE/CAD innovation with EPLAN P8. In Telecommunications Forum Telfor (TELFOR), 2015 23rd (pp. 835-838). IEEE.

Lumby, A. (2014). *The 10 best-selling video games of 2014*. Retrieved from The Fiscal Times website: http://www.thefiscaltimes.com/2014/12/12/10-Best-Selling-Games-2014-Why-Big-Studios-Should-Take-Page-Indie-Games

Luo, X., Zhang, J., & Duan, W. (2013). Social Media and Firm Equity Value. *Information Systems Research, 24*(1), 146–163. doi:10.1287/isre.1120.0462

Lu, Y. (2017). Industry 4.0: A survey on technologies, applications and open research issues. *Journal of Industrial Information Integration, 6*, 1–10. doi:10.1016/j.jii.2017.04.005

Lynch, M. (2002). Capital punishment as moral imperative: Pro-death-penalty discourse on the internet. *Punishment & Society, 4*(2), 213–236. doi:10.1177/14624740222228554

Mackrous, I., Lavalliere, M., & Teasdale, N. (2014). Adaptation to simulator sickness in older drivers following multiple sessions in a driving simulator. *Gerontechnology (Valkenswaard), 12*(2), 101–111. doi:10.4017/gt.2013.12.2.004.00

Madigan, S., Ly, A., Rash, C. L., Van Ouytsel, J., & Temple, J. R. (2018). Prevalence of multiple forms of sexting behavior among youth: A systematic review and meta-analysis. *JAMA Pediatrics, 172*(4), 327–335. doi:10.1001/jamapediatrics.2017.5314 PMID:29482215

Magnier-Watanabe, R., Yoshida, M., & Watanabe, T. (2010). Social network productivity in the use of SNS. *Journal of Knowledge Management, 14*(6), 910–927. doi:10.1108/13673271011084934

Majid, S., & Kassim, G. M. (2000). Information-seeking behaviour of international Islamic University Malaysia Law faculty members. *Malaysian Journal of Library and Information Science, 5*(2), 1–17.

Malone, T. B., Kirkpatrick, M., Mallory, K., Eike, D., Johnson, J. F., & Walker, R. W. (1980). *Human factors evaluation of control room design and operator performance at Three Mile Island -2* (Technical Report NUREG/CR-1270). Retrieved from https://tmi2kml.inl.gov/

Mangalindan, J. P. (2014). *How third-world tech can help the U.S.* Retrieved July 22, 2018 from http://fortune.com/2014/09/12/how-third-world-tech-can-help-the-u-s/

Marcus, M. B. (2016, Feb 9). Fitbit fitness tracker detects woman's pregnancy. *CBS News.* Accessed at http://www.cbsnews.com/news/fitbit-fitness-tracker-tells-woman-shes-pregnant/

Martinez-Prather, K., & Vandiver, D. M. (2014). Sexting among teenagers in the United States: A retrospective analysis of identifying motivating factors, potential targets, and the role of a capable guardian. *International Journal of Cyber Criminology*, *8*, 21–35.

Maslow, A. H. (1943). A theory of human motivation. *Psychological Review*, *50*(4), 370–396. doi:10.1037/h0054346

Matas, N. A., Nettelbeck, T., & Burns, N. R. (2015). Dropout during a driving simulator study: A survival analysis. *Journal of Safety Research*, *55*, 159–169. doi:10.1016/j.jsr.2015.08.004 PMID:26683559

Materstvedt, L. J., Clark, D., Ellershaw, J., Førde, R., Boeck Gravgaard, A.-M., & Müller-Busch, H. C. (2003). Euthanasia and physician-assisted suicide: A view from an EAPC Ethics Task Force. *Palliative Medicine*, *17*(2), 97–101. doi:10.1191/0269216303pm673oa PMID:12701848

Mather, M., & Carstensen, L. L. (2003). Aging and attentional biases for emotional faces. *Psychological Science*, *14*(5), 409–415. doi:10.1111/1467-9280.01455 PMID:12930469

Mather, M., & Carstensen, L. L. (2005). Aging and motivated cognition: The positivity effect in attention and memory. *Trends in Cognitive Sciences*, *9*(10), 496–502. doi:10.1016/j.tics.2005.08.005 PMID:16154382

Matthews, G., Emo, A. K., Funke, G., Zeidner, M., Roberts, R. D., Costa, P. T. Jr, & Schulze, R. (2006). Emotional intelligence, personality, and task-induced stress. *Journal of Experimental Psychology. Applied*, *12*(2), 96–107. doi:10.1037/1076-898X.12.2.96 PMID:16802891

Mayser, C., Piechulla, W., Weiss, K. E., & König, W. (2003, May). Driver workload monitoring. In *Proceedings of the Internationale Ergonomie-Konferenz der GfA, ISOES und FEES* (pp. 7-9). Academic Press.

Mazman, S. G., & Usluel, Y. K. (2010). Modeling educational usage of Facebook. *Computers & Education*, *55*(2), 444–453. doi:10.1016/j.compedu.2010.02.008

McBride, T., & Nief, R. (2010). *Beloit college mindset list, entering class on 2014*. Retrieved from http://www.beloit.edu/mindset/

McCusker, K., & Gunaydin, S. (2015). Research using qualitative, quantitative or mixed methods and choice based on the research. *Perfusion*, *30*(7), 537-542. doi:10.1177/0267659114559116

McDaniel, B. T., & Drouin, M. (2015). Sexting among married couples: Who is doing it, and are they more satisfied? *Cyberpsychology, Behavior, and Social Networking*, *18*(11), 628–634. doi:10.1089/cyber.2015.0334 PMID:26484980

McLachlan, H. V. (2008). The ethics of killing and letting die: Active and passive euthanasia. *Journal of Medical Ethics*, *34*(8), 636–638. doi:10.1136/jme.2007.023382 PMID:18667657

McLaughlin, A. C., Matalenas, L. A., & Gandy Coleman, M. (2018). Design of human centered augmented reality for managing chronic health conditions. In R. Pak & A. C. McLaughlin (Eds.), *Aging, Technology, and Health* (pp. 261–196). Cambridge, MA: Elsevier. doi:10.1016/B978-0-12-811272-4.00011-7

McPhee, L. C., Scialfa, C. T., Dennis, W. M., Ho, G., & Caird, J. K. (2004). Age difference in visual search for traffic signs during a simulated conversation. *Human Factors, 46*(4), 674–685. doi:10.1518/hfes.46.4.674.56817 PMID:15709329

McVeigh, K. (2013). Drone strikes: Tears in Congress as Pakistani family tells of mother's death. *The Guardian.* Retrieved from: https://www.theguardian.com/world/2013/oct/29/pakistan-family-drone-victim-testimony-congress

Meagher, D. K., & Balk, D. E. (Eds.). (2013). *Handbook f thanatology: The essential body of knowledge for the study of death, dying, and bereavement.* New York, NY: Routledge. doi:10.4324/9780203767306

Medicalchain. (2018). *MedcialChain Whitepaper.* Retrieved from https://medicalchain.com/en/whitepaper/

Medicalchain. (2018, June 18). *Medicalchain Announces Joint Working Agreement with Mayo Clinic.* Retrieved from https://medium.com/medicalchain/medicalchain-announces-joint-working-agreement-with-mayo-clinic-9cfb474dcf0f

Meier, D. E., Emmons, C.-A., Wallenstein, S., Quill, T., Morrison, R. S., & Cassel, C. K. (1998). A national survey of physician-assisted suicide and euthanasia in the United States. *The New England Journal of Medicine, 338*(17), 1193–1201. doi:10.1056/NEJM199804233381706 PMID:9554861

Melenhorst, A. S., Rogers, W. A., & Bouwhuis, D. G. (2006). Older adults' motivated choice for technological innovation: Evidence for benefit-driven selectivity. *Psychology and Aging, 21*(1), 190–195. doi:10.1037/0882-7974.21.1.190 PMID:16594804

Meng, J. (2009). *Living in internet time.* Retrieved from http://www.ocf.berkeley.edu/~jaimeng/techtime.html

Men, L. R., & Tsai, W. H. S. (2013). Beyond Liking or Following: Understanding Public Engagement on Social Networking Sites in China. *Public Relations Review, 39*(1), 13–22. doi:10.1016/j.pubrev.2012.09.013

Mercer, K., Giangregorio, L., Schneider, E., Chilana, P., Li, M., & Grindrod, K. (2016). Acceptance of commercially available wearable activity trackers among adults aged over 50 and with chronic illness: A mixed-methods evaluation. *JMIR mHealth and uHealth, 4*(1), e7. doi:10.2196/mhealth.4225 PMID:26818775

Merriman, N. A., Ondřej, J., Rybicki, A., Roudaia, E., O'Sullivan, C., & Newell, F. N. (2016). Crowded environments reduce spatial memory in older but not younger adults. *Psychological Research, 82*(2), 407–428. doi:10.100700426-016-0819-5 PMID:27783147

Meyer, J. (2009). Designing in-vehicle technologies for older adults. *The Bridge, 39*(1), 21–26.

Mezghani, E., Exposito, E., Drira, K., Da Silveira, M., & Pruski, C. (2015). A semantic big data platform for integrating heterogeneous wearable data in healthcare. *Journal of Medical Systems, 39*(12), 185. doi:10.100710916-015-0344-x PMID:26490143

Mienaltowski, A. (2013). Everyday problem solving across the adult life span: Solution diversity and efficacy. *Annals of the New York Academy of Sciences, 1235*(1), 75–85. doi:10.1111/j.1749-6632.2011.06207.x PMID:22023569

Miller, K. J., Adair, B. S., Pearce, A. J., Said, C. M., Ozanne, E., & Morris, M. M. (2014). Effectiveness and feasibility of virtual reality and gaming system use at home by older adults for enabling physical activity to improve health-related domains: A systematic review. *Age and Ageing, 43*(2), 188–195. doi:10.1093/ageing/aft194 PMID:24351549

Mitchell, K. J., Finkelhor, D., Jones, L. M., & Wolak, J. (2011). Prevalence and characteristics of youth sexting: A national study. *Pediatrics, 129*, 1–10. PMID:22144706

Mitzner, T. L., Boron, J. B., Fausset, C. B., Adams, A. E., Charness, N., Czaja, S. J., ... Sharit, J. (2010). Older adults talk technology: Technology usage and attitudes. *Computers in Human Behavior, 26*(6), 1710–1721. doi:10.1016/j.chb.2010.06.020 PMID:20967133

Mitzner, T. L., Chen, T. L., Kemp, C. C., & Rogers, W. A. (2014). Identifying the potential for robotics to assist older adults in different living environments. *International Journal of Social Robotics, 6*(2), 213–227. doi:10.100712369-013-0218-7 PMID:24729800

Mitzner, T. L., & Rogers, W. A. (2006). Reading in the dark: Effects of age and contrast on reading speed and comprehension. *Human Factors, 48*(2), 229–240. doi:10.1518/001872006777724372 PMID:16884045

Mix. (2018, January 17). *How BitConnect pulled the biggest exit scheme in cryptocurrency.* Retrieved from https://thenextweb.com/hardfork/2018/01/17/bitconnect-bitcoin-scam-cryptocurrency/

Miyazaki, R., Kotani, K., Tsuzaki, K., Sakane, N., Yonei, Y., & Ishii, K. (2015). Effects of a year-long pedometer-based walking program on cardiovascular disease risk factors in active older people. *Asia-Pacific Journal of Public Health, 27*(2), 155–163. doi:10.1177/1010539513506603 PMID:24174388

Molenaar, I., Sleegers, P., & Boxtel, C. (2014). Metacognitive scaffolding during collaborative learning: A promising combination. *Metacognition and Learning, 9*(3), 309–332. doi:10.100711409-014-9118-y

Moline, T. (2010). Video games as digital learning resources: Implications for teacher-librarians and for researchers. *School Libraries Worldwide, 16*(2), 1–15.

Monostori, L. (2014). Cyber-physical production systems: Roots, expectations and R&D challenges. *Procedia Cirp, 17*, 9–13. doi:10.1016/j.procir.2014.03.115

Moon, D. G. (2008). Concepts of "culture.". In M. Asante, Y. Miike, & J. Yin (Eds.), *The global intercultural communication reader* (pp. 11–26). Routledge.

Moqbel, M., Nevo, S., & Kock, N. (2013). Organizational Members' Use of Social Networking Sites and Job Performance: An Exploratory Study. *Information Technology & People*, 26(3), 240–264. doi:10.1108/ITP-10-2012-0110

Morozov, E. (2012). *The net delusion: The dark side of internet freedom*. PublicAffairs.

Morris, M. R., Teevan, J., & Panovich, K. (2010, April). *What Do People Ask Their Social Networks, and Why*. Paper presented at the SIGCHI Conference on Human Factors in Computing Systems, New York, NY. 10.1145/1753326.1753587

Mourdoukoutas, P. (1988). Seasonal employment, seasonal unemployment and unemployment compensation: The case of the tourist industry of the Greek islands. *American Journal of Economics and Sociology*, 47(3), 315–329. doi:10.1111/j.1536-7150.1988.tb02044.x

Müller-Busch, H. C., Oduncu, F. S., Woskkanjan, S., & Klaschik, E. (2004). Attitudes on euthanasia, physician-assisted suicide and terminal sedation – A survey of the members of the German Association for Palliative Medicine. *Medicine, Health Care, and Philosophy*, 7(3), 333–339. doi:10.100711019-004-9349-9 PMID:15679025

Müller-Oehring, E. M., Schulte, T., Rohlfing, T., Pfefferbaum, A., & Sullivan, E. V. (2013). Visual search and the aging brain: Discerning the effects of age-related brain volume shrinkage on alertness, feature binding, and attentional control. *Neuropsychology*, 27(1), 48–59. doi:10.1037/a0030921 PMID:23356596

Mumford, L. (1958). The highway and the city. In L. Mumford (Ed.), *The highway and the city* (pp. 234–246). New York: Harcourt, Brace & World.

Mumporeze, N., & Prieler, M. (2017). Gender digital divide in Rwanda: A qualitative analysis of socioeconomic factors. *Telematics and Informatics*, 34(7), 1285–1293. doi:10.1016/j.tele.2017.05.014

Nakamoto, S. (2008, October 31). *Bitcoin: A Peer-to-Peer Electronic Cash System*. Retrieved from https://bitcoin.org/bitcoin.pdf

Nakamoto, S. (2009, January 10). *Bitcoin v0.1 released*. Retrieved from https://satoshi.nakamotoinstitute.org/emails/cryptography/16/

National Campaign to Prevent Teen and Unplanned Pregnancy & CosmoGirl.com. (2008). *Sex and tech: Results from a survey of teens and young adults*. Retrieved May 14, 2018 from http://www.thenationalcampaign.org/sextech/pdf/sextech_summary.pdf

National Eye Institute. (2018a). *Cataracts*. Retrieved August 20, 2018 from https://www.nei.nih.gov/eyedata/cataract

National Eye Institute. (2018b). *Glaucoma, open-angle.* Retrieved August 20, 2018 from https://www.nei.nih.gov/eyedata/glaucoma

National Highway Traffic Safety Administration (NHTSA). (2008). National motor vehicle crash causation survey: Report to congress. *National Highway Traffic Safety Administration technical report DOT HS, 811,* 059.

National Highway Traffic Safety Administration (NHTSA). (2016). *2016 fatal motor vehicle crashes: Overview.* Retrieved from https://crashstats.nhtsa.dot.gov/Api/Public/Publication/812456

National Highway Traffic Safety Administration (NHTSA). (2017). *Automated driving systems 2.0: A vision for safety.* Retrieved from https://www.nhtsa.gov/document/automated-driving-systems-20-voluntary-guidance

National Institutes of Health. (2016). *World's older population grows dramatically.* Retrieved from: https://www.nih.gov/news-events/news-releases/worlds-older-population-grows-dramatically

National Safety Council. (2017). *CarTech VR360* [Smartphone app]. Retrieved August 9, 2018 from https://appadvice.com/app/cartech-vr360/1200913564

Navigant Research. (2018, January 16). *Leaderboard report: Automated driving.* Retrieved from https://www.navigantresearch.com/research/navigant-research-leaderboard-automated-driving-vehicles

Nees, M. A., & Walker, B. N. (2011). Auditory displays for in-vehicle technologies. *Review of Human Factors and Ergonomics, 7*(1), 58–99. doi:10.1177/1557234X11410396

Neisser, U., & Becklen, R. (1975). Selective looking: Attending to visually specified events. *Cognitive Psychology, 7*(4), 480–494. doi:10.1016/0010-0285(75)90019-5

Neri, S. G. R., Cardoso, J. R., Cruz, L., Lima, R. M., de Oliveira, R. J., Iversen, M. D., & Carregaro, R. L. (2017). Do virtual reality games improve mobility skills and balance measurements in community-dwelling older adults? Systematic review and meta-analysis. *Clinical Rehabilitation, 31*(10), 1292–1304. doi:10.1177/0269215517694677 PMID:28933612

Nesset, V. (2008). *The information-seeking behaviour of grade-three elementary school students in the context of a class project.* McGill University.

New York City Department of Transportation (NYC DOT). (2018, June). *New York City mobility report.* Retrieved from http://www.nyc.gov/html/dot/downloads/pdf/mobility-report-2018-print.pdf

Newzoo. (2018, April). *2018 Global Games Market.* Retrieved from https://newzoo.com/key-numbers/

Ngo, D. (2018, March 8). *UK Groves Medical Group Partners With Medicalchain To Pilot Blockchain Platform.* Retrieved from https://coinjournal.net/uk-groves-medical-group-partners-with-medicalchain-to-pilot-blockchain-platform/

Nicol, N., & Wiley, H. (2005). *Between the dying and the dead: Dr. Jack Kevorkian's life and the battle to legalize euthanasia.* Madison, WI: University of Wisconsin Press.

Nielsen Group. (2009). *Americans watching more tv than ever; web and mobile video up too.* Retrieved from http://blog.nielsen.com/nielsenwire/online_mobile/americans-watching-more-tv-than-ever/

Nielsen, J. (2006). *Digital divide: The 3 stages.* Retrieved July 20, 2018 from https://www.nngroup.com/articles/digital-divide-the-three-stages/

Nielsen-Englyst, L. (2003). Game design for imaginative conceptualisation. *Proceedings of the international workshop on experimantal interactive learning in industrial management,* 149–164.

Nielsen, J. (1994). *Usability Engineering.* San Diego, CA: Academic Press Inc.

Nishijima, M., Ivanauskas, T. M., & Sarti, F. M. (2017). Evolution and determinants of digital divide in Brazil (2005–2013). *Telecommunications Policy, 41*(1), 12–24. doi:10.1016/j.telpol.2016.10.004

Niva, S. (2013). Disappearing violence: JSOC and the Pentagon's new cartography of networked warfare. *Security Dialogue, 44*(3), 185–202. doi:10.1177/0967010613485869

Norman, D. (2013). *The design of everyday things: Revised and expanded edition.* Philadelphia, PA: Basic Books.

Norry, A. (2017, November 17). *The History of Silk Road: A Tale of Drugs, Extortion & Bitcoin.* Retrieved from https://blockonomi.com/history-of-silk-road/

Norton, P. D. (2011). *Fighting traffic: The dawn of the motor age in the American city.* MIT Press.

Nyberg, L., Bäckman, L., Erngrund, K., Olofsson, U., & Nilsson, L.-G. (1996). Age differences in episodic memory, semantic memory, and priming: Relationships to demographic, intellectual, and biological factors. *The Journals of Gerontology: Series B, 51B*(4), 234–P240. doi:10.1093/geronb/51B.4.P234 PMID:8673644

Oh, O., Agrawal, M., & Rao, H. R. (2013). Community Intelligence and Social Media Services: A Rumor Theoretic Analysis of Tweets During Social Crises. *Management Information Systems Quarterly, 3*(2), 407–426. doi:10.25300/MISQ/2013/37.2.05

Oktay, E., (2002). *Makro İktisat Teorisi ve Politikası.* Maltepe Üniversitesi İ.İ.B.F. Yayınları No: 2, 3. Baskı, Ege Reklam Basım Sanatları Ltd. Şti., Eylül, İstanbul.

Omaye, S. (2002). Metabolic modulation of carbon monoxide toxicity. *Toxicology, 180*(2), 139–150. doi:10.1016/S0300-483X(02)00387-6 PMID:12324190

Orlu, A. D. (2016). Information seeking behaviour of masters students: Affective and behavioural dimensions. *Library Philosophy and Practice (e-journal),* 1-56.

Ortega, A., Pérez, F. A., & Turianskyi, Y. (2018). *Technological justice: A G20 agenda (No. 2018-58).* Economics Discussion Papers.

Osborne, J., Simon, S., & Collins, S. (2003). Attitudes towards science: A review of the literature and its implications. *International Journal of Science Education, 25*(9), 1049–1079. doi:10.1080/0950069032000032199

Owsley, C., & McGwin, G. Jr. (2004). Association between visual attention and mobility in older adults. *Journal of the American Geriatrics Society, 52*(11), 1901–1906. doi:10.1111/j.1532-5415.2004.52516.x PMID:15507069

Özkan, M., Al, A., & Yavuz, S. (2018). Uluslararası Politik Ekonomi Açısından Dördüncü Sanayi-Endüstri Devrimi'nin Etkileri ve Türkiye. *Siyasal Bilimler Dergisi, 1*(1), 1–30. doi:10.14782/marusbd.418669

Padula, G. (2008). Enhancing the innovation performance of firms by balancing cohesiveness and bridging ties. *Long Range Planning, 41*(4), 395–419. doi:10.1016/j.lrp.2008.01.004

Papadimitriou, J. D., Skiadas, P., Mavrantonis, C. S., Polimeropoulos, V., Papadimitriou, D. J., & Papacostas, K. J. (2007, January). Euthanasia and suicide in antiquity: Viewpoint of the dramatists and philosophers. *Journal of the Royal Society of Medicine, 100*(1), 25–28. doi:10.1177/014107680710000111 PMID:17197683

Parker, T., Blackburn, K., Perry, M., & Hawks, J. (2013). Sexting as an intervention: Relationship satisfaction and motivation considerations. *The American Journal of Family Therapy, 41*(1), 1–12. doi:10.1080/01926187.2011.635134

Park, N., Kee, K. F., & Valenzuela, S. (2009). Being immersed in social networking environment: Facebook groups, uses and gratifications, and social outcomes. *Cyberpsychology & Behavior, 12*(6), 729–733. doi:10.1089/cpb.2009.0003 PMID:19619037

Park, S.-H., Huh, S.-H., Oh, W., & Han, S. P. (2012). A Social Network-Based Inference Model for Validating Customer Profile Data. *Management Information Systems Quarterly, 36*(4), 1217–1237. doi:10.2307/41703505

Pearson, J. (2017, July 19). *'THIS IS NOT A DRILL:' A Hacker Allegedly Stole $32 Million in Ethereum.* Retrieved from Motherboard: https://motherboard.vice.com/en_us/article/zmvkke/this-is-not-a-drill-a-hacker-allegedly-stole-dollar32-million-in-ethereum

Peercoin. (2018). Retrieved from https://peercoin.net/

Penprase, B. E. (2018). *Higher Education in the Era of the Fourth Industrial Revolution.* Singapore: Springer.

Pereira, J. (2011). Legalizing euthanasia or assisted suicide: The illusion of safeguards and controls. *Current Oncology (Toronto, Ont.), 18*(2), e38–e45. doi:10.3747/co.v18i2.883 PMID:21505588

Pfannenstiel, A., & Chaparro, B. S. (2015, August). An investigation of the usability and desirability of health and fitness-tracking devices. In *International Conference on Human-Computer Interaction* (pp. 473-477). Springer. 10.1007/978-3-319-21383-5_79

Pfeiffer, S. (2017). The vision of "Industrie 4.0" in the making—A case of future told, tamed, and traded. *NanoEthics*, *11*(1), 107–121. doi:10.100711569-016-0280-3 PMID:28435474

Phillips, E. K., & Jentsch, F. G. (2017). Supporting situation awareness through robot-to-human information exchanges under conditions of visuospatial perspective taking. *Journal of Human-Robot Interaction*, *6*(3), 92–117. doi:10.5898/JHRI.6.3.Phillips

Phua, J., Jin, S. V., & Kim, J. J. (2017). Uses and gratifications of social networking sites for bridging and bonding social capital: A comparison of Facebook, Twitter, Instagram, and Snapchat. *Computers in Human Behavior*, *72*, 115–122. doi:10.1016/j.chb.2017.02.041

Pîrvu, B. C., & Zamfirescu, C. B. (2017, August). Smart factory in the context of 4th industrial revolution: Challenges and opportunities for Romania. *IOP Conference Series. Materials Science and Engineering*, *227*(1), 012094. doi:10.1088/1757-899X/227/1/012094

Plunkett, J. (2017, August 28). *What was the Great Video Game Crash of 1983?* Retrieved from https://www.bugsplat.com/great-video-game-crash-1983

Pool, I. D. S., & Kochen, M. (1979). Contacts and Influence. *Social Networks*, *1*(1), 5–51. doi:10.1016/0378-8733(78)90011-4

Population Reference Bureau. (2016, January 13). *Factsheet: Aging in the United States*. Retrieved from https://www.prb.org/aging-unitedstates-fact-sheet/

Porter, K., & Warburton, K. G. (2018). Physicians' views on current legislation around euthanasia and assisted suicide: Results of surveys commissioned by the Royal College of Physicians. *Future Healthcare Journal*, *5*(1), 30–34.

Poushter, J., Bishop, C., & Chwe, H. (2018). Social media use continues to rise in developing countries but plateaus across developed ones. *Global Attitudes and Trends*. Retrieved July 22, 2018 from http://www.pewglobal.org/2018/06/19/social-media-use-continues-to-rise-in-developing-countries-but-plateaus-across-developed-ones/

Preddy, M. (2014, April). *Automakers rediscover and create for boomers*. Retrieved from https://www.aarp.org/auto/trends-lifestyle/info-2015/car-buying-for-older-drivers.html

Prensky, M. (2011). Digital natives, Digital immigrants. *On the Horizon*, *9*(5), 1–6. doi:10.1108/10748120110424816

Price, R. (2015, February 6). Uber drivers keep just 50% of what you pay. *Business Insider UK*. Retrieved from http://uk.businessinsider.com/uber-customer-cost-breakdown-morgan-stanley-2015-2

Puentes, R., & Tomer, A. (2008, December). *The road... less traveled: an analysis of vehicle miles traveled trends in the US*. Brookings Institute. Retrieved from https://rosap.ntl.bts.gov/view/dot/18145

Putnam, R. D. (2000). *Bowling alone: The collapse and revival of American community*. Simon & Schuster Paperbacks.

Putnam, R. D. (2007). E Pluribus Unum: Diversity and Community in the Twenty-first Century The 2006 Johan Skytte Prize Lecture. *Scandinavian Political Studies, 30*(2), 137–174. doi:10.1111/j.1467-9477.2007.00176.x

Qian, M., & Clark, K. R. (2016). Game-based learning and 21st century skills: A review of recent research. *Computers in Human Behavior, 63*, 50–58. doi:10.1016/j.chb.2016.05.023

Rakower, L. H. (2011). Blurred line: Zooming in on google street view and the global right to privacy. *Brooklyn Journal of International Law, 37*(1), 317–348.

Ramsay, J. H. R. (1994). A king, a doctor, and a convenient death. *British Medical Journal, 308*(6941), 1445. doi:10.1136/bmj.308.6941.1445 PMID:11644545

Ransbotham, S., Kane, G. C., & Lurie, N. (2012). Network Characteristics and the Value of Collaborative User-Generated Content. *Marketing Science, 31*(3), 387–405. doi:10.1287/mksc.1110.0684

Ratcliff, R., Spieler, D., & McKoon, G. (2000). Explicitly modeling the effects of aging on response time. *Psychonomic Bulletin & Review, 7*(1), 1–25. doi:10.3758/BF03210723 PMID:10780018

Rauschnabel, P. A., Brem, A., & Ivens, B. S. (2015). Who will buy smart glasses? Empirical results of two pre-market-entry studies on the role of personality in individual awareness and intended adoption of Google Glass wearables. *Computers in Human Behavior, 49*, 635–647. doi:10.1016/j.chb.2015.03.003

Regalado, A. (2013, March 5). Is this why Google doesn't want you to drive? *MIT Technology Review*. Retrieved from https://www.technologyreview.com/s/512091/is-this-why-google-doesnt-want-you-to-drive/

Rehm, M., & Leichtenstern, K. (2012). Gesture-based mobile training of intercultural behavior. *Multimedia Systems, 18*(1), 33–51. doi:10.100700530-011-0239-8

Remidez, H., & Jones, N. B. (2012). Developing a Model for Social Media in Project Management Communications. *International Journal of Business and Social Science, 3*(3), 33–36.

Rendon, A. A., Lohman, E. B., Thorpe, D., Johnson, E. G., Medina, E., & Bradley, B. (2012). The effect of virtual reality gaming on dynamic balance in older adults. *Age and Ageing, 41*(4), 549–552. doi:10.1093/ageing/afs053 PMID:22672915

Rennie, E. (2018). Policy experiments and the digital divide: Understanding the context of internet adoption in remote Aboriginal communities. In M. Dezuanni, M. Foth, K. Mallan, & H. Hughes (Eds.), *Digital Participation through Social Living Labs* (pp. 299–313). Cambridge, MA: Chandos Publishing. doi:10.1016/B978-0-08-102059-3.00016-2

Rensink, R. A. (2005). Change blindness. In L. Itti, G. Ress, & J. K. Tsotsos (Eds.), *Neurobiology of Attention* (pp. 76–81). Cambridge, MA: Academic Press. doi:10.1016/B978-012375731-9/50017-3

Rice, E., Craddock, J., Hemler, M., Rusow, J., Plant, A., Montoya, J., & Kordic, T. (2018). Associations Between Sexting Behaviors and Sexual Behaviors Among Mobile Phone-Owning Teens in Los Angeles. *Child Development, 89*(1), 110–117. doi:10.1111/cdev.12837 PMID:28556896

Rice, E., Gibbs, J., Winetrobe, H., Rhoades, H., Plant, A., Montoya, J., & Kordic, T. (2014). Sexting and sexual behavior among middle school students. *Pediatrics, 134*(1), e21–e28. doi:10.1542/peds.2013-2991 PMID:24982103

Rice, E., Rhoades, H., Winetrobe, H., Sanchez, M., Montoya, J., Plant, A., & Kordic, T. (2012). Sexually explicit cell phone messaging associated with sexual risk among adolescents. *Pediatrics, 130*(4), 667–673. doi:10.1542/peds.2012-0021 PMID:22987882

Richards, R. D., & Calvert, C. (2009). When sex and cell phones collide: Inside the prosecution of a teen sexting case. *Hastings Communication and Entertainment Law Journal, 32*, 1–39.

Roberts, D. (2015, June 3). Sergey Brin: Here's why Google is making self-driving cars. *Fortune.* Retrieved from http://fortune.com/2015/06/03/google-self-driving-cars/

Rogers, K. (2017). *Kansas City was first to embrace Google Fiber, now Its broadband future Is 'TBD'.* Retrieved July 20, 2018 from https://motherboard.vice.com/en_us/article/xwwmp3/kansas-city-was-first-to-embrace-google-fiber-now-its-broadband-future-is-tbd

Rogers, W. A., Essa, I. A., & Fisk, A. D. (2007). Designing a technology coach. *Ergonomics in Design, 15*(Summer), 17–23. doi:10.1177/106480460701500303 PMID:22545001

Rogers, W. A., Fisk, A. D., McLaughlin, A. C., & Pak, R. (2005). Touch a screen or turn a knob: Choosing the best device for the job. *Human Factors, 47*(2), 271–288. doi:10.1518/0018720054679452 PMID:16170938

Rojko, A. (2017). Industry 4.0 concept: Background and overview. *International Journal of Interactive Mobile Technologies, 11*(5), 77–90. doi:10.3991/ijim.v11i5.7072

Rooksby, J., Baxter, G., Cliff, D., Greenwood, D., Harvey, N., Kahn, A. W., . . . Sommerville, I. (2009). *Social Networking and the Workplace.* Pew Research Center. Retrieved from http://www.lscits.org/pubs/HOReport1b.pdf

Rose, C. L., Murphy, L. B., Byard, L., & Nikzad, K. (2002). The role of the Big Five personality factors in vigilance performance and workload. *European Journal of Personality, 16*(3), 185–200. doi:10.1002/per.451

Rosenberger, M. E., Buman, M. P., Haskell, W. L., McConnell, M. V., & Carstensen, L. L. (2016). 24 hours of sleep, sedentary behavior, and physical activity with nine wearable devices. *Medicine and Science in Sports and Exercise, 48*(3), 457–465. doi:10.1249/MSS.0000000000000778 PMID:26484953

Rosenberger, M. E., Haskell, W. L., Albinali, F., Mota, S., Nawyn, J., & Intille, S. (2013). Estimating activity and sedentary behavior from an accelerometer on the hip or wrist. *Medicine and Science in Sports and Exercise, 45*(5), 964–975. doi:10.1249/MSS.0b013e31827f0d9c PMID:23247702

Rosenbloom, S. (2009). Meeting transportation needs in an aging-friendly community. *Journal of the American Society on Aging, 33*(2), 33–43.

Rothacker, R. (2015). *Google Fiber: Kansas City offers Charlotte 'Digital Divide' lessons.* Retrieved July 22, 2018 from https://www.thecharlotteobserver.com/news/business/article13806530.html

Royakkers, L., & Olsthoorn, P. (2018). Lethal military robots: Who is responsible when things go wrong? In The Changing Scope of Technoethics in Contemporary Society (pp. 106-123). IGI Global.

Royakkers, L., & van Est, R. (2015). A literature review on new robotics: Automation from love to war. *International Journal of Social Robotics, 7*(5), 549–570. doi:10.100712369-015-0295-x

Rudner, J., McDougall, C., Sailam, V., Smith, M., & Sacchetti, A. (2016). Interrogation of patient smartphone activity tracker to assist arrhythmia management. *Annals of Emergency Medicine, 68*(3), 292–294. doi:10.1016/j.annemergmed.2016.02.039 PMID:27045694

Rüßmann, M., Lorenz, M., Gerbert, P., Waldner, M., Justus, J., Engel, P., & Harnisch, M. (2015). Industry 4.0: The future of productivity and growth in manufacturing industries. Boston Consulting Group.

Ryan, T., Chester, A., Reece, J., & Xenos, S. (2014). The uses and abuses of Facebook: A review of Facebook addiction. *Journal of Behavioral Addictions, 3*(3), 133–148. doi:10.1556/JBA.3.2014.016 PMID:25317337

Sadock, B. J., & Sadock, V. A. (2008). *Kaplan & Sadock's concise textbook of clinical psychiatry.* Philadelphia, PA: Lippincott Williams & Wilkins.

Safahieh, H., & Singh, D. (2006). *Information needs of international students at a Malaysian University.* Academic Press.

Saffer, D. (2010). *Designing for interaction* (2nd ed.). San Francisco, CA: New Riders Book.

Salen, K., & Zimmerman, A. (2003). *Rules of play: Game design fundamentals.* Chicago: MIT Press.

Salthouse, T. A. (1996). The processing-speed theory of adult age differences in cognition. *Psychological Review, 103*(3), 403–428. doi:10.1037/0033-295X.103.3.403 PMID:8759042

Samovar, L. A., & McDaniel, E. R. (2007). *Communication between cultures.* Thomson Learning.

Sawyer, B. D., Calvo, A. A., Finomore, V. S., & Hancock, P. A. (2015, August). Serendipity in Simulation: Building Environmentally Valid Driving Distraction Evaluations of Google Glass™ and an Android™ Smartphone. In *Proceedings 19th Triennial Congress of the IEA* (Vol. 9, p. 14). Academic Press.

Sawyer, B. D., & Hancock, P. A. (2012). Development of a linked simulation network to evaluate intelligent transportation system vehicle to vehicle solutions. *Proceedings of the Human Factors and Ergonomics Society Annual Meeting, 56*(1), 2316–2320. doi:10.1177/1071181312561487

Schaller, B. (2017a). *Empty seats, full streets: Fixing Manhattan's traffic problem.* Schaller Consulting. Retrieved from http://www.schallerconsult.com/rideservices/emptyseats.htm

Schaller, B. (2017b). *Unsustainable? The growth of app-based ride services and traffic, travel and the future of New York City.* Schaller Consulting. Retrieved from http://www.schallerconsult.com/rideservices/unsustainable.htm

Schaller, B. (2018, July 25). *The New Automobility: Lyft, Uber and the future of American cities.* Schaller Consulting. Retrieved from http://www.schallerconsult.com/rideservices/automobility.htm

Scherr, A. (2007). Schools and cultural difference. In H. Kotthoff & H. Spencer-Oatey (Eds.), Handbook of intercultural communication (pp. 301–321). Hal.

Schuh, G., Gartzen, T., Rodenhauser, T., & Marks, A. (2015). Promoting work-based learning through industry 4.0. *Procedia CIRP, 32*, 82–87. doi:10.1016/j.procir.2015.02.213

Schwab, K. (2016). The 4th industrial revolution. In *World Economic Forum*. New York: Crown Business.

Schwartz, A. V., Vittinghoff, E., Sellmeyer, D. E., Feingold, K. R., De Rekeneire, N., Strotmeyer, E. S., ... Faulkner, K. A. (2008). Diabetes-related complications, glycemic control, and falls in older adults. *Diabetes Care, 31*(3), 391–396. doi:10.2337/dc07-1152 PMID:18056893

Schwieterman, J. P., Livingston, M., & Van Der Slot, S. (2018, August 1). *Partners in transit: A review of partnerships between transportation network companies and public agencies in the United States.* Chaddick Institute for Metropolitan Development. Retrieved from https://las.depaul.edu/centers-and-institutes/chaddick-institute-for-metropolitan-development/research-and-publications/Pages/default.aspx

Scialfa, C. T., Jenkins, L., Hamaluk, E., & Skaloud, P. (2000). Aging and the development of automaticity in conjunction search. *The Journals of Gerontology. Series B, Psychological Sciences and Social Sciences, 55B*(1), 27–P46. PMID:10728122

Securing America's Future Energy (SAFE). (2018, June). *America's workforce and the self-driving future.* Retrieved from https://avworkforce.secureenergy.org/wp-content/uploads/2018/06/Americas-Workforce-and-the-Self-Driving-Future_Realizing-Productivity-Gains-and-Spurring-Economic-Growth.pdf

Seibert, S. E., Kraimer, M. L., & Liden, R. E. (2001). A Social Capital Theory of Career Success. *Academy of Management Journal, 44*(2), 219–237.

Selkie, E. M., Kota, R., Chan, Y. F., & Moreno, M. (2015). Cyberbullying, depression, and problem alcohol use in female college students: A multisite study. *Cyberpsychology, Behavior, and Social Networking, 18*(2), 79–86. doi:10.1089/cyber.2014.0371 PMID:25684608

Selwyn, N. (2007). Web 2.0 applications as alternative environments for informal learning-a critical review. *Paper for CERI-KERIS International Expert Meeting on ICT and Educational Performance.*

Seo, N. J., Kumar, J. A., Hur, P., Crocher, V., Motawar, B., & Lakshminarayanan, K. (2016). Usability evaluation of low-cost virtual reality hand and arm rehabilitation games. *Journal of Rehabilitation Research and Development, 53*(3), 321–334. doi:10.1682/JRRD.2015.03.0045 PMID:27271199

Sepúlveda, C., Marlin, A., Yoshida, T., & Ullrich, A. (2002). Palliative care: The World Health Organization's global perspective. *Journal of Pain and Symptom Management, 24*(2), 91–96. doi:10.1016/S0885-3924(02)00440-2 PMID:12231124

Ševčíková, A. (2016). Girls' and boys' experience with teen sexting in early and late adolescence. *Journal of Adolescence, 51*, 156–162. doi:10.1016/j.adolescence.2016.06.007 PMID:27391169

Shah, N. (2014). A move within the Shadows: Will JSOC's control of drones improve policy? In P. L. Bergen & D. Rothenberg (Eds.), *Drone Wars: Transforming conflict, law and policy* (pp. 160–184). Cambridge, UK: Cambridge University Press. doi:10.1017/CBO9781139198325.012

Shapiro, E. (2015, Sep 22). How an Apple Watch May Have Saved a Teen's Life. *ABC News.* Accessed at http://abcnews.go.com/US/apple-watch-saved-teens-life/story?id=33944550

Shared-Use Mobility Center (SUMC). (2015). *Shared-use mobility reference guide.* Retrieved from http://sharedusemobilitycenter.org/publications/

Shared-Use Mobility Center (SUMC). (2016). *Shared mobility and the transformation of public transit.* Report to the American Public Transportation Association. Retrieved from http://sharedusemobilitycenter.org/publications/

Sharkey, A. (2017). Can we program or train robots to be good? *Ethics and Information Technology*, 1–13.

Sharkey, N. (2007). Automated killers and the computing profession. *Computer, 11*, 122–124.

Shih, P. C., Han, K., Poole, E. S., Rosson, M. B., & Carroll, J. M. (2015). Use and adoption challenges of wearable activity trackers. *IConference 2015 Proceedings.*

Shipps, B., & Phillips, B. (2013). Social Networks, Interactivity and Satisfaction: Assessing Socio-Technical Behavioral Factors as an Extension to Technology Acceptance. *Journal of Theoretical and Applied Electronic Commerce Research, 8*(1), 35–52. doi:10.4067/S0718-18762013000100004

Shiroishi, Y., Uchiyama, K., & Suzuki, N. (2018). Society 5.0: For Human Security and Well-Being. *Computer, 51*(7), 91–95. doi:10.1109/MC.2018.3011041

Shi, Z., & Whinston, A. B. (2013). Network Structure and Observational Learning: Evidence from a Location-Based Social Network. *Journal of Management Information Systems, 30*(2), 185–212. doi:10.2753/MIS0742-1222300207

Shrouf, F., Ordieres, J., & Miragliotta, G. (2014, December). Smart factories in Industry 4.0: A review of the concept and of energy management approached in production based on the Internet of Things paradigm. In *Industrial Engineering and Engineering Management (IEEM), 2014 IEEE International Conference on* (pp. 697-701). IEEE.

Shuping, X. (2016). How the diversity of values matters in intercultural communication. *Theory and Practice in Language Studies, 6*(9), 1836–1840. doi:10.17507/tpls.0609.16

Siegfried, B. (2011). *Sisyphus, or the limits of education*. Berkeley, CA: University of California Press.

Silva, R. B., Teixeira, C. M., Vasconcelos-Raposo, J., & Bessa, M. (2016). Sexting: Adaptation of sexual behavior to modern technologies. *Computers in Human Behavior, 64*, 747–753. doi:10.1016/j.chb.2016.07.036

Simpson, J. A. (1990). Influence of attachment styles on romantic relationships. *Journal of Personality and Social Psychology, 59*(5), 971–980. doi:10.1037/0022-3514.59.5.971

Siniscarco, M. T., Love-Williams, C., & Burnett-Wolle, S. (2017). Video conferencing: An intervention for emotional loneliness in long-term care. *Activities, Adaptation and Aging, 41*(4), 316–329. doi:10.1080/01924788.2017.1326763

Sin, S.-C. J. (2015). Demographic Differences in International Students' Information Source Uses and Everyday Information Seeking Challenges. *Journal of Academic Librarianship, 41*(4), 466–474. doi:10.1016/j.acalib.2015.04.003

Sin, S.-C. J., & Kim, K.-S. (2013). International students' everyday life information seeking: The informational value of social networking sites. *Library & Information Science Research, 35*(2), 107–116. doi:10.1016/j.lisr.2012.11.006

Sisson, P. (2017). *Kansas City wants to be the city of the future; Has Google helped it get there?* Retrieved July 20, 2018 from https://www.curbed.com/2017/1/17/14298148/kansas-city-google-fiber-tech-hub

Skeels, M. M., & Grudin, J. (2009, May). *When social networks cross boundaries: a case study of workplace use of Facebook and LinkedIn*. Paper presented at the ACM 2009 international conference on Supporting group work, Sanibel Island. 10.1145/1531674.1531689

Smart, K. L., & Csapo, N. (2007). Learning by doing: Engaging students through learner-centered activities. *Business Communication Quarterly, 70*(4), 451–457. doi:10.1177/10805699070700 040302

Sohn, S. Y., & Jo, Y. K. (2003). A study on the student pilot's mental workload due to personality types of both instructor and student. *Ergonomics*, *46*(15), 1566–1577. doi:10.1080/0014013031000121633 PMID:14668175

SolonO.SiddiquiS. (2017, October 31). Retrieved from https://www.theguardian.com/technology/2017/oct/30/facebook-russia-fake-accounts-126-million

Sookhtanlo, M., Mohammadi, H. M., & Rezvanfar, A. (2009). Library information-seeking behaviour among undergraduate students of agricultural extension and education in Iran. *DESIDOC Journal of Library and Information Technology*, *29*(4), 12–20. doi:10.14429/djlit.29.256

Sparrow, R., & Howard, M. (2017). When human beings are like drunk robots: Driverless vehicles, ethics, and the future of transport. *Transportation Research Part C, Emerging Technologies*, *80*, 206–215. doi:10.1016/j.trc.2017.04.014

Spencer-Oatey, H., & Franklin, P. (2009). *Intercultural interaction: A multidisciplinary approach to intercultural communication. Palgrave* Macmillan. doi:10.1057/9780230244511

Spitzer, B., Stanhope, J., Scott, M., Ries, T., Moore, M., McKenzie, B., . . . Elliott, L. J. (2016). *Digital Inclusion App User Testing.* Paper presented to Code for Kansas City, Kansas City, MO.

Sprague, R. (2011). Invasion of the social networks: Blurring the line between personal life and the employment relationship. *University of Louisville Law Review*, *50*(1), 1–34.

Spreckels, J., & Kotthoff, H. (2007). Communicating identity in intercultural communication. In H. Kotthoff & H. Spencer-Oatey (Eds.), Handbook of intercultural communication (pp. 415–439). Hal.

Statista. (2018). *Number of available apps in the Apple App Store from July 2008 to January 2017.* Retrieved September 23, 2018 from https://www.statista.com/statistics/263795/number-of-available-apps-in-the-apple-app-store/#0

Steg, L. (2005). Car use: Lust and must. Instrumental, symbolic and affective motives for car use. *Transportation Research Part A, Policy and Practice*, *39*(2-3), 147–162. doi:10.1016/j.tra.2004.07.001

Steinfield, C., Ellison, N. B., & Lampe, C. (2008). Social capital, self-esteem, and use of online social network sites: A longitudinal analysis. *Journal of Applied Developmental Psychology*, *29*(6), 434–445. doi:10.1016/j.appdev.2008.07.002

Stellabelle. (2017). *Cold Wallet Vs. Hot Wallet: What's The Difference?* Retrieved from https://medium.com/@stellabelle/cold-wallet-vs-hot-wallet-whats-the-difference-a00d872aa6b1

Stephen, A. T., & Toubia, O. (2010). Deriving Value from Social Commerce Networks. *JMR, Journal of Marketing Research*, *47*(2), 215–228. doi:10.1509/jmkr.47.2.215

Stewart, R., & Wingfield, A. (2009). Hearing loss and cognitive effort in older adults' report accuracy for verbal materials. *Journal of the American Academy of Audiology*, *20*(2), 147–154. doi:10.3766/jaaa.20.2.7 PMID:19927677

Stocker, A., & Shaheen, S. (2018, July). Shared Automated Vehicle (SAV) Pilots and Automated Vehicle Policy in the US: Current and Future Developments. In *Automated Vehicles Symposium 2018* (pp. 131-147). Springer.

Stock, T., & Seliger, G. (2016). Opportunities of sustainable manufacturing in industry 4.0. *Procedia Cirp, 40*, 536–541. doi:10.1016/j.procir.2016.01.129

Stowers, K., Leyva, K., Hancock, G. M., & Hancock, P. A. (2016). Life or Death by Robot? *Ergonomics in Design, 24*(3), 17–22. doi:10.1177/1064804616635811

Strawser, B. J. (2010). Moral predators: The duty to employ uninhabited aerial vehicles. *Journal of Military Ethics, 9*(4), 342–368. doi:10.1080/15027570.2010.536403

Street, A., & Kissane, D. W. (2000). Dispensing death, desiring death: An exploration of medical roles and patient motivation during the period of legalized euthanasia in Australia. *Omega, 40*(1), 231–248. doi:10.2190/JB07-5GCR-BH81-J2QN PMID:12578011

Stuart, H., & Gay, P. (2010). *Questions of Cultural Identity*. London: Sage.

Stuart, M., Turman, A. B., Shaw, J., Walsh, N., & Hguyen, V. (2003). Effects of aging on vibration detection thresholds at various body regions. *BMC Geriatrics, 3*(1), 1. doi:10.1186/1471-2318-3-1 PMID:12600276

Suberg, W. (2015). *Factom's Latest Partnership Takes on US Health-care*. Retrieved from https://cointelegraph.com/news/factoms-latest-partnership-takes-on-us-healthcare

Suh, A., Shin, K., Ahuja, M., & Kim, M. S. (2011). The Influence of Virtuality on Social Networks Within and Across Work Groups: A Multilevel Approach. *Journal of Management Information Systems, 28*(1), 351–386. doi:10.2753/MIS0742-1222280111

Sullivan, B. (2013). Poverty in America: Millions of families too broke for bank accounts. *NBC News*. Retrieved September 26, 2018 from https://www.nbcnews.com/feature/in-plain-sight/poverty-america-millions-families-too-broke-bank-accounts-v17840373

Sullivan, H. S. (1953). *The Interpersonal Theory of Psychiatry*. New York: Norton.

Sun, C. (2012). Application of RFID technology for logistics on internet of things. *AASRI Procedia, 1*, 106–111. doi:10.1016/j.aasri.2012.06.019

Sung, T. K. (2018). Industry 4.0: A Korea perspective. *Technological Forecasting and Social Change, 132*, 40–45. doi:10.1016/j.techfore.2017.11.005

Sun, Q., Townsend, M. K., Okereke, O. I., Franco, O. H., Hu, F. B., & Grodstein, F. (2010). Physical activity at midlife in relation to successful survival in women at age 70 years or older. *Archives of Internal Medicine, 170*(2), 194–201. doi:10.1001/archinternmed.2009.503 PMID:20101015

Suwana, F., & Lily. (2017). Empowering Indonesian women through building digital media literacy. *Kasetsart Journal of Social Sciences, 38*(3), 212–217. doi:10.1016/j.kjss.2016.10.004

Swan, M. (2015). *Blockchain: Blueprint for a New Economy*. O'Reilly Media.

Szabo, N. (1996). *Smart Contracts: Building Blocks for Digital Markets.* Retrieved from http://www. fon.hum.uva.nl/rob/Courses/InformationInSpeech/CDROM/Literature/LOTwinterschool2006/ szabo.best.vwh.net/smart_contracts_2.html

Tabak, R. J., & Lane, J. M. (1989). The execution of injustice: A cost and lack-of-benefit analysis of the death penalty. *Loyola of Los Angeles Law Review, 23,* 59–146.

Taylor, T. L. (2008). Becoming a player: networks, structure, and imagined futures. In Beyond Barbie & mortal kombat: new perspectives on gender and gaming (pp. 51–66). MIT Press.

Tefft, B. C. (2017). Rates of motor vehicle crashes, injuries and deaths in relation to driver age, United States, 2014-2015. *AAA Foundation for Traffic Safety.* Retrieved from http://aaafoundation. org/rates-motor-vehicle-crashes-injuries-deaths-relation-driver-age-united-states-2014-2015/

Tesla. (2018). *Tesla Autopilot.* Retrieved from https://www.tesla.com/autopilot/

Tett, G. (2018, April 9). A shortage of US truck drivers points to bigger problems. *Financial Times,* p. 11.

The Centre for Computing History. (2018). *Atari Pong.* Retrieved from http://www.computinghistory. org.uk/det/4007/Atari-PONG/

Tikhomirov, S., Voskresenskaya, E., Ivanitskiy, I., Takhaviev, R., Marchenko, E., & Alexandrov, Y. (2018). SmartCheck: Static Analysis of Ethereum Smart Contracts. *WETSEB'18: WETSEB'18:IEEE/ACM 1st International Workshop on Emerging Trends in Software Engineering for Blockchain.* Retrieved from http://orbilu.uni.lu/bitstream/10993/35862/1/smartcheck-paper.pdf

Tirado-Morueta, R., Aguaded-Gómez, J. I., & Hernando-Gómez, Á. (in press). The socio-demographic divide in Internet usage moderated by digital literacy support. *Technology in Society.*

Treisman, A. M., & Gelade, G. (1980). A feature-integration theory of attention. *Cognitive Psychology, 12*(1), 97–136. doi:10.1016/0010-0285(80)90005-5 PMID:7351125

Trub, L., & Starks, T. J. (2017). Insecure attachments: Attachment, emotional regulation, sexting and condomless sex among women in relationships. *Computers in Human Behavior, 71,* 140–147. doi:10.1016/j.chb.2017.01.052

Tsai, H. H., & Tsai, Y. F. (2011). Changes in depressive symptoms, social support, and loneliness over 1 year after a minimum 3-month videoconference program for older nursing home residents. *Journal of Medical Internet Research, 13*(4), e93. doi:10.2196/jmir.1678 PMID:22086660

Tsai, W. (2000). Social Capital, Strategic Relatedness and the Formation of Intraorganizational Linkages. *Strategic Management Journal, 21*(9), 925–939. doi:10.1002/1097-0266(200009)21:9<925::AID-SMJ129>3.0.CO;2-I

Tschabitscher, H. (2017). *How many emails are sent every day?* Retrieved from http://www. radicati.com/

Tun, P. A., Williams, V. A., Small, B. J., Hafter, E. R. (2012). The effects of aging on auditory processing and cognition. *American Journal of Audiology, 21*(2), 344-350. doi:(2012/12-0030 doi:10.1044/1059-0889

Tyree, G. M., & McLaughlin, A. C. (2016). Older adult engagement in activities: All motivations are not created equal. *Proceedings of the Human Factors and Ergonomics Society Annual Meeting, 56*(1), 135–139. doi:10.1177/1071181312561005

U. S. Department of Transportation (DOT). (2018). *Comprehensive Management Plan for Automated Vehicle Initiatives.* Retrieved from https://www.transportation.gov/policy-initiatives/automated-vehicles/usdot-comprehensive-management-plan-automated-vehicle

Unay, C. (2001). *Makro Ekonomi.* Bursa: Vipaş.

Underwood, B. J. (1974). *Individual differences as a crucible in theory construction.* A distinguished scientific contribution award address presented at the annual meeting of the American Psychological Association, New Orleans, LA.

UNESCO. (n.d.). *Glossary: International (or internationally mobile) students.* Retrieved 25 July, 2018, from http://uis.unesco.org/node/334686

United States Census Bureau. (2018, March 13). *From pyramid to pillar: A century of change, population of the U.S.* Retrieved from https://www.census.gov/library/visualizations/2018/comm/century-of-change.html

Van Aalst-Cohen, E. S., Riggs, R., & Byock, I. R. (2008). Palliative care in medical school curricula: A survey of United States medical schools. *Journal of Palliative Medicine, 11*(9), 1200–1202. doi:10.1089/jpm.2008.0118 PMID:19021481

Van Deursen, A. J. A. M., & Van Dijk, J. A. G. M. (2010). Measuring internet skills. *International Journal of Human-Computer Interaction, 26*(10), 891–916. doi:10.1080/10447318.2010.496338

Van Deursen, A. J. A. M., & Van Dijk, J. A. G. M. (2014). The digital divide shifts to differences in usage. *New Media & Society, 16*(3), 507–526. doi:10.1177/1461444813487959

Van Dijck, J. (2013). *The Culture of Connectivity. A Critical History of Social Media.* New York: Oxford University Press. doi:10.1093/acprof:oso/9780199970773.001.0001

Van Dijk, J. A. (2005). *The deepening divide: Inequality in the information society.* Thousand Oaks, CA: Sage Publications.

Van Dijk, J. A. (2006). Digital divide research, achievements and shortcomings. *Poetics, 34*(4-5), 221–235. doi:10.1016/j.poetic.2006.05.004

Van Krevelen, D. W. F., & Poelman, R. (2010). A survey of augmented reality technologies, applications and limitations. *International Journal of Virtual Reality, 9*(2), 1.

Van Ouytsel, J., Van Gool, E., Ponnet, K., & Walrave, M. (2014). Brief report: The association between adolescents' characteristics and engagement in sexting. *Journal of Adolescence, 37*(8), 1387–1391. doi:10.1016/j.adolescence.2014.10.004 PMID:25448834

Vanderelst, D., & Winfield, A. (2018). An architecture for ethical robots inspired by the simulation theory of cognition. *Cognitive Systems Research, 48,* 56–66. doi:10.1016/j.cogsys.2017.04.002

Varadarajan, R., Freeman, R. A., & Parmar, J. R. (2016). Aid-in-dying practice in Europe and the United States: Legal and ethical perspectives for pharmacy. *Research in Social & Administrative Pharmacy, 12*(6), 1016–1025. doi:10.1016/j.sapharm.2015.11.008 PMID:26711140

Varatharajan, R., Manogaran, G., Priyan, M. K., & Sundarasekar, R. (2017). Wearable sensor devices for early detection of Alzheimer disease using dynamic time warping algorithm. *Cluster Computing,* 1–10.

Velasco, D. (2015). Evaluate, analyze, describe (EAD): Confronting underlying issues of racism and other prejudices for effective intercultural communication. *IAFOR Journal of Education, 3*(2), 82–93. doi:10.22492/ije.3.2.05

Veletsianos, G., & Navarrete, C. C. (2012). Online Social Networks as Formal Learning Environments: Learner Experiences and Activities. *International Review of Research in Open and Distance Learning, 13*(1), 144. doi:10.19173/irrodl.v13i1.1078

Venkatesh, V., & Bala, H. (2008). Technology Acceptance Model 3 and a research agenda on interventions. *Decision Sciences, 39*(2), 273–315. doi:10.1111/j.1540-5915.2008.00192.x

Venkatesh, V., & Davis, F. D. (2000). A theoretical extension of the technology acceptance model: Four longitudinal field studies. *Management Science, 46*(2), 186–204. doi:10.1287/mnsc.46.2.186.11926

Venkatesh, V., Morris, M. G., Davis, G. B., & Davis, F. D. (2003). User acceptance of information technology: Toward a unified view. *Management Information Systems Quarterly, 27*(3), 425–478. doi:10.2307/30036540

Venkatesh, V., Thong, J. Y., Chan, F. K., Hu, P. J. H., & Brown, S. A. (2011). Extending the two-stage information systems continuance model: Incorporating UTAUT predictors and the role of context. *Information Systems Journal, 21*(6), 527–555. doi:10.1111/j.1365-2575.2011.00373.x

Verhaeghen, P., & Cerella, J. (2002). Aging, executive control, and attention: A review of meta-analyses. *Neuroscience and Biobehavioral Reviews, 26*(7), 849–857. doi:10.1016/S0149-7634(02)00071-4 PMID:12470697

Verhagen, A. A., Sol, J. J., Brouwer, O. F., & Sauer, P. J. (2005). Deliberate termination of life in newborns in The Netherlands; Review of all 22 reported cases between 1997 and 2004. *Nederlands Tijdschrift voor Geneeskunde, 149*(4), 183–188. PMID:15702738

Verhagen, E., & Sauer, P. J. J. (2005). The Groningen Protocol – euthanasia in severely ill newborns. *The New England Journal of Medicine, 352*(10), 959–962. doi:10.1056/NEJMp058026 PMID:15758003

Vigdor, J. L., Ladd, H. F., & Martinez, E. (2014). Scaling the digital divide: Home computer technology and student achievement. *Economic Inquiry, 52*(3), 1103–1119. doi:10.1111/ecin.12089

Virtanen, M., Kivimäki, M., Joensuu, M., Virtanen, P., Elovainio, M., & Vahtera, J. (2005). Temporary employment and health: A review. *International Journal of Epidemiology, 34*(3), 610–622. doi:10.1093/ije/dyi024 PMID:15737968

Vitak, J. (2012). The Impact of Context Collapse and Privacy on Social Network Site Disclosures. *Journal of Broadcasting & Electronic Media, 56*(4), 451–470. doi:10.1080/08838151.2012.732140

Volvo. (2015). *Future of driving*. Retrieved from https://www.futureofdriving.com

Vooijs, M., Alpay, L. L., Snoeck-Stroband, J. B., Beerthuizen, T., Siemonsma, P. C., Abbink, J. J., ... Rövekamp, T. A. (2014). Validity and usability of low-cost accelerometers for internet-based self-monitoring of physical activity in patients with chronic obstructive pulmonary disease. *Interactive Journal of Medical Research, 3*(4), e14. doi:10.2196/ijmr.3056 PMID:25347989

Vries, A. d. (2018). Bitcoin's Growing Energy Problem. *Joule*, 801-809.

Wallace, L., Warkentin, M., & Benbasat, I. (2018, January). *How Do You Handle It? Developing a Theory of Facebook Affordances and Envy*. Paper presented at the 51st Hawaii International Conference on System Sciences. Retrieved from http://hdl.handle.net/10125/50544

Walport, M. (2016, January). *Distributed ledger technology: beyond block chain, U.K. Government Office Sci., London, U.K., Tech. Rep.* Retrieved from https://cointelegraph.com/news/factoms-latest-partnership-takes-on-us-healthcare

Walsh, T. (2017). Expert and Non-Expert Opinion about Technological Unemployment. *International Journal of Automation and Computing*, 1-6.

Walsh, C. (2010). Systems-based literacy practices: Digital games research, gameplay and design. *Australian Journal of Language and Literacy, 33*(1), 24–40.

Walton, D. (1976). Active and passive euthanasia. *Ethics, 86*(4), 343–349. doi:10.1086/292010 PMID:11662292

Wamuyu, P. K. (2017). Bridging the digital divide among low income urban communities leveraging use of community technology centers. *Telematics and Informatics, 34*(8), 1709–1720. doi:10.1016/j.tele.2017.08.004

Wang, Y., & Kulich, S. J. (2015). Does context count? Developing and assessing intercultural competence through an interview and model-based domestic course design in China. *International Journal of Intercultural Relations, 48*, 38–57. doi:10.1016/j.ijintrel.2015.03.013

Warrior, L. C. (2015). Drones and targeted killing: Costs, accountability, and U.S. civil-military relations. *Orbis, 59*(1), 95–110. doi:10.1016/j.orbis.2014.11.008

Warwick, K., Xydas, D., Nasuto, S. J., Becerra, V. M., Hammond, M. W., Downes, J. H., ... Whalley, B. J. (2010). Controlling a Mobile Robot with a Biological Brain. *Defence Science Journal, 1*(60), 5–14. doi:10.14429/dsj.60.11

Watts, D. J., & Strogatz, S. H. (1998). Collective dynamics of 'small-world' networks. *Nature, 393*(6684), 440–442. doi:10.1038/30918 PMID:9623998

Watts, D. T., & Howell, T. (1992). Assisted suicide is not voluntary active euthanasia. *Journal of the American Geriatrics Society, 40*(10), 1043–1046. doi:10.1111/j.1532-5415.1992.tb04484.x PMID:1401679

Weaver, N. (2018). Risks of cryptocurrencies. *Communications of the ACM, 61*(6), 20–24. doi:10.1145/3208095

Web of Science. (n.d.). Retrieved from www.webofknowledge.com

WEFORUM. (2017). *The world's most popular social networks, mapped.* Retrieved September 29th, 2017 from https://www.weforum.org/agenda/2017/03/most-popular-social-networks-mapped/

Weinberg, B. D., Ruyter, K., Dellarocas, C., Buck, B., & Keeling, D. I. (2013). Destination Social Business: Exploring an Organization's Journey with Social Media, Collaborative Community and Expressive Individuality. *Journal of Interactive Marketing, 27*(4), 299–310. doi:10.1016/j.intmar.2013.09.006

Weis, C., & Axhausen, K. W. (2009). Induced travel demand: Evidence from a pseudo panel data based structural equations model. *Research in Transportation Economics, 25*(1), 8–18. doi:10.1016/j.retrec.2009.08.007

Wellman, B. (1988). Structural Analysis: From Method and Metaphor to Theory and Substance. In B. Wellman & S. D. Berkowitz (Eds.), *Social Structures: A Network Approach* (pp. 19–61). Cambridge, UK: Cambridge University Press.

Wells, J. D., Campbell, D. E., Valacich, J. S., & Featherman, M. (2010). The effect of perceived novelty on the adoption of information technology innovations: A risk/reward perspective. *Decision Sciences, 41*(4), 813–843. doi:10.1111/j.1540-5915.2010.00292.x

Wesolko, D. (2016). *Peter Morville's user experience honeycomb.* Retrieved September 26, 2018 from https://medium.com/@danewesolko/peter-morvilles-user-experience-honeycomb-904c383b6886

Wetmore, J. (2009). Implementing Restraint: Automobile safety and the US debate over technological and social fixes. In J. Conley & A. T. McLaren (Eds.), *Car troubles: Critical studies of automobility and auto-mobility* (pp. 111–125). Routledge.

Wiener, N. (1954). *The human use of human beings: Cybernetics and society.* Da Capo Press.

Willems, D. L., Groenewoud, J. H., & van der Wal, G. (1999). Drugs used in physician-assisted death. *Drugs & Aging, 15*(5), 335–340. doi:10.2165/00002512-199915050-00001 PMID:10600041

Williams, D. (2006). On and Off the 'Net: Scales for Social Capital in an Online Era. *Journal of Computer-Mediated Communication, 11*(2), 593–628. doi:10.1111/j.1083-6101.2006.00029.x

Williams, K. N., Herman, R., Gajweski, B., & Wilson, K. (2010). Elderspeak communication: Impact on dementia care. *American Journal of Alzheimer's Disease and Other Dementias, 24*(1), 11–20. doi:10.1177/1533317508318472 PMID:18591210

Wilson, J. (2009). Social networking: The business case. *Engineering & Technology, 4*(10), 54–56. doi:10.1049/et.2009.1010

Wilson, K. G., Scott, J. F., Graham, I. D., Kozak, J. F., Chater, S., Viola, R. A., ... Curran, D. (2000). Attitudes of terminally ill patients toward euthanasia and physician-assisted suicide. *Archives of Internal Medicine, 160*(16), 2454–2460. doi:10.1001/archinte.160.16.2454 PMID:10979056

Wisniewski, P., Islam, A. K. M. N., Lipford, H. R., & Wilson, D. C. (2016). Framing and Measuring Multi-dimensional Interpersonal Privacy Preferences of Social Networking Site Users. *Communications of the Association for Information Systems, 38*, 235–258. doi:10.17705/1CAIS.03810

Wohlsen, M. (2012). *Google Fiber splits along Kansas City's digital divide*. Retrieved July 22, 2018, from https://www.wired.com/2012/09/google-fiber-digital-divide

Wolak, J., Finkelhor, D., Walsh, W., & Treitman, L. (2018). Sextortion of minors: Characteristics and dynamics. *The Journal of Adolescent Health, 62*(1), 72–79. doi:10.1016/j.jadohealth.2017.08.014 PMID:29055647

Wolfe, J. M., & Horowitz, T. S. (2014). What attributes guide the deployment of visual attention and how do they do it? *Nature Reviews. Neuroscience, 5*(6), 495–501. doi:10.1038/nrn1411 PMID:15152199

Wong, J. I. (2017, December 4). *The ethereum network is getting jammed up because people are rushing to buy cartoon cats on its blockchain*. Retrieved from https://qz.com/1145833/cryptokitties-is-causing-ethereum-network-congestion/

Woodall, B. (2016, August 18). Uber buys self-driving truck startup Otto; teams with Volvo. *Reuters.* Retrieved from https://www.reuters.com/article/us-uber-tech-volvo-otto-idUSKCN10T1TR

Wright, M. (2018). Cyberbullying Victimization through Social Networking Sites and Adjustment Difficulties: The Role of Parental Mediation. *Journal of the Association for Information Systems, 19*(2), 113–123. doi:10.17705/jais1.00486

Ybarra, M. L., & Mitchell, K. J. (2014). "Sexting" and its relation to sexual activity and sexual risk behavior in a national survey of adolescents. *The Journal of Adolescent Health, 55*(6), 757–764. doi:10.1016/j.jadohealth.2014.07.012 PMID:25266148

Yi, Z. (2007). International student perceptions of information needs and use. *Journal of Academic Librarianship, 33*(6), 666–673. doi:10.1016/j.acalib.2007.09.003

Yrjölä, S. (2017). Analysis of Blockchain Use Cases in the Citizens Broadband Radio Service Spectrum Sharing Concept. *International Conference on Cognitive Radio Oriented Wireless Networks*, 128-139.

Yun, Y. H., Han, K. H., Park, S., Park, B. W., Cho, C.-H., Kim, S., ... Chun, M. (2011). Attitudes of cancer patients, family caregivers, oncologists and members of the general public toward critical interventions at the end of life of terminally ill patients. *Canadian Medical Association Journal*, *183*(10), E673–E679. doi:10.1503/cmaj.110020 PMID:21624907

Zen, A. (2017, November 28). *CryptoKitties: The World's First Ethereum Game Launches Today*. Retrieved from https://www.prnewswire.com/news-releases/cryptokitties-the-worlds-first-ethereum-game-launches-today-660494083.html

Zhang, D., Yu, Z., Guo, B., & Wang, Z. (2014). Exploiting Personal and Community Context in Mobile Social Networks. In A. Chin & D. Zhang (Eds.), *Mobile Social Networking. Computational Social Sciences*. New York, NY: Springer. doi:10.1007/978-1-4614-8579-7_6

Zhang, X. (2010). Charging children with child pornography–Using the legal system to handle the problem of "sexting.". *Computer Law & Security Review*, *26*(3), 251–259. doi:10.1016/j.clsr.2010.03.005

Zhang, Y., Qiu, M., Tsai, C. W., Hassan, M. M., & Alamri, A. (2017). Health-CPS: Healthcare cyber-physical system assisted by cloud and big data. *IEEE Systems Journal*, *11*(1), 88–95. doi:10.1109/JSYST.2015.2460747

Zheng, Z., Dai, H.-N., Xie, S., Wang, H., & Wang, H. (2017). An Overview of Blockchain Technology: Architecture, Consensus, and Future Trends. *ResearchGate*, 557-564.

Zhou, K., Liu, T., & Zhou, L. (2015, August). Industry 4.0: Towards future industrial opportunities and challenges. In *Fuzzy Systems and Knowledge Discovery (FSKD), 2015 12th International Conference on* (pp. 2147-2152). IEEE.

Zimmer, J. (2016, September 18). The third transportation revolution: Lyft's vision for the next 10 years and beyond. *Medium*. Retrieved from https://medium.com/@johnzimmer/the-third-transportation-revolution-27860f05fa91

Zong, J., & Batalova, J. (2016, May 12). *International students in the United States*. Retrieved from http://www.migrationpolicy.org/article/international-students-united-states

About the Contributors

Heather C. Lum is an assistant professor at Penn State Erie, The Behrend College. She earned her Ph.D. in applied experimental and human factors psychology from the University of Central Florida in 2011. Her primary research interests focus on perceptions of technology, specifically the ways in which technology is impacting the way we interact with each other as humans. Other areas of interest include the use of psychophysiological measures such as eye tracking and vocal analyses to better determine and study the critical applied cognitive and experimental topics of interest such as spatial cognition, human-human and human-robot team interactions. She has also turned her attention to the use of games for training and educational purposes. In addition to her research pursuits, Dr. Lum is a faculty advisor for Psych Club, the Behrend chapter of Psi Chi, is chair-elect for the Cognitive Engineering & Decision Making Technical Group and former program chair for the Education Technical Group Since coming to Penn State, she has advocated for the advertisement of human factors as the discipline within the university. She has successfully proposed an undergraduate interdisciplinary certificate in human factors, a course in the psychology of gaming, an interdisciplinary course in human factors in design and art, and a minor in game development on campus.

* * *

Nahla Absumara is an Ed.D candidate in the program of Curriculum and Instruction at Indiana University of Pennsylvania. Her area of research is the use of technology in education. Specifically, Ms. Abusamra examines the role of virtual reality and serious games in creating anchored instruction for foreign language and culture education programs. She also investigates the plausibility of using social media as a learning management system in higher education.

Mehmet Aktan is a professor and the chair at the Department of Industrial Engineering, Necmettin Erbakan University, Turkey. He received his Ph.D. from The University of Wisconsin-Madison, his M.S. from The University of Iowa, and his B.S. from Bogazici University. He is the author and co-author of many academic publications in several research areas such as decision making, artificial intelligence, engineering statistics and financial engineering.

Chris Niyi Arasanmi is a senior lecturer at the Faculty of Business Management, Toi Ohomai Institute of Technology, Rotorua, New Zealand, where he teaches strategic management, management practice, digital business and research methodology. He received a PhD in Business Information Systems from Auckland University of Technology (AACSB accredited), Auckland, New Zealand. His doctoral research was in the area of skills transfer in enterprise systems. His research interests are in enterprise systems and implementation training, enterprise resource planning, information systems adoption, mobile and e-learning and digital commerce. He has contributed articles to international refereed journals, like Enterprise Information Systems and American Conference on Information Systems (AMCIS), Pacific Conference on Information Systems (PACIS) and Australasian Conference on Information Systems (ACIS).

Isabel Azevedo holds a Ph.D. in Informatics Engineering from the Faculty of Engineering - University of Porto, Porto. She is an Associate Professor in the Department of Informatics Engineering of ISEP and a senior researcher at the GILT - Games, Interaction and Learning Technologies research center. Isabel Azevedo previously worked in the Documentation Service of Aveiro University, and in the Faculty of Engineering of the University of Porto as a software and system programmer in the area of Technological Infrastructures.

Suparna Dhar is a senior manager in an IT organization with focus on developing IT solutions for the Fintech space and exploring emerging technologies. She takes interest in academic research on application, adoption and use of emerging technologies in business; covering analytics, social media technologies, cloud computing, distributed processing and blockchain. She is pursuing her PHD on Information Systems Management from Aligarh Muslim University.

Samuel Ehrenreich is an Assistant Professor in the Human Development and Family Studies program at the University of Nevada, Reno. His research interests focus on how digital communication shapes adolescents' development and relationships.

338

Samuel Ekundayo is a lecturer at Eastern Institute of Technology in New Zealand. He holds a PhD in Business Information Systems from Auckland University of Technology (AUT), New Zealand; a Master of Science in Knowledge Management from Nanyang Technological University (NTU), Singapore and a Bachelors degree from Coventry University (CU), United Kingdom in Engineering Business Management. His research interests include Knowledge-Based Economies, Educational Technology, Activity theory, Human-Computer Interaction, ICT in Education, ICT4D, Social Media, Pedagogy, Open and Distance Learning, and Mobile Development.

Lisa Jo Elliott earned a PhD in Engineering Psychology from New Mexico State University. She is a former usability practitioner (IBM). She researches and teaches usability. Her former students work as usability practitioners at small and large technology firms/design studios throughout the U.S.

Jing Feng is an Assistant Professor in the Human Factors and Applied Cognition Program at the Department of Psychology, North Carolina State University. Her research focuses on integrating theories of attention and relevant applications in human factors.

Gabriella Hancock is an Assistant Professor at California State University - Long Beach. Her research interests include human performance under workload and stress (with an emphasis on cognitive neuroscience methods) and human-technology interaction. She graduated with her Ph.D. in Applied Experimental and Human Factors Psychology, M.S.I.E. in Industrial Engineering, and B.S. in Psychology from the University of Central Florida. She earned her M.S. in Applied Physiology and Kinesiology from the University of Florida.

Anne Collins McLaughlin is an associate professor of psychology at North Carolina State University in Raleigh, NC. She received her PhD from the Georgia Institute of Tech- nology in 2007. She directs the Learning, Aging, and Cognitive Ergonomics Lab and codirects the Gains Through Gaming Lab.

Diana J. Meter is an Assistant Professor of Human Development and Family Studies at Utah State University. She trained as a Post Doctoral Research Associate in the School of Behavioral and Brain Sciences at The University of Texas at Dallas and earned her PhD and MS in Family Studies and Human Development from the University of Arizona. Her research focuses on peer relations among children and adolescents in person and online and how peer relationships can be affected by and also affect parent-child relationships, school factors, and adjustment.

Alexis Neigel received her Ph.D. in Applied Experimental and Human Factors Psychology and her M.S. in Modeling and Simulation from the University of Central Florida. She earned her B.S. in Psychology with a focus on Gerontology from Washington State University. Her research interests include human perception, attention, and decision making.

Makenzie Pryor received her BA in psychology from New College of Florida in 2013. She is currently pursuing a PhD in Human Factors and Applied Cognition at North Carolina State University. She is interested in using human factors to support healthy aging.

Ben D. Sawyer is the Director of The Laboratory for Brain-Autonomy Exchange (LabX) and an Assistant Professor in the Department of Industrial Engineering and Management Systems (IEMS) within the College of Engineering and Computer Science (CECS) at The University of Central Florida (UCF). At the time of this work, Dr. Sawyer was with The Center for Transportation and Logistics (CTL) and AgeLab at the Massachusetts Institute of Technology (MIT). Dr. Sawyer is known for using brainwaves, eye movements, and mathematical theory to build better human-machine teams. His startups and academic work have been covered by Forbes, Reuters, Fast Company, Techcrunch, and The BBC. His PhD in Human Factors is from UCF. More information at bendsawyer.com.

Michael Schwartz is the founder of the Wearable Electronics/Augmented Reality (WEAR) Lab. His research has two main tracks. The first is how the human centered design of consumer products can reduce users' workload, especially for people with disabilities. The second area focuses on quality of life issues, particularly activities of daily living, throughout the aging and rehabilitation processes.

Duarte Teles holds a Bachelor of Informatics Engineering in addition to a master's degree in Informatics Engineering with specialization in Computer Systems. He has a deep interest in everything related to Blockchain. He recently developed a proof-of-concept which focused on data protection and privacy and the Ethereum Blockchain. Currently, he works as a Blockchain Software Engineer in Porto, Portugal.

David Thurlow is a strategic advisor for technology adoption and policy. His work centers on understanding future impacts and making the proactive choices now that can help organizations and communities prepare for new disruptive changes. His primary focus is new transportation technologies, with a specific emphasis on the potential applications of automated vehicles. David holds a master's degree in

Science and Technology Studies from York University in Toronto. He has also been a partner in two internet startups, both centering on helping entrepreneurs succeed in bringing their products to market, and is the founder of an advocacy group promoting the safe and positive uses of unmanned aircraft systems. He is a licensed pilot of both airplanes and helicopters. He lives with his wife in Toronto.

Tuba Ulusoy is currently working as a Research Assistant at the Industrial Engineering Department of Necmettin Erbakan University (Konya, Turkey). She received the B.Sc. and M.Sc., degrees in Industrial Engineering at Erciyes University (Kayseri, Turkey) and Necmettin Erbakan University (Konya, Turkey), respectively. Her research interests are mathematical modeling, optimization, and supply chain management.

Marion K. Underwood serves as Dean of the College of Health and Human Sciences at Purdue University. Dr. Underwood's research examines developmental origins and outcomes of social aggression, and how adolescents' digital communication relates to qualities of relationships and adjustment. Dr. Underwood's work has been published in numerous scientific journals and her research program has been supported by the National Institutes of Health since 1995. In 2003, she authored a book, Social Aggression among Girls. Since 2003, she and her research group have been conducting a longitudinal study of origins and outcomes of social aggression, and how adolescents use digital communication. Before participants began their 9th grade year and continuing through their high school years, all were given BlackBerry devices configured to capture the content of their electronic communication to a secure archive: text messaging, email, and Facebook communication. Dr. Underwood earned her undergraduate degree from Wellesley College and her doctoral degree in clinical psychology from Duke University in 1991. She began her faculty career at Reed College in Portland, Oregon, earned tenure there, then moved to the University of Texas at Dallas in 1998, where she was named the Ashbel Smith Professor of Psychological Sciences and served as Graduate Dean and Associate Provost from 2015-2018. Dr. Underwood received the 2001 Chancellor's Council Outstanding Teacher of the Year Award, was granted a FIRST Award and a K02 Mid-Career Independent Scientist Award from the National Institute of Mental Health, and is a Fellow of the Association for Psychological Science. She enjoys administrative work because relishes the challenge of thinking creatively about how to build the strengths of other people and how to improve large systems.

Esra Yaşar is a research assistant at KTO Karatay University in Department of International Trade and Logistics. She graduated from Selçuk University Department of Industrial Engineering in 2012. She received a Master's degree in Industrial Engineering from the Necmettin Erbakan University Institute of Natural and Applied Sciences in 2017. She is a Ph.D. student at Eskişehir Teknik University in the Department of Industrial Engineering.

Ahmed Yousof is currently an assistant teaching professor at Pennsylvania State University. Yousof teaches classes in advanced video game design, game art, multimedia, and animation. Having been born and raised in Belgium lived in the Middle East, and studied in the U.S., Yousof is interested in intercultural communication and the effective use of video games in enhancing the intercultural competency of people from different cultures. Yousof's research focuses on the examination and production of effective computer-mediated and mixed-reality instructional approaches to solve challenging learning problems related to intercultural communication. Through considering the necessary factors in the instructional design of video games and virtual reality, Yousof tackles how dynamic learning environments made possible by 3D games and virtual reality can contribute to better development and acquisition of intercultural communication and foreign language, respectively. Yousof's research about gaming and communication has received an international award for New Media and Mobile Learning in 2013 from Education Without Borders Conference in Dubai.

Index

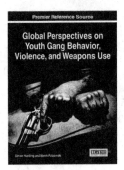

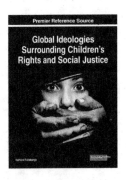
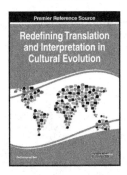

Ensure Quality Research is Introduced to the Academic Community

Become an IGI Global Reviewer for Authored Book Projects

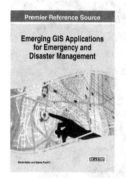

The overall success of an authored book project is dependent on quality and timely reviews.

In this competitive age of scholarly publishing, constructive and timely feedback significantly expedites the turnaround time of manuscripts from submission to acceptance, allowing the publication and discovery of forward-thinking research at a much more expeditious rate. Several IGI Global authored book projects are currently seeking highly qualified experts in the field to fill vacancies on their respective editorial review boards:

Applications may be sent to:
development@igi-global.com

Applicants must have a doctorate (or an equivalent degree) as well as publishing and reviewing experience. Reviewers are asked to write reviews in a timely, collegial, and constructive manner. All reviewers will begin their role on an ad-hoc basis for a period of one year, and upon successful completion of this term can be considered for full editorial review board status, with the potential for a subsequent promotion to Associate Editor.

If you have a colleague that may be interested in this opportunity, we encourage you to share this information with them.

Printed in the United States
By Bookmasters